CORRESPONDENCE

OF THE

AMERICAN REVOLUTION.

VOL. I.

G. Washington

CORRESPONDENCE

OF THE

AMERICAN REVOLUTION;

BEING

LETTERS OF EMINENT MEN

TO

GEORGE WASHINGTON,

FROM

THE TIME OF HIS TAKING COMMAND OF THE ARMY

TO

THE END OF HIS PRESIDENCY.

EDITED FROM THE ORIGINAL MANUSCRIPTS

BY JARED SPARKS.

VOLUME I.

BOOKS FOR LIBRARIES PRESS
FREEPORT, NEW YORK

First Published 1853
Reprinted 1970

STANDARD BOOK NUMBER:
8369-5486-6

LIBRARY OF CONGRESS CATALOG CARD NUMBER:
78-126259

PRINTED IN THE UNITED STATES OF AMERICA

PREFACE.

WHILE I was employed in preparing "Washington's Writings" for the press, I made a selection from letters written to him, and copies were taken from the autographs. It was then my intention to publish the letters thus selected, as a sequel to that work, but various causes have intervened to delay the publication till the present time.

In making the selection from several thousand letters, it was not possible to adopt any precise rule, but it was the aim to choose such as would enlarge the reader's knowledge of the events, characters, and opinions of the period which they embrace. All the letters are here printed entire. Having been written by various hands, and on different subjects, they are not, in any instance, repetitions of each other; and hence there was no occasion to omit any parts of them on this account, as in the case of Washington's own letters; nor was there the same reason for omissions to save space, in order to secure more valuable materials, and exhibit a continuous chain of events. In fact,

such an attempt would be impracticable in a series
of disconnected and miscellaneous letters. The
editorial revision has been performed with such
care, as the condition of the manuscripts admitted
or required. Errors of grammar, and obvious
blunders, the result of hasty composition, have been
corrected.

The letters from Count Rochambeau were written in English, either by himself, or by a Secretary who had but an imperfect knowledge of the
language. Hence the style partakes of the French
idiom. The same characteristic appears in the
letters of Lafayette and some of the other foreign officers. A large portion of the original
letters from Lafayette were returned to him from
Mount Vernon, at some time after Washington's
death. A copy of these was furnished to me in
part by Lafayette himself, and the remainder by
his son. Such of them as are selected for this
work, are printed from that copy. The letters
from Gouverneur Morris, written while he was in
Europe, were copied from his letter-books. In
most instances, the translations of letters written
in a foreign language are the same that were
found in the files at Mount Vernon.

The remarkable letter from the Reverend Jacob Duché, written from Philadelphia in October,
1777, soon after the British took possession of
that city, was transmitted by Washington to the
President of Congress. As the original is not to
be found among the papers of that time in the

Department of State, it has probably been lost. In the present work it is reprinted from Rivington's Gazette. There are discrepances, of minor importance, between this copy and another published a few years ago from a manuscript copy, the origin of which was not known. As Rivington's Gazette was in the British interest, the letter may be presumed to have been inserted in that paper with the knowledge of the author; but it has evidently suffered from the carelessness of transcribers or printers.

Although these volumes are intended to illustrate various parts of Washington's Writings, yet their contents have an independent value as conveying numerous original facts of history, drawn from the highest sources. The writers were among the most prominent actors in the political and military events of the time, and, as they wrote with a full understanding of what was passing around them, and generally on topics of immediate importance, their statements possess a weight of authority and a freshness, which insure their accuracy, and enhance their interest. Moreover, the characters of the writers, their respective qualifications, and relative agency and influence in public affairs, are here unfolded in a clear and impressive manner by the best of all testimony, a personal declaration of their acts, opinions, and designs. As authentic records of history, and as faithful memorials of eminent patriots, these letters may be equally valued.

The Appendixes to the first and second volumes comprise miscellaneous letters, designed to contribute additional facts concerning some of the large operations of the war, in which Washington was not engaged, except by a general supervision as Commander-in-chief, but which affected in a greater or less degree his own movements and plans. A few of these letters have been printed before, but they have mostly been taken from originals among the papers of Generals Schuyler, Gates, Lee, Lincoln, Sullivan, Stark, and others. Together they will be found to lend some new aids towards filling out the narrative, and explaining the events to which they relate.

CAMBRIDGE, March 1, 1853.

CORRESPONDENCE

RELATING TO THE

AMERICAN REVOLUTION.

FROM NICHOLAS COOKE, GOVERNOR OF RHODE ISLAND.

Providence, 12 July, 1775.

SIR,

I beg leave to congratulate your Excellency upon your being appointed General of the Armies of the United Colonies, which hath given sincere pleasure to every friend of America, and will, I hope, prove glorious to yourself, and be attended with essential advantages to your country.*

The General Assembly of this Colony have the deepest sense of the necessity of a strict union, and the most vigorous efforts, of the Colonies to preserve them from unlimited servitude; and their utmost exertions in the common cause may be depended upon.

I also assure your Excellency, that I shall give you every possible assistance in my power; and that I am with very great regard, Sir, your Excellency's

Most obedient humble servant,

NICHOLAS COOKE.

---

* Washington arrived in Cambridge on the 2d of July, and took command of the army there the next day.

FROM JONATHAN TRUMBULL, GOVERNOR OF CONNECTICUT.

Lebanon, 13 July, 1775.

SIR,

Suffer me to join in congratulating you, on your appointment to be General and Commander-in-Chief of the troops raised, or to be raised, for the defence of American liberty. Men, who have tasted freedom, and who have felt their personal rights, are not easily taught to bear with encroachments on either, or brought to submit to oppression. Virtue ought always to be made the object of government. Justice is firm and permanent.

His Majesty's ministers have artfully induced the Parliament to join in their measures, to prosecute the dangerous and increasing difference between Great Britain and these Colonies with rigor and military force; whereby the latter are driven to an absolute necessity to defend their rights and properties by raising forces for their security.

The Honorable Congress have proclaimed a Fast to be observed by the inhabitants of all the English Colonies on this continent, to stand before the Lord in one day, with public humiliation, fasting, and prayer, to deplore our many sins, to offer up our joint supplications to God, for forgiveness, and for his merciful interposition for us in this day of unnatural darkness and distress.

They have, with one united voice, appointed you to the high station you possess. The Supreme Director of all events hath caused a wonderful union of hearts and counsels to subsist among us.

Now, therefore, be strong and very courageous. May the God of the armies of Israel shower down the blessings of his Divine Providence on you, give you wisdom and fortitude, cover your head in the day of battle and danger, add success, convince our enemies of their mistaken measures, and that all their attempts to deprive these Colonies of their inestimable constitutional rights and liberties are injurious and vain. I am, with great esteem and regard, Sir,

Your most obedient humble servant,

JONATHAN TRUMBULL.

FROM MAJOR-GENERAL PHILIP SCHUYLER.

Saratoga, 15 July, 1775.

DEAR SIR,

Since I did myself the honor to write to your Excellency from New York, nothing very material occurred until yesterday, when I received the inclosed letters. The accounts contained in that marked Number One are truly alarming, in the present defenceless state of the counties of Tryon and Albany, and especially as the assistance I can afford them either of men or money is next to nothing; the few troops at Ticonderoga, &c., being at too great a distance, and not more than sufficient to guard the posts they occupy. I should have been at Ticonderoga this day, had not the information from Tryon county arrived, which may make my presence there absolutely necessary, if it should be confirmed. I therefore propose remaining here until to-morrow, when I hope to be further informed.

I wish I may be able to proceed to Ticonderoga, as I am very much wanted there, the greatest confusion having taken place in the controversy between the officers claiming the command in that quarter. Some have taken the liberty to disband troops, others refused to serve unless this or that particular person commanded. The sloop is left without either captain or pilot, both of which are dismissed or come away; much provision wasted or embezzled, and on the 7th instant only one barrel of flour at Ticonderoga. I shall have an Augean stable to clean there.

I do myself the honor to inclose a return of the forces in this colony.* It is doubtless imperfect, as I have been under a necessity of forming it out of the returns which were evidently so. I hope soon to send you a more complete one.

Be assured, my General, that I shall use my best endeavours to establish order and discipline in the troops under my command. I wish I could add, that I had a prospect of much success in that way. It is extremely difficult to introduce a proper subordination amongst a people where so little distinction is kept up.

Our accounts of the disposition of the Canadians and Canada Indians continue to be favorable, though the intelligence is nothing very authentic. I am your Excellency's

Obedient and most humble servant,

PHILIP SCHUYLER.

FROM GOVERNOR TRUMBULL.

Lebanon, 17 July, 1775.

SIR,

On the 1st instant I met the Honorable Assembly of this Colony, to deliberate on the request and pressing reasons sent us from the Massachusetts for an

---

* See this return in Washington's Writings, Vol. III. p. 43.

immediate augmentation of troops from this Colony. Our Assembly agreed to augment with two regiments of seven hundred men each, who are now raising to join the Continental Army. It was wished that we could have the advice and direction of the Congress, or your Excellency, before we took this step, but thought the present critical situation of our affairs would not admit the delay of obtaining it. Since your arrival at camp before Boston, views and considerations of their situation and circumstances, I shall gladly be advised, and shall attend your request for the hastening and marching the men.

There are thirteen hundred and ninety-one barrels of flour come to the care of Colonel Jedediah Huntington, at Norwich, for the use of the army, which I have ordered forward. The busy season with the farmers renders its speedy transportation difficult. Please to advise of the need of hurry, and where it shall be ordered to be delivered.

Our Assembly supplied Major-General Schuyler with fifteen thousand pounds in cash, and forty barrels of another necessary article. Accounts from the northward are favorable. The brig Nancy, Thomas Davis, master, which arrived at Stonington with molasses, is removed to Norwich. She hath on board eighteen or nineteen thousand gallons. The Committee of Inspection and Correspondence, I trust, will take proper care respecting both vessel and cargo.

The road by my door being the nearest for post-riding from Cambridge to Philadelphia, I shall be obliged, whenever your Excellency has occasion to send to that city, if the rider may be directed this way, and to call on me, for the convenience of any despatches I may have occasion to forward by him. Fessenden has passed this way more than once.

1*

I am, with great esteem and regard, Sir, your obedient and most humble servant,

JONATHAN TRUMBULL.

FROM MAJOR-GENERAL SCHUYLER.

Ticonderoga, 18 July, 1775.

DEAR SIR,

I do myself the honor to inform your Excellency of my arrival at this place early this morning; and, as a person is just going to Hartford, I sit down to give you the little information I have procured.

A Canadian, who twelve days ago left St. John's, advises me that General Carleton has about four hundred men at that place; that he has thrown up a strong intrenchment, covered with *chevaux-de-frise;* picketed the ditch, and secured it with an *abatis;* that he has an advanced post of fifty men, intrenched a league on this side; that there are many Indians in Canada; but believes neither they, nor the Canadians, will join him; the latter he is sure will not, unless compelled by force.

You will expect that I should say something about this place and the troops here. Not one earthly thing for offence or defence has been done; *the commanding officer has no orders, he only came to reinforce the garrison, and he expected the General.* But this, my dear General, as well as what follows in this paragraph, I pray may be *entre nous,* for reasons I need not suggest. About ten, last night, I arrived at the landing-place at the north end of Lake George; a post occupied by a Captain and one hundred men. A sentinel, on being informed I was in the boat, quitted his post to go and awaken the guard, consisting of three men, in which he had no success. I walked up and came to another, a sergeant's guard. Here the sentinel challenged, but suffered me to come up to him, the whole guard, like the first, in the soundest sleep. With a penknife only I could have cut off both guards, and then have set fire to the block-house, destroyed the stores and starved the people here. At this post I have pointedly recommended vigilance and care, as all the stores from Fort George must necessarily be landed there. But I hope to get the better of this inattention. The officers and men are all good-looking people, and decent in their deportment, and I really believe will make good soldiers as soon as I can get the better of this *nonchalance* of theirs. Bravery, I believe, they are far from wanting. As soon as I am a little settled, I shall do myself the honor to send you a return of my strength both on land and water.

I inclose to your Excellency a copy of a letter from Colonel Johnson, with a copy of an examination of a person lately from Canada, contradictory of the accounts I gave you in my last from Saratoga. You will perceive that he is gone to Canada. I hope Carleton, if he should be able to procure a body of Indians, will not be in a hurry to pay us a visit. I wish to be a little more decently prepared to receive him; in doing which be assured I shall lose no time.

I have no way of sending you any letters, with a probable hope of their coming to hand, unless by express, or by the circuitous route of Hartford; by which only I can expect to be favored with a line from you.

Generals Lee and Gates share with you in my warmest wishes. I shall devote the first hour I can call my own to do myself the honor to write them. I am, most sincerely, your Excellency's

    Obedient and humble servant,

      PHILIP SCHUYLER.

P. S. Permit me, Sir, through you, to inquire the health of Colonel Reed, Major Mifflin, and Mr. Griffin.

FROM MAJOR-GENERAL SCHUYLER.

Ticonderoga, 31 July, 1775.

DEAR GENERAL,

Since my last I have been most assiduously employed in preparing materials for building boats to convey me across the Lake. The progress has hitherto been slow, as with few hands I had all the timber to cut, mills to repair, to saw the plank, and my draught-cattle extremely weak for want of feed, the drought having scorched up every kind of herbage. I have now one boat on the stocks, which I hope will carry near three hundred men; another is putting up to-day. Provisions of the bread kind are scarce with me, and therefore I have not dared to order up a thousand men that are at Albany, lest we should starve here.

I have had no intelligence from Canada since my last to you. Major Brown has been gone nine days, and I expect him back, if all is well, by Saturday next.*

2 August.

I have not had a return from General Wooster since my arrival. I am therefore under the necessity of making you a return of the troops here only.

---

* See Major Brown's letter to Governor Trumbull, August 14th, in the APPENDIX.

I inclose your Excellency copies of two affidavits made by persons from Canada. I have transmitted other copies to the Congress.

I am extremely anxious to hear from your part of the world. Reports prevail that a body of troops have left Boston, and are gone to Canada. If so, I fear we shall not be able to penetrate into Canada, or even attack St. John's with success, though at all events I am ordered to go there. I am

> Your Excellency's most obedient
> and most humble servant,
> PHILIP SCHUYLER.

P. S. I wish I could make you a regular return even of the troops at this place and Crown Point, but I have not yet got these people to be regular in any thing, and therefore beg you to dispense with the following statement.

Fit for duty,—one colonel, three majors, nine captains, one captain-lieutenant, twenty-one subalterns, thirty-four sergeants, eighteen drums and fifes, ninety-three rank and file, one chaplain, two adjutants, one quarter-master, one surgeon, and two mates. Sick,— one lieutenant, four sergeants, two drums, one hundred and three rank and file.

FROM GOVERNOR TRUMBULL.

Lebanon, 31 July, 1775.

SIR,

By the resolve in Congress of the 19th instant, it is recommended to the New England Colonies to complete the deficiencies in the regiments belonging to them respectively.

I have not been informed of any deficiency in the number of troops sent from Connecticut. It is recommended also to this Colony to complete and send forward to the camp before Boston, as soon as possible, the fourteen hundred men lately voted by our Assembly. The 25th instant I sent orders to the Colonels of the last raised regiments to march forthwith to the camp before Boston, by subdivisions, if all were not in readiness. I expect many of the companies will begin their march this day, and that the whole will move forward very soon.

The Honorable President Hancock, in his favor of the 22d instant, informs that you had recommended, and the Congress have appointed, Mr. Joseph Trumbull Commissary-General of the American Army. I am also informed that you have taken Mr. John Trumbull into your service and family.* These instances of kindness shown them justly claim my most grateful acknowledgments. A performance of their duty, answerable to your expectation, will meet your approbation and continuance of regard, and afford me peculiar satisfaction and pleasure.

The Rose, Swan, and Kingfisher, ships of war, with a small tender, the 26th instant came into the harbour at New London. On the 27th some men landed near the light-house, broke off the nuts, and plugged up with old files three or four cannon. They sailed out again on Friday last. It is reported Mr. Collector Stuart is packing up his effects, in order to leave that port. I am, with great truth and regard, your Excellency's

Most obedient and humble servant,

JONATHAN TRUMBULL.

---

* Mr. John Trumbull is the same, who was afterwards celebrated as an artist.

FROM GOVERNOR COOKE.

Providence, 31 July, 1775.

SIR,

I am favored with your Excellency's letter of the 26th instant. Having just before the receipt of it had accounts by a private hand of the sailing of a number of men-of-war and transports from Boston, which I conjectured were designed to supply the enemy with fresh provisions, I immediately sent the intelligence to Block Island, together with a quantity of powder, ball, and flints, to enable them to defend their property, and give them assurances of further assistance if necessary.

We have no account of this fleet from any part of our coast; so that I think it probable they were destined to the eastward.

I desire your Excellency to oblige me with a return of the army; and when any thing of importance occurs, I shall esteem an early communication of it a favor. I am, with great truth and regard, Sir, your Excellency's

Most humble and most obedient servant,

NICHOLAS COOKE.

FROM RICHARD HENRY LEE.*

Philadelphia, 1 August, 1775.

DEAR SIR,

After the fatigue of many days, and of this in particular, I should not sit down, at eleven o'clock at night, to write to a gentleman of whose goodness of heart I

---

* A member of the Continental Congress from Virginia.

have less doubt than I have of yours; but well knowing
that you will pardon what flows from good intentions,
I venture to say that my hopes are, you will find from
what the Congress has already done, and from what I
hope they will do to-morrow, that it has been a capital
object with us to make your arduous business as easy
to you as the nature of things will admit. The business
immediately before us being finished, the approaching
sickly season here, and the great importance of our
presence in the Virginia Convention, have determined a
recess of a month, it standing now, that the Congress
shall meet here again on the 5th of September. The
capital object of powder we have attended to as far as
we could by sending you the other day six tons, and
to-morrow we shall propose sending six or eight tons
more, which, with the supplies you may get from Connecticut, and such further ones from here as future
expected importations may furnish, will, I hope, enable
you to do all that this powerful article can in good
hands accomplish.

We understand here, that batteries may be constructed at the entrance of the Bay of Boston, so as
to prevent the egress and regress of any ships whatever. If this be a fact, would it not, Sir, be a signal stroke to secure the fleet and army in and before
Boston, so as to compel a surrender at discretion?
While I write this I assure you my heart is elated
with the contemplation of so great an event; a decisive thing that would at once end the war, and vindicate the injured liberties of America. But your
judgment, and that of your brave associates, will
best determine the practicability of this business.

I think we have taken the most effectual measures
to secure the friendship of the Indians all along our
extensive frontiers, and, by what we learn of the spirit

of our Convention now sitting at Richmond, a spirit prevails there very sufficient to secure us on that quarter. The particulars of their conduct I refer you to Mr. Frazer for, who comes fresh from thence, and who goes to the camp a soldier of fortune. You know him better than I do, and I am sure you will provide for him as he deserves.

We are here as much in the dark about news from England as you are, the London ships having been detained long beyond the time they were expected. The indistinct accounts we have, tell us of great confusion all over England, and a prodigious fall of the stocks. I heartily wish it may be true, but if it is not so now, I have no doubt of its shortly being the case.

I will not detain you longer from more important affairs, than to beg the favor of you, when your leisure permits, to oblige me by a line by post, to let us know how you go on.

There is nothing I wish so much as your success, happiness, and safe return to your family and country, because I am with perfect sincerity, dear Sir, your affectionate friend and countryman,*

RICHARD HENRY LEE.

FROM MAJOR-GENERAL SCHUYLER.

Ticonderoga, 6 August, 1775.

I thank you, my dear General, for your very kind and polite letter of the 28th ultimo, which I just had the honor to receive.†

---

* See the answer to this letter in Washington's Writings, Vol. III. p. 68.
† Washington's Writings, Vol. III. p. 41.

Immediately on my arrival here, I issued such orders respecting the provisions and stores, (which I found had been most scandalously embezzled or misapplied,) as I hoped would effectually have brought matters into a right train; but it is the misfortune of the people here, that they do not know how to obey, although they should be willing.

I have therefore directed the Deputy Commissary-General to send up a person, (whom I named and knew to be equal to the business,) to examine the Commissaries at the several posts on the communication, and to give them such directions as will, I hope, introduce regularity in future. Mr. John N. Bleeker is now employed in that essential business.

With respect to the returns of the army, you will see, by the last letter I had the honor to write you, that I have had no success in getting them properly made, although I have drawn and given them forms, which I thought so clear that no possibility of mistaking them remained.

I foresaw, my dear Sir, that you would have a Herculean labor, in order to introduce that proper spirit of discipline and subordination, which is the very soul of an army; and I felt for you with the utmost sensibility, as I well knew the variety of difficulties you would have to encounter, and which must necessarily be extremely painful and disgusting to you, accustomed to order and regularity. I can easily conceive, that my difficulties are only a faint semblance of yours. Yes, my General, I will strive to copy your bright example, and patiently and steadily persevere in that line, which only can promise the wished-for reformation.

Since my last I have had a verbal confirmation, by one of my scouts, of the intelligence contained in the affidavits which I sent you. I am prepared, with the utmost diligence, to obey my orders and move against the enemy, unless your Excellency or Congress should direct otherwise. In the course of a few days I expect to receive the ultimate determination. Whatever it may be, I shall try to execute it in such a manner as will best promote the just cause in which we are engaged.

Not a man from this Colony has yet joined me, except those I returned to you, and who were raised and paid by the Committee of Albany. Nor have I yet received those necessary supplies, which I begged the New York Provincial Congress to send me as long ago as the 3d of last month, and which the Continental Congress had desired them to do.

The troops here are destitute of tents. They are crowded in vile barracks, which, with the natural inattention of the soldiery to cleanliness, has already been productive of disease, and numbers are daily rendered unfit for duty.

I am so unfortunate as not to have one carriage for field artillery, so that if I am ordered to attack St. John's, and am able to get down the Sorèl River, I shall labor under vast difficulty to bring up the cannon through a very swampy country. They will be few, indeed, as I shall have less than a ton of powder, when the troops are completed to twenty-four rounds a man.

Congress has appointed Commissioners for Indian Affairs. As one of them, I have ordered messengers to be sent into their country, to invite them to a conference at Albany. I have also requested the Caghnawagas to meet me at this place. The whole family of the late Sir William Johnson have held a line of conduct, that evinces the most inimical sentiments to the American cause. Sir John Johnson has had four hundred men, partly Scotch Highlanders, in arms, to protect a scoundrel sheriff, who had repeatedly insulted the good inhabitants of that country, which at length they retaliated. The inhabitants have, however, drove off the sheriff, and made the knight promise he would interfere no further. I should not have hesitated one moment to have secured him and his adherents, had I not been apprehensive of evil consequences from the Indians. I therefore thought it most prudent to advise Congress of the whole matter.

Although, Sir, I am much in want of men, and would wish to have the three New Hampshire companies, mentioned in the copy of your letter of the 27th ultimo; yet they are so happily posted, either to awe the Missisque and St. François Indians, or to march to the relief of the inhabitants of this Colony, living to the westward of where these troops are now posted, on what are commonly called the New Hampshire Grants, that in case of an attack from the savages I have mentioned, who, if any, are most our enemies, I could wish them to remain under orders there for that purpose.

I am extremely happy to learn that you are so well supplied with provisions. I have now a tolerable stock of flour, but very little pork. Fat cattle are, however, coming up, so that I do not apprehend we shall suffer in that article.

My best wishes attend Colonel Reed and Major Mifflin. I am, most respectfully, your Excellency's obedient

Very humble servant,
PHILIP SCHUYLER.

FROM GOVERNOR COOKE.

Providence, 8 August, 1775.

SIR,

Last evening Colonel Porter delivered me your letter of the 4th instant, to which I have paid all the attention the importance of it demands.

This Colony, the last fall, not confiding entirely in the precarious supply of powder that might be expected from the merchants, imported a considerable quantity, though not so large as was ordered. The supplying the inhabitants, who were in a manner utterly destitute, the army near Boston, and our armed vessels, has so exhausted this stock, that the powder now left, which is all in this place, is greatly insufficient to resist even a short attack upon it. Our situation is the same with respect to lead. So that at present none of either article can be spared from the Colony.

By a vessel, which arrived here on the 30th ultimo from Cape Francois, we are informed that the captain of the vessel, sent from this port to the Cape for a quantity of warlike stores, in which the Committee of Safety for the Colony of the Massachusetts had interested themselves, had executed his commission, and was to sail with a large quantity in a day or two, so that she may be hourly expected. This Colony, about four weeks ago, despatched a suitable vessel with money to purchase fifteen tons of powder and other warlike stores, which may also soon be expected. Of these vessels we have the highest reason to think the enemy have gained intelligence; the ships of war upon this station having for several days past cruised continually off

2 *

Block Island, and from thence to Montauk Point, and up the Sound.

This hath made us think it absolutely necessary to send the smallest of our armed sloops to cruise without the ships of war, and endeavour, at all hazards, to speak with the vessels expected with powder, and order them to another port. She will sail this day. The other armed sloop, by being within the river, prevents the cutters and barges from committing depredations, so that she cannot be spared; nor, indeed, is a vessel of her force required for the enterprise you mention.

We have, in this harbour, a very fine sailing packet that would answer the purpose extremely well; which might be equipped with swivels, manned with about twenty men, and be ready to sail in less than two days. But as I do not think it prudent that her sole dependence should be upon getting powder at Bermuda, it will be necessary to send a sum of money to purchase a quantity at some other port, in case of a disappointment at Bermuda. In the present state of the Colony, I do not think it probable that a sufficient sum can be procured here for that purpose before the sitting of the General Assembly; and therefore advise that application be made to the General Court of the Massachusetts Bay to advance part of the sum necessary. I believe we may be able to supply one half the sum here. Colonel Porter hath been at Bedford, and along the Eastern Shore, but can hear nothing of Harris. He is now bound as far as New London, to endeavour to meet with him; but is greatly apprehensive that he is fallen into the hands of the enemy.

We have information that several ships of war and transports were, the day before yesterday, at New

London; and that the country round were alarmed and mustering. We also hear that they have taken some stock off the east end of Long Island.

Sensible of the great scarcity of lead in the country, I some time ago wrote to the Congress of the Massachusetts Bay, and to our delegates at the Continental Congress, recommending that a part of the large quantity of lead at Ticonderoga should be immediately brought down; and still think the measure necessary.

I shall immediately give orders to the Committee of Safety to purchase, for the use of the Colony, all the tow-cloth that can be had.

If the powder, supposed to be at Bermuda, be private property, it must be immediately paid for. If not, I imagine it will be settled with our other disputes. This is a matter that ought to be known and provided for.

Upon further consideration, I am very doubtful whether a vessel can be immediately provided with men here; and therefore am of opinion that twenty-five or thirty sailors had better be drafted from the army, and held in readiness to embark immediately upon the arrival of Harris.

This letter waits upon you by my son, whom I beg leave to recommend to your favorable notice. I am, with very great esteem,

Sir, your most obedient

And most humble servant,

NICHOLAS COOKE.

FROM GOVERNOR COOKE.

Providence, 11 August, 1775.

SIR,

Since my last to you, Mr. Ward, one of the Delegates, hath returned from the Congress. He informs me that some of the Bermudians had been at Philadelphia, soliciting for liberty to import provisions for the use of the Island. They gave information of the powder mentioned in your letter to me, and were of opinion it might be easily obtained. They were told by the Delegates, that every vessel they should send to the northward with powder should be permitted to carry provisions to the Island. Whether their situation will not probably prevent them from bringing the powder, I submit to your Excellency. Mr. Porter and Mr. Harris are both here. To Mr. Porter, who can fully inform you in the matter, I refer you.

I have forwarded about thirteen hundred pounds of lead, which is all that can be procured at present, that article being extremely scarce among us. In my last to you, I mentioned that I thought it might be brought from Ticonderoga with more ease than it can be procured in any other way; I am still of the same opinion.

I have given orders to the Committee of Safety to purchase all the tow-cloth that is to be bought in the Government; but I am afraid the quantity will be small, the scarcity of coarse linens in the Colony having occasioned a great use of that article in families. I am, with great esteem, Sir, your Excellency's

Most obedient humble servant,

NICHOLAS COOKE.

FROM GOVERNOR TRUMBULL.

Lebanon, 11 August, 1775.

SIR,

Yesterday, at twelve o'clock, I received your letter by Major Johnson. I immediately gave the necessary directions. Some companies I ordered to New London; others to New Haven; Colonel Webb, with the companies that way, if not marched, to take his station at Greenwich. Same day, at eleven o'clock, I received a letter from Brigadier-General Wooster, dated the 9th, at the Oyster Ponds, on Long Island. He had with him four hundred and fifty men, besides militia, designing to preserve the stock at that place. The people on the Island had left it. He applied to me for three hundred pounds of powder, before I had made my answer and order for the powder, which I gave, notwithstanding our exhausted condition. On receipt of yours, I inserted an extract from it, for his observation.

I am informed a quantity of powder for the camp is to be at Hartford this evening, and more to follow soon. We have none lately arrived, which is daily expected. I request your direction, that of the next quantity that comes to Hartford, there may be lodged there so much as you shall judge expedient. Of what is expected do arrive in the mean time, I shall have no occasion to use your allowance.

I am, most respectfully,

JONATHAN TRUMBULL.

FROM MAJOR-GENERAL SCHUYLER.

Albany, Sunday, 27 August, 1775, 6 o'clock.

DEAR SIR,

Your Excellency's favors of the 15th and 20th instant were delivered me last night.*

I left Ticonderoga on Thursday, the 17th instant, and hoped to have returned in four days; but, on my arrival at Saratoga, I received information, that a large body of Indians of the Six Nations were to be here on Tuesday last, and that my presence was indispensably necessary. I therefore attended, and on Wednesday the congratulatory ceremony was performed, and on Friday the treaty, agreeably to their request, was opened by them, by giving an answer to the messages that had been sent them by the Committee of this place. In this speech they anticipated part of what we had in charge to deliver them. Being (as we conceived) apprehensive that we should request them to take up arms in our cause, they explicitly declared, that, as it was a family quarrel, they would not interfere, but remain neuter, and hoped we would not desire more of them.

We have not got above half through what we are directed to say to them, and, although I hardly know how to leave them, yet such is the nature of the intelligence contained in the papers, which I do myself the honor to inclose to your Excellency, I consider myself under the necessity of leaving the Indian business to my colleagues, and repairing immediately to the army.

That Governor Carleton and his agents are exert-

---

* Washington's Writings, Vol. III. pp. 60, 62.

ing themselves to procure the savages to act against us, I have reason to believe from the various accounts which I have received, but I do not believe he will have any success with the Canada tribes, though I make no doubt that he is joined by some of the more remote Indians, who, I believe, will assist him as scouts from St. John's. I should, therefore, not hesitate one moment to employ any Indians that might be willing to join us.

I thank your Excellency for the honor you have done me in communicating to me your plan for an expedition into Canada. The inclosed information of fires, which corroborates not only the information of Major Brown (that contained in the two affidavits), but every other we have had, leaves not a trace of doubt on my mind, as to the propriety of going into Canada, and to do it has been my determined resolution (unless prevented by my superiors), for some time; and I have, accordingly, since my arrival here, requested General Montgomery to get every thing in the best readiness he could, for that I would move immediately, weak and ill-appointed as we were; and I learn with pleasure, that he has, since the receipt of Griffin's information, ordered the cannon to be embarked, and he will probably be off from Ticonderoga so soon, that I shall only be able to join him at Crown Point. Such being my intentions, and such the ideas I have formed of the necessity of penetrating into Canada without delay, your Excellency will easily believe that I felt happy to learn your intentions, and only wished that the thought had struck you sooner. The force I shall carry is far short of what I could wish. I believe it will not exceed seventeen hundred men, and this will be a body insufficient to attempt Quebec with, after leaving the necessary detachments, (at St. John's, Chamblee, and Montreal, should we succeed and carry those places,) which would be respectable to keep an open and free communication with Crown Point, &c.

Having now given your Excellency the time, force, and latest intelligence I have had, together with my opinion of the sentiments of the Canadians, I proceed to inform you of the enemy's strength, as far as I have been able to learn it; three hundred and fifty or four hundred at St. John's; one hundred and fifty or two hundred at Chamblee; about fifty at Montreal; and one company at Quebec. These are regular troops, besides between three hundred and five hundred Indians, Scotchmen, and some few Canadians with Colonel Johnson at La Chine. Of this party the Indians that are at St. John's are a part. Whether any ships of war are at Quebec, I cannot say. As none have been mentioned to me, I am rather inclined to believe there are none. Should the detachment of your body penetrate into Canada, and we meet with success, Quebec must inevitably fall into our hands. Should we meet with a repulse, which can only happen from foul play in the Canadians, I shall have an opportunity to inform your party of it, that they may carry into execution any orders you may give, in case such an unfortunate event should arise.

Your Excellency will be pleased to be particular in your orders to the officer that may command the detachment, that there may be no clashing, should we join.

I shall leave orders at Ticonderoga to forward all the lead that can be spared.

Excuse these scraps of paper. Necessity obliges me to use them, having no other fit to write on.

Be pleased to make my compliments to the gentlemen of your suite. Colonel Reed will be so good as to excuse my not answering his letter, as I really cannot find time. I am, dear Sir, with the most respectful sentiments,

Your Excellency's obedient humble servant,

PHILIP SCHUYLER.

FROM BRIGADIER-GENERAL WOOSTER.

Oyster Ponds, Suffolk County, 29 August, 1775.

SIR,

I have with me at this place four hundred and fifty of my regiment. I should before this time have returned to my station at Haerlem, but General Schuyler having ordered the three companies raised upon this end of Long Island for the Continental service to join their regiment at Ticonderoga, the County Committee requested me to remain here till the return of an express, which they sent to New York, to beg of their Congress, if possible, to prevent the three companies from being removed. The express has now returned, with liberty for the companies to remain here ten days from last Friday. It is thought best that I keep my station near New York, though I shall not return there till I know the destination of the fleet, which I understand, from your Excellency's information to Governor Trumbull, has sailed out of Boston. I hope and expect such measures will be pursued, as will prevent their taking the stock from this, or the adjacent islands.

The inhabitants here think that, had General Schuyler known their very exposed situation, he would not have ordered the companies away. The New York Congress suppose they have no right to counteract his orders. They might indeed have sent to him, and received an answer in season, but they are so refined in their policy, have so many private views to answer, and take such infinite pains to keep out of the plain path, conscious, perhaps, of their own superior wisdom, that they do nothing like other people. It is now too late to send to General Schuyler. The Committee of Safety have therefore desired me to request your Excellency to continue their troops upon this station. I shall only say, that I know of no place so much exposed to the ravages of the enemy; and if the companies raised here, who have a great part of the good arms in the country, should be removed, and their places not supplied, I know of none so defenceless as this. It is my opinion, after all the soldiers are gone, that two hundred men might ravage the country, notwithstanding all the inhabitants could do to prevent it. From this representation I doubt not your Excellency will think proper to continue the troops raised here upon this station, or order others in their room. I am, with great truth and regard, your Excellency's

Most obedient humble servant,

DAVID WOOSTER.

FROM GOVERNOR COOKE.

Providence, 30 August, 1775.

SIR,

Your Excellency's letter of the 14th instant is now before me, the contents of which I have duly considered. When it came to hand, our small sloop of war was out upon the cruise which I mentioned to your Excellency in a former letter. She hath since returned. The sending her on the enterprise you propose could not be done without some new and further powers from the General Assembly, which sat here last week; and the nature of the business was such, that I did not think proper to lay it before so large a body. I therefore procured a committee to be appointed to transact all business necessary for the common safety during the recess of the Assembly, particularly with power to employ the two vessels of war in such service as they should think necessary. The committee is summoned to meet this day, before whom I shall lay your letter. At present the undertaking appears to me extremely difficult. The most suitable man we have for the purpose is confined to his bed by sickness.

We have accounts that a number of vessels have sailed lately from Boston, which we apprehend are designed to plunder the stock along the coast. The General Assembly have ordered it all to be removed from all the islands in this Colony, excepting Rhode Island. We have now about three hundred men employed in that business. I am requested, by the General Assembly, to apply to you to give direction to the Commissary-General, that all the stock taken from the islands that are fit to kill be taken for the use of the army, in preference to any stock which is secure in the country. The drought hath been so severe along the sea-coast this summer, that there is no possibility of providing for this stock in any other way.

The scarcity of coarse linens hath caused such a demand for tow-cloth for family use, that upon inquiry I find there is scarcely any of that article to be had in the Government at any rate.

The vessel our small sloop was cruising for, arrived on the 28th instant at Norwich. She hath brought powder, lead, flints, and small arms. What quantity of each I am not certain. They are now on their way by land.

This letter waits upon your Excellency by Captain Joseph Brown, who is an eminent merchant here, a true friend to the liberties of his country, extremely well respected among us, and noted for his superior mechanical genius. If he hath any thing to propose for the service of the common cause, I have no doubt of your paying attention to it, and giving it the weight it shall appear to you to deserve. I am, with very great esteem and regard, Sir, your Excellency's most obedient and

Most humble servant,
Nicholas Cooke.

<hr>

FROM MAJOR-GENERAL SCHUYLER.

Ticonderoga, 31 August, 1775.

Dear Sir,

I arrived here last night, and immediately received orders for sending you the lead (my former ones not having come to hand). It will leave Crown Point this afternoon, and be forwarded without loss of time to you.

General Montgomery leaves Crown Point to-day, with twelve hundred men and four twelve-pounders. I follow him this evening, and have ordered the whole strength I can spare to join me at Isle aux

Noix without delay. When they arrive there, which I hope will be in five days, I shall then be near two thousand strong. I am still of opinion that the Canadians and Indians will be friendly to us, unless [for] the imprudence of a Captain Baker, who, without my leave, went upon a scout, and, contrary to the most pointed and express orders, seeing some people in a boat that belonged to us, attempted to fire on them, but, his gun missing, he was instantly shot through the head and expired. His party consisted of five men, and the other of an equal number, one of which, an Indian, was only seen to paddle away.

I will neither detain your Excellency, nor waste my time (which is precious) in giving you a detail of the many wants I labor under. I hope they will serve for an evening chat at some future day.

You would have cause to blame me for not sending a return of the forces under my command, but I cannot get one that may in the least be depended upon. I know the reason, but so critical is my situation, that I sacrifice every thing to the grand object. I have sent on only six   ; but I have promised not to complain. Adieu, my dear General. I am, with the most respectful sentiments,

Your most obedient servant,
PHILIP SCHUYLER.

P. S. My situation will apologize for this utter scrawl. Since writing the above, I have received the papers, of which a copy is inclosed.

3 *

FROM GOVERNOR COOKE.

Providence, 2 September, 1775.

SIR,

I am favored with your Excellency's letter, of the 31st of last month, by Captain Baylor, who hath purchased the warlike stores imported by Messrs. Clarke & Nightingale. The prices appear to be very high; but, considering the cost, expenses, and risk, I believe they are as low as can reasonably be expected.

In the letter I did myself the honor to write you by Mr. Brown, I mentioned the extreme scarcity of tow-cloth in the Colony. There is indeed none to be purchased.

The Committee, appointed to act during the recess of the General Assembly, have given your proposal for taking the powder from Bermuda a full consideration, and have come to a resolution to make the attempt. Captain Abraham Whipple, the commander of the two armed vessels in the service of this Colony, who hath been very ill, but is now upon the recovery, hath been consulted, and will undertake the enterprise as soon as his health will permit. He is deemed the most suitable person to conduct it that we have. He requests your Excellency to give him a line under your hand, assuring the people of Bermuda that, in case of their assistance, you will recommend it to the Continental Congress to permit them to fetch provisions for the use of the Island. He does not propose to make any use of it, unless he shall find it utterly impracticable to obtain the powder without their assistance. I am, with much esteem and respect, Sir, your most obedient   Humble servant,

NICHOLAS COOKE.

FROM GOVERNOR TRUMBULL.

Lebanon, 5 September, 1775.

SIR,

Your Excellency's favor of the 2d instant was delivered to me last night.* This afternoon I received General Schuyler's, of the 31st of August. He has ordered the lead to Albany, with directions to forward it by the most direct route to your camp.

We are infested by ministerial ships and transports. I gave your Commissary-General a narrative yesterday, and beg leave to refer you to him, from the haste of this express. Our coasts are kept in continual alarm. Three ships of war, with thirteen other vessels of divers sorts, were seen off Fisher's Island, and in the Sound, yesterday. They have gained no provisions from the main. Have heard nothing from Montauk, or any part of Long Island. New London is in great fears, and Stonington expects another attack. I have ordered the new-raised levies to guard and defend those two places, and the coasts as far as Connecticut River. There are likewise four companies of them beyond the river, for defence in those parts. This appears absolutely necessary for their security at present. Hope this use of them, till these dangers are over, will neither injure nor hinder any of your operations.

Whether these are the same ships your Excellency noticed us of, remains uncertain. Yesterday, ordered the best intelligence to be gained, to render that matter more certain.

Lord's day morning, constrained by the weather,

---

* Washington's Writings, Vol. III. p. 74.

came into the harbour at New London a schooner, taken by the Rose, Captain Wallace, at Stonington; four hands on board; one, a white man, sent to Windham gaol; the other three, negroes, two belonging to Governor Cooke and one to Newport, ordered to be returned to their masters, and the schooner to her owner. General Schuyler's army is moved forward; a few days will determine the event.

I have ordered our Commissaries in the several counties to send to your camp all the hunting shirts they can procure. I am, with great esteem and regard, Sir, your very obedient and

Most humble servant,
JONATHAN TRUMBULL.

FROM PEYTON RANDOLPH.*

6 September, 1775.

DEAR SIR,

I have it in command to transmit to you the thanks of the Convention of Virginia for the faithful discharge of the important trust reposed in you, as one of their Delegates to the Continental Congress. Your appointment to an office of much consequence to America, and incompatible with your attendance on this duty, was the only reason that could have induced them not to call you to the Convention. Your brother Delegates were unanimous in their acknowledgments; and you will believe it gives me the greatest satisfaction to convey to you the sentiments

* The first President of the Continental Congress, and at this time President of the Convention of Virginia.

of your countrymen, and at the same time to give you every testimony of my approbation and esteem.

The Convention appointed Mr. Henry Colt Commander-in-Chief of the army of observation to be raised, which is to consist of one thousand men, to be divided into two regiments. Mr. William Woodford commands the second. The Lieutenant-Colonels are Christian and Scott. Besides these, the Colony being divided into sixteen districts, each district is to be trained and disciplined, and to be paid during the time of training, and while in actual service. Mr. Henry is excluded from the Congress, the Convention having resolved that an officer commanding in the military shall not be a member of the Congress, Convention, or Committee of Safety. Mr. Pendleton and Mr. Bland both resigned, and in their room Colonel Nelson, Mr. Wythe, and Colonel Frank Lee,* are appointed delegates to the Congress.

I am much obliged to you for your letters. That relating to the action of the men-of-war and transports did not come to hand till the account had been in Virginia some time.

I shall be much obliged to you to remember me to Edmund.

I am your obedient servant,
PEYTON RANDOLPH.

---

* Francis Lightfoot Lee.

Providence, 9 September, 1775.

Sir,

I am to acknowledge the receipt of your Excellency's letter of the 6th instant, and to inform you, that, zealous to do every thing in our power to serve the common cause of America, the Committee have determined, instead of the small armed sloop, to send the large vessel, with fifty men, upon the Bermuda enterprise; with orders to Captain Whipple to cruise ten days off Sandy Hook for the packet expected from England; and, if he is so fortunate as to meet her, to put the letters ashore at South Hampton, and send them by express to your Excellency. She will sail, wind and weather permitting, the beginning of the week.

There is in this town a Mr. De Ville, a Frenchman, who hath made several voyages from this port during the last four or five years, and is esteemed a person every way well qualified, and to be depended upon, for the execution of the plan he proposes. He was with Captain Hopkins the last voyage, when he imported the ammunition, &c., lately purchased of Messrs. Clarke & Nightingale for the army; and hath brought with him a set of papers to qualify a brig as a French bottom.

His scheme is to proceed to Bayonne, in France, where he is well acquainted, and there to take in a load of powder, which he says can be effected in three days. This despatch will be so great, that intelligence of the vessel cannot be sent to England timely enough for any measures to be taken to intercept her upon her return. I think the plan practicable, and likely to be attended with success. We have here a brig, a fast sailer, and otherwise a suitable vessel for the voyage, which will bring about eighty tons, and we will undertake to fit one quarter of her, and to supply the money to purchase one quarter part of the quantity of powder; which is the most we can do here.

I have written to Governor Trumbull upon this subject, and desired him, if the plan meets with his approbation, to despatch a trusty person to confer with you upon it, who can return through Providence, and let me know the result, so that we may immediately equip the vessel for the voyage.

I have communicated to Messrs. Clarke & Nightingale that part of your letter that related to them. They desire me to present to you their respectful thanks for the polite notice you have taken of them.

I have the honor to be, with much esteem and regard, &c., &c.,

NICHOLAS COOKE.

FROM GOVERNOR COOKE

Providence, 14 September, 1775.

SIR,

I am favored with a letter from Governor Trumbull, in answer to mine proposing a voyage to Bayonne, in which he informs me that the Council of the Colony of Connecticut are summoned to meet this day to take the scheme into consideration. This, Sir, is the time to exert ourselves in sending to Europe for powder, as the vessels may perform their voyages and return upon this coast in the winter, when the enemy's ships are unable to cruise. I have written to our Delegates, strongly recommending it to them to use their influence, that measures may be taken to procure sufficient quantities of that necessary article. I have also advised them to move in Congress for opening some lead mines immediately, as the depending upon a precarious supply by sea, when we have such quantities in our own country, seems to me very preposterous. And I believe the article in this way will cost us less money than it can be imported for.

Captain Whipple sailed on Tuesday, with sixty-one men on board; his vessel being clean, and every way in good order. I have given him instructions to cruise fourteen days off Sandy Hook for the packet, and, if he is so fortunate as to meet her, to take her at all events; to take out of her the arms, ammunition, and warlike stores, and to land the letters at South Hampton, and forward them immediately by express. After the taking of the packet, or the expiration of the time, he is immediately to proceed to Bermuda, and, if possible, take the powder into possession, without any communication with the inhabitants. I have given to him strictly in charge not to make any use of your Address, unless in case of absolute necessity.*

The noble example set by the Lord Mayor, Aldermen, and Livery of London, in their late Address to the King, will, I hope, have a good effect in the other parts of the kingdom, and, together with the disaffection of the people of Ireland to the iniquitous

---

* See the Address to the Inhabitants of Bermuda, and a further account of Captain Whipple's cruise, in Washington's Writings, Vol. III. p. 77.

measures now pursuing against the Colonies, added to our own efforts, compel the ministry to depart from their favorite plan of establishing arbitrary power in America.

This letter waits on you by Joshua Babcock, Esq. He is a gentleman of a genteel fortune, a member of our General Assembly, and hath highly distinguished himself in the glorious cause in which America is embarked. I beg leave to recommend him to your Excellency's notice, and am, with great esteem and regard, Sir,

Your most obedient humble servant,
NICHOLAS COOKE.

FROM GOVERNOR TRUMBULL.

Lebanon, 15 September, 1775.

SIR,

I have received your Excellency's letter of the 8th instant by the express, who was detained by sickness, and did not deliver it till the 12th, in the evening; and my own bodily indisposition is some hinderance. Your peremptory requisition is fully complied with; all our new levies will be at your camp with all convenient expedition.

At the time they were by your direction to remain in the Colony on some reason to suspect a remove from Boston to New York, that they might be able to give them more speedy opposition, I ordered Colonel Webb, of our seventh regiment, his men being raised in the western part of the Colony, to take his station, with three or four companies, at Greenwich, the nearest town of this Colony to New

York; his Lieutenant-Colonel and company at New Haven; the residue of his and Colonel Huntington's, who were forward in their march, one company to Norwich and the rest to New London. Last week I sent orders to Colonel Webb to march the companies with him to New Haven, to be on his way so much nearer to your camp.

I am surprised that mine of the 5th instant was not received, or not judged worthy of notice, as no mention is made of it.

Stonington has been attacked and severely cannonaded, and by Divine Providence marvellously protected.

New London and Stonington are still so menaced by the ministerial ships and troops, that the militia cannot be thought sufficient for their security, and it is necessary to cast up some intrenchments. We are obliged actually to raise more men for their security, and for the towns of New Haven and Lyme. I hoped some of the new levies might have been left here till these dangers were over, without injury to your own operations. I own that must be left to your judgment; yet it would have given me pleasure to have been acquainted that you did consider it.

I thank Divine Providence and you for this early warning to great care and watchfulness, that so the union of the Colonies may be settled on a permanent and happy basis.

I have before me your more acceptable letter of the 9th instant. The necessities of the Colony to supply our two armed vessels, to furnish the men necessarily raised for defence of our seaports and coasts, and to raise the lead ore, which appears very promising, prevent our being able to spare more than half a ton, which is ordered forward with expedition. Before the necessity of raising more men appeared, we intended to send a ton.

You may depend on our utmost exertions for the defence and security of the constitutional rights and liberty of the Colonies, and of our own in particular. None have shown greater forwardness, and thereby rendered themselves more the objects of ministerial vengeance. I am, with great esteem and regard for your personal character, Sir, your most obedient and
Very humble servant,

JONATHAN TRUMBULL.

P. S. The Glasgow and Rose men-of-war are now at Newport, and threaten that, on the return of the Swan from Boston, probably with men for the purpose, they will attack New London and Stonington. All the regiments in the Colony, at a great expense, have been disciplined; and one quarter of them on the sea-coast are situated, equipped, and held in readiness as minute-men for every emergency.*

FROM MAJOR-GENERAL SCHUYLER.

Ticonderoga, 20 September, 1775.

DEAR SIR,

The day after I did myself the honor to write your Excellency from Albany, I set out for this place and arrived here on the 30th ultimo, much

---

* See the answer to this letter in Washington's Writings, Vol. III. p. 96.

indisposed with a bilious fever. Next day I followed General Montgomery, whom I overtook on the 4th instant at the Isle-la-Motte, he having been detained by adverse winds and rainy weather. On that day we moved on to Isle-aux-Noix, twelve miles south of St. John's. On the 5th I drew a Declaration, (but was so ill that it is not such as I could wish, a copy of which you have inclosed,) which I sent into Canada by Major Brown and Mr. Allen; and as we judged that going to St. John's, weak as we were, (our numbers not exceeding one thousand, and the little artillery we had not come up,) might have a good effect on the Canadians and encourage them to join us, we resolved upon the measure, and landed our baggage and provisions, except for four days, and early on the 6th embarked, and, without any obstructions, proceeded towards St. John's. When we arrived in sight of it, and at the distance of about two miles, the enemy began to cannonade, but did us no damage. We approached half a mile nearer and then landed without opposition, in a close, deep swamp, which extended to very near the fort.

Here we formed, and marched in the best order we could towards the fort, to reconnoitre. Major Hobby, of Waterbury's, with a detachment flanked the left wing, and was something advanced before the main body, when he was attacked, in crossing a deep muddy brook, by a party of Indians, from whom he received a heavy fire; but our men pushing on, they soon gave way and left us the ground. In the rencounter we had a sergeant, a corporal, and three privates killed, and one missing; eight privates wounded, three of whom died the ensuing night; Major Hobby shot through the thigh, Captain Mead through the shoulder, and Lieutenant Brown in the hand. These gentlemen are all out of danger. Night coming on, and the swamp being almost impassable, we drew our men together, and cast up a small intrenchment to defend ourselves in case of an attack in the night. In the evening a gentleman, Mr. ———— (whose name I can only mention to your Excellency, not having even ventured it to the Congress, and therefore beg you to erase the scored part of the letter after persual,) came to me and gave me the following account; — "That there were no regular troops in Canada, but the twenty-sixth regiment; that all these, except fifty at Montreal, were at St. John's and Chamblee; that there were then at St. John's about one hundred Indians, and that there was a considerable body with Colonel Johnson; that the fortifications were complete and strong, and plentifully furnished with cannon; that the vessel was launched, and had one mast in and the other ready to raise; that she would be ready to sail in three or four days, and is to carry sixteen guns; that he does not believe that our army will be joined by one Canadian; that they wish to be neuter on the occasion, but if we should penetrate into Canada, it would not displease them, provided their persons and properties were safe, and we paid them in gold and silver for what we had; that in the situation we were in he judged it would be imprudent to attack St. John's, and advised us to send some parties amongst the inhabitants, and the remainder of the army to retire to the Isle-aux-Noix, from whence we might have an intercourse with Laprairie. He told me that in the afternoon's engagement five Indians were killed and four badly wounded, besides several others the condition of whose wounds he did not know, and

4 *

Captain Tyce, of Johnstown, who was badly wounded in the belly."

On the 7th, in the morning, (having been undisturbed through the night excepting by a few shells, which did no other damage than slightly wounding Lieutenant Mills,) I called a council of war of all the field officers present, to whom I communicated the information I had received, and inclose a copy of their opinion, which, being perfectly consonant to my own, I immediately ordered the troops to embark, and we retired.

On my return to Isle-aux-Noix I immediately began to fortify the place, and to throw a boom across the channel, until my artillery should come up. On the 9th I received a letter from Canada, without signature, but which I knew to be written by Mr. James Livingston (copy inclosed). As I had through other channels a corroboration of the intelligence contained in the former part of his letter, I resolved, as I had not yet my artillery, to detach five hundred men into Canada, and gave orders on the 9th for their embarkation on the 10th, with an additional number of about three hundred, to cover their landing and bring back the boats. (Copy of my instructions to the commanding officer inclosed.)

For the event of this intended expedition, see the paper which was drawn and delivered me by one of the party, and, from what I can learn, is just.

This body returned on Monday, the 11th. On Tuesday, the 12th, I found I had upwards of six hundred sick, Waterbury's regiment being reduced to less than five hundred. General Montgomery (for I was too ill to leave my bed) perceived, however, with pleasure, that the men were unable to bear the reproach of their late unbecoming behaviour; and, taking advantage of this happy return to a sense of their duty, on the 13th I issued the orders contained in the paper Number Six. The 14th proved rainy, and retarded the embarkation of the cannon. On this day Colonel Allen arrived and made the report, Number Seven; and I found myself so much better that I had hopes of moving with the army, but by ten at night my disorder reattacked me with double violence, and every fair prospect of a speedy recovery vanished. Great part of the 15th rainy, the embarkation much retarded by it. On the same day I received the letter of which Number Eight is a copy. On the 16th I was put into a covered boat, and left Isle-aux-Noix; and as it rained part of the day, I do not suppose that General Montgomery could move until the 17th, which proved fair.

The mode of the intended attack on St. John's, as judged best both by General Montgomery and myself, was as follows; — to land as near the fort as we did the first time we went down; the two row-galleys carrying a twelve-pounder each, and well manned; the sloop and schooner and ten bateaux with picked men, to lay in the river, ready to attack the enemy's schooner (which is complete and carries sixteen guns) in case she should attempt to destroy our boats, or get to the southward of them, and thereby effectually cut off all communication between this place and the army. After this naval arrangement (which will take three hundred and fifty men), five hundred men to be sent as a corps of observation to intercept any succours between St. John's and Chamblee, and to keep as near the former as possible; two hundred men at the proposed landing to cover the boats and secure a retreat for the men in the vessels and boats, should the enemy's vessel [intercept them]; the remainder of the army to invest the place, make the, approaches, and erect the batteries.

You will perceive, by Number Five, that some of the enemy's boats fired on our people. Captain Douglas, who commands one of our armed boats, pointed and fired a twelve-pounder, loaded with ball and grape-shot, at them, and we have accounts that about thirty of the unfriendly Canadians were killed or drowned. In the first engagement, on the 7th, we killed them six Indians, two Caghnawagas, as many Mohawks, (Daniel, and William, a bastard son of Sir William Johnson's,) one Connasadago, and one Huron; and we are informed, by a Caghnawaga and Huron whom I left at Isle-aux-Noix, that not an Indian remained at St. John's, and which I believe to be true. Four deputies, who were sent by the Six Nations, and left Isle-aux-Noix on the 10th, to request the Canadian Indians to remain neuter, were not returned when I left Isle-aux-Noix. I have taken the liberty to desire General Montgomery to make a present, in the name of the Congress, to the Canadian Indians, if he should think it necessary.

Since the affair of the 10th, the army at Isle-aux-Noix, which then consisted of thirteen hundred and ninety-four effectives, all ranks included, has been reinforced by Captain Livingston's company of New Yorkers, nearly complete; on the 16th, by Colonel Warner, whom I met, an hour after my departure with one hundred and seventy Green Mountain Boys (being the first that have appeared of that boasted corps); he left this with about fifty more, but they mutinied, and the remainder are at Crown Point. Captain Allen's company, of the same corps, arrived here last night, every man of which was raised in Connecticut. About one hundred men of Colonel Bedel's, from New Hampshire, (his corps was to have been up a fortnight before, the remainder, one hundred and fifty of that body, were yet to come) joined, the 16th, at night; and I suppose the artillery company, under Captain Lamb, will join them to-day. These last were indispensably necessary, as we had none that knew any thing of the matter; so that the whole reinforcement consists of about four hundred. Yesterday I sent off sixty of Easton's, and one hundred and forty more are just embarking; this is the whole of that corps. About one hundred and twenty-five, of the first New York battalion, will embark early to-morrow, together with the company of Green Mountain Boys, consisting of about seventy.

Two hundred and sixty, of the third New York battalion, remain here, which I will forward on as soon as I can procure craft, which is building slowly, as most of the carpenters are gone home sick.

Your Excellency's letter, of the 8th instant, I received yesterday. I am happy to learn that the troops under the command of Colonel Arnold were to march so soon. I hope our people will commit no depredations in Canada; all possible care will be taken of it; but yet I have many fears on that score, as they stole thirty-two sheep at Isle-aux-Noix, contrary to the most pointed orders.

Be assured, Sir, that I shall not fail of giving you the most early intelligence of every occurrence worthy your attention.

I find myself much better, as the fever has left

me, and hope soon to return where I ought and wish to be, unless a barbarous relapse should dash this cup of hope from my lips.

The number of sick is incredible, and I have very little assistance to afford them. I wish I could make you a return of the army under my command; but I cannot get one; a great deal of foul play is carrying on.

I am indebted to General Lee and Colonel Reed for a letter, but I am too feeble to write. Be pleased to assure them of my respect, and be so good as to make my compliments acceptable to all the gentlemen of your suite. I am, dear Sir, your Excellency's

Most obedient and most

Humble servant,

PHILIP SCHUYLER.

FROM COLONEL ARNOLD.

Fort Western,* 25 September, 1775.

MAY IT PLEASE YOUR EXCELLENCY,

My last, of the 19th instant, from Newburyport, advising of the embarkation of the troops, I make no doubt your Excellency received.

The same day we left Newbury, and arrived safe in the river next morning, except a small vessel which ran on the rocks, but is since off without damage, and arrived safe. I found the bateaux completed, but many of them smaller than the directions given, and very badly built; of course I have been

---

* On the Kennebec River, opposite the present town of Augusta.

obliged to order twenty more, to bring on the remainder of the provisions, which will be finished in three days. Many of the vessels were detained in the river by running aground and head winds, which delayed us a day or two. The 23d instant I despatched Lieutenant Steel, of Captain Smith's company, with six men, in two birch canoes, to Chaudière Pond, to reconnoitre, and get all the intelligence he possibly could from the Indians, who I find are hunting there. The same day I despatched Lieutenant Church and seven men with a surveyor and pilot, to take the exact courses and distances to the Dead River, so called, a branch of the Kennebec; and yesterday, the three companies of riflemen, under the command of Captain Morgan, embarked with forty-five days' provisions, as an advanced party to clear the roads over the carrying-places. Colonel Greene and Major Bigelow march to-day with the second division of three companies. Major Meigs goes off to-morrow with the third division, and Colonel Enos the next day with the remainder. As soon as the whole are embarked, I propose taking a birch canoe and joining the advanced party. I have found it necessary to divide the detachment for the conveniency of passing the carrying-places, at the first of which there are some carriages to be procured. I design Chaudière Pond as a general rendezvous, and from thence to march in a body.

Inclosed is a letter to Mr. Coburn, from the party I sent to Quebec, by which your Excellency will see all the intelligence I have received. I have conversed with the party, who saw only one Indian, one Natanis, a native of Norridgewock, a noted villain; and very little credit, I am told, is to be given to his information.

The Indians with Higgins set out by land, and are not yet arrived. I have engaged a number of good pilots, and believe, by the best information I can procure, we shall be able to perform the march in twenty days; the distance about one hundred and eighty miles.

I intended Colonel Greene should have gone on with the first division of one company of riflemen, and two companies of musketeers. This was objected to by the Captains of the rifle companies, who insist on being commanded by no other persons than Captain Morgan and myself. This, Captain Morgan tells me, was your Excellency's intention; but, as I was not acquainted with it before I came away, I should be very glad of particular instructions on that head, that I may give satisfaction to the field-officers with me. There is at present the greatest harmony among the officers, and no accident has happened except the loss of one man, supposed to be wilfully shot by a private, who is now taking his trial by a court-martial.

Major Mifflin could not send money for the bateaux. The Commissary has been obliged to pay for them, with one hundred pounds I have lent him, out of the pay received for the month of September, and has been obliged to draw an order in favor of the bearer, Mr. John Wood, who has engaged to deliver this to your Excellency. I have promised him his time and expenses paid. I should be glad the manifestoes might be forwarded on by him, if not sent with the last intelligence from General Schuyler, to whom I intend sending one of the Indians as soon as they arrive. I have the honor to be, very respectfully, your Excellency's most obedient

Humble servant,

BENEDICT ARNOLD.

P. S. Since writing the foregoing, I have received a letter from Colonel Reed, with the manifestoes;* and the court-martial have condemned the man who shot the other, to be hanged, which sentence I have approved, but have respited him until your Excellency's pleasure in the matter is known, and design sending him back in one of the transports. Inclosed are all the papers relative to the matter, with his confession at the gallows before respited.

The three first divisions of my detachment are gone forward ; the last goes to-morrow, when I shall join Captain Morgan as soon as possible.

FROM GOVERNOR COOKE.

Providence, 26 September, 1775.

SIR,

In consequence of your letter of the 18th instant, we have sent out our small armed vessel with orders to Captain Whipple to relinquish the voyage to Bermuda, and to prolong his cruise for the packet to the 6th day of October.

Agreeably to your advice I have communicated the proposed adventure to Bayonne to the Congress, and most heartily wish it may be pursued, as the ability and integrity of De Ville are perfectly relied upon here. The following extract from Governor Trumbull's letter to me, of the 18th instant, will inform you of his sentiments respecting the enterprise, and his reasons for declining to take a part in it.

---

* Being an Address to the Inhabitants of Canada. See Washington's Writings, Vol. III. p. 92.

"In mine of the 11th instant, in answer to your esteemed favor of the 9th, I acquainted you with my purpose to lay your letter before my Council, on Thursday, the 14th, which I did. They approve your proposition; the way appears to them promising; at the same time we have advanced money so largely for that article, and have great reason to expect a supply in a similar method, that they judge it not expedient for us to proceed further at this time. It is an article which requires our attention, and wish every method, that appears probable to obtain it, may be pursued. I hope General Washington will hearken to your application, and suitably encourage and promote your generous design."

The time for which the combined army was enlisted being nearly expired, it is of great importance to provide some method of reënlisting them, in order to keep up a sufficient force to restrain the enemy during the winter, and to take the field in the spring. My anxious concern on this head, which appears to me to be of the last importance, will excuse my suggesting to you the necessity of giving it the earliest attention, as I greatly fear difficulties may arise which will require time to obviate, and I can safely assure you of the concurrence of this Colony in every prudent measure for the effecting this most essential point. I am, with great truth and respect, Sir, your Excellency's most humble and

Most obedient servant,
NICHOLAS COOKE.

P. S. Since the sailing of the small vessel, I observe, in the New York papers, that a packet is arrived there from Falmouth, which I take to be the same that Captain Whipple was sent after. If so, the opportunity is lost; but by extending his cruise a little longer, he may have a chance for the August packet.

FROM RICHARD HENRY LEE.

Philadelphia, 26 September, 1775.

DEAR SIR,

Two days ago I arrived here from Virginia, which the late short adjournment just allowed me time to visit and return from. I brought two letters from thence for you, which come with this. Having some business with Colonel Mason, I travelled that road, and having sent to your lady to know if she had any commands this way, had the pleasure to learn that all were well at Mount Vernon. As I suppose it will be agreeable to you to know what is passing in Virginia, I have inclosed you the proceedings of our last Convention, with two of Purdie's Gazettes.

I am greatly obliged to you for your favor of August the 29th, and you may be assured I shall pay great attention to it. When I mentioned securing the entrance of the harbour of Boston, it was more in the way of wishing it could be done, than as conceiving it very practicable. However, the reasons you assign are most conclusive against the attempt. I assure you, that so far as I can judge from the conversation of men, instead of there being any who think you have not done enough, the wonder seems to be, that you have done so much. I believe there is not a man of common sense, and who is void of prejudice, in the world, but greatly approves the discipline you have introduced into the camp; since reason and experience join in proving, that without discipline armies are fit only for the contempt and slaughter of their enemies. Your labors are no doubt great, both of mind and body, but if the praise of the present and future times can be any compensation, you will have a plentiful portion of that. Of one thing you may certainly rest assured, that the Congress will do every thing in their power to make your most weighty business easy to you. I think you could not possibly have appointed a better man to his present office than Mr. Mifflin. He is a singular man, and you certainly will meet with the applause and support of all good men, by promoting and countenancing real merit and public virtue, in opposition to all private interests and partial affections. You will see, in the proceedings of our Convention, that they have agreed to raise the pay of our rifle officers and men to the Virginia standard. It may, perhaps, encourage them to be told this.

We have no late accounts from England; but from what we have had that can be relied on, it seems almost certain, that our enemies there must shortly meet with a total overthrow. The entire failure of all their schemes, and the rising spirit of the people, strongly expressed by the remonstrance of the Livery of London to the King, clearly denote this. The ministry had their sole reliance on the impossibility of the Americans' finding money to support an army, on the great aid their cause would receive from Canada, and consequent triumph of their forces over the liberties and rights of America. The reverse of all this has happened; and very soon, now, our commercial resistance will begin sorely to distress the people at large.

The ministerial recruiting business in England has
entirely failed them; the ship-builders in the royal
yards have mutinied; and now they are driven, as
to their last resort, to seek for soldiers on the Highlands of Scotland. But it seems the greatest willingness of the people there cannot supply more
than one or two thousand men, a number rather calculated to increase their disgrace, than to give success
to their cause.

I beg your pardon for engaging your attention so
long, and assure you that I am, with unfeigned
esteem, dear Sir,

Your affectionate friend and countryman,
RICHARD HENRY LEE.

FROM MAJOR-GENERAL SCHUYLER.

Ticonderoga, 26 September, 1775.

SIR,

I did myself the honor to address you in a long
letter of the 20th, which I hope will come safe to
hand.

The day before yesterday I was favored with a
letter from General Montgomery (copy of which inclosed), on the contents of which, and on the report
of the Indian deputies, I do myself the pleasure to
congratulate your Excellency. I have made some
explanatory notes on General Montgomery's letter,
which I conceived might be necessary for you.* I
made a short speech to the Indian deputies, gave
them a present, and they left me in high good humor,
and with a very good opinion of our army.

* See this letter, in the Appendix, dated 19th September.

5 *

The vexation of spirit under which I labor, that a barbarous complication of disorders should prevent me from reaping those laurels for which I have unweariedly wrought, since I was honored with this command; the anxiety I have suffered since my arrival here, lest the army should starve, occasioned by a scandalous want of subordination and inattention to my orders, in some of the officers that I left to command at the different posts; the vast variety of disagreeable and vexatious incidents, that almost every hour arise in some department or other, — not only retard my cure, but have put me considerably back for some days past. If Job had been a General in my situation, his memory had not been so famous for patience. But the glorious end we have in view, and which I have confident hope will be attained, will atone for all.

I have discharged, or ordered to be discharged, every man that was so ill as to be rendered unfit for further service during this campaign, and that was able to return to the place of his abode. Those that were not, I have sent to the hospital. The former already amount to seven hundred and twenty-six, as per the inclosed return.

My best wishes attend your Excellency and the gentlemen with you. I am, dear Sir, with the most sincere esteem,

Your very obedient humble servant,
PHILIP SCHUYLER.

FROM THE PRESIDENT OF CONGRESS.

Philadelphia, 30 September, 1775.

Sir,

Your letters, Numbers Four and Five, and two other letters not numbered, with the inclosures, have been duly received and laid before the Congress.

As there are sundry matters contained in your letters, which are of great importance, and on which the Congress, before they come to a final determination, are desirous to have the advantage of your experience and knowledge, they have appointed three of their members, namely, Mr. Lynch, Dr. Franklin, and Mr. Harrison, to wait on you, and confer with you and the Governors of Connecticut and Rhode Island, the Council of Massachusetts Bay, and the President of the Convention of New Hampshire, to whom I have wrote on the subject, by order of Congress, and such other persons as to the said Committee shall seem proper, touching the most effectual method of continuing, supporting, and regulating a Continental Army. They will set out as soon as possible, and expect to be with you by the 12th of next month.

I have the honor to be, with the greatest esteem, Sir, &c.,

JOHN HANCOCK, *President.*

Philadelphia, 5 October, 1775.

Sir,

The Congress having this day received certain intelligence of the sailing of two north-country-built brigs, of no force, from England, on the 11th of August last, loaded with six thousand stand of arms, and a very large quantity of powder and other stores for Quebec, without convoy; and as it is of great importance, if possible, to intercept them, I am ordered by the Congress to give you this information, and to desire you immediately to apply to the Council of Massachusetts Bay for two armed vessels in their service, and despatch the same, with a sufficient number of people, stores, and particularly a number of oars, in order, if possible, to intercept said brigs and their cargoes, and secure the same for the use of the Continent. It is also their desire, that you give orders to the commanders of the vessels you send on this service, to seize and take any other transports, laden with ammunition, clothing, or other stores, for the use of the Ministerial Army or Navy in America, which they may meet with, and secure them in the most convenient places for the purpose above mentioned; that you give the commander or commanders such instructions as are necessary, and also proper encouragement to the marines and seamen that shall be sent on this enterprise; that the instructions you shall give be delivered to the commander or commanders, sealed up, with orders not to open the same until out of sight of land, on account of secrecy.

If the vessels in the service of the Massachusetts

Bay can be readily obtained, you are to employ them, and others, if you should think more necessary, to effect the purposes aforesaid; if they cannot, you will employ such as can be soonest fitted out. At the same time I am directed to inform you, that the Rhode Island and Connecticut vessels of force, if possible, will be sent directly after, to the assistance of those you send out; for which purpose I write, by order of Congress, to those governments, by this conveyance.

For the encouragement of the men employed in this service, I am to inform you that the Congress have determined that, on this occasion, the master, officers, and seamen, shall be entitled to one half of the value of the prizes by them taken, the wages they receive from their respective Colonies notwithstanding. It is farther resolved, that the ships or vessels of war, employed in this service, are to be on the Continental risk and pay during their being thus employed.

For further intelligence I must refer you to the inclosed, which I have not time to copy, as I am ordered immediately to despatch the express.

I have the honor to be, &c.,

JOHN HANCOCK, *President.*

P. S. The inclosed please to order to be delivered to the Council of Massachusetts Bay.

FROM GOVERNOR COOKE.

Providence, 10 October, 1775.

SIR,

I have this moment received, by express, orders from the Honorable Continental Congress to despatch the two armed vessels belonging to the Colony, on a cruise after two brigs that sailed from England on the 11th of August last for Quebec, with six thousand stand of arms, powder, &c. I think it my duty to inform your Excellency, that the large sloop hath not yet returned from her Bermuda expedition, and that the small one is unfit for service, unless it be in our rivers; so that it is not in my power to take any measures for intercepting those vessels. I also give the same information to Governor Trumbull. I am, Sir,

Your Excellency's most humble servant,

NICHOLAS COOKE.

FROM MAJOR-GENERAL SCHUYLER.

Ticonderoga, 12 October, 1775.

DEAR SIR,

I did myself the honor to write your Excellency on the 26th ultimo, which I sent by the way of Albany. On the 4th instant I received the originals of the inclosed, except that marked Number Two, which came to hand yesterday. It chagrins me much, that I have not more frequent opportunities of addressing myself to you.

I am extremely apprehensive that a want of powder will be fatal to our operations. I have sent express to Albany and New York, but have not yet learnt whether I shall be supplied or not.

The army is now supplied with provisions to the 30th instant, but all the pork that is to be had is gone; and although we have a sufficiency of fat cattle, I fear we shall want salt.

I inclose your Excellency a return of the discharged men from this army. Exclusive of this, one hundred and fifty, at least, occupy the general hospital at Fort George, and I fear as many more are ready to enter it.

I begin to gather strength; my fever has left me, and I hope soon to be able to join the army. General Wooster's regiment, I suppose, will be this evening at Fort George; they will be pushed off immediately on their arrival here.

Be pleased to make my best respects to General Lee, General Gates, and the gentlemen of your suite. I hope we shall all meet at a merry Christmas.

Adieu, my dear General; my best wishes attend you through life, happy if I can have an opportunity of evincing how sincerely I am, dear Sir,

Your most obedient humble servant,
PHILIP SCHUYLER.

P. S. This moment your Excellency's despatches of the 4th came to hand. Captain Buell waits for this; can therefore only thank you for them.

Second Portage from Kennebec to the Dead River,
13 October, 1775.

MAY IT PLEASE YOUR EXCELLENCY,

A person going down the river presents the first
opportunity I have had of writing to your Excellency
since I left Fort Western; since which we have had
a very fatiguing time. The men in general not understanding bateaux, have been obliged to wade, and
haul them more than half way up the river. The
last division is just arrived; three divisions are over
the first carrying-place, and as the men are in high
spirits, I make no doubt of reaching the River Chaudière in eight or ten days, the greatest difficulty
being, I hope, already past. We have now with us
about twenty-five days' provisions for the whole detachment, consisting of about nine hundred and fifty
effective men. I intend making an exact return, but
must defer it until I come to Chaudière.

I have ordered the Commissary to hire people acquainted with the river, and forward on the provisions left behind (about one hundred barrels) to the
Great Carrying-place, to secure our retreat. The expense will be considerable, but when set in competi-
tion with the lives or liberty of so many brave men,
I think it trifling; and if we succeed, the provisions
will not be lost. I have had no intelligence from
General Schuyler, and expect none till I reach Chaudière Pond, where I expect a return of my express,
and to determine my plan of operation, of which, as
it is to be governed by circumstances, I can say no
more than, if we are obliged to return, I believe we
shall have a sufficiency of provisions to reach this

place, where the supply I ordered the Commissary to send forward will enable us to return on our way home, so far that your Excellency will be able to relieve us. If we proceed on, we shall have a sufficient stock to reach the French inhabitants (where we can be supplied), if not Quebec.

Your Excellency may possibly think we have been tardy in our march, as we have gained so little; but when you consider the badness and weight of the bateaux, and large quantity of provisions, &c., we have been obliged to force up against a very rapid stream, where you would have taken the men for amphibious animals, as they were a great part of the time under water; add to this the great fatigue in portage; you will think I have pushed the men as fast as they could possibly bear. The officers, volunteers, and privates in general, have acted with the greatest spirit and industry. I am, with the greatest respect, your Excellency's

Most obedient humble servant,

BENEDICT ARNOLD.

P. S. I have inclosed a copy of my journal, which I fancied your Excellency might be glad to see.*

---

* Many of Colonel Arnold's letters, written to various persons during this expedition, may be found in the Collections of the Maine Historical Society, Vol. I. p. 357. Major Meigs's Journal of the daily occurrences in the course of the expedition is printed in the Massachusetts Historical Collections, Second Series, Vol. II. p. 227. See also Sparks's Life of Arnold, Chapters III. and IV.

Gunston Hall, Virginia, 14 October, 1775.

Dear Sir,

I wrote you in July, a little before my being ordered to the Convention, congratulating you upon
an appointment which gives so much satisfaction to
all America, and afterwards, in August, from Richmond ; since which I have to acknowledge your
favor of the 20th of August, which nothing but want
of health should have prevented my answering sooner,
as I shall always think myself honored by your correspondence and friendship. I hinted to you, in my
last, the parties and factions which prevailed at Richmond. I never was in so disagreeable a situation, and
almost despaired of a cause which I saw so ill conducted. Mere vexation and disgust threw me into such
an ill state of health, that, before the Convention rose,
I was sometimes near fainting in the House. Since
my return home, I have had a severe fit of sickness,
from which I am now recovering, but am still very
weak and low.

During the first part of the Convention, parties
ran so high, that we had frequently no other way of
preventing improper measures, but by procrastination,
urging the previous question, and giving men time
to reflect. However, after some weeks, the babblers
were pretty well silenced, a few weighty members
began to take the lead, several wholesome regulations
were made, and, if the Convention had continued to
sit a few days longer, I think the public safety
would have been as well provided for as our present
circumstances permit. The Convention, not thinking
this a time to rely upon resolves and recommenda-

tions only, and to give obligatory force to their proceedings, adopted the style and form of legislation, changing the word *enact* into *ordain*; their ordinances were all introduced in the form of bills, were regularly referred to a Committee of the whole House, and underwent three readings before they were passed.

I inclose you the ordinance for raising an armed force, for the defence and protection of this Colony; it is a little defaced, by being handled at our District Committee, but it is the only copy I had at present by me. You will find some little inaccuracies in it; but, upon the whole, I hope it will merit your approbation. The minute plan I think is a wise one, and will, in a short time, furnish eight thousand good troops, ready for action, and composed of men in whose hands the sword may be safely trusted. To defray the expense of the provisions made by this ordinance, and to pay the charge of the last year's Indian War, we are now emitting the sum of three hundred and fifty thousand pounds, in paper currency. I have great apprehensions, that the large sums in bills of credit, now issuing all over the Continent, may have fatal effects in depreciating the value; and therefore opposed any suspension of taxation, and urged the necessity of immediately laying such taxes as the people could bear, to sink the sum emitted as soon as possible; but was able only to reduce the proposed suspension from three years to one. The land and poll tax (the collection of which is to commence in June, 1777,) will sink fifty thousand pounds per year; and instead of the usual commissions for emitting and receiving, the Treasurer is allowed an annual salary of six hundred and twenty-five pounds.

Our friend, the Treasurer, was the warmest man in the Convention, for immediately raising a standing army of not less than four thousand men, upon constant pay. They stood a considerable time at three thousand, exclusive of the troops upon the western frontiers; but, at the last reading, (as you will see by the ordinance), were reduced one thousand and twenty, rank and file; in my opinion, a well-judged reduction, not only from our inability to furnish, at present, such a number with arms and ammunition, but I think it extremely imprudent to exhaust ourourselves before we know when we are to be attacked. The part we have to act, at present, seems to require our laying in good magazines, training our people, and having a good number of them ready for action. An ordinance is passed for regulating an annual election of members to the Convention and County Committees; for encouraging the making saltpetre, sulphur, and gunpowder; for establishing a manufactory of arms, under the direction of Commissioners; and for appointing a Committee of Safety, consisting of eleven members, for carrying the ordinances of the Convention into execution, directing the stations of the troops, and calling the minute-battalions and drafts from the militia into service, if necessary, &c.

There is also an ordinance establishing articles for the government of the troops, principally taken from those drawn up by the Congress, except that about martial law upon life and death is more cautiously constituted, and brought nearer to the principles of the common law.

Many of the principal families are removing from Norfolk, Hampton, York, and Williamsburg, occasioned by the behaviour of Lord Dunmore, and the commanders of the King's ships and tenders upon this station.

Whenever your leisure will permit, it will always give me the greatest pleasure to be informed of your welfare, and to hear what is doing on the great American theatre.

I most sincerely wish you health and success equal to the justice of our cause; and am, with great respect, dear Sir,

Your affectionate and obedient servant,

GEORGE MASON.

P. S. I beg the favor of you to remember me kindly to General Lee, and present him my respectful compliments.

FROM RICHARD HENRY LEE.

Philadelphia, 22 October, 1775.

DEAR SIR,

I thank you for your obliging favor of the 13th, and assure you, that no man living approves the vigorous measures you mention, more than myself. Great bodies, you know, move slow, and it is as sure, that the most palpable and glorious events may be delayed, and the best causes finally lost by slow, timid, and indecisive counsels. We must be content, however, to take human nature as we find it, and endeavour to draw good out of evil. You will, no doubt, have heard the disgraceful conduct of our Norfolk [people], in suffering Lord Dunmore, with a few men, to take away their printing-press.

It happened when the good men of that place

6 *

were all away, and none but Tories and negroes remained behind. Virginia is much incensed, and five hundred men are ordered immediately down to Norfolk. I expect, by every post, to hear of the demolition of that infamous nest of Tories.

By a vessel in twenty days from Quebec, which I believe brings us later intelligence than you had from thence when the last express left camp, we learn that the Lieutenant-Governor had twelve companies of Canadians in training, and that they were generally on their guard. But the same account says, the Government was so suspicious of the attachment of its troops, that they were trusted with no more than four rounds of cartridges. This still gives us some hopes of success in that quarter. Before this reaches you, you will have heard of Colonel Allen's unlucky and unwise attempt upon Montreal; nor have we, from the last accounts, much prospect of success from St. John's. The ministerial dependence on Canada is so great, that no object can be of greater importance to North America, than to defeat them there. It appears to me, that we must have that country with us this winter, cost what it will. Colonel Stephens writes me from Fort Pitt, that the Indians on that quarter came slowly in to the Commissioners, and that they evidently appear to be waiting the event of things in Canada, when they will surely, according to custom, join the strongest side. We have so many resources for powder, that I think we cannot fail of getting well supplied with that most necessary article.

Remember me, if you please, to General Gates, and to all my acquaintances with you. I am, with great esteem and sincerity, dear Sir, your affectionate and obedient servant,

RICHARD HENRY LEE.

P. S. *Monday Morning.* 'T is with infinite concern I inform you, that our good old Speaker, Peyton Randolph, Esquire, went yesterday to dine with Mr. Harry Hill, was taken, during the course of the dinner, with the dead palsy, and at nine o'clock at night died without a groan. Thus has American liberty lost a powerful advocate, and human nature a sincere friend!

FROM GOVERNOR COOKE.

Providence, 25 October, 1775.

Sir,

Captain Whipple returned here from his voyage to Bermuda on Friday last. He had received authentic intelligence of the arrival of the packet at New York, before the first time limited for his cruise was expired, and immediately sailed for Bermuda. He had light, flattering winds for several days, and when near the Island met with a violent gale, which drove him three or four degrees to the southward, and occasioned his having a long voyage. He put in at the west end of the Island, where the inhabitants, taking him to be an armed vessel belonging to the King, were thrown into the utmost confusion, and the women and children fled into the country; but upon showing his commission and instructions, were satisfied, and treated him with great cordiality and friendship. They informed him, that, upon the powder being removed, the Governor had given General Gage an account of the part they had taken in the transaction, who had despatched a sloop of war, and a transport of six hundred tons, to take all the pro-

visions sent to the Island. They then lay at George-
town, and treated the islanders as rebels. Captain
Whipple had five of the King's Council on board
his sloop, who all assured him, that the inhabitants
were hearty friends of the American cause, and
heartily disposed to serve it. As the assistance they
gave in the removal of the powder hath made them
obnoxious to the enemy, and reduced them to a disagreeable situation, I think they ought to be treated
with every mark of friendship. I submit to your
Excellency the propriety of our representing their
case to the Continental Congress, and recommending
them to favor.

We are fitting out Captain Whipple for a cruise to
the Eastward, with all possible expedition, which I
hope will prove more fortunate than his last. I am,
with acknowledgment of the polite treatment I received from you at Cambridge, and with great respect,
Sir,

Your humble, and most obedient servant,

NICHOLAS COOKE.

P. S.   I inclose your Address to the inhabitants
of Bermuda.

FROM MAJOR-GENERAL SCHUYLER.

Ticonderoga, 26 October, 1775.

DEAR SIR,

At two, this afternoon, an express from General
Montgomery arrived at this place. Copy of his
letter, with copies of the papers it inclosed, I do
myself the honor to transmit your Excellency by

express.   The irresistible force of necessity having drove us to arms, success cannot be attended without pleasure; and, therefore, I congratulate your Excellency on the good account these papers contain. The reduction of Chamblee will, in all probability, be followed by that of St. John's, especially as General Montgomery has now a supply of powder, of which he stood in such need, that a very few days more would have expended his all.

I wrote your Excellency that I should not send on General Wooster; but, as his regiment refused to go without him, I was obliged to suffer him to go. But, lest any detriment should accrue to the service, I thought it proper to write him a letter, of which I inclose a copy, as also a copy of his answer.

I am in hopes that the next accounts I receive will announce the arrival of Colonel Arnold (whose success seems now certain), and the reduction of St. John's.   I have requested General Montgomery to send me an express, as soon as he receives any certain intelligence from Colonel Arnold.   As I can easily conceive that your Excellency's anxiety must be extreme, I shall forward what intelligence I receive by express.   The great dread I was in, lest we should suffer for provisions, induced me to have all brought up that could be got; and it was very lucky, as the late heavy rains have carried away almost all the bridges between Fort George and Albany, and rendered the roads impassable, in which state they will continue at least a week hence.

I am, dear Sir, with the best wishes for your health, your happiness, and prosperity,

Your Excellency's most obedient humble servant,

PHILIP SCHUYLER.

FROM BRIGADIER-GENERAL SULLIVAN.

Portsmouth, 29 October, 1775.

MAY IT PLEASE YOUR EXCELLENCY,

I arrived here in about twenty-four hours after I left you; have collected powder, so as to make up near thirty barrels, and have since been preparing to set an example to the other seaports, by setting the fleet at defiance. Upon my arrival, I was surprised to find that the boom, so much talked of, was not prepared; that the bridge intended for crossing from the main to the islands, whereon stands the principal fort (called Fort Washington), had nothing more done than one pier sunk; that there was not a foot of the parapet, over which a man might fire, or even see his enemy; that the embrasures at the foot were horizontal, as well as the top of the parapet; and, in short, not a moment's defence could be made, or annoyance given to the enemy, either with cannon or small arms.

I immediately collected a number of gondolas, moored them head and stern, laid pieces from one to the other, and plank across, and soon completed the bridge. I then turned my attention to the boom, and in two days got it across, but found it could not stand the rapidity of the tide; it soon broke, and we have again fixed it, so that I hope it may hold; but lest it should deceive us, I have taken a number of ships, and moored them above, with a great quantity of combustible matter in them, and shall to-morrow have them chained together, and, in case the boom should give way, set those vessels in flames. I have also a great number of fire-rafts, ready to let loose upon them.

I have altered the works, and I trust made them fit for defence, and I doubt not will, in two or three days more, be completely prepared. I am extremely thankful to your Excellency for the riflemen sent to our assistance; it has indeed filled our people with gratitude; and that my coming down was equally agreeable, your Excellency will see by the inclosed letter from their Committee of Safety.

I have seen some men that were on board the fleet after the destruction of Falmouth. Captain Mowat showed his orders, which were, to burn all the seaports east of Boston.* When he departed from Falmouth, he told them that he must go to Boston, and take a recruit of shells, carcasses, &c., and then would visit Portsmouth. I expect him daily, but in case he does not arrive in a few days, shall despair of his coming. I must beg your Excellency to give me intelligence of any movement of their ships, with any orders you may think proper with respect to my conduct while here. I shall give the earliest intelligence of any thing material; and remain, with great esteem,

Your Excellency's most obedient servant,
JOHN SULLIVAN.

P. S. I inclose a letter from the eastward, which was inclosed in one to me, signed by one Major Goodwin, of Pownalborough. That infernal crew of Tories, who have laughed at the Congress, despised the friends of liberty, endeavoured to prevent fortifying this harbour, and strove to hurt the credit of

---

* For important particulars relating to the burning of Falmouth, see Washington's Writings, Vol. III. p. 520.

the Continental money, and are yet endeavouring
it, walk the streets here with impunity, and will,
with a sneer, tell the people in the streets, that all
our liberty-poles will soon be converted into gal-
lowses.   I must entreat your Excellency to give
some directions, what to do with those persons, as I
am fully convinced, that if an engagement was to
happen, they would, with their own hands, set fire
to the town, expecting a reward from the ministry
for such hellish service.   Some, who have for a long
time employed themselves in ridiculing and discouraging those, who were endeavouring to save the
town, have now turned upon me, and are flying
from one street to another, proclaiming that you
gave me no authority to take the ships to secure
the entrance of the harbour, or did any thing more
than send me here, to see the town reduced to
ashes, if our enemies thought proper.   Sir, I shall
wait your directions respecting these villains, and
see that they are strictly complied with.

FROM JOSIAH QUINCY.

Braintree, 31 October, 1775.

MAY IT PLEASE YOUR EXCELLENCY,

My worthy and dear friend, Dr. Franklin, the Honorable Mr. Bowdoin, Dr. Winthrop, and Dr. Cooper,
were the last week so kind as to honor me with
a friendly visit.   The conversation naturally turned
upon the savage cruelty we are daily suffering
from the unrelenting vengeance of a tyrannical Government.   In the course of it, the stopping up
the harbour of Boston, as one salutary measure,

was thought well worthy the attention of our State pilots; and upon my saying I had once, if not more than once, hinted the scheme to your Excellency, they desired me to communicate my sentiments to you once more, in writing, especially as I had lately received a letter from the Honorable John Adams, Esquire, in Philadelphia, in answer to one of mine, which seemed to throw new light upon the subject. This, Sir, I beg may be a sufficient apology for transmitting to you the following extracts of those letters, with what has further occurred to my mind since they were wrote. In my letter I thus write.

"In my former letter I said, 'the harbour might be blocked up, and both seamen and soldiers made prisoners at discretion;' which seems to you incredible. Please to read, at your leisure, the following explanation. There are but two channels through which ships of burden can safely pass to and from Boston. One of them runs between the west head of Long Island and the Moon (so called), and is about a mile across. This is too shallow for any ship of war above twenty guns. The other is called the ship-channel, and runs between the east head of Long Island and the south point of Deer Island, and is something better than a mile, from side to side. This, the only channel through which capital ships can pass, leads, outward bound, through the Narrows between Gallop's Island and Lovell's Island, where the channel is not wider than the length of a fifty-gun ship. In the opening between Gallop's Island and George's Island is Nantasket Road, where one frigate is always stationed, to guard the Narrows from being stopped up. Upon these facts I thus reason; —

"The Moon Island communicates, at low water, with Squantum Neck, almost dry-shod. A defensible fort, therefore, may be so placed upon Squantum as to cover the retreat not only from the Moon, but from Squantum to the main. One upon the east head of the Moon, and another on the west head of Long Island, secure that passage, and cover the retreat from the latter to the former. Another upon the summit, in the middle of Long Island, covers the shore on both sides, so as that no force can land without being greatly annoyed, if not entirely prevented. Another strong fort, with heavy cannon, at the east head of Long Island, would command not only the ship-channel that runs by it, but the Narrows and Nantasket Road, so that no ship could remain there with safety; and consequently we might, by sinking hulks in the Narrows, prevent any ship of force from going out or coming in. If the passage through the Narrows is not stopped, I am sensible that a ship, with a fresh gale of wind and flood tide, which is rapid between Long Island and Deer Island, might run through without any great hazard; but, after the east head of Long Island is fortified, I can foresee nothing to hinder the Narrows being reduced to such a depth of water as that no vessel of force can pass through there.

"This being effected, as I said above, both seamen and soldiers, if they do not escape by a timely flight, must become prisoners at discretion. I have been told there is, in one of the late English Magazines, an accurate draught of the harbour, which, upon examination, will enable you to determine, with precision, the bearings and distances from island to island, and the depth of water between them; and, consequently, whether such a scheme is practicable or not."

Mr. Adams, in answer, writes thus:

"I am much obliged by your kind explanation of your opinion, that the harbour might be blocked up. I must confess, although I was born so near it, I never understood before the course of the channel, and the situation of the harbour, so well. I have carefully compared your description of Squantum, the Moon, Long Island, Gallop's Island, Lovell's Island, and George's, the Narrows, and Nantasket Road, with 'A Plan of the Town and Chart of the Harbour of Boston, exhibiting a view of the Islands, Castle Fort, and Entrances into the said Harbour,' which was published in London last February. This plan I knew to be inaccurate in some particulars, and the chart may be so in others; but, by the best judgment I can make, upon comparing your facts with the chart, and considering the depths of water marked on this chart, I think it extremely probable, with you, that nothing but powder and cannon are wanting to effect the important purposes you mention, that of making soldiers and sailors prisoners at discretion.

"Dr. Franklin's row-galleys are in great forwardness; seven of them are completely manned, armed, &c. I went down the river the other day, with all of them. I have as much confidence in them as you have.* But the people here have made machines, to be sunk in the channel of Delaware River. Three rows of them are placed in the river, with large timbers, barbed with iron. They are frames of timber, sunk with stone; machines very proper for our channel in the Narrows."

---

* "I had wrote largely to Mr. Adams upon the subject, but have not copied it, for fear of being tedious."

Dr. Franklin says they may be made in the form of a *chevaux-de-frise,* and used to great advantage.

I have wrote to Mr. Adams for a model of the machines he mentions, with explicit directions how to sink and secure them from being weighed or destroyed by the enemy's ships. For my own part, since I have read what my friend has wrote, I am more than ever convinced of the practicability of not only securing the harbour, but relieving the town of Boston, by making the present possessors of it our prisoners, and that without shedding much more human blood, provided we can once possess and fortify Long Island.

I doubt not your Excellency will readily agree with me, that these are become objects of much greater importance, since the destruction of Falmouth demonstrates the malicious resolution of our barbarously civilized enemies, to destroy all the rest of our maritime towns, if they can.

If your Excellency should think the above sentiments worthy of your attention, and, for maturing your judgment, conclude it necessary to take an ocular view of the harbour and islands, please to accept of my cordial invitation to refresh or repose yourself at my house, where my happiness will be in proportion to the freedom with which you receive the friendly salutations of

Your Excellency's most obedient humble servant,

JOSIAH QUINCY.

FROM MAJOR-GENERAL SCHUYLER.

Ticonderoga, 6 November, 1775.

DEAR GENERAL,

Your Excellency's favor of the 26th ultimo I had the honor to receive on the 3d instant.*

I have long since signified to Congress the necessity of a delegation from them to this place; and in their last to me, of the 12th ultimo, they (unfortunately for me) say that it did not appear necessary then. I took the liberty to lament, that they were not in sentiment with me on the subject, and to add that I thought it absolutely necessary that one should be sent, so that I hope soon to see some of the gentlemen here. A variety of regulations are necessary to be made in this quarter; a task to which I feel myself greatly inadequate, but which, if I had even judgment enough to arrange with propriety, the shattered condition of my constitution is such, that matters so momentous as these should not be left to so precarious an event as that of my being able to support the fatigue; for General Montgomery, though endowed with shining abilities, will have his time so totally engrossed with other matters, that he will not be able to attend to these.

Should success crown our endeavours at St. John's, of which there seems to be little doubt, the entire reduction of Canada will, in all probability, be the consequence; an event which will open new scenes. An army to be formed and properly disposed of in that quarter; provisions, ammunition, and every necessary to be procured for it; preparations to be

* Washington's Writings, Vol. III. p. 132.

made for the next campaign; proper places to be determined on, and fortifications to be erected, to defend that Province against any attacks that may be made on it in the ensuing year; small craft to be constructed here, that a reënforcement may be speedily sent into Canada, in case it should be found necessary to support what troops may be stationed there; galleys, carrying heavy artillery, to prevent vessels of force from coming up the St. Lawrence; a mode of government to be adopted in a country, where all will be anarchy and confusion without it; and probably a variety of other interesting regulations to take place, that do not just now occur to me.

Your Excellency will do me the justice to believe that I feel, in the most sensible manner, the favorable opinion you are pleased to entertain of me; and I am confident General Montgomery will not be less affected on what you observe of him. I do myself the pleasure, this day, to write that gentleman, and shall convey to him your best wishes and respects.

The vast benefit that would result from a successful conclusion of the campaign in this quarter, has been so deeply impressed upon me, that I have often regretted that the operations were not commenced at an earlier period, and, when commenced, that so much tardiness prevailed in sending up the necessary stores and troops. That you, my dear General, should feel an anxiety to induce you to ask those questions, which you have done in so polite and friendly a manner, is what I can easily suppose.

The difficulties, under which General Montgomery has labored, have been in the extreme, and which he most pathetically laments in a letter to me of the

13th ultimo, an extract of which I do myself the honor to inclose your Excellency, together with the opinion of a Council of War held on that day, and which I forgot to transmit you in the hurry with which I sent off my last. And in his letter of the 23d ultimo he says;—" Our reënforcements not yet arrived; at this instant I have not in my camp above seven hundred and fifty men, and I wish much to send a strong detachment to the Island of Montreal"; a manœuvre which would have taken place sooner, had it been in his power, or been prudent to have gone into; neither of which I think it was, and shall beg leave to make the following observations in support of this opinion.

At no period, until this, has it appeared to me that it would have been prudent to have passed St. John's, although a sufficient force could have been left for forming a blockade; for [it would have been hazardous] previous to the reduction of Chamblee, and the success of our troops in repulsing the attack of Monsieur Regouville, who was sent from Montreal with two hundred and forty men, and expected to be joined by the inhabitants of three of the most populous parishes on the south side of the St. Lawrence, in which he was disappointed to a man, and which has in some measure evinced the temper of the Canadians towards us, and given us better assurances than any we have had of their friendly disposition, for until then their real sentiments were problematical; and about this time, too, we sunk their best armed vessel, so that we can now spare more men for an attack upon Montreal, which, if not prevented by other obstacles, was General Montgomery's intention, as soon as the reënforcement above alluded to should arrive, which took place on the 26th or 27th, and consisted of General Wooster's, of three hundred and thirty-five, and Major Tuthill, of Colonel Holmes's, with two hundred and twenty-five, officers of both included. In the numbers, however, he will be disappointed, as General Wooster had returned four hundred and eighty-four effectives from Albany, but discharged ninety-nine between this and Albany, and left fifty-one sick here; and the others, too, fell greatly short of what I expected

If a blockade had been formed before the above-mentioned events took place, it must have been sufficiently strong, not only to have guarded against the danger of a sortie, but to have prevented the enemy's armed vessels, which greatly surpassed ours in strength, from getting to the southward of us, and thereby effectually cutting off every possibility of retreat; which, if they had been able to accomplish, the Canadians, I do firmly believe, would immediately have joined Mr. Carleton. But if a sufficient body had been left, that to make the attempt on Montreal would have been too weak for such a service; and if they had met with a repulse, the Canadians, in that case, would not have hesitated one moment to have acted against us, (as Colonel Allen, in his report to me, observes,) and all our hopes in Canada would have been at an end. But another difficulty presented itself, and which I do not know how the detachment which General Montgomery proposed to send, or has sent, will even now surmount,—the want of craft to convey a body of troops, sufficient to promise success, to the Island of Montreal, across the St. Lawrence, (which is deep, rapid, and wide,) as no craft can pass the fort at St. John's to go down the Sorel; which obstacles would be immediately removed on the reduction of that fortress, which I hope has taken place by this time, and then I shall have the fullest confidence that our labors will be at an end in this quarter, except from what difficulties may arise from the intemperate desire our people have to return to their habitations; my fears on which account I have expressed to Congress.

If we had passed it wholly, and could have got to and succeeded against Montreal, St. John's would undoubtedly have fallen. But what a vast risk! No less than that of the loss of the whole Army, the command of Lake Champlain, Ticonderoga, and Crown Point; for no retreat could possibly have taken place; the dependence on the Canadians uncertain. And if they had found us incapable of passing to Montreal for want of boats, or of retreating on the same account, it is certain we should have found them opposed to us.

In this view of things, I hope it will be thought that either attempt would have been injudicious.

I do myself the honor to inclose you sundry extracts of my letters to Congress, with extracts of their answers, by which your Excellency will perceive that I have hinted at several things, which I conceived claimed the attention of Congress. I inclose you, also, a list of the officers made prisoners at St. John's. The return of the non-commissioned officers and privates is either mislaid or by mistake inclosed to Governor Trumbull.

Be so good as to assure the gentlemen of your family that they have my best wishes. I have the honor to be your Excellency's

Most obedient and very humble servant,
PHILIP SCHUYLER.

FROM THOMAS LYNCH.

Philadelphia, 13 November, 1775.

My Dear Sir,

In consequence of your favor by Colonel Reed, I applied to the Chief Justice, who tells me the Supreme Courts were lately held, and that it will be some time before their term will return ; that he knows of no capital suit now depending, and that it is very easy for Colonel Reed to manage matters so as not to let that prevent his return to you. I am sure Mr. Chew is so heartily disposed to oblige you, and to serve the cause, that nothing in his power shall be wanting.

I fear, however, that you will be some time in want of your Secretary, as I did not find him in haste to return, when I mentioned to him what is just now related ; he, doubtless, has many private affairs to transact ; the loss must be greatly increased by Mr Randolph's absence, who, I hear, came to town last night.

I am happy to inform you, that Congress has agreed to every recommendation of the Committee,* and have gone beyond it, in allowing the additional pay to the officers. I rejoice at this, but can't think with patience, that the pitiful wretches, who stood cavilling with you, when entreated to serve the next campaign, should reap the benefit of this addition ; they will now be ready enough, but hope you will be able to refuse them with the contempt they deserve, and find better in their room. Could not some

---

* The Committee of Congress, consisting of Dr. Franklin, Mr. Lynch, and Colonel Harrison, who had recently visited Cambridge, to assist the Commander-in-chief in a new organization of the army.

of the gentlemen at the camp enlist the New England men, who have been persuaded to leave you? Frazier told me he could; it would be a capital point to convince the world, that it is not necessary to have bad officers of that country in order to raise men there. I can scarce bear their tyranny.

I have a letter, from undoubted authority, that assures me that the destruction of the Parliamental army in America will certainly produce peace; and by another, that the seizing Quebec will produce the same effect. I have no doubt America stands now indebted to her General for the one, and will, before the return of spring, for the other. Mistake me not; I have not altered my mind one jot since I left you. I mean not to anticipate your determinations, but only to approve your design to hover like an eagle over your prey, always ready to pounce it, when the proper time comes. I have not forgot your proposition relative to that city. I try to pave the way for it, and wait for the season as you do.

No appearance of peace on the part of the enemy, unless produced by necessity; every human feeling seems to have forsaken them; fear and interest are only listened to.

We hear seven tons of powder are arrived at Rhode Island, and as many at Portsmouth. I hope it is true, as it will possess us of advantageous grounds, and begin the enemy's destruction. It is suspected, in England, that Howe's army will give you the slip, and land at Long Island; which God, in his infinite mercy, grant! We wait with impatience to hear of the total reduction of Canada.

Your Virginians, we hear, have drubbed Lord Dunmore, killed and took fifty men, and sunk one of his vessels; may all such villains so perish!

A Mr. Richard Hare, brother to the porter brewer, sailed in the transport for Quebec. As you have or must take him, let me recommend him to your civilities while with you, and to send him to his friends here.

The articles of war have all the amendments we reported. You will enforce them; you will not now suffer your officers to sweep the parade with the skirts of their coats, or the bottoms of their trowsers; to cheat or to mess with their men; to skulk in battle, or sneak in quarters; in short, being now paid, they must do their duty, and look, as well as act, like gentlemen. Do not bate them an ace, my dear General, but depend upon every support of your friends here. I have strove to keep two battalions now raising in the Jerseys, and one here, quite disengaged, that they may be ready on a call to join you, should those you have desert you. I have not been quite unsuccessful. The winter is our own; Boston will not, during that season, be reënforced; at least we have reason to think so.

I want the return I desired from Gates exceedingly. Compliments to him, Lee, Putnam, Mifflin, &c.

It is so dark I can't read this letter over, or I would save you the trouble of deciphering it.

Dear Sir, your most obedient servant,

THOMAS LYNCH.

P. S. Ought not that spirit of independence, and separation from all other authority, which appeared in the case of Captain Dyer, to be abolished? Will it be right to keep your heroes for wood-cutters?

Ticonderoga, 28 November, 1775.

My Dear General,

The evening before General Montgomery landed on the Island of Montreal, Mr. Carleton embarked his garrison on board of some vessels and small craft, and made two attempts to pass our batteries, near the mouth of Sorel, but was drove back by Colonel Easton, who has behaved with bravery and much alertness. On the 19th, Mr. Carleton, disguised *en Canadien*, and accompanied by six peasants, found means to make his escape. Brigadier-General Prescott surrendered next day by capitulation. What terms General Montgomery has given him, I do not know, as he was so hurried, in preparing to move immediately to Quebec, that he could not find time to send them. Prescott and the officers arrived here at four to-day. I have just received a return of the officers, men, vessels, and stores taken, which I do myself the honor to inclose.

Your Excellency's favor, of the 16th of November, I received two days ago. I believe some cannon and mortars may be spared; but none, except what I have sent across Lake George, can be got down until that or this lake freezes over. I have a very fine thirteen-inch mortar here, and I will make a push to get her over the Lake. But where will you get shells? We have none here.

Mr. Livingston, Mr. Langdon, and Mr. Paine, arrived here at seven this evening. The season was so far advanced that I could not wait the orders of Congress upon sundry matters, which appeared to me absolutely necessary to be carried into immediate execution. I am, however, happy to find, that every measure I have pursued corresponds with the instructions given to the Committee.

I am informed that Prescott has used poor Walker and Allen with a shameful brutality. Of this I shall acquaint Governor Trumbull, to whose Colony I shall send him.

I believe our army in Canada consists of about one thousand and nine hundred men, including Colonel Arnold's corps. I have suggested to Congress, that I thought it necessary that they should be completed to three thousand, in the course of the winter, that they may be ready, early in the spring, to put Quebec (of which I make no doubt we shall possess ourselves) into a proper state of defence, to prevent the enemy from regaining that important place. I have added, that I thought it necessary that preparation should be made here to throw in a reënforcement early in the spring, if they should be wanted.

I expect to leave this in a few days for Albany. I am, Sir, your Excellency's

Most obedient and very humble servant,

PHILIP SCHUYLER.

FROM COLONEL KNOX.*

Fort George, 5 December, 1775.

MAY IT PLEASE YOUR EXCELLENCY,

I arrived here yesterday, and made preparation to go over the Lake this morning, but General Schuyler

---

* Colonel Knox was sent from the camp at Cambridge, to procure cannon, mortars, and other military supplies from Ticonderoga and Crown Point. See the instructions to him for this object, in Washington's Writings, Vol. III. p. 160.

reaching here before day, prevents my going over for an hour or two. He has given me a list of stores on the other side, from which I am enabled to send an inventory of those which I intend to forward to camp. The garrison at Ticonderoga is so weak, the conveyance from the fort to the landing is so difficult, the passage across the Lake so precarious, that I am afraid it will be ten days, at least, before I can get them on this side. When they are here, the conveyance from hence will depend entirely on the sledding; if that is good, they shall immediately move forward; without sledding, the roads are so much gullied, that it will be impossible to move a step.

General Schuyler will do every thing possible to forward this business. I have the honor to be, with the greatest respect, your Excellency's

Most obedient humble servant,
HENRY KNOX.

P. S. General Schuyler assures me, that although the navigation through Lake George should be stopped, yet, if there is any sledding, they shall move on another way.

FROM COLONEL ARNOLD.

Before Quebec, 5 December, 1775.

MAY IT PLEASE YOUR EXCELLENCY,

My last, of the 20th ultimo, from Point-aux-Trembles, advising of my retiring from before Quebec, I make no doubt your Excellency has received. I continued at Point-aux-Trembles until the 3d instant, when, to my great joy, General Montgomery joined us, with artillery, and about three hundred men. Yesterday we arrived here, and are making all possible preparation to attack the city, which has a wretched motley garrison of disaffected seamen, marines, and inhabitants; the walls in a ruinous situation, and cannot hold out long.

Inclosed is a return of my detachment, amounting to six hundred and seventy-five men, for whom I have received clothing of General Montgomery. I hope there will soon be provision made for paying the soldiers' arrearages, as many of them have families who are in want. A continual hurry has prevented my sending a continuation of my journal. I am, with very great respect, your Excellency's

Most obedient humble servant,

BENEDICT ARNOLD.

FROM RICHARD HENRY LEE.

Philadelphia, 6 December, 1775.

DEAR SIR,

The inclosed letter, from Colonel Pendleton, came to hand two days ago, and, as it will save a good deal of unnecessary writing, I send it to you.

The proclamation, there alluded to, we have seen. It proclaims martial law through Virginia, and offers freedom to all the slaves, calling their masters rebels, &c. It seems this unlucky triumph over Hutchings, with his less than half-armed militia, so dispirited the miserable wretches in that neighbourhood, that many have taken an oath of Lord Dunmore's prescribing, reprobating Congress, Committees, &c.   Long before this, Colonel Woodford, with eight hundred good men, must be arrived in those parts; and I make no doubt has forced his Lordship on board his ships again. All this would have been prevented, if our troops could have crossed James River, in proper time; but they were obstructed, and forced to march high up, by the men-of-war; and indeed, such is the nature of our water-intersected country, that a small number of men, provided with naval force, can harass us extremely.

I have good reason to hope, that in a few weeks the state of things in Virginia will be greatly altered for the better.   I thank you for your list of armed vessels, but at present no use can be made of them. I hope some of them will be fortunate enough to meet with prizes eastward.

I had not heard of your improvements on the Kanawha being destroyed, and unless Mr. Lund Washington has received very accurate information on this head, I am inclined to doubt it; because I see, in the treaty lately concluded with all the Ohio Indians, they first inform the Commissioners of the Kanawha fort being burnt by some of their rash young men; but they promise to punish the offenders, and prevent repetition of the like offence.   They are very precise in their information, and mention only the fort, as well as I remember.   I hope, therefore, that your property may yet be safe.   This treaty with the Indians is more likely to last, as Connolly, with his little corps of officers, is now in close custody in Maryland, having been arrested there, as they were stealing through the country to Pittsburg, from whence they were to proceed to Detroit, and with the troops in those western parts, Indians, &c., he was

8 *

to have done wonders. This wonderful man is now in close jail.*

I congratulate you on the surrender of Montreal; and from General Montgomery's letter, giving an account of that event, I think we have room to expect that Quebec is fallen before now. A Committee of Congress, some time since sent to Canada, have direction to raise a regiment in that country, to invite delegates to this Congress, and give the strongest assurances of protection to their civil and religious rights. I am glad to hear of your getting Cobble Hill, and I hope it will prove useful to you. We are told that your enemy's troops are very uneasy on Bunker's Hill. God grant that their uneasiness may increase to their ruin. No accounts yet from England, but ships are daily expected. I am, with much esteem, dear Sir,

Your affectionate and obedient servant,

RICHARD HENRY LEE.

FROM THE PRESIDENT OF CONGRESS.

Philadelphia, 8 December, 1775.

SIR,

Your letter of the 28th of November, by Captain Blewer, being received, was immediately laid before Congress.

By my letter of the 2d instant, which I hope you will in due time receive, you will perceive the Congress have, in a great measure, prevented your wishes,

---

* See the particulars of Connolly's case in Washington's Writings, Vol. III. p. 212.

having written to New York, and given orders to General Schuyler to supply you with, and to forward, with all possible expedition, what cannon can be spared. They have also directed General Schuyler to make diligent search for lead; and, retaining so much as may be wanted there, to send the remainder to your camp. However, it is hoped the gentlemen you have sent will expedite that business.

By order of Congress, I forward a commission for Mr. Knox, who is appointed Colonel of the Regiment of Artillery. The Congress also have relieved your difficulties with respect to the two battalions of Marines, having ordered that the raising them out of the army be suspended. It is the desire of Congress that such a body of forces may be raised; but their meaning is, that it be in addition to the army voted; and they expect you will think of proper persons to command that corps, and give orders for enlisting them wherever they may be found.

The Congress are sensibly affected with your situation, and regret the backwardness of the troops to reënlist. In addition to what I had the honor of transmitting you the 2d instant, they have desired me to inclose you a copy of a resolution passed yesterday, and to write to the Council of Massachusetts Bay, the Convention of New Hampshire, and the Governors of Rhode Island and Connecticut, acquainting them with the present state of the army, and inclosing copies of the resolutions of this Congress relative to your being empowered to call forth the militia of those Governments on any emergency, and requesting those Colonies to exert themselves in defence of our common liberties, by affording you all the aid in their power, and to comply with your request for the assistance of the militia, whenever you may find it necessary to call for it.

The gentlemen with the money set out to-day. I hope the arrival of this will relieve some of your difficulties; and that the payment of the arrears, and the month's advance, which you are empowered to offer, will induce many to reënlist; who seem not to be actuated by nobler motives.

By letters, received yesterday, we learn that Colonel Arnold, after a fatiguing march, had reached Canada, where he was well received by the inhabitants; that, on the 14th of November, he had reached Point Levi, and was preparing to pass the river that night; that, notwithstanding his being deserted by Colonel Enos, he had great hopes of gaining possession of Quebec, as both the English and Canadian inhabitants were well affected to our cause; that Carleton, with the ships under his command, was stopped in his passage down the river by a fort in our possession, at the mouth of the Sorel, and some row-galleys; and that General Montgomery was preparing to attack him from Montreal. But of these matters you will doubtless be more fully informed by an express, which we understand was despatched to you from Ticonderoga.

I have the honor to be, &c.,

JOHN HANCOCK, *President.*

FROM MAJOR ROBERT ROGERS.

Medford, (Porter's Tavern), 14 December, 1775.

SIR,

I sailed from Gravesend the 4th of June last, in a merchant ship, bound to Baltimore, in Maryland, which was, at the time I came away, the nighest passage I could get to Philadelphia, where I waited on the gentlemen that compose the Continental Congress, in order to obtain their permit to settle my private affairs, being much encumbered with debts, chiefly contracted in the Province of New York; in which settlement my brother, Colonel James Rogers, who lives in the Province of New York, about twenty miles west of Connecticut River, was deeply concerned, being bound for me in several sums of money, which made it necessary for me to visit him in my way home; and for that purpose came by the way of New York and Albany to my brother's, and from thence to Portsmouth, to my wife and family (a pleasure long wished for), having been six years in Europe.

I have taken the earliest opportunity that would permit to come to this town (where I arrived this morning), in order to lay before your Excellency the passport I received at Philadelphia, from the Committee of Safety there, a copy of which is transmitted at the bottom of this letter, together with the minutes made thereon by the Committees of Safety at New York and New Hampshire. I do sincerely entreat your Excellency for a continuance of that permission for me to go unmolested where my private business may call me, as it will take some months from this time to settle with all my creditors.

I have leave to retire on my half-pay, and never expect to be called into the service again. I love North America; it is my native country, and that of my family, and I intend to spend the evening of my days in it.

I should be glad to pay you my respects personally, but have thought it prudent to first write you this letter, and shall wait at this place for your Ex-

cellency's commands.   I am, Sir, your Excellency's
most obedient and

Most humble servant,

ROBERT ROGERS.

FROM COLONEL KNOX.

Fort George, 17 December, 1775.

MAY IT PLEASE YOUR EXCELLENCY,

I returned from Ticonderoga to this place on the
15th instant, and brought with me the cannon, &c.; it
having taken nearly the time I conjectured it would
to transport them here.   It is not easy to conceive
the difficulties we have had in getting them over the
Lake, owing to the advanced season of the year, and
contrary winds; three days ago it was very uncertain whether we could have gotten them over until
next spring; but now, please God, they shall go.   I
have made forty-two exceedingly strong sleds, and
have provided eighty yoke of oxen, to drag them as
far as Springfield, where I shall get fresh cattle to
carry them to camp.

The route will be from here to Kinderhook, from
thence into Great Barrington, in Massachusetts Bay,
and down to Springfield.   There will scarcely be any
possibility of conveying them hence to Albany or
Kinderhook, but on sleds, the road being very much
gullied.   At present the sledding is tolerable to Saratoga, about twenty-six miles; beyond that, there is
none.   I have sent for the sleds and teams to come
up, and expect to begin to move them to Saratoga on
Wednesday or Thursday next; trusting that between
this and that period we shall have a fine fall of snow,

which will enable us to proceed further and make the carriage easy. If that should be the case, I hope in sixteen or seventeen days to be able to present to your Excellency a noble train of artillery, the inventory of which I have inclosed. I have been particular with respect to their dimensions, that no mistake may be made in making their carriages, as there are none here, or implements of any kind. I also send a list of those stores, which I desired Colonel McDougall to send from New York. I did not then know of any thirteen-inch mortars, which was the reason of my ordering but few shells of that size; but I now write to him for five hundred one-inch, two hundred five-and-seven-tenths inches, and four hundred seven-and-one-half inches. If these sizes could be had there, as I believe they can, I should imagine it would save time and expense, rather than have them cast. If you should think otherwise, or have made provisions for them elsewhere, you will please to countermand this order.

There is no other news here of Colonel Arnold, than that, from Colonel McLean's having burnt the houses round Quebec, Colonel Arnold was obliged to go to Point-aux-Trembles, about six miles from the city, and that General Montgomery had gone to join him with a considerable body of men, and a good train of artillery, mortars, &c.

There are some timid, and some malevolent spirits, who make this matter much worse; but from the different accounts which I have been able to collect, I have very little doubt that General Montgomery has Quebec now in his possession. I am, with the utmost respect, your Excellency's

Most obedient, humble servant,

HENRY KNOX.

Camp on Winter Hill, 17 December, 1775.

MUCH RESPECTED GENERAL,

Agreeably to your order, have again waited on Major Rogers, and strictly examined him. Have seen his several permits, and think them genuine, and in every respect agreeable to the copy sent you. He says he left New York about the 10th of October, being ill with the fever-and-ague, was ten days in getting to Albany; that there, and at the place called Stone Arabia, he tarried ten days more; he then passed through Hoosick, Standford, Draper, and Hinsdale, in his way to his brother, who lives in Kent; he was three days in performing this route, and tarried with his brother five or six days more; he was then three days in going to Westminster, and in his way passed through by Dartmouth College, and saw Mr. Wheelock; from thence he went to his farm in Pennicook, where he tarried six or eight days; from thence he went to Newbury, and from thence to Portsmouth, and, after tarrying there some few days, laid his permit before the Committee of Safety.

He owns every thing in Mr. Wheelock's letter except that of his having been in Canada, which he warmly denies, and says he can prove the route he took, and prove himself to have been in the several towns at or near the days he has mentioned. I asked him why he came to the camps, as he had no business with any particular persons, and had no inclination to offer his service in the American cause; to which he replied, that he had voluntarily waited upon the Committees of several Colonies, as he thought it a piece of respect due to them, and would probably prevent his being suspected and treated as a person unfriendly to us; that he likewise thought it his duty to wait on your Excellency, and acquaint you with the situation of his affairs, and, if he could, to obtain your license to travel unmolested.

These, Sir, are the facts as handed to me by him. What may be his secret designs I am unable to say, and what steps are most proper to be taken respecting him, your Excellency can best judge. I am far from thinking that he has been in Canada; but, as he was once Governor of Michilimackinac, it is possible he may have a commission to take that command, and stir up the Indians against us, and only waits for an opportunity to get there; for which reason I would advise, lest some blame might be laid upon your Excellency in future, not to give him any other permit, but let him avail himself of those he has; and, should he prove a traitor, let the blame centre upon those who enlarged him. I beg pardon for intruding my opinion; and subscribe myself

Your Excellency's most obedient servant,

JOHN SULLIVAN.*

FROM GOVERNOR COOKE.

Providence, 19 December, 1775.

SIR,

I have your Excellency's letter of the 17th, which I have laid before the General Committee.   Should

---

* For other particulars concerning Major Rogers, see Washington's Writings, Vol. III. p. 208.

the force sailed from Boston be destined for Rhode Island, I tremble for the consequences, as the Colony, in its present exhausted state, cannot, without assistance, defend the Island. At their unanimous request, I apply to your Excellency for a detachment from the Continental Army, of one regiment, to be stationed upon Rhode Island, and that you would please to appoint a general officer to take the command of the whole force there. They also desired me to inform you, that General Lee will be very acceptable to the Colony, and to request that the general officer who may be appointed may set out immediately, to take the command of the troops upon the Island, and put it in the best posture of defence.

We have, at head-quarters, about two hundred and fifty men, and shall immediately place on there about four hundred more, and hold as many more in readiness as possible. I need not point out to you the importance of the Island, and the inability of the Colony. I am, in great haste,

Your very humble servant,
NICHOLAS COOKE.

P. S. Captain Wallace hath hinted, to some of his friends, that he expects a reënforcement daily.

FROM THE PRESIDENT OF CONGRESS.

Philadelphia, 22 December, 1775.

SIR,

Your letters of the 30th of November, and of the 4th, 7th, and 11th of December, being duly received, were laid before Congress. To prevent the ill conse-

quences that might ensue from the backwardness of
the men, in the present service, to reënlist, the Congress, as I informed you in my last, have written to
the Governors of Connecticut and Rhode Island, the
Council of Massachusetts Bay, and the President of
the Convention of New Hampshire.   In consequence
of which letters, they have strong hopes and confidence that measures will be taken to complete your
army.   As to the article of butter, the Congress, desirous to obviate whatever may have a " tendency to
give the soldiery room for complaint," have instructed
me to inform you, that the same may be continued
until further order.

The Congress receive, with great satisfaction, your
congratulations on the success of Captain Manly. By
the inclosed resolves, you will perceive their determination on the captures already made, as well as
those which may be made hereafter.   It is expected
the several Colonies will erect Courts of Admiralty,
and that the Judges in those courts will regulate their
decisions by the law of nations, except where it is
relaxed by the inclosed resolutions.

I am further directed to inform you, that the Congress approve your taking such of the articles, found
on board the Concord, as are necessary for the army.
The necessity of the case will, they apprehend, justify the measure, even though the vessel upon trial
should, contrary to their expectation, be acquitted.

I am authorized to inform you, that it is the pleasure of Congress that Mr. Mifflin, the Quartermaster-
General, hold the rank of Colonel in the Army of
the United Colonies, and that you establish his rank
accordingly.

I must beg leave to refer you to the inclosed resolutions of Congress for your future proceedings,

which I am directed to transmit to you. You will notice the last resolution relative to an attack upon Boston.* This passed, after a most serious debate, in a Committee of the whole House, and the execution was referred to you; and may God crown your attempt with success. I most heartily wish it, though individually I may be the greatest sufferer.

I have paid Mr. Fessenden, the express, in full for his three journeys as express to Philadelphia, deducting only sixty dollars, which he says you ordered him; so that there will be no pay due to him for services performed heretofore, only for his expenses now from this place to you. If this adjustment be not right, please to inform me.

I have the honor to be, with sincere sentiments of esteem, Sir,

Your most obedient, humble servant,
JOHN HANCOCK, President.

P. S. Fessenden being indisposed, I have sent a special express, as Congress were anxious their resolves should reach you as quick as possible.

FROM JAMES LYON.

Machias, 25 December, 1775.

SIR,

You doubtless remember to have seen an application from the Committee of Safety in this place, for

---

* *In Congress, December* 22d. "Resolved, That if General Washington and his Council of War should be of opinion, that a successful attack may be made on the troops in Boston, he do it in any manner he may think expedient, notwithstanding the town and property in it may thereby be destroyed."

leave to go against Nova Scotia, which might probably have been taken then with very little difficulty. But we were informed that such an expedition could not be carried on, at that time, with proper secrecy, and that there was imminent danger from the King's ships. The same difficulties may possibly lie in the way now, if any troops are collected, and sent from any part near the head-quarters. I apprehend that secrecy is as necessary now as ever it was, and if only one proper person, at a suitable place, be ordered to conduct the whole affair, it will probably succeed.

There have been many applications, I dare say, from many persons and places; but were I to point out a suitable place, I should mention this, as it is near to Nova Scotia. I should be more at a loss for a proper person to conduct the enterprise. I know of fitter persons than myself in many respects, but they are strangers to the province and people. But I have dwelt there for years, and have a personal acquaintance with almost all the principal men, and know the country well. I should rejoice, therefore, in the appointment to this necessary business; and if your Excellency, together with those only who must necessarily be acquainted with the appointment (for I choose none but they should know any thing of the matter), in your great wisdom, should see fit to appoint me, I will conduct the expedition with the utmost secrecy, and, *Deo adjuvante*, will add to the dominions of the Continental Congress another province, before our enemies are able to defend it. All I require is sufficient authority to collect as many troops as I see fit, in this eastern country, not exceeding one thousand men, and vessels to convey them to the place of action, and blank commissions for the necessary officers of a thousand more, to be

9 *

filled up as I shall find expedient in Nova Scotia, where the men are to be raised, put into the Continental pay, and left there to defend the country, when taken; and farther, that a sufficient quantity of provisions, ammunition, arms, &c., be sent here, about the middle of March.

Your Excellency may inquire as much about me as you please, of Benjamin Foster, Esq., Captain Stephen Smith, Captain O'Brien, and Mr. Shannon; for these gentlemen I should choose to have as companions, but do not choose that they, or any other persons living, should know any thing of the design, if this petition is granted, till it is time to embark, except those persons only who have authority to appoint. The above-mentioned gentlemen know nothing of this application.

The reduction of Nova Scotia is a matter of great importance, and lies near my heart, on account of my many suffering friends in that province, and on account of the many advantages that would arise from it to this Colony, and to this place in particular. But should the Government appoint another person to conduct the expedition, I shall cordially acquiesce, and pray for his success, as I ever do, that God may smile on all the American arms, till all our enemies are subdued before us.

Your Excellency will not take amiss what my zeal for the honor and safety of my country constrained me to write. I am, most respectfully, your Excellency's

Very humble and obedient servant,

James Lyon.

FROM GOVERNOR TRUMBULL.

Lebanon, 1 January, 1776.

SIR,

I received, the 20th of last month, your Excellency's favor of the 15th, inclosing a list of the officers and companies under the new arrangement, with the number of men enlisted; and, at the same time, another of the 17th, with the information from several persons who then had lately come out of Boston. I return my thanks for both.

By accounts received from the various parts of the Colony, the recruiting officers, for the Continental service, have good success in enlisting men.

The Assembly have granted Chaplains the same pay given last campaign, with the addition of forty shillings per month each, to enable them to supply their pulpits.

Brigadier-General Prescott is not arrived. Shall give particular directions to prevent his escape, if he comes into this Colony.

The 23d, yours of the 14th of December came to hand, per Messieurs Penet and De Pliarne. Every necessary assistance, for expediting their journey, was afforded without delay; they set out the next morning. You shall be made acquainted with the expense incurred on their account, when the same is known.

The 28th instant, at evening, our General Assembly adjourned. There is great unanimity in our common cause. Among others, they passed an act for raising and equipping one fourth part of the militia of this Colony, to be forthwith selected by voluntary enlistment, with as many other ablebodied, effective men, not included in any militia-roll, as are inclined to enlist, to stand in readiness as minute-men, for the defence of this and the rest of the United Colonies, with proper encouragement. Another act, for restraining and punishing persons who are inimical to the liberties of this and the rest of the United Colonies, and for directing proceedings therein. No person to supply the Ministerial army or navy; to give intelligence; to enlist, or procure others to enlist in their service; to undertake to pilot any of their vessels, or in any other ways to aid or assist them, on the penalty of forfeiting all his estate, and imprisonment in any of the jails in this Colony, not exceeding three years. No one to speak, write, &c., against the doings of the Honorable General Congress, or acts of our Assembly, on the penalty of being disarmed, and rendered incapable to hold or serve in any office, civil or military; and be further punished, either by fine, imprisonment, disfranchisement, or to find surety of the peace and good behaviour.

Any person or persons, who put, or shall continue to hold, or screen themselves under, the protection of the Ministerial army or navy, or aid or assist in carrying into execution the present Ministerial measures against America, their estates to be seized for the use of the Colony.

A resolve to provide, so that we shall have two armed vessels, one of sixteen carriage-guns, the other fourteen; with a schooner called the Spy, of four carriage-guns; and four row-galleys.

An act to exempt the polls of soldiers from taxes, for the last, and ensuing campaigns. Another act, for encouraging the manufactories of saltpetre and gunpowder.

Hope to collect saltpetre and manufacture a considerable quantity of gunpowder early in the spring. The furnace, at Middletown, is smelting lead, and likely to turn out twenty or thirty tons. Ore is plenty.

Please to favor me with an account of the quantity of lead received from Crown Point. From thence I received one hundred and eighty old gunbarrels, which are fitting up here, and will make one hundred and fifty stands of good arms. We are put to difficulty for gunlocks. Hearing that those stands, taken in the ordnance store-ship, had each a spare lock, thought proper to mention to you, that, if it be so, whether it may not be well to furnish a number for the arms fitting here.

On the 29th, at evening, I met, at Hartford, on my returning from the General Assembly, yours of the 23d December, and immediately sent to Captain Wadsworth, a person employed by the Commissary-General, and much acquainted, to see if any blankets could be purchased, and found there are none. Many of our new-enlisted men, I am told, will bring blankets with them, which they get from private families. Those lost at the Bunker Hill fight were furnished in that manner, and our minute-men will supply themselves in that way; but I am very doubtful of success, if attempted. Lieutenant-Colonel Durkee this day mentioned to me your direction to him on this head. Shall lay the same before the Committee at our next meeting.

Inclosed is a copy of an Act empowering the Commander-in-chief, &c., to administer an oath. Also, Minutes of the ordnance taken from the Ministerial troops at the several northern posts, from the 1st of May to the 13th of November, 1775.

I remain, with great truth and regard, and with the proper salutations of this day, your Excellency's Most obedient, humble servant,

JONATHAN TRUMBULL.

P. S. Inclosed is a copy of a letter from President Wheelock, at Dartmouth College.

FROM MAJOR-GENERAL CHARLES LEE.

January 5, 1776.

DEAR GENERAL,

The consequences of the enemy's possessing themselves of New York have appeared to me so terrible, that I have scarcely been able to sleep from apprehensions on the subject. These apprehensions daily increase. You have it in your power, at present, to prevent this dreadful event. If I do not mistake, the Congress have given you authority to take any step in that place, as well as here, which you shall think necessary for the public service; but if they have not given you expressly and literally authority with respect to the city of New York, I am confident that any measure you think right to plan and put in execution will be approved of.

I have the greatest reason to believe, from the most authentic intelligence, that the best members of the Congress expect that you would take much upon yourself; as referring every matter of importance to them is, in fact, defeating the project. We have an instance of this in the fate of the motion for seizing the person of Mr. Tryon. To you they look up for decision;

by your conduct they are to be inspired with decision. In fact, your situation is such that the salvation
of the whole depends on your striking, at certain
crises, vigorous strokes, without previously communicating your intention. On this principle I venture to
propose the following scheme, and to offer myself for
the execution.

New York must be secured; but it will never, I am
afraid, be secured by direct order of the Congress, for
obvious reasons. They find themselves awkwardly
situated on this head; you must step in to their relief.
I am sensible that no men can be spared from the
lines in our present circumstances; but I would propose that you should detach me into Connecticut, and
lend your name for collecting a body of volunteers.
I am assured that I shall find no difficulty in assembling a sufficient number for the purposes wanted.
This body, in conjunction (if there should appear occasion to summon them) with the Jersey Regiment
under the command of Lord Stirling, now at Elizabethtown, will effect the security of New York, and
the expulsion or suppression of that dangerous banditti of Tories, who have appeared in Long Island,
with the professed intention of acting against the
authority of the Congress. Not to crush these ser-
pents, before their rattles are grown, would be ruinous.

I am assured, likewise, that the Connecticut volunteers, who will offer themselves for the service, will
expect no pay, but, at most, the expenses of their
provisions and perhaps of carriages for the conveyance
of their baggage. When once we have secured the
place with strict fortifications, and engaged the Friends
of Liberty so far that they cannot recede, purged the
City and Long Island of the leading Tories, the resi-

dence of these Connecticut volunteers will be no longer necessary; for there is no reason to doubt that the Congress will detach troops from Pennsylvania to garrison the place, although, from reasons hinted at, they may not choose to commence the operation. This manœuvre I not only think prudent and right, but absolutely necessary to our salvation; and if it meets, as I ardently hope it will, with your approbation, the sooner it is entered upon the better. Indeed, the delay of a single day may be fatal. I am, dear General,

Yours most respectfully,

CHARLES LEE.*

FROM MAJOR-GENERAL SCHUYLER.

Albany, 5 January, 1776.

I do not hesitate a moment to answer my dear General's question in the affirmative, by declaring that now or never is the time for every virtuous American to exert himself in the cause of liberty and his country; and that it is become a duty cheerfully to sacrifice the sweets of domestic felicity, to attain the honest and glorious end America has in view; and I can, with a good conscience, declare, that I have devoted myself to the service of my country, in the firmest resolution to sink or swim with it, unanxious how I quit the stage of life, provided that I leave to my posterity the happy reflection that their ancestor was an honest American.

* General Lee's plan was adopted by the Commander-in-chief, and he was sent to New York to carry it into execution. See the instructions to him in Washington's Writings, Vol. III. p. 230.

Here, my dear Sir, you will ask, why then do you wish to retire from a public office? Not because I am deterred by any difficulties I have experienced, or any that might hereafter present themselves; for I have had repeated experience, in the course of life, that what the greater part of mankind deem impossibilities exist only in idea, and are surmountable by a steady perseverance; but, because I think I should prejudice my country by continuing any longer in this command. The favorable opinion that you are pleased to entertain of me, obliges me to an explanation, which I shall give you in confidence. I have already informed you of the disagreeable situation I have been in during the campaign, but I would waive that, were it not that it has chiefly arisen from prejudice and jealousy; for I could point out particular persons of rank in the Army, who have frequently declared that the General commanding in this quarter ought to be of the Colony from whence the majority of the troops came. But it is not from opinions or principles of individuals that I have drawn the following conclusion, that troops from the Colony of Connecticut will not bear with a General from another Colony. It is from the daily and common conversation of all ranks of people from that Colony, both in and out of the army; and I assure you, that I sincerely lament that a people of so much public virtue should be actuated by such an unbecoming jealousy, founded on such a narrow principle, a principle extremely unfriendly to our righteous cause, as it tends to alienate the affections of numbers in this Colony, in spite of the most favorable constructions that prudent men, and real Americans amongst us, attempt to put upon it. And, although I frankly avow that I feel a resentment, yet I shall continue to sacrifice it to a nobler object, the weal of that country in which I have drawn the breath of life, resolved ever to seek, with unwearied assiduity, for opportunities to fulfil my duty to it.

I shall to-morrow write to General Montgomery to collect the evidence in support of the charge against Prescott, and entreat him to be very particular. As the prisoners taken on board the vessels in the St. Lawrence are not yet passed, it is probable that I may, by their means, be able to furnish your Excellency with some accounts of the usage Allen received.

Since the receipt of your Excellency's, of the 18th, Major Rogers is come to this town. I sent to him, and, amongst a variety of passes, he produced a late one from the Committee of New Hampshire, to pass unmolested to New York, for which place he sets out to-day. I believe there is no truth in the intelligence sent by Mr. Wheelock; for I find, upon inquiry, that Rogers arrived at this place after St. John's was invested, and that he went from hence to New England. I shall, however, make further inquiries. I shall forward the account against Captain Morgan to Colonel Arnold by next post.

You will perceive, by the inclosed, that the junction of General Montgomery and Colonel Arnold has taken place; but their force is so small, and the weather has been so severe, that I fear they have not been able to possess themselves of Quebec. Should an attempt have been made to storm it, and have proved fruitless, and accidents have happened to Montgomery and Arnold, I tremble lest Canada should be lost. If I could procure any men, I would send them to Canada immediately; but I know not where to get any. Even Ticonderoga and Fort George are by this time, I fear, left to the care of the Commissary of Provisions and Conductor of Artillery. The officers, to whom I had issued warrants to raise four companies, meet with no success.

The first of the cannon arrived here on Wednesday, and the whole is on its way, but detained by the weakness of the ice in Hudson's River, occasioned by the uncommon mildness of the weather for several days past. One frosty night, if not deferred too long, will, however, put every thing in order, and I hope you will soon have the pleasure of seeing all at Cambridge.

To-morrow thirteen of the Caghnawaga tribe, under the care of Major Wales, will set out for Cambridge on a visit.

Your letter to General Howe gave me great pleasure, and his answer must convince mankind of your superiority.* His affectation is trifling, and unbecoming a gentleman. His letter, I believe, will be eventually a censure on General Carleton.

I shall immediately forward to your Excellency what clothing can be spared from here; great part of it is not yet made up.

Sunday, January 7th. Yesterday a frost came on, and this morning I had the satisfaction to see the first division of sleds, with cannon, cross the river. Should there be snow all the way to Cambridge, they will probably arrive there about this day week.

A Mr. Gamble, who was made prisoner with Brigadier Prescott, and who was a Deputy-Quartermaster-General in Canada, has entreated me to intercede with your Excellency to get him exchanged. He

---

* Washington's Writings, Vol. III. pp. 201, 203.

urges that he must be ruined unless he can get back to Canada. Although I by no means wish to prejudice an individual, yet I do not think it prudent that he should go to Quebec, unless it is in our possession. When that happens, I can see no inconveniency in exchanging him, or permitting him to go, and shall esteem it as a favor if he can then procure your leave, and if you can get him exchanged, that he may not lose his office. He writes to General Lee on the subject. I have expressly informed him that I did not think he could be permitted to go to Quebec until after its reduction.

Be pleased to accept the compliments of the season, and my best wishes. I have the honor to be, with unfeigned esteem, your Excellency's most obedient, and

Most humble servant,
PHILIP SCHUYLER.

FROM JOHN ADAMS.

Watertown, 6 January, 1776.

DEAR SIR,

As your Excellency has asked my opinion of General Lee's plan, as explained in his letter of the 5th instant, I think it my duty to give it, although I am obliged to do it in more haste than I could wish.

I suppose the only questions, which arise upon that letter, are, whether the plan is practicable; whether it is expedient; and whether it lies properly within your Excellency's authority, without further directions from Congress.

Of the practicability of it, I am very ill qualified

to judge; but were I to hazard a conjecture, it would be that the enterprise would not be attended with much difficulty. The Connecticut people, who are very ready upon such occasions, in conjunction with the Friends of Liberty in New York, I should think, might easily accomplish the work.

That it is expedient, and even necessary to be done, by some authority or other, I believe will not be doubted by any friend of the American cause, who considers the vast importance of that City, Province, and the North River, which is in it, in the progress of this war, as it is the *nexus* of the northern and southern Colonies, as a kind of key to the whole continent, as it is a passage to Canada, to the Great Lakes, and to all the Indian nations. No effort to secure it ought to be omitted.

That it is within the limits of your Excellency's command, is, in my mind, perfectly clear. Your commission constitutes you commander of all the forces now raised, or to be raised, and of all others who shall voluntarily offer their service, and join the army for the defence of American liberty, and for repelling every hostile invasion thereof; and you are vested with full power and authority to act as you shall think for the good and welfare of the service.

Now if upon Long Island there is a body of people, who have arms in their hands, and are intrenching themselves, professedly to oppose the American system of defence, who are supplying our enemies both of the army and navy, in Boston and elsewhere, as I suppose is undoubtedly the fact, no man can hesitate to say that this is an hostile invasion of American liberty, as much as that now made in Boston. Nay, those people are guilty of the very invasion in Boston, as they are constantly aiding, abet-

10*

ting, comforting, and assisting the army there, and
that in the most essential manner, by supplies of
provisions.

If in the city a body of tories are waiting only
for a force to protect them, to declare themselves on
the side of our enemies, it is high time that city was
secured. The Jersey troops have already been ordered
into that city by the Congress, and are there undoubtedly under your command, ready to assist in
this service. That New York is within your command, as much as the Massachusetts, cannot bear a
question. Your Excellency's superiority in the command over the Generals in the Northern Department,
as it is called, has been always carefully preserved
in Congress, although the necessity of despatch has
sometimes induced them to send instructions directly
to them, instead of first sending them to your Excellency, which would have occasioned a circuit of many
hundreds of miles, and have lost much time.

Upon the whole, Sir, my opinion is, that General
Lee's is a very useful proposal, and will answer many
good ends. I am, with great respect, your Excellency's

Most obedient, humble servant,

JOHN ADAMS.

FROM MAJOR-GENERAL SCHUYLER.

Albany, 13 January, 1776.

I wish I had no occasion to send my dear General
this melancholy account. My amiable friend, the gallant Montgomery, is no more; the brave Arnold is

wounded; and we have met with a severe check in an unsuccessful attempt on Quebec. May Heaven be graciously pleased that the misfortune may terminate here! I tremble for our people in Canada; and nothing, my dear Sir, seems left to prevent the most fatal consequences, but an immediate reënforcement that is nowhere to be had but from you; and the only route, that which I have pointed out in my letter to Congress, copy of which you have inclosed. Nor do I think that a less number than I have mentioned will suffice. Should your Excellency think proper to send the troops, you will please to let me know it by express, that I may send provisions to Onion River.*

Congress has wrote to me on the subject of my request to retire. Our affairs are much worse than when I made the request. This is motive sufficient for me to continue to serve my country in any way I can be thought most serviceable; but my utmost can be but little, weak and indisposed as I am. The clothing is gone to Cambridge.

I am your Excellency's most obedient and most humble servant,

PHILIP SCHUYLER.

---

* No troops could be spared from the main army for this service; but a regiment from each of the Colonies of Massachusetts, New Hampshire, and Connecticut, was raised and sent to Canada. See Washington's Writings, Vol. III. pp. 248, 253.

FROM COLONEL ARNOLD.

Camp before Quebec, 14 January, 1776.

DEAR SIR,

I make no doubt you will soon hear of our misfortune on the 31st ultimo, and be very anxious to know our present situation. Our loss and repulse struck an amazing panic into both officers and men, and, had the enemy improved their advantage, our affairs here must have been entirely ruined. It was not in my power to prevail on the officers to attempt saving our mortars, which had been placed in St. Roque's. Of course they fell into the hands of the enemy. Upwards of one hundred officers and soldiers instantly set off for Montreal, and it was with the greatest difficulty I could persuade the rest to make a stand.

The panic soon subsided. I arranged the men in such order, as effectually to blockade the city, and enable them to assist each other if attacked. It was urged, by the officers, to move our ammunition and artillery stores, of which we had a large quantity; and, though the risk was great, I could not approve the measure, as it would undoubtedly have made unfavorable impressions on the minds of the Canadians, and induced them to withdraw their assistance, which must have ended in our utter ruin. I therefore put the best face on matters, and betrayed no marks of fear. I have withdrawn the cannon from our battery, and placed them round the magazine.

Our present force is only seven hundred. I am in daily expectation of a reënforcement from Montreal of two or three hundred men. I expected General Wooster, but find he cannot leave Montreal. Colonel

Clinton is just arrived. I have put on foot the raising a regiment of two or three hundred Canadians, which I make no doubt of effecting. Our finances are very low. However, I hope we shall be able to rub along. Mr. Price is our only resource, and has exerted himself. I wait with great anxiety the arrival of a reënforcement from below. I have wrote the Honorable Congress my opinion, that five thousand men will be necessary to insure us Quebec, though it may possibly be reduced with a less number; it appears a blockade may answer the purpose. I think Quebec an object of too much consequence to trust it to the event. If reduced, five thousand men will be necessary for a garrison.

Your favor of the 5th ultimo is just come to hand. It gives me a most sensible pleasure, to have your approbation of my conduct. I beg you would accept my thanks for the notice you have been pleased to take of me and my officers in your new establishment. Most of them are provided for in an unexpected manner, not very pleasing to me. Inclosed is a list of the killed and wounded. Both officers and men behaved with the greatest intrepidity, and had not the General been basely deserted by his troops, we should doubtless have carried the town. My detachment had carried the first battery. My being wounded, and the loss of their guides, retarded them much. After the death of the General, they sustained the force of the whole garrison for a considerable time, who fired from under cover, and had every advantage of situation. Their retreat was cut off by the enemy's gaining a narrow defile, through which they were obliged to pass. They were overpowered by numbers and obliged to resign, though deserving a better fate. Governor Carleton treats them with humanity, and has given leave for their baggage to be sent in to them.

I heartily congratulate you on the success of your privateers. I think the balance of the last year's account is still in our favor, though we have met a severe check here. I hope soon to have the pleasure of seeing General Lee, or some experienced officer, here. I heartily wish you the protection and blessing of the Almighty; and am, with very great respect and esteem, dear Sir,

Your obedient, humble servant,
BENEDICT ARNOLD.

FROM GOVERNOR TRUMBULL.

Lebanon, 15 January, 1776.

SIR,

I have received your agreeable letter, of the 7th instant, per Captain Sears. The condition and circumstances of the Colony of New York give me pain, lest the friends to American liberty in that Colony should be too much neglected and become disheartened, and the inimical designs and mischievous operations of others succeed. I have received credible information that the Provincial Congress there had spent some time, just before they adjourned to the 1st of February, in debating whether they should not address Mr. Tryon for the purpose of calling the General Assembly of that Colony, to revive the old scheme of adopting the Parliamentary insult of the 20th of February last, which was rejected. Surely our friends want to be strengthened, and our enemies to be checked.

The following is an extract from a letter from one of our friends to another, dated December 27th, 1775. "Just after you left town, the Phœnix, a forty-gun ship, arrived and anchored just before Mr. Drake's, and in two or three days after, the Asia, in company of the Duchess of Gordon, came and anchored opposite to Peck's slip, so that we are highly honored. General Dalrymple is on board the Phœnix, and it is rumored that they have two hundred troops concealed on board, which has, for near a week past, kept us on pretty hard duty. The Colonel has slept in the barracks two or three nights. If they come I hope to give a good account of them. We have some excellent field-pieces, and if they visit us the gates will be opened, and we will welcome them with a few resolves of the *Continental Congress*, which is the name of one of the pieces."

I wrote a letter to President Hancock, dated the 6th of January, and another to one of our Delegates at Congress, requesting that more effectual measures may be taken for the security of New York, to prevent our enemies from being supplied with provisions, furnished with intelligence, and from having an opportunity to use every artifice to insult and injure us from that quarter.   It therefore gave me sensible pleasure to find, that you have adopted the measures mentioned in yours, and with great cheerfulness called my council, and, with their advice, appointed Colonel Waterbury, Lieutenant-Colonel Bradley, and Major Hobby, field-officers for one regiment; Colonel Ward, Lieutenant-Colonel Lewis, and Major Douglas for another.   Sent a proclamation to the two Colonels, and orders to them with the rest of the field-officers, by voluntary enlistment, to raise seven hundred and fifty men each, to join and assist Major-General Lee, with encouragement that they should be entitled to the same pay, wages, and billeting allowed the troops before Boston, during the time they served, and to be dismissed soon, when the service would conveniently admit.

The field-officers of each regiment to select captains and subalterns from those in the standing militia; if needful, to request the chief officer of the militia companies to call their companies together for the purpose of enlisting the men with expedition; and, to prevent difficulty for want of ammunition, have ordered Captain Niles, Commander of our armed schooner, the Spy, to take on board half a ton of powder, and transport four hundred pounds to New Haven, two hundred pounds to Norwalk, and four hundred pounds to Stamford, with orders to him to follow such directions as Major-General Lee may give for the service he is employed in, and to execute the same, until dismissed by him, or further orders from me. Wished, but failed, to have the pleasure of a short interview with him. When my orders were ready, very early on Saturday morning last, Captain Sears took them, and I apprehend he got to Hartford by noon. I wrote to Major-General Lee, informing of what was done by me. I have no doubt but the men at the westward part of this Colony will readily and expeditiously engage in the service. May the Supreme Director of all events add His blessing on our endeavours to preserve, support, and maintain the constitutional liberties of these Colonies, which he hath made it our duty to do.

Thirteen Indians, of the Caghnawaga tribe, came to visit me on the 13th, and seemed well pleased to have a conference on our affairs, and expressed their belief of my information, and that they were friends and brothers, and yesterday proceeded on their way to you. I am, with great esteem and regard, your Excellency's most obedient, humble servant,

JONATHAN TRUMBULL.

FROM THE PRESIDENT OF CONGRESS.

Philadelphia, 16 January, 1776.

Your letters of the 25th and 31st of December, and 4th of January, have been duly received, and laid before Congress.

By the inclosed resolutions, you will perceive that the Congress, in providing for the defence of Canada, have directed that two battalions should be raised out of the troops now serving there. This they did in testimony of their approbation of the services of those brave men, apprehending, at the same time, that it would be both agreeable to the officers and men to have the honor of defending a country, which their valor had rescued from slavery. And the Congress have a firm confidence, that General Montgomery, who has a warm and just sense of their merit and services, will cheerfully embrace the present opportunity to continue and promote the officers of that corps, and, as far as in his power, to reward with office and command, in those battalions, such volunteers and others as have distinguished themselves.

The Committee, to whom your letters were referred, this day brought in a partial report; on which the Congress came to certain resolutions, which you will see in the inclosed extracts. I am just to acquaint you, that it is expected, when the Paymaster draws any bills, he will observe to make them payable some few days after sight. The Committee have desired leave to sit again, which is granted. As soon as they have completed their report, and the Congress have come to a determination thereon, I shall do myself the pleasure of transmitting it to you. The money last voted, is now ready ; and the persons who have the charge of conveying it will, I expect, set out with it to-morrow.

I have the pleasure to inform you, that the Committee have purchased the saltpetre, and have agreed with the owners of mills to manufacture it into powder. One of the mills, it is expected, will make near a ton a week, and another near half a ton. I hope you will soon receive the powder ordered to be purchased at New York. There were, as we are informed, eight tons in the same vessel imported for that Colony.

The public papers will inform you, that Lord Dunmore has endeavoured to exercise the same barbarity against the defenceless town of Norfolk, as was exercised against Falmouth. By these repeated instances of inhumanity, so contrary to the rules of war, and so long exploded by all civilized nations, it would seem as if the rancorous Ministry, despairing of their measures to conquer and enslave, had determined to glut their revenge with destruction and devastation.* For my part, I shall not be surprised to hear, that in their frenzy of rage, and to effect their dark purposes, they have proceeded to murder, under forms of law, those prisoners whom the tools of their vengeance have chanced to take, and whom, with officious zeal, they have sent to England.

---

* It has been ascertained that the British Ministry were in no degree responsible for the burning of Falmouth. It was the wanton act of a naval officer, unknown to the Ministry at the time, and disapproved by them afterwards. Washington's Writings, Vol. III. p. 520.

As it is now apparent that our enemies mean to exert their whole force against us next summer, the Congress are taking measures for putting the middle and southern Colonies in a posture of defence. We shall doubtless suffer much in this great struggle; but I trust no losses or sufferings will induce us to desert the defence of our liberty; and that, cost what it may, we will persevere, with unremitting vigor, to maintain that inestimable jewel which we received from our ancestors, and transmit the same, with un-sullied lustre, to our posterity.

January 18*th.* The Committee, to whom your letter of the 31st of December was referred, desire to be informed whether the companies stationed at Chelsea and Malden are regimented; and whether, if those at Hingham, Weymouth, and Braintree, were withdrawn, it would be necessary to replace them out of the Continental Army.

Since writing the above, we have received a letter from Messrs. Philip Livingston, Alsop, and Lewis, by which we find, to our mortification, that we were misinformed with regard to the large quantity of powder arrived at New York, and that there were only four hundred and sixty-two quarter casks, which were imported for the use of that Colony, and of which a great part is distributed among several Counties.

Before this comes to hand, you will doubtless receive an account of the disagreeable news from Quebec, on which I sincerely condole with you. The express arrived here last evening. To-day I expect the Congress will take it into consideration. The result of their deliberations you will have in my next letter.   I am, &c.

JOHN HANCOCK, *President.*

New Haven, 16 January, 1776.

DEAR GENERAL,

We have been so baffled by the weather, that we only arrived here last night. I believe we shall find no difficulties in procuring a sufficient body of volunteers for the New York expedition. The unhappy accounts from Canada seem to animate these people, rather than depress. Indeed, we have new occasion for exertion and decision. I am apprehensive that the Congress must be inspired by you. They have just given a strong, and, I think, unfortunate instance of indecision. Colonel Waterbury had raised a regiment. The regiment was equipped, and ready for embarkation. They were to have landed in Oyster Bay, to have attacked the Tories in Long Island. Lord Stirling was to have attacked them on the other side. All this by order of Congress;—when suddenly Colonel Waterbury received an order to disband his regiment; and the Tories are to remain unmolested till they are joined by the King's assassins.

Governor Trumbull, like a man of sense and spirit, has ordered this regiment to be reassembled. I believe it will be ready on Sunday, the day on which I shall march from this town. I shall send immediately an express to the Congress, informing them of my situation, and, at the same time, conjuring them not to suffer the accursed Provincial Congress of New York to defeat measures so absolutely necessary to salvation.

The affairs of Canada will, I suppose, very soon, if not instantly, require a very considerable force from this Province. Neither will the circumstances of New

York admit of its being too much stripped of men, for which reason I should think it advisable immediately to raise some additional regiments in Massachusetts Bay. Adieu, dear General. God prosper you and the arms of virtue!

Yours, most sincerely,
CHARLES LEE.

FROM THOMAS LYNCH.

Philadelphia, 16 January, 1776.

DEAR SIR,

I am happy to be at last able to write you, that every thing you desired me to get done is accomplished, for the present. Our President assures me he has sent you the determination of Congress concerning the trial of captures. Courts of Admiralty have been appointed in the Colony for that purpose. Colonel Frye has been appointed Brigadier in your army (Mr. Arnold precedes him in that of Quebec); and I inclose copies of the resolutions for the direction of the postmaster, relative to letters of officers and soldiers in our service.

The delays in procuring the money have given me much concern, being sensible of the injury occasioned thereby to the service; but the calls for money, from every quarter, so far outrun the diligence of the signers, that my reiterated solicitations could get the sum no sooner.

We have resolved to raise, exclusive of your army, in New Hampshire one battalion, in Connecticut one, in New York one, in Jersey three, in Pennsylvania

11*

five, in the Lower Counties one, in Virginia six, in North Carolina three, and South Carolina three, in Georgia one, and in Canada two, exclusive of Canadians. Besides these, I have no doubt New York will have four more, and Maryland two, which, with the regiments of artillery, will be sixty-two or three battalions, and the expense not less than ten millions of dollars. How quick a transfer of property, from the rich to the poor, such an expenditure must produce, you are well able to judge. The prospect is far from receiving light, when it is considered how each Colony lavishes away its private treasure at the same time, or when we view the amazing and unaccountable supineness of all our Governments. Not a single individual, anywhere in a civil department, seems to consider himself as interested in public matters, unless he can get money by them. The idea of all the paper being mortgages on their private estates is totally lost and forgotten.

In this state of things I have, besides my dependence on the continuance of the favor of Heaven, trust in two supports alone; the one, on your vigorous exertions; the other, on the weakness of our enemies. Should they lose footing in America this winter, I should despise their thirty thousand Russians,* scattered by storms, arriving, one transport after another, fatigued and debilitated by the fatal effects of a long voyage, without a spot to collect and recruit themselves for the field, and depending, for every necessary, on supplies from a country three thousand miles distant.

---

* It was reported, at this time, that the British Government had obtained, or was about to obtain, military aid from Russia; but the report was unfounded.

Do not the speeches of the King and his Ministers hold very different language from those of the last year? America is no longer the abject, cowardly, and defenceless wretch she was then; now his Lordship, [who] would have despised [them], had they not bravely supported their rights, seems to approve their vigorous support of them, and offers the terms of 1763. A gentleman, well known to Maryland, Lord Drummond, just from England, assures me he will give much more; he tells me that he has had many conversations with Ministry on this subject, and showed me a paper, approved by each of them, and which he is sure will be supported in both Houses. The substance of it is, America to be declared free in point of taxation and internal police; Judges to be approved by the Judges of England, and commissioned during good behaviour, upon stated and sufficient support being statedly assigned by the Colonies; all charters to be held sacred; that of Boston restored; Britain to regulate trade *sub modo*; all duties, laid for the purpose of regulation, to be paid into the Colony Treasury where they arise, applicable to its uses by its own Legislature; in lieu of which America shall, by duties on such articles as will probably keep pace in consumption with the rise or declension of the Colony, laid by each Legislature by permanent act of Assembly, grant towards the general support of the empire, annual sums in proportion to five thousand pounds sterling for this Colony. As this sum is little more than half of what did arise by duties heretofore paid in this place, I doubted his information; but was assured that Ministry wanted nothing but a show of revenue to hold up to Parliament, as they are afraid to propose reconciliation without saving what the stiff old Englishmen call the honor of the nation.*

His Lordship came hither through Halifax, Boston, and York, where, I fancy, he saw what induced him to hint, once or twice, at beginning with a suspension of arms, to which I turned a very deaf ear, well knowing that the winter season is ours, and that much may be done by April next. I sincerely wish I had your sentiments on these heads. I shall propose them to the consideration of Congress, as soon as the most urgent affairs are over; I think they merit it.

Congress has ordered you fifteen tons of gunpowder from New York, and we have saltpetre enough here to make eighty tons more, so that I hope we shall not soon want again; larger quantities are every day expected. I beg you will make our compliments to your lady, and to the rest of your family, and all my friends.

Dear sir, your most obedient
THOMAS LYNCH.

P. S. We have just heard, from Charleston, that they have mounted on the batteries there above one hundred and sixty cannon, from twelve to forty-two pounders, and seventy more in different parts of the Province; that the party raised by Kirkland and his gang are totally suppressed. He is come, but I have not yet seen him.

---

* A full account of Lord Drummond's projects for a reconciliation may be seen in Washington's Writings, Vol. III. p. 525.

Philadelphia, 20 January, 1776.

SIR,

In my former letter, I mentioned the disagreeable news received from Canada. The Congress have taken that matter into consideration; and, having examined Mr. Antill, and duly deliberated on the situation of our affairs in that quarter, they have come to sundry resolutions, which I have the honor to inclose.

I would just observe, that, by Mr. Antill's examination, it appears our loss is greater than what is set forth in the despatches he brought, a copy of which was transmitted to you. Almost the whole of General Arnold's gallant detachment are taken prisoners, having, after four hours' resistance, been obliged to surrender at discretion. However, we have the satisfaction to hear the prisoners are treated with humanity.

The Congress are anxious, as well from motives of policy as of justice and humanity, to repair our losses in that quarter, and, if possible, to gain possession of Quebec, and drive our enemies out of that country before they can be reinforced in the spring. An active, able General is wanted to take the command there, and if such an one can be spared from the service at Cambridge, it is their desire you should send him.

The battalion from Pennsylvania, and that from New Jersey, will set forward the beginning of next week.

As it is of great importance, as well for the security and relief of our friends as for confirming the wavering, that speedy succours should arrive, I am directed to request you to detach, from the camp at Cambridge, one battalion, if the service there will permit you to spare one, with orders to march, with the greatest expedition possible, to Canada. If this cannot be complied with, you will use your utmost endeavours in stimulating the Governor of Connecticut and the Convention of New Hampshire, to whom I write by this opportunity, to forward, with the utmost despatch, the very first companies that can be raised in those Colonies. You can easily conceive what effect the arrival of even one company will have on the minds of our friends, especially when they shall be satisfied it will soon be followed by more.

The Colony of South Carolina has been so fortunate as to oblige Lord William Campbell, with the vessels of war, to quit their harbour. Being earnestly desirous of providing for their defence, they have resolved to fit out some armed vessels, but not having seamen among themselves, they have despatched Captain Cochran to the northward, to enlist a number of seamen for the service of that Colony. Lest the offers he was empowered to make might prejudice the service, the Congress have chalked out a plan for him to go by, as you will see in the inclosed extracts, and I am directed to desire you will please to forward this service.

Yesterday Dr. J. Smith, who made his escape from Frederick, was brought to this town. He was taken at the Little Meadows, on his way to Detroit, and had with him letters from Connolly to the commanding officer there.

I hinted to you, in my former letter, that the Congress were taking measures for the defence of the Middle and Southern Colonies. For this purpose, over and above those destined for Canada, they have ordered four battalions to be raised in the Colony of New York, two in New Jersey, four in Pennsylvania, one in the Counties on Delaware, six in Virginia, three in North Carolina, three in South Carolina, and one in Georgia, each to consist of seven hundred and twenty-eight men, including officers, making in the whole, with those for Canada, thirty-four battalions.

I have the honor to be, &c.

JOHN HANCOCK, *President.*

FROM GOVERNOR COOKE.

Providence, 21 January, 1776.

SIR,

Your favor of the 6th instant I received, and laid before the General Assembly. It had great weight; and I believe that no supplies to the enemy's ships would have been permitted, had it not appeared to us that the members of the Continental Congress were of opinion that they should be continued. The following is an extract from our Delegates on that subject. "A Memorial from the Town of Newport, forwarded to us by express, having been referred to the General Assembly, we now inclose that, with the papers pertinent thereto. We should not do justice to the benevolence of Congress, or to the distressed situation of the town, if we did not acquaint you that all the gentlemen, who spoke in this debate, expressed the most tender regard for the distressed people, and gave it as their opinion that, as long as the ships of war now in the harbour could be supplied with fresh provisions, beer, and such like necessaries for their own immediate support, consistently with the great principles of the general good and safety of America, the town ought to be permitted to furnish them; the greatest care being taken by government that no more than the barely necessary supplies be furnished from time to time, lest the common enemy in other parts of the Continent should, through them, obtain provisions." In consequence of which the General Assembly have ordered that Captain Wallace should be supplied, as you will see by the inclosed vote. But, as he may cannonade, and even burn the town, a discretionary power, by a private vote, which it is designed should be kept a profound secret, is given to the commander of the forces on Rhode Island to permit supplies in cases of imminent danger, until the next session, to be holden on the last Monday in next month.

Similar measures to those taken by Connecticut, as mentioned in your letter, have been adopted by this Colony. Besides which, the commanding officer of any body of Continental troops is empowered to impress carriages, &c.

The General Assembly ordered an Address to the Congress, a copy of which I do myself the honor to inclose you. We are not without hopes that the Congress will take the whole brigade into their service, especially as the necessity, arising from so powerful an invasion, of establishing the whole force we have ordered, is clear and manifest. From the nature of the war, and the circumstances of the Colonies, I think every idea of partial and Colonial defence ought to be given up. There must be a supreme, superintending power, to exert and direct the force of the whole, for the defence and safety of all; otherwise the exertions and burdens will not only be very unequal, to the greatly endangering the union, upon which the welfare of America depends, but Colony after Colony may be subdued without the chance of making resistances.   I shall only add, on this head, that unless the Continent enter upon the defence of the Colony, it must be abandoned, to the great detriment of the common cause.   I beg the favor of your Excellency seriously to consider this matter, and to give us your assistance with the members of the Congress for procuring such a body of forces as the interest of this and the United Colonies in general shall require.

We had procured upwards of an hundred blankets, which were designed for the army under your immediate command; but the descent upon Prudence obliged us to send forty of them to our troops upon that Island; and to supply the additional forces, ordered to be raised, will demand every blanket that can be spared in the Colony.   I am, with great respect and esteem, Sir, your Excellency's

Most obedient and most humble servant,

NICHOLAS COOKE.

FROM BRIGADIER-GENERAL WOOSTER.

Montreal, 21 January, 1776.

SIR,

I herewith inclose a letter just received from Colonel Arnold, and take this opportunity most heartily to condole with you for the loss of the brave and most amiable General Montgomery, and the other brave officers and soldiers who fell with him, and for the failure of success in the unfortunate attack upon Quebec, the particulars of which you will doubtless have received before this reaches you.

I should have gone down, immediately upon hearing of the defeat, to the camp before Quebec, but the necessity of securing this place and the country round in our interest, induced all the officers, and our friends here, to request me not to leave this place till we should have a reënforcement from the Colonies. When they arrive, I expect to proceed on with them. We have many enemies in this Province, particularly among the clergy, who are using every artifice to excite the Canadians to take up arms against us; but I hope to be able to prevent any thing of the kind. I have called in many of the commissions given by Governor Carleton, and have given out new ones under the Congress, and expect soon to have them spread through the country, which I expect, and indeed I perceive already, that it answers very salutary purposes. After receiving new commissions, they look upon themselves as bound, and, unless we succeed, they will all be treated as traitors. I allow each parish to choose their own captains, a circumstance which pleases them much, and there have been but few instances that they have not chosen a zealous friend to our cause. The taking of Quebec must be a matter of the greatest consequence to the Colonies, but at present we are very ill provided for it. The place is strong. I believe they are determined to defend it to the last extremity. We have but about four tons of powder in the Province. We have, I believe, a sufficiency of small cannon, none larger than twelve-pounders, except two brass twenty-fours, which are at St. John's. We have expectations of having shot and shells cast at Three Rivers.

In my opinion it will not only be necessary to forward men and powder from the Colonies, but also a number of heavy cannon, such as thirty-two pounders and one thirteen-inch mortar, if no more, and some small ones, if to be had. I understand that the large mortar from Ticonderoga, with a number of pieces of cannon, are gone to your camp. It is of the greatest importance that whatever is sent from the Colonies should be here by the middle of March at furthest, for, after that time, the gentlemen here inform me, it will be impossible to transport any thing from this place to Quebec, on account of the river being filled with ice, and the water, of consequence, overflows the flat country. Therefore, if any of our wants can be supplied from your camp, I could wish that whatever is sent may be forwarded as expeditiously as possible. I am, Sir, with the greatest esteem and respect,

Your most obedient servant,
DAVID WOOSTER.

FROM MAJOR-GENERAL LEE.

Stamford, 24 January, 1776.

DEAR GENERAL,

It was unnecessary sooner to trouble you with my scrawl, as I could give you no information the least interesting. I find the people through this Province more alive and zealous than my most sanguine expectation. I believe I might have collected ten thousand volunteers. I take only four companies with me, and

Waterbury's regiment, which is so happily situated on the frontier. Ward's regiment I have ordered to remain at their respective homes, until they hear further. These Connecticutians are, if possible, more eager to go out of their country, than they are to return home, when they have been out for any considerable time.

Inclosed I send you my letter to the General Congress. That of the Provincial Congress of New York to me, with my answer, I hope will have your approbation.

The Whigs, I mean the stout ones, are, it is said, very desirous that a body of troops should march and be stationed in their city. The timid ones are averse, merely from the spirit of procrastination, which is the characteristic of timidity. The letter of the Provincial Congress, you will observe, breathes the very essence of this spirit. It is wofully hysterical. I conclude I shall receive the orders of the General Congress before, or immediately on, my arrival; otherwise I should not venture to march into the Province, as, by their late resolve, every detachment of the Continental troops is to be under the direction of the Provincial Congress in which they are; a resolve, I must say with submission to their wisdom, fraught with difficulties and evils. It is impossible, having two sovereigns, that any business should be carried on.

Have you seen the pamphlet, *Common Sense?* I never saw such a masterly, irresistible performance. It will, if I mistake not, in concurrence with the transcendent folly and wickedness of the ministry, give the *coup-de-grace* to Great Britain. In short, I own myself convinced by the arguments, of the necessity of separation. Poor brave Montgomery! But it it is not a time to cry, but to revenge. God bless you, my dear General, and crown us with the success I am sure we merit, from the goodness of our cause. My love to the ladies. I shall write a long letter to Gates, when I have time and materials. Adieu.

Yours, most affectionately,

CHARLES LEE.

FROM GOVERNOR TRUMBULL.

Lebanon, 24 January, 1776.

SIR,

Your letters, of the 20th and 21st instant, are received. I thought fit this morning to acquaint Colonel Burrell, appointed to command the regiment destined to Canada from hence, that a month's pay will be advanced to officers and men by you. This additional encouragement will enliven them to the service. Also to inform, that I understood the route of the Massachusetts and New Hampshire regiments would probably be by Number Four* to Onion River, with a Commissary to attend such as went that way. A month's pay was promised the men by my proclamation, and, on being acquainted with the readiness of the men, one of the Committee of the Pay-Table should attend for the payment thereof at Litchfield, to prevent delay. I am unable to inform how and when the money from you may be received.

The men in that quarter are well spirited and zealous, but have yet received no intelligence of the progress made in the business. Shall give you every necessary intelligence as it comes to my knowledge.

---

* Charlestown, in New Hampshire.

12*

Every necessary requisite for the march of this regiment will be provided on the best terms in my power. Shall forward the three regiments destined for your camp, without delay. I am, with sincere esteem and regard, your Excellency's

Most obedient and humble servant,

JONATHAN TRUMBULL.

FROM THE PRESIDENT OF CONGRESS.

Philadelphia, 29 January, 1776.

SIR,

The Congress have received your letter of the 19th instant, and highly commend your prudence and zeal in applying to the Governments of New Hampshire, Massachusetts Bay, and Connecticut, to raise forces for the service of Canada at this exigency. They have fond hopes, by the zeal and alacrity of those Colonies, troops will be forwarded with such expedition as will not only succour our friends, but in some measure retrieve our loss, and put us in possession of Quebec, before our enemies can receive reënforcements.

The Congress have agreed to add the Massachusetts regiment to the forces they at first destined for Canada. This is the more necessary, as it is now uncertain whether two battalions, as was expected, can be raised out of the troops in that country. But they do not, by this, mean to weaken your army. They have, therefore, ordered that the three regiments you applied for from Massachusetts Bay, New Hampshire, and Connecticut, shall be exclusive of the thirteen wanted for the army at Cambridge.

By the latest advices from England, it appears that Administration are determined to exert themselves, and to send a considerable force against us next spring, though at the same time they pretend to say, that they will offer terms of accommodation, and mean only by their armament to enforce their terms.

It behooves us, therefore, to be ready to receive them; for, should an accommodation take place, the terms will be severe or favorable in proportion to our ability to resist.

The Congress highly approve your sending General Lee to the assistance of New York, as a measure judicious and necessary, and have also appointed three of their body to repair to New York and confer with General Lee and the Committee of Safety of New York, on the subject of putting that Colony in a posture of defence.

General Prescott arrived here last Thursday, and is this day ordered into close confinement in the jail of this city.

I must beg leave to refer you to the inclosed resolutions. I send, by this express, commissions for the Massachusetts battalion, and the money ordered to the Assembly. I have the honor to be, with the greatest esteem, Sir,

Your most obedient, humble servant,
JOHN HANCOCK, *President.*

FROM MAJOR-GENERAL LEE.

New York, 5 February, 1776.

MY DEAR GENERAL,

I arrived here yesterday, but not without some diffi-

culty. My disorder increased rather than diminished, so that I was under the necessity of being carried in a litter a considerable part of the way. I
consider it as a piece of the greatest good fortune
that the Congress have detached a Committee to this
place, otherwise I should have made a most ridiculous figure, besides bringing upon myself the enmity
of the whole Province. My hands were effectually
tied up from taking any step necessary for the public service by the late resolve of the Congress, putting every detachment of the Continental forces under the command of the Provincial Congress where
such detachment is.

I should apprise you that General Clinton arrived
almost at the same instant with myself. He has
brought no troops with him, and pledges his honor
that none are coming. He says it is merely a visit
to his friend Tryon. If it is really so, it is the most
whimsical piece of civility I ever heard of. He informs us that his intention is for North Carolina,
where he expects five regiments from England; that
he only brought two companies of light infantry from
Boston. This is certainly a droll way of proceeding.
To communicate his full plan to the enemy is too
novel to be credited.

The Congress Committees, a certain number of the
Committee of Safety, and your humble servant, have
had two conferences. The result of these conferences
is such as will agreeably surprise you. It is, in the
first place, agreed, and justly, that to fortify the town
against shipping, is impracticable; but we are to fortify lodgments in some commanding part of the city
for two thousand men. We are to erect inclosed batteries on both sides the water near Hell Gate, which
will answer the double purpose of securing the town

against piracies through the Sound, and secure our communication with Long Island, now become a more capital point than ever, as it is determined to form a strong fortified camp of three thousand men on the Island, immediately opposite to New York. The pass in the Highlands is to be made as respectable as possible, and guarded by a battalion. In short, I think the plan judicious and complete. The two brass pieces and other articles will be sent down as you request. You have heard of the fate of the cannon near King's Bridge. As I write with pain, you will excuse my abrupt conclusion.

Yours, dear General,
Charles Lee.

P. S. My love to Gates and the rest, female and male.*

FROM GOVERNOR TRUMBULL.

Lebanon, 5 February, 1776.

Sir,

Inclosed is account of the charges and expenses incurred by providing for Messrs. Penet and De Pliarne, in their journey to Philadelphia, by your Excellency's direction. I have sent forward to you the bills, showing how the account arose. Please to order payment to be made, and sent to me by the post who brings this.

The battalion raising in this Colony, to march to

---

* Mrs. Washington, and her son Mr. Custis, and his wife, were at this time at head-quarters.

the assistance of our friends at Canada, are enlisted to serve until the 1st of February next, with bounty, pay, wages, and allowances, agreeable to resolve of Congress, sent me by the express who last came to you this way.

Our Treasury was exhausted, and knew not how to set the troops forward, until Saturday. Intelligence came to me that twelve thousand five hundred dollars were received from the Honorable Congress for that purpose. My proclamation was out some time before, and I hear that men enlist freely, and hope they will be on their march soon; have ordered them to go off by divisions, and hope nothing will retard them.

Through fear of delay, I wrote, last week, to you on the head of our payment of the troops that served under you last season; the pay-rolls are to meet your approbation and order for payment; and although provision is received for those going to Canada, yet there remain innumerable calls we are unable to answer without further supplies, and apprehend payment is to be made by you on those rolls.

Three battalions, raised and marching to your camp, will come on soon; three dollars a man was paid, in part of wages, to enable them to make necessary provisions. I hear that two or three companies are gone forward, and the rest going this week.

I received a letter from Major-General Lee, dated at Stamford, January 31st, wherein he writes;—"A most unexpected and severe attack of the rheumatism or gout has seized me here, and prevented me personally proceeding. I have sent Colonel Waterbury on, as he is sufficiently strong in numbers betwixt his own regiment and the volunteers. I thought it prudent to order back Ward's regiment, till they received your Honor's further orders." In another scrip, he says; — "There is a late resolve of the Continental Congress, which, had I seen before, would have stopped me. It is, that every detachment of the army is to act under the direction of the Provincial Congress where it is. What then will be the use of a detachment at New York? I answer by asking, is New York to be left to be more inimical to us than even the Province of Quebec? The policy of many there is strained to the utmost against our rights. However, I hope better things of their Congress, if not perverted by artful threats and craft."

Since writing thus far, I am informed that General Lee was carried into New York in a litter, and three members of the Continental Congress are to meet him there, to settle measures of conduct.

I am, with great truth and regard, Sir, your obedient, humble servant,

JONATHAN TRUMBULL.

FROM GOVERNOR TRUMBULL.

Lebanon, 12 February, 1776.

SIR,

I received your two favors of the 8th instant; have also received, per Bacon, the remittance for the expenses of the French gentlemen to Philadelphia. I had no design to have ever called on you for the money paid our troops under your immediate command, but to have accounted with the Congress, had we not been unexpectedly drained of cash, and had pressing calls upon us two or three ways at once. That to the northward could not possibly have been answered, but for the seasonable arrival of the Continental supply, just sufficient for that purpose. Our other demands for the common service are many. The men, for the short service with you, could not have marched without some money, which they have, I trust, wholly expended for necessary clothing, &c. I therefore could have wished it had been in your power to have remitted the sum advanced by our Pay-Table, but shall do every thing in my power, that the common interest do not suffer.

I am greatly concerned for the scarcity of powder and arms. We have not half a sufficiency for ourselves, as the circumstances may be; yet, anxious to furnish you, for the common good, with every supply in our power, have ordered a quantity of gunpowder lately arrived at Bedford, in Dartmouth, carted to and now lying at Providence, on account of this Colony, to be sent you, with all possible expedition. Three thousand weight of this we conclude to order to Major Thompson, Agent for the Massachusetts Colony, on account of money he supplied to Mr. Shaw, the importer, for that end, and you will consult him or them concerning the use of it. I suppose the whole to be upwards of six thousand weight; the residue, on account of this Colony, for which shall expect payment, or to be replaced, as shall be hereafter chosen by us. I shall send you this week twenty or thirty stands of good arms. I have not certain advice from every quarter, but I believe our three regiments are all on the march to your camp, except those already arrived there.

I have much more agreeable intelligence from General Lee, and the New York Congress, than I expected. I cannot but hope propitious Heaven will smile success on that most timely and judicious exertion of your Excellency, to prevent our enemies possessing themselves of that important station. I have the pleasure to inclose you a copy of General Lee's letter. In compliance with his request, we have already sent orders to Colonel Ward to repair again forthwith to New York.

I am, Sir, with the greatest esteem and regard, your most obedient, humble servant,

JONATHAN TRUMBULL.

FROM MAJOR-GENERAL LEE.

New York, 14 February, 1776.

DEAR GENERAL,

I should have written to you more constantly, but really had no means of conveying my letter. A Mr. Buchanan and Tolby, bound for head-quarters, will deliver you this. You will excuse the conciseness, as my time is short. The Governor and Captain of man-of-war had threatened perdition to the town if the cannon were removed from the batteries and wharves; but I ever considered their threats as a *brutum fulmen*, and even persuaded the town to be of the same way of thinking. We accordingly conveyed them to a place of safety in the middle of the day, and no cannonade ensued. Captain Parker publishes a pleasant reason for his passive conduct. He says it was manifestly my intention, and that of the New England men under my command, to bring down destruction on this town, so hated for their loyal principles; but that he was determined not to indulge us, so remained quiet out of spite. The people here laugh at his nonsense, and begin to despise the menaces which formerly used to throw them into convulsions. To do them justice, the whole show a wonderful alacrity; and in removing the cannon, men and boys, of all ages, worked with the greatest zeal and pleasure. I really believe that the generality are as well affected as any on the Continent.

The Provincial Congress have ordered on fifteen hundred minute-men. A number equal to two battalions are coming from Pennsylvania and the Jerseys. Lord Stirling's regiment is already here, but not complete. When the major part, or a sufficient number, arrive, we shall begin our works. My intention is to pull down that part of the fort on the town side, to prevent its being converted into a citadel for the enemy, and to erect a battery on a traverse in the street, to prevent their making a lodgment in it. A redoubt and battery at the pass of Hell Gate will prevent their ships and tenders passing and repassing to and from the Sound.

We have fixed on a spot in Long Island for a retrenched camp, which I hope will render it impossible for them to get footing on that important Island. As this camp can always be reënforced, it is our intention to make it so capacious as to contain four thousand men. The batteries on the pass of Hudson's River will be secured as soon as possible. Some of the heavy cannon from hence must be sent up for the purpose. It is really a fine train we are in possession of. You shall have a return of the guns as well as stores by the post.

Captain Smyth is an excellent, intelligent, active officer, and I take the liberty of commending him to your protection. Captain Badlam, of the artillery, is likewise a man of great merit in his way. You must pardon me, dear General, for a liberty I have taken. You know that Sears was to collect our volunteers in Connecticut, but he thought he could not succeed unless he had some nominal office and rank. I accordingly, most impudently, by the virtue of the power deputed by you to me (which power you never deputed), appointed him assistant Adjutant-General, with rank of Lieutenant-Colonel, for the expedition. It can have no bad consequences. The man was much tickled, and it added spurs to his heat.* He is a creature of much spirit and public virtue, and ought to have his back clapped.

With respect to the Canada expedition, which you indirectly propose to me, I have only one answer to make. Wherever I can be of most service, there I should choose to be. I have, indeed, just at this instant, one objection, which is, I am not without apprehensions that facing the cold may throw me into a relapse, so as not only to render me unfit for service there, but everywhere else. I am, indeed, much better, but extremely tender. I begin to walk — it has been a d—d attack; a constant violent fever attending it. I neither ate nor slept for eight days; but my fever is passed, and I begin to eat; a week I hope will set me up.

Several members of Congress have indicated a desire I should go to Canada. I have explained to them my apprehensions, but assured them most honestly of my willingness; but, in fact, unless they expedite an army, and some heavy artillery, it will be in vain to trouble their heads about a General. Colonel Richmore, who lately left Montreal, tells us that what few troops are now there will infallibly

---

* This word is so obscurely written, in the original manuscript, that it is difficult to decide whether it is *heat*, *hat*, or *head*.

return home early in April. He is gone to the Congress, and I hope will give them (as he is capable) the necessary lights; but whatever steps they take, be assured, dear General, that I am, with the greatest readiness, prepared to receive and execute your and their commands. Canada is, I confess, if I am only to be ably accoutred, a glorious field, which must flatter the ambition of

Yours, most sincerely,
CHARLES LEE.

FROM COLONEL LACHLAN MⁱCINTOSH.*

Savannah, 16 February, 1776.

SIR,

My country having honored me with the command of the Continental battalion, ordered to be raised by the General Congress for the protection and defence of this Colony (though I fear too partial to my poor abilities), it becomes my duty to inform your Excellency of the state of our Province, as far as it concerns the service, as well as of the troops to be immediately under my command.

---

* Lachlan McIntosh was a native of Scotland, and, in 1736, when he was nine years old, he came to Georgia with his father, who accompanied General Oglethorpe. Early in 1776, the Assembly of Georgia passed a resolution to raise a battalion of Continental troops, and, on the 4th of February, Lachlan McIntosh was appointed to the command, with the rank of Colonel. (McCall's History of Georgia, Vol. II. p. 65.) On the 16th of September, of the same year, he was appointed by Congress a Brigadier-General in the Continental Army. He served in the Western Department for some time, having his head-quarters at Pittsburg, and was afterwards at the siege of Savannah. He retired from the service before the close of the war.

Our Province has a front along the sea-coast of above one hundred miles, covered by a range of islands divided from each other by eight rivers from the main land, which makes as many good inlets and harbours, most of them capable of receiving any frigate, and, as some say, much larger ships. Our settlements extend back to the north-west above two hundred miles; in other parts, to the southward, not above ten, and very thinly inhabited. Indeed, this large space of land altogether has not more than three thousand men, chiefly in the back country, and many disaffected and doubtful in our cause, especially the men of the greatest property among us. Our slaves will be above fifteen thousand souls, mostly within twenty miles of the sea-coast, and make above thirty-five thousand tierces of rice annually, besides many other articles of provision, which, with our fine harbours, makes the security of this Colony, though weak in itself, of the utmost consequence to the whole Continent of America. And we have every reason to think our enemies intend to make it a place of general rendezvous and supplies.

We are bounded south by the garrisoned Province of East Florida, who have now, as I am well informed, five hundred regulars in St. Augustine, and one thousand more expected there daily from Europe. On the west of us is the Province of West Florida, the numerous nations of the Creek, Choctaw, and Cherokee Indians, besides lesser tribes, supposed to have at least ten thousand gun-men, brave, intrepid, and eager for war, whom we shall have the utmost difficulty to keep at peace, as we want every article of their usual supply, and now furnished them in great plenty from the two Floridas.

Our metropolis is situated in the north corner of

13 *

the Province, upon a bluff or sand-hill thirty feet high or more above the water, and fifteen miles up the river Savannah from the inlet of Tybee, where five ships of war, the Syren, the Scarborough, the Raven, the Tamar, and Cherokee, besides tenders, are now lying, and two large transports, having, it is said, above three hundred men on board, and expecting more daily; with what design, whether for this Colony only, or Carolina, or both together, we are not yet informed. Our Province has declared itself in a state of alarm, and resolved not to supply the men-of-war with provision, and ordered a draft of half the militia to the town of Savannah, to oppose the landing of any troops.

Our Provincial Congress, having accepted the battalion ordered for their protection and defence, chose the officers the 29th and 30th ultimo (a return of whom shall accompany this), and made them sign the inclosed test before their commissions were delivered; and I have this day issued general orders for recruiting, which has been hitherto prevented by many obstacles in providing money for that and other necessary services, and I fear will yet be attended with some difficulty. We expect very few in our own Province. That of South Carolina is said to be already drained of such people as will enlist by their Provincial regiments; besides, their bounty, subsistence, &c., is so much better than ours. Therefore, I expect we must have recourse, distant as it is, to North Carolina, with this additional disadvantage, that our currency passes in no other Colony but our own, and we have received very little Continental money yet.

I have received no kind of orders or instructions from the General Congress, or your Excellency; nor have I yet been able to obtain even a copy of the American Articles of War, which makes me at a loss how to act in many cases. Therefore I shall wish any orders or directions your Excellency will please to send me, to be as full and frequent as possible; also to be informed how far we are under the control of the Provincial Congress, &c., of this or any other Province, when we are upon duty, and what rank we hold when acting with militia or Provincial troops.

I shall take the liberty of appointing surgeons to the battalion, which are so indispensably necessary that I suppose the neglect of not naming any must be owing to our Delegates; and also make Captain Colson's a rifle company, when raised, which I think will be useful, and hope will meet with your Excellency's approbation, and I doubt we shall be obliged to arm more with such guns, for want of others, which are very scarce.

I have the honor to be your Excellency's
                    Most obedient
                        And most humble servant,
                            LACHLAN MCINTOSH.

———

FROM MAJOR-GENERAL LEE.

New York, 19 February, 1776.
DEAR GENERAL,

I am extremely happy that there is any opening for a more comfortable establishment for poor Palfrey than his present. He is a valuable and capable man, and the pittance of a simple Aid-de-Camp-ship is wretched for a man, who has a family to support.

On this principle, and in obedience to your commands, I shall send him to head-quarters without delay. I must, at the same time, confess that the loss will be irreparable to me, particularly if I am detached to Canada, of which there is the greatest probability, as I have received letters from divers members of the Congress, expressing their wishes that I should be employed in that department. Messrs. Griffin and Byrd are very good young men, but pretty much in the predicament of your Baylor. They can ride, understand, and deliver verbal orders, but you might as well set them the task of translating an Arabic or Irish manuscript as expect that they should, in half a day, copy a half sheet of orders. However, I must bustle through the difficulties, and not keep Palfrey out of the channel of a better provision. If I go to Canada, I suppose I shall be allowed secretaries, one French and one English. I do not see now it is possible to manage matters with less. *Apropos*, my dear General, if this is to be my province, shall you take it ill if I apply for one of my two Brigadiers, either Greene or Sullivan? It is a pleasure to have some officer about us in whom we can place confidence.

The ships of war, which were here, have been frightened away. The Asia lies betwixt Nutten's and Bedloe's Islands; the Duchess of Gordon, with his Excellency Governor Tryon, is under her stern; the Phœnix is stationed a league below the Narrows. The Mercury and General Clinton must inevitably fall into the hands of our fleet, unless they are fast asleep. We have taken strong hold of Hell Gate, so that the passage betwixt Long Island and the continent is absolutely blocked up to the enemy. I wait for some more force to prepare a post, or retrenched en-

campment, on Long Island, opposite to the city, for
three thousand men. This is, I think, a capital object; for, should the enemy take possession of New
York, when Long Island is in our hands, they will
find it almost impossible to subsist. The Jerseys are
two well manned, and Connecticut, you know, will
not furnish them with any thing.

What to do with the City, I own, puzzles me. It
is so encircled with deep, navigable water, that who-
ever commands the sea must command the town.
To-morrow I shall begin to dismantle that part of
the fort next to the town, to prevent its being converted into a citadel. I shall barrier the principal
streets, and, at least, if I cannot make it a Continental garrison, it shall be a disputable field of battle.

Inclosed I send you a return of the good and indifferent pieces of cannon. The number of the bad,
those, I mean, totally unfit for service, is, I believe,
about sixty. As no Commissary of Stores has been
appointed until this instant, it is impossible to give
you a return of the other stores by this post, but
you shall have it by the next. Lord Stirling is a
great acquisition. He is a most zealous, active, and
accurate officer.

A captain of a ship from Cadiz, who is a very intelligent person, tells us that Lord Howe and Captain
Barrington, or Admiral Barrington, are appointed Commissioners to propose terms to the Congress. This
he had from the Consul Hardy. What d——d fools
the Ministry are! How does your recruiting go on
for the standing army? Be so good as to tell Gates,
to whom I shall write by the next post, that Mr.
Nourse inclosed no letters for him. If little Eustace
is not provided for in your army, and I should go
to Canada, I think he had better be sent to me, and

I will consign him to his uncle. I am got quit of my gout and fever, but remain extremely weak and tender. God preserve you, my dear General, from all disorders, at least until we have trampled Satan under our feet.

My love to Mrs. Washington and all the ladies.

Adieu. Yours, most faithfully,

CHARLES LEE.

FROM BRIGADIER-GENERAL ARNOLD.

Camp before Quebec, 27 February, 1776.

DEAR GENERAL,

I wrote you the 14th ultimo, of our situation and prospects, since which nothing of consequence has occurred here. The enemy, to the number of about five hundred, have twice sallied out at Palace Gate, with design of seizing our field-pieces (near the Nunnery); but, on our troops advancing to attack them, they made a precipitate retreat under cover of their guns. Desertions from the garrison are frequent, by which we learn they are much distressed for fuel, and must soon burn their houses and ships. Two officers, taken at St. John's, were lately sent with a flag to the walls, with a view of getting their families at liberty, but were refused admittance, which, I am told by several deserters, incensed the inhabitants very much, and caused a great uneasiness in the garrison, who, I believe begin to grow heartily tired of salt provisions and confinement. We have received a reinforcement of four hundred men; many are daily coming in. I hope, in the course of this month, we shall have four or five thousand men. I am fearful we shall not be supplied with shot, shells, mortars, &c. I am therefore preparing ladders for an assault, if necessary. The extensiveness of the works I think will render their defence impracticable.

I have this minute the pleasure of your favor of the 27th ultimo. I am greatly obliged to you for your good wishes, and the concern you express for me. Sensible of the vast importance of this country, you may be assured my utmost exertions will not be wanting to effect your wishes in adding it to the United Colonies. I am fully of your opinion, that the balance will turn in whose favor it belongs. The repeated successes of our raw, undisciplined troops over the flower of the British army, the many unexpected and remarkable occurrences in our favor, are plain proofs of the overruling hand of Providence, and justly demand our warmest gratitude to Heaven, which I make no doubt will crown our virtuous efforts with success. No doubt Administration will exert themselves in sending a large force this way in the spring; but if we are fortunate enough to reduce the city before they arrive, I make no doubt of keeping it, as we shall have the interest of the country in general, to which the raising two regiments of Canadians (which Congress have ordered) will not a little conduce.

I am sorry to inform you, notwithstanding every precaution that could be used, the smallpox has crept in among the troops. We have near one hundred men in the hospital. In general it is favorable; very few have died. I have moved the inhabitants of the vicinity of Quebec into the country, and hope to prevent its spreading any further.

The severity of the climate, the troops very illy clad, and worse paid, the trouble of reconciling matters among the inhabitants, and lately an uneasiness among the New York and some other officers, who think themselves neglected in the new arrangement, while those who deserted the cause and went home last fall have been promoted; in short, the choice of difficulties I have had to encounter, has rendered it so very perplexing, that I have often been at a loss how to conduct matters.

As General Schuyler's ill state of health will not permit his coming this way, I was in hopes General Lee, or some experienced officer, would have been sent to take the command here. The service requires a person of greater abilities and experience than I can pretend to. General Wooster writes me his intention of coming down here. I am afraid he will not be able to leave Montreal.

I have the pleasure to inform you my wound is entirely healed, and I am able to hobble about my room. Though my leg is a little contracted and weak, I hope soon to be fit for action. We are waiting impatiently, expecting to hear of some capital blow being struck with you. I beg my compliments to the gentlemen of your family; and am, with great respect and esteem, dear General,

Your obedient and very humble servant,
BENEDICT ARNOLD.

FROM MAJOR-GENERAL LEE

New York, 29 February, 1776.

DEAR GENERAL,

I am now so far recovered, though far from well, that I shall set out in two days. The stripping

Ticonderoga so entirely of its heavy cannon, is a most unfortunate circumstance, as the transportation of them from this place is a business of monstrous difficulties, expense, and labor.

The Congress have, as yet, not taken the least step for the security of this place. The instant I leave it, I conclude the Provincial Congress and inhabitants in general will relapse into their former hysterics; the men-of-war and Mr. Tryon will return to their old station at the wharves; and the first regiments, who arrive from England, will take quiet possession of the town and Long Island. I have written letters till I am tired, on the subject, to the Congress, but have received no answer. The Committee of three, who were here to confer with me, agreed it was necessary that five thousand men should be in the place. They left us, and no notice has been taken of the affair since. Great and extensive works were resolved upon; and we have scarcely sufficient numbers to mark out the ground, much less to throw up the works. In short, I know not what to make of this apathy on so important a subject.

Messrs. Price, Walker, and, since them, the volunteer Melchior, are arrived from Canada. It is very lucky, for they can communicate all the necessary lights to the Congress with respect to the measures which must be taken in that country. By their accounts, nothing is so much wanted as artillerymen. Captain Lamb's company were all taken prisoners. I wish, indeed it is necessary, you should spare us a company from Boston. We cannot possibly do without them. We have none here. I entreat, dear General, you would detach Captain Badlam's company. The Captain and I are now well acquainted, and agree wonderfully. The Pennsylvania and Jersey troops march for Canada; are good and strong in numbers. The spirit of enlisting prevails through the whole country. I am told, but cannot believe it, that the New England Delegates oppose the enlisting for a year. They say, by means of a shorter engagement the whole country would be soldiers. A curious whim this. Who the d—l can fill their heads with such nonsense? I should think a letter from you on the subject, to either of the Adamses, would have a good effect.

I have this moment received yours of the 22d. It is a sort of reprimand for not having more exactly informed you of the occurrences here. I do assure you, General, that I have wrote fully and frequently. It is true, I believe, two posts have carried no letters from me, but I would not trouble you when I had nothing material to communicate. I shall not intrench myself behind the parade of great business, for my first business is to be attentive to my General. Nor shall I make a plea of the loss of Palfrey, since whose departure I have been obliged to write with my own hand every the most trifling note. But, in fact, though I confess I am naturally remiss, I have not neglected my duty in this point. I have suffered no safe opportunity to escape me. But enough of this.

I shall now give you a detail of what we have been doing, and in what circumstances we are. Our force, including the minute-men, amounts to about seventeen hundred men. Ward's regiment, which is the strongest, I have stationed on Long Island. They are employed in making fascines, and preparing other materials for constructing three redoubts, one of which will, in great measure, (in correspondence with a battery which I have sunk opposite to it in the city), secure the entrance of the East River. Waterbury's and Stirling's regiments are quartered in the city; the former in the upper barracks, the latter in the lower. Two hundred minute-men are likewise lodged in the town. Drake's regiment of minute-men, and one more company (in all about two hundred), are stationed at Horen's Hook, which commands the pass of Hell Gate. They are employed in throwing up a redoubt to contain three hundred men.

As to the town, having few hands, and the necessary duty being hard, I have been able to effect little. I have indeed thrown down the side of the fort next the town, to prevent its being converted into a citadel for the use of the enemy. It was absolutely impossible to be moulded into any thing which could annoy their ships. I have likewise thrown a traverse, or barrier, across the Broadway, two hundred yards in the rear of the fort, with four pieces of cannon, to prevent the enemy lodging themselves in the remains of the fort, and repairing it. It is likewise my intention to barricade all the streets leading into the Broadway, both on the right and left, to secure us against being taken in reverse. Batteries are to be erected on the eminence behind Trinity Church, to keep their ships at so great a distance as not to injure the town. As we are surrounded by navigable waters, I consider inclosed works as rather dangerous. It was, therefore, my intention to throw up a great number of large *flèches* or *redans* at certain distances, one behind another, so as to render it a disputable field of battle against any force. King's Bridge, being a most important pass, without the command of which we could have no communication with Connecticut, I had resolved to make as strong as possible.

Such were my schemes; but as the Congress have not furnished the force which I was taught to expect from Philadelphia, we have not had it in our power to effect more than I have related. Governor Tryon and the Asia still continue betwixt Nutten's and Bedloe's Islands. It has pleased his Excellency, in violation of the compact he had made, to seize several vessels from Jersey, laden with flour. It has, in return, pleased my Excellency to stop all provision from the city, and cut off all intercourse with him, a measure which has thrown the Mayor, Council, and Tories into agonies. The propensity, or rather rage, for paying court to this great man, is inconceivable. They cannot be weaned from him. We must put wormwood on his paps, or they will cry to suck, as they are in their second childhood.

Captain Smith is just returned from Fort Constitution. He gives me a most terrible account of it. The expense of its construction has been enormous. Its defects, both in point of situation, laying out, finishing, &c., are numerous. He has made the plan of another, which will command, as far as I can judge from it on paper, the river effectually.

I have now related, as minutely as necessary, our situation. As I shall set out very soon, it will probably be my last from this place. I must entreat, once more, dear General, that you will spare us a company of artillery. Badlam seems rather averse, on proposing it.

Adieu, dear Sir. Yours, with the greatest respect and affection,

CHARLES LEE.

FROM MAJOR-GENERAL LEE.

New York, 3 March, 1776.

Dear General,

My destination is altered. Instead of going to Canada, I am appointed to command at the southward. There has been a great promotion of Brigadier-Generals; Armstrong, Thompson, Lewis, Moore, Stirling, and Howe, are the six. Four are to serve under my orders, namely, Armstrong, Lewis, Moore, and Howe. As I am the only general officer on the Continent, who can speak and think in French, I confess I think it would have been more prudent to have sent me to Canada; but I shall obey with alacrity, and hope with success. Griffin has resigned, as he flatters himself he can do better in the commercial line. I have, in his room, appointed one of the sons of Lewis Morris, to whom I was under a sort of engagement. Lord Stirling will take the command until the arrival of Schuyler. His Lordship is active and distinct.

In my last I gave you my plan of defence for this city and environs; but, from want of men, I shall be obliged to leave it in a poor condition. A regiment of Associators are, I am told, ordered from Philadelphia. I have likewise sent for a battalion from the Jerseys; but, on the other hand, Ward's and Waterbury's regiments will, I suppose, according to their laudable custom, leave the place the moment their time is expired, which is the 12th of this month. I heartily pray that you may give Mr. Howe a handsome salute on his leaving Boston. I am not yet informed who is to take the command in Canada. No time, I am sure, is to be lost. As I am ordered away

14*

immediately, I must consign the affairs of New York to Lord Stirling. He will acquit himself well. I have nothing material to trouble you with at present, further than to assure you that I am, and ever shall be, dear General,

Yours, most sincerely,

CHARLES LEE.

FROM JOSEPH REED.

Philadelphia, 3 March, 1776.

MY DEAR GENERAL,

I have not been favored with any thing from you since my two last; but that never makes any difference in my writing, as your claims of friendship and gratitude upon me are superior to all others. The Congress have made an appointment of Generals, as by the inclosed paper. Armstrong is ordered to South Carolina, Thompson to New York. The others keep their present situations. General Lee's destination is changed to Virginia, from undoubted authority that it will be a principal scene of action. The Congress have acceded to the proposition respecting myself; so that unless some new event, unforeseen and very important, should happen, I shall be with you this summer. I must beg your indulgence till I can get my family into some convenient situation, and settle my affairs. In the mean time, I am forwarding your camp equipage, which I have extended, in many small particulars, beyond your order.

Arnold is to be intrusted with the affairs of Canada, Wooster having either resigned, or been superseded, I know not which. Melchior is come from

Quebec in twelve days, where he left our little army strengthened to fifteen hundred men, in good spirits, and still pleasing themselves with the hope of being masters of the town. I have not yet seen him, so that I can give you no further particulars; but I understand they are like to want battering cannon and mortars. No arrivals of powder or arms since my last, or any account of our fleet, though, from their present cruising ground, we hope they will fall in with Lord Cornwallis and the transports.

Notwithstanding the act of Parliament for seizing our property, and a thousand other proofs of a bitter and irreconcilable spirit, there is a strange reluctance, in the minds of many, to cut the knot which ties us to Great Britain, particularly in this Colony and to the southward. Though no man of understanding expects any good from the Commissioners, yet they are for waiting to hear their proposals before they declare off. However, yesterday I was informed letters had been sent to France to know what encouragement we might expect from that quarter. Our coast is yet clear; it is a golden opportunity to make provision for the war, which, I hope, will not be lost. If the other Provinces had done any thing like this in the making of arms, this winter we should have been tolerably provided. We shall, by the 1st April, have made four thousand stands since last October, every part done here. We are casting cannon, and there is more saltpetre made than in all the Provinces put together. Six powder-mills are erecting in different parts. The two near this city deliver twenty-five hundred pounds per week, and are now in very good order. Many attempts have been made to get a bounty for the New England troops, but without effect. The Congress are resolved that you shall aban-

don the lines, and give up their country to be ra-
vaged, if they will not defend it upon the same terms
as those enlisted here (such as marched to Canada
only excepted).

The Assembly have it under consideration to raise
two thousand men for the defence of this Province;
but I doubt its taking. Perhaps there may be half
the number. I am told we can easily raise two or
three more battalions, if we had arms, &c., for them.

I do not think I shall bring any person with me
when I come. Mr. Webb has long had an inclination
to be in your family. If the post should be agreeable to him, and he is agreeable to you, I believe I
should prefer him to any other. The post is just
going; so that I have only time to add, that I am,
my dear Sir,

Yours, most affectionately,

JOSEPH REED.

FROM THE PRESIDENT OF CONGRESS.

Philadelphia, 6 March, 1776.

SIR,

Since my last, I have had the honor of receiving
your letters of the 24th and 30th of January, 9th,
14th, 18th, 21st, and 26th of February, which were
communicated to Congress. On the settlements and
adjustments of accounts, the Congress have not yet
come to any determination; nor have they yet had
time to contrive expedients for remedying the inconveniences mentioned in that of the 9th, which is referred to, and will be taken up, in a Committee of
the Whole.

The Congress highly approve your care and attention in stopping Lord Drummond's letter, and entirely concur with you in sentiment with regard to his Lordship's officious and unwarrantable zeal.

The situation of the Middle and Southern Colonies hath engaged the attention of Congress. These are divided into two departments; — the Middle, comprehending New York, New Jersey, Pennsylvania, Delaware, and Maryland, under the command of a Major-General and two Brigadier-Generals; the Southern, comprehending Virginia, North and South Carolina, and Georgia, under the command of a Major-General and four Brigadier-Generals. As there is reason to think that the force of our enemies will be directed against the Colonies in the Southern Department, Major-General Lee is appointed to that command. The Brigadier-Generals are, John Armstrong, William Thompson, Andrew Lewis, James Moore, Esq., Lord Stirling, and Robert Howe, Esq.

Of these gentlemen, General Armstrong is directed to repair to South Carolina; General Lewis and General Howe to Virginia; General Moore to North Carolina; and General Thompson and Lord Stirling to New York. And, that our affairs in Canada may be under the direction of an able officer, and General Schuyler's health not permitting him to go thither, or, if he could, as his presence is so necessary in New York, the Congress have promoted Brigadier-General Thomas to the rank of a Major-General, and directed him to repair to Canada, and take the command of the Continental forces in that quarter. I have accordingly inclosed him his commission, and am to desire you will give him orders to repair, with all expedition, to his post. To enable him to execute the purposes Congress have in view in Canada,

they have ordered twelve battering cannon to be sent
from New York, and have forwarded ten tons of
powder.

Of this article, we have lately received several supplies, and have, some time ago, ordered five tons and
a half to be sent to you; which, if you have not
already received, will, I hope, soon reach you. The
Congress have also ordered ten tons more of powder
to be sent to you, which will set out to-morrow or
next day. Besides this, in the beginning of last
month they ordered ten tons of saltpetre to be sent
to Mr. Wisner's powder-mill, in the Colony of New
York; and, on the 12th of the same month, ten tons
to Mr. Livingston's mill, in the same Colony; and
ten tons to the Council of Massachusetts, with a desire to have it manufactured into gunpowder with all
possible expedition, and sent to you for the use of
the army under your command. Besides this, I have
the pleasure to inform you, that the powder-mills in
this Colony are employed, and more mills are building, which will be employed; so that I have strong
hopes we shall soon have a plentiful supply of that
necessary article.

With regard to arms, I am afraid we shall, for a
time, be under some difficulty. The importation is
now more precarious and dangerous. To remedy this,
a Committee is appointed to contract for the making
arms; and, as there is a great number of gunsmiths
in this and the neighbouring Colonies, I flatter myself we shall soon be able to provide ourselves without
risk or danger. But we must, like other States engaged in the like glorious struggle, contend with
difficulties. By perseverance, and the blessing of
God, I trust, if we continue to deserve freedom, we
shall be enabled to overcome them. To that Being,

in whose hands is the fate of nations, I recommend you and the army under your command.

I have the honor to be, with every sentiment of esteem,

Sir, your most obedient, humble servant,

JOHN HANCOCK, *President.*

P. S.   The inclosed letter I request the favor you will please order to be delivered to Mr. Cushing.

FROM COLONEL MᶜINTOSH.

Savannah, Georgia, 8 March, 1776.

SIR,

I did myself the honor to write to your Excellency the 16th ultimo, which, for want of conveyance, lies here still, as our Continental post is not well regulated, this length, yet. It is hardly worth troubling you with any report of our battalion, as I have heard from very few of our recruiting officers, and we have only between twenty and thirty men of them in town ; but the transactions here, since that time, may deserve some notice. The men-of-war at Tybee, though still giving out they had no hostile intentions against this Colony, were encouraging our slaves to desert to them, pilfering our sea islands for provisions ; and our Governor broke his parol of honor, and went privately, in the night, with his family, aboard the Scarborough, Captain Barclay, which gave us every reason to expect they meant to land at or near the town, destroy it, and carry off about twenty sail of shipping lying in the river, having, among other articles, near three thousand tierces of rice on board.

Between three and four hundred of our own militia, and one hundred from South Carolina, were all that could be got to defend an open, straggling, defenceless, and deserted town, with numberless avenues leading to it, and those men under no control or command whatsoever; and, to add to the anarchy and confusion we were in, our Council of Safety had not met for some time, having differed about the meaning of a resolve of the Continental Congress respecting the ships sailing the 1st of March.

In this desperate state of affairs, I ventured to take the command of the militia, lest the Colony should be tamely given up, though, I must acknowledge, with some reluctance; and, after examining very particularly, as I was unacquainted, around the town, I placed guards everywhere the enemy could land, and ambushes in the different roads leading to it, which made the duty very severe, and reduced our number in town greatly. In the mean time, the Cherokee, the two transports, the armed vessels and boats, came up the river within two and a half miles of town, near where we sunk a hulk in the channel of the river, and opposite to Brewton's plantation, where I placed a detachment of one hundred and fifty men, under command of Colonel Bullock, expecting they would attempt to land there. The enemy were parading with their boats for several days within gunshot of our sentinels, who, though they were ordered not to fire unless they were fired upon first, or they attempted to land, gave them several shot, but were not returned.

Our Council of Safety were got together, and resolved the shipping should not sail, and ordered they should be unrigged. The evening of the 2d of March one of the transport ships (the schooner Hinchinbrook), and sloop St. John, of eight or ten guns each, with some boats, sailed in our sight up the North River, back of Hutchinson's Island, lying opposite to the town of Savannah, but so far off that a little battery we had below the town, which played upon them, could do no damage to them. Expecting the enemy intended coming round Hutchinson's Island, and down the south side of it, to make their landing good at Yamacraw (a village three or four hundred yards above the town), I had three four-pounders carried there, a little battery erected in haste, and threw up intrenchments, and withdrew part of the guard at Brewton's, without weakening too much, or withdrawing any of our ambushes on that side, lest it might be a feint to deceive us.

About the middle of the same night, as we were afterwards informed, the Commodore, Barclay, and Majors Grant and Maitland, with about three hundred men, as it was said, landed on the back of Hutchinson's Island, with some howitzers and field-pieces, and, with the assistance and contrivance of all our own seafaring people, and many from the town, crossed the Island and hid themselves aboard of our merchant ships, which were previously hauled close to the Island, a little above our battery at Yamacraw, for that purpose. Early on Sunday, the 3d, the two armed vessels, intending to cover the enemy's landing, had come round the Island, and, coming down on the south side, were attacked by parties of riflers ordered for that purpose, and kept smartly engaged on both sides most of the day, until they lost the tide and got aground; while two sailors (Americans), at the risk of their lives, stole ashore and

informed me the enemy were hid on board our merchant-men, and had taken Joseph Rice prisoner, who
was employed to unrig them that morning.

To confirm this intelligence, Messrs. Demeré and
Roberts were ordered to go only alongside the vessels, and, without arms, to demand our fellow-citizen,
Mr. Rice ; but, to our astonishment, they were also
forced on board and kept, which convinced us our
information was true ; and immediately our little battery of three guns began to play upon them, which
they returned ; and was continued very smartly with
ball, langrage, and small arms, from both sides for
several hours. Our men were inflamed, particularly
at our own people, who had treacherously joined the
enemy against us, and were eager to board them ;
but we had neither boats, sailors, or arms, proper for
the attempt, and the oars of the few boats we had
were previously stolen away. The general cry then
was, to set all the shipping on fire ; in attempting
of which, many of our people showed great resolution
and bravery ; but, unfortunately, the first ship set
fire to (valued at twenty thousand pounds sterling),
was so large that she grounded before she got up to
the others. Afterwards a sloop was fired, which
burned two others, while the rest were cutting away,
amidst the shot of our rifles and langrage, and
slipping higher up the river, out of our reach, with
the last of the flood. In the mean time, many of
the soldiers hastily landed on the Island, in great
confusion, running in the marsh in a laughable manner, for fear of our rifles, though far past their reach,
until they got aboard a tier of ships higher up the
river, and out of the reach of our guns, near the
armed vessels. In this manner ten sail of our vessels
went along with the enemy round the upper end of

the Island (a channel never known before), with six-teen hundred barrels of rice, with the utmost anxiety and fear.

After being foiled in their scheme upon the town, the Commodore and Majors eagerly and repeatedly solicited a cessation of hostilities, for which they promised immediately to repair to Tybee, and not molest us again ; which was at length granted them, with seeming difficulty, though the truth was, we had no means of annoying them by water. The rest of the shipping we hauled close to the wharves, con-fined some of their Captains, for acting against us, with our Chief Justice and some Councillors, until they released our fellow-citizens, Demeré, Roberts, and Rice, and sent them up from Tybee, where our enemies are all now gone.

Whether they intend to try us again or not, I am not able to inform your Excellency. In this, I think, they rather lost than gained any reputation, and have done us great honor, by being the second Pro-vince on the continent which they attacked, and were shamefully foiled. We had, in all our different engagements, but two white men and one Indian wounded slightly. They must have many both kill-ed and wounded, though they acknowledge but six. Several were seen to fall.

I have the honor to be, your Excellency's most obedient and most humble servant,

LACHLAN McINTOSH.

P. S. The ships of war have taken all the rice (sixteen hundred barrels) out of the merchant-men, that so treacherously went down with them, and put it aboard their two transport ships, without paying a farthing for it. They claim one eighth for "wresting them out of the hands of the rebels," as the Commodore's certificate expresses it; but I doubt they will keep the other seven eighths also.

FROM BRIGADIER-GENERAL LORD STIRLING

New York, 11 March, 1776.

My dear General,

General Lee left this place on Thursday evening last for Philadelphia, on his way for Virginia, where he is to command. This has thrown a heavy load on my shoulders, and very unexpectedly; but I am likely soon to be relieved from it, as I hear Brigadier-General Thompson is to be here in a day or two.

The sudden departure of the post prevents my saying any thing at present relative to the situation of this place; and will only inform you that last night three gentlemen landed here from on board a packet, nine weeks out from Falmouth. They say that seven regiments of foot, amounting to about four thousand men, were embarked and ready to sail from Cork, about the 6th of January, bound to the southern Colonies; that Great Britain had engaged four thousand Hanoverians and six thousand Hessians, for the American service, and were in treaty for ten thousand Russians; that the French Ambassador at London had declared to the English Ministry, that his master did not mean to meddle with the quarrel between Great Britain and her Colonies, while it was carried on with its own force; but that he could not be an idle spectator, if any foreign aid was made use of (it was not then known, in London, that the French had any troops in the West India Islands); that it was not likely any more British troops would be sent out, for they had them not to spare.

If these things should be true, I am in hopes we shall have an easy summer's work to secure the whole Continent. The Commissioners, whose number is reduced to twenty, were to embark about the middle of January. It was said that they were to endeavour to treat with the Assemblies of Colonies separately, if possible; and even to retail out corruption to single towns or families; but if this could not succeed, they were to swallow the bitter pill, and treat with Congress.

Adieu, my dear General; the post waits. But yet, present my best regards to Mrs. Washington, Mr. and Mrs. Custis, Palfrey, &c.; and I am, with the highest esteem and regard,

Your most humble servant,
STIRLING.

FROM BRIGADIER-GENERAL LORD STIRLING.

New York, 20 March, 1776.

MY DEAR GENERAL,

I received your letter, by express, of the 14th, and your letter of the same date to General Lee, which I opened and forwarded, agreeably to the directions he left me. I am happy to find that the aid I called in from New Jersey and Connecticut exactly concords with your sentiments.

The two regiments of Connecticut now here, consisting of about five hundred rank and file each, are

15 *

impatient to go home, as many of them are farmers, who want to mark out their summer's work. The time of their engagement with General Lee ends next Monday. I have used my best endeavours to prevail on them to stay till their places are supplied from that quarter; but it is still doubtful whether they will consent to it. Of this I have apprised Governor Trumbull, and have requested him to supply their places, and to make the whole two thousand from that Colony. From New Jersey I have requested one thousand men; about two hundred of them are come in. About one thousand are ordered from the northern counties of this Province; none of them are yet arrived. We have now in this place and in Long Island about twenty-five hundred men, including the above two Connecticut regiments. The militia in town amount to about as many more. Near one half of the whole are on fatigue every day, carrying into execution the plan of defence formed by General Lee. They go on with great spirit and industry.

The Congress have ordered eight thousand men for the defence of this City and Province. The corps to make up this number are four regiments from Pennsylvania, one from New Jersey, and four of this Province, none of which are yet arrived, and most of them are incomplete and unfit to march, especially the latter, of which not above two hundred are yet in town, and some of them I find are to be employed on Hudson's River, and the northern parts of this Province. From this state of the matter, you will see that, if the Ministerial troops leave Boston and move this way, how necessary it will be to detach a large part of your army to this place, which, undoubtedly, is the most important object in North America.

On receiving your last letter, I had determined to detain at this place the eleven tons of powder designed for your camp; but, lest the manœuvres at Boston should prove a feint, I have ordered five tons of it to proceed to-morrow morning. The rest will follow according to the intelligence we receive.

Ten o'clock, P. M. Brigadier-General Thompson is arrived here this day, and of course takes the command. My utmost industry will be exerted to assist him in it. My most sincere and best wishes attend you. I have the honor to be, my dear General,

Your most obedient, humble servant,

STIRLING.

FROM THE PRESIDENT OF CONGRESS.

Philadelphia, 25 March, 1776.

SIR,

I had the honor of receiving, yesterday, yours of the 19th, containing the agreeable information of the Ministerial troops having abandoned Boston. The partial victory we have obtained over them, in that quarter, I hope will turn out a happy presage of a more general one. Whatever place may be the object of their destination, it must certainly give a sincere pleasure to every friend of this country, to see the most diligent preparations everywhere making to receive them. What may be their views, it is indeed impossible to tell with any degree of exactness. We have all the reason, however, from the rage of disappointment and revenge, to expect the worst. Nor have I any doubt that, as far as their power extends, they will inflict every species of calamity upon us. The same Providence that has baffled their attempt against the Province of Massachusetts Bay will, I trust, defeat the deep-laid scheme they are now meditating against some other part of our country.

The intelligence that our army had got possession of Boston, you will readily suppose gave me heartfelt pleasure. I beg, Sir, you will be pleased to accept my warmest thanks for the attention you have showed to my property in that town. I have only to request that Captain Cazneau will continue to look after it, and take care that it be no ways destroyed or damaged.

This success of our arms naturally calls on me to congratulate you, Sir, to whose wisdom and conduct it has been owing. Permit me to add, that, if a constant discharge of the most important duties, and the fame attending thereon, can afford genuine satisfaction, the pleasure you feel must be the most rational and exalted.

I have it in charge from Congress to direct, that you send an account of the troops in your camp, who are deficient in arms, to the several Assemblies or Conventions of the Colonies to which those men belong, and request them to send a sufficient number of arms for the men coming from the respective Colonies; and that, if arms cannot be procured, such as have not arms be dismissed the service.

The Congress being of opinion, that the reduction of Quebec and the general security of the Province of Canada, are objects of great concern, I am commanded to direct that you detach four battalions into Canada from the army under your command, as soon as you shall be of opinion, that the safety of New York and the Eastern service will permit.

Your several letters are at this time under the consideration of a Committee. As soon as any determination is made thereon, I will immediately forward it to you. I have the honor to be, with the greatest esteem, Sir, your most obedient and very humble servant,

JOHN HANCOCK, *President.*

FROM JOHN ADAMS.

Philadelphia, 1 April, 1776.

DEAR SIR,

The bearer of this letter (Francis Dana, Esq., of Cambridge) is a gentleman of family, fortune, and education, returned in the last packet from London, where he has been about a year. He has ever maintained an excellent character in his country, and a warm friendship for the American cause. He returns to share with his friends in their dangers and their triumphs. I have done myself the honor to give him this letter for the sake of introducing him to your acquaintance, as he has frequently expressed to me a desire to embrace the first opportunity of paying his respects to a character so highly esteemed and so justly admired throughout all Europe as well as America. Mr. Dana will satisfy you that we have no reason to expect peace from Britain.

I congratulate you, Sir, as well as all the friends of mankind, on the reduction of Boston; an event, which appeared to me of so great and decisive importance, that the next morning after the arrival of the news, I did myself the honor to move for the thanks of Congress to your Excellency, and that a medal of gold should be struck in commemoration of it. Congress have been pleased to appoint me, with two other gentlemen, to prepare a device. I should be very happy to have your Excellency's sentiments concerning a proper one.

I have the honor to be, with very great respect, Sir, your most obedient and affectionate servant,

JOHN ADAMS.

FROM GEORGE MASON.

Gunston Hall, Virginia, 2 April, 1776.

DEAR SIR,

We have just received the welcome news of your having, with so much address and success, dislodged the Ministerial troops, and taken possession of the town of Boston. I congratulate you most heartily upon this glorious and important event; an event which will render General Washington's name immortal in the annals of America, endear his memory to the latest posterity, and entitle him to those thanks, which Heaven appointed as the reward of public virtue.

It is the common opinion here, that we shall have a visit from General Howe in some of the Middle or Southern Colonies; but it does not seem well founded. I am very unable to judge of military affairs; but it appears to me that if General Howe acts the part of a wise man, and an experienced officer, he will not venture a sickly, worn-out, disgusted, and disgraced army, in a country where he must meet immediate opposition, and where any misfortune might produce a mutiny or general desertion. I think it much more probable that he will retire to Halifax, give his troops a little time, by ease and refreshment, to recover their spirits, and be in readiness, as soon as the season permits, to relieve Quebec; keeping some ships of war cruising off Boston harbour, to protect and direct the transports which may arrive. New York, or any of the Northern United Provinces, are too near Cambridge; for, if he could not maintain the advantageous and strongly-fortified post of Boston, what reasonable hope has he of gaining and maintaining a new one in the face of a superior army?

You will perhaps smile at these speculative and idle suggestions upon a subject which will probably be reduced to a certainty, one way or another, long before this reaches your hands; but, when I am conversing with you, the many agreeable hours we have spent together recur upon my mind. I fancy myself under your hospitable roof at Mount Vernon, and lay aside reserve. May God grant us a return of those halcyon days, when every man may sit down at his ease, under the shade of his own vine and his own fig-tree, and enjoy the sweets of domestic life! Or, if this is too much, may he be pleased to inspire us with spirit and resolution to bear our present and future sufferings becoming men determined to transmit to our posterity, unimpaired, the blessings we have received from our ancestors.

Colonel Caswell's victory in North Carolina, and the military spirit which it has raised, will be an obstacle to any attempts in that quarter. Maryland and Virginia are at present rather unprepared, but their strength is daily increasing. The late levies here have been made with surprising rapidity, and the seven new regiments are already in a manner complete, except as to arms, in which they are very deficient; but arms are coming in, in small quantities, from different parts of the country, and a very considerable manufactory is established at Fredericksburg. Large ventures have been lately made for military stores; for which purpose we are now loading a ship for Europe, with tobacco, at Alexandria. Her cargo is all on float, and I hope to have her under sailing in a few days. Notwithstanding the natural plenty of provisions in this Colony, I am very apprehensive of a great scarcity of beef and pork among our troops this summer, occasioned by the people's not expecting a market until the slaughter season was past. I find it extremely difficult to lay in a stock for about three hundred men, in the marine department of this river.

Ill health, and a certain listlessness inseparable from it, have prevented my writing to you so often as I would otherwise have done; but I trust to your friendship to excuse it. The same cause disabled me from attending the Committee of Safety this winter, and induced me to entreat the Convention to leave me out of it. I continue to correspond constantly with that Board, and I hope am no less usefully employed, thinking it, in such times as these are, every man's duty to contribute his mite to the public service.

I have, in conjunction with Mr. Dalton, the charge of providing and equipping armed vessels for the protection of this river. The thing is new to me, but I must endeavour to improve by experience. I am much obliged to the Board for joining Mr. Dalton with me. He is a steady, diligent man, and without such assistance I could not have undertaken it. We are building two row-galleys, which are in considerable forwardness; and have purchased three sloops for cruisers. Two of them, being only from forty to fifty tons burden, are to mount eight carriage-guns each, three and four-pounders; they are not yet fitted up, and we are exceedingly puzzled to get cannon for them.

The other, the *American Congress*, is a fine stout vessel, of about one hundred and ten tons burden, and has such an easy draft of water as will enable her to run into most of the creeks, or small harbours, if she meets with a vessel of superior force. She mounts fourteen carriage-guns, six and four-pounders, though we have thoughts of mounting two nine-pounders upon her main beam, if we find her able, as we think she is, to bear them. Her guns are mounted, and to be tried to-morrow. We have twenty barrels of powder, and about a ton of shot ready; more is making; swivels we have not yet been able to procure, but she may make a tolerable shift without, until they can be furnished. We have got some small arms, and are taking every method to increase them, and hope to be fully supplied in about a week more. Her company of marines is raised, and have been for some time exercised to the use of the great guns. Her complement of marines and seamen is to be ninety-six men. We are exerting ourselves to the utmost, and hope to have her on her station in less than a fortnight, and that the other vessels will quickly follow her, and be able to protect the inhabitants of this river from the piratical attempts of all the enemy's cutters, tenders, and small craft.

Immediately upon receipt of your former letters, I applied to some of the Maryland Committees, as well as those on this side; in consequence of which, the several most convenient places on this river were sounded, and thoroughly examined; but effectual batteries were found, in our present circumstances, impracticable. Mr. Lund Washington tells me he sent you the draughts and soundings taken upon this occasion. A regiment, commanded by Colonel Mercer, of Fredericksburg, is stationed on this part of the river, and I hope we shall be tolerably safe, unless a push is made here with a large body of men. I think we have some reason to hope the Ministry will bungle away another summer, relying partly upon force, and partly upon fraud and negotiation.

The family here join with me in presenting their best compliments to yourself and lady, as well as to Mr. Custis and his. If, in any of your affairs here, I can render you any acceptable service, I beg you will use that freedom with which I wish you to command, dear Sir,

Your affectionate and obedient servant,
GEORGE MASON.

FROM MAJOR-GENERAL LEE.

Williamsburg, 5 April, 1776.

MY DEAR GENERAL,

I most sincerely congratulate you, I congratulate the public, on the great and glorious event, your possession of Boston. It will be a most bright page in the annals of America, and a most abominable black one in those of the beldam Britain. Go on, my dear General; crown yourself with glory, and establish the liberties and lustre of your country on a foundation more permanent than the Capitol Rock.

My situation is just as I expected. I am afraid that I shall make a shabby figure, without any real demerits of my own. I am like a dog in a dancing-school. I know not where to turn myself, where to fix myself. The circumstances of the country, intersected by navigable rivers, the uncertainty of the enemy's designs and motions, who can fly in an instant to any spot with their canvas wings, throw me, or would throw Julius Cæsar, into this inevitable dilemma. I may possibly be in the North, when, as Richard says, I should serve my sovereign in the West. I can only act from surmise, and have a very good chance of surmising wrong.

I am sorry to grate your ears with a truth; but must at all events assure you that the Provincial Congress of New York are angels of decision, when compared with your countrymen, the Committee of Safety assembled at Williamsburg. Page, Lee, Mercer, and Payne are indeed exceptions; but from Pendleton, Bland, the Treasurer, and Company, — *libera nos, Domine!*

I shall not trouble you with a detail of the army, ordnance, stores; but compendiously say, that the regiments in general are very complete in numbers, the men (those that I have seen) fine, but a most horrid deficiency of arms, no intrenching tools, no guns (although the Province is pretty well stocked) for service. Had I only eight eighteen-pounders, I would immediately, at all events, take post on Craney Island, by which measure I should drive out the enemy, and exclude them from the finest and most advantageous port in America. I have ordered, with this view, the artificers to work night and day. If I succeed, I shall come in for a sprig of laurels.

This essential measure might have been effected

long ago, but the same apathy and oblique squinting towards what the milk-and-water people call reconciliation, the prodigious flattering prospect opened by the appointment of Commissioners, were strong arguments against the expense of gun-carriages and intrenching tools.

But this is not all. They have distributed their troops in so ingenious a manner as to render every active offensive operation impossible. An equal number of their battalions are stationed on the different necks. They say, very acutely, that, as the expense is equal, the security ought to be equal. I cannot help persuading myself, that their object will be to take possession of Williamsburg, not only from its tempting advantageous situation, commanding, in great measure, two fine rivers, and a country abundant in all the necessaries for an army; but the possession of the Capital would give an air of dignity and decided superiority to their arms, which, in this slave country, where dominion is founded on opinion, is a circumstance of the utmost importance. Perhaps I may be mistaken, but, as the surmise is not irrational, I have called three regiments down the country.

You will excuse, my dear General, the blots and scratches of this letter, for the post is just going out. By the next, I will inform you of the steps we have taken for the security of this place. I have been desired to recommend Colonel Grayson as a man of extraordinary merit. He sets out soon to make application to the Congress for an establishment. If we have, as we must, a Continental Hospital in the Southern Department, Dr. McClary, I suppose, will be the man to direct it. I need not mention his qualifications, they are so well known. I beg you will make somebody write to me from time to time.

Indeed, I think I may modestly insist on Mr. Palfrey's pen being employed often in this service. Adieu, dear General.

Yours, most respectfully and sincerely,

CHARLES LEE.

FROM MAJOR-GENERAL THOMAS.

Albany, 7 April, 1776.

SIR,

I arrived at Albany in five days after I left the camp at Roxbury, at which place I have been detained to this time by reason of the Lakes being impassable. The troops here and at Lake George are about eleven hundred, and I hear some few are at Ticonderoga and Crown Point, prevented going forward, as the Lakes are partly blocked up. What number are in Canada, I cannot ascertain; but am sensible, from the best intelligence, will be much short of the number required, as I find the regiments are very incomplete. General Schuyler thinks they will be much short of five thousand; and should the Ministerial troops there be reënforced, and Quebec remain in their hands, so small a number must be thought to be inadequate for the defence of that quarter. Your Excellency will judge whether a reënforcement will not be necessary.

The last from Canada was about the 25th of March, at which time things there remained *in statu quo*. Dr. Franklin and others, of the Committee of Congress, arrived here this morning. As the weather this day or two is moderate, I am in hopes the Lake may be passed in a few days. I determine to set

16*

off for the Lake tomorrow. I am, Sir, with the greatest respect, your Excellency's most obedient and

Most humble servant,

JOHN THOMAS.

FROM MAJOR-GENERAL SCHUYLER.

Fort George, 12 April, 1776.

DEAR GENERAL,

Yesterday I had the honor to receive your favor of the 3d instant, by Bennet, who overtook me on my way to this place. All is in readiness to move, as soon as the Lakes open, which, I hope, will be in a day or two. General Thomas is here, six companies of Burrell's regiment from Connecticut, two companies of the First Pennsylvania Battalion, and three of the New Jersey. The remainder of these corps are gone on, whereof two companies are about forty-five miles below Crown Point; the rest have reached Canada. We have also here two companies of Van Schaick's, of this Colony; and five companies of the Second Pennsylvania Battalion are at Fort Edward, waiting for the Lake to open, as I have no quarters for them at this place. The remainder of Van Schaick's are not yet raised; and two companies of the First Pennsylvania Battalion are on their way from New York.

I should be extremely happy, my dear General, to pay my devoirs to you at New York; but I do not see a possibility of quitting this quarter, without risking all in Canada. Unless some other general officer should relieve me, I shall, therefore, presume to remain, unless I receive your further orders.

Four o'clock, P. M. This moment the post from Canada is arrived. I inclose you copies of all the papers I received. The intelligence they afford is so alarming, that I beg leave to repeat my wish that a considerable body of troops should be immediately sent up.

I have stopped the courier at this place, and he goes back immediately to advise our friends in Canada, that the troops now here will soon be in Canada; and I have presumed to add, that they will be followed by three or four thousand more. This intelligence will keep up their spirits, and intimidate our enemies.

I have, heretofore, observed to your Excellency, that I had never received a return of the army in Canada. I am, on that account, still incapable of letting you know the strength of our army there. I am equally in the dark with respect to the arrangement made in officering the two regiments that were to be raised out of the troops that wintered there.

The provisions at these posts are very trifling. None of what General Lee has contracted for is come to Albany; and, unless a speedy supply is sent up, our troops in Canada must suffer. I have written on this subject to General Thompson before I left Albany; and although I make not the least doubt but that he will forward it, if he can, yet I beg leave to mention it, lest he should forget to mention it on the arrival of his superior officer at New York.

I am seized with a copious scorbutic eruption, which I have frequently experienced, and imagined it threw off some other more disagreeable disorder. I believe it will not confine me, or prevent me from doing my duty. I am, dear General, most sincerely,

Your obedient, humble servant,
PHILIP SCHUYLER.

Philadelphia, 23 April, 1776.

Sir,

I am to acknowledge the receipt of your favor of the 19th of April, inclosing several papers; all which were immediately laid before Congress.

The important intelligence they contain makes it necessary that the most vigorous measures should be adopted, as well to defend our troops against the Canadians themselves, as to insure success to the expedition. The Congress being determined on the reduction of Quebec, and the security of that country, for reasons too obvious to be mentioned, have left nothing undone which can any ways contribute to that end. Whatever may be the causes of the late insurrection, good policy requires, that while we endeavour to prevent every thing of the kind for the future, we should also make provision in case it should happen. Accordingly Congress have come into sundry resolutions calculated to quiet the minds of the Canadians, and to remove the sources of their uneasiness and discontent. They have likewise ordered six more battalions to be sent into Canada from the army at New York, as you will see by the inclosed resolve. Whether any further additional forces will be wanted there, is a matter of some uncertainty with Congress. Should you, from your knowledge of facts, the state of Canada, the possibility that General Howe will attempt to relieve General Carleton, and, comparing all circumstances together, be of opinion that an additional force is still necessary, you will please to signify it to Congress, and at the same time inform them whether, in that case, such additional force can be spared from the army now at New York.

I transmit, herewith, sundry resolves of Congress for your direction; and have the honor to be, Sir, your

Most obedient and very humble servant,
JOHN HANCOCK, *President*.

P. S. The inclosed letter for Commodore Hopkins, I leave unsealed for your perusal *only ;* after which I beg of you the favor to seal and forward it by Fessenden, or a fresh express. I have paid Mr. Fessenden twelve dollars, which you will please to note on settlement with him.

FROM MAJOR-GENERAL THOMAS.

Montreal, 27 April, 1776.

SIR,

I have been so unfortunate, by reason of the Lake being blocked up with ice, as not to be able to reach this city until last evening; and the troops which were at Albany and Fort George, waiting for the opening of the Lakes, have not yet arrived on this side; but as they are on their way, I hope to see them in a few days.

I have endeavoured to inform myself from General Arnold, and other gentlemen in this city, of the state of our army before Quebec, and in other parts of the Province of Canada. I find that the troops, who engaged only to the 15th of April, are mostly on their return home, and cannot be prevailed on to continue longer in the country; and, by the information given me, have no reason to expect, that when those who are on their way here shall arrive, the

whole will much exceed four thousand, exclusive of
a small number of Canadians, who have and are
likely to engage in the Continental service. The
artillery, powder, &c., are not yet arrived, and little
or no preparation made, as I expected there would
have been, for the defence of the country; not an
artificer, as I can find, for building boats or floating
batteries, which are, in my opinion, very necessary
to defend the river; nor a person who understands
the use of artillery, except those who are confined in
Quebec.

The provisions are not more than sufficient to vict-
ual the troops to the 10th of May, and the Continental currency has but little credit, which makes it
extremely difficult to discharge the debts contracted
among the inhabitants, whose dispositions are not so
friendly as heretofore, owing partly to their not being
paid so punctually for their services as they were
promised, and partly to their disappointment in not
seeing the number of troops coming into the country,
which they have been taught to expect. When I
mention the quantity of provisions, I mean the provisions already here, exclusive of three hundred barrels
of pork, which General Schuyler is sending forward.

The Committee of Congress have not yet arrived;
and unless, on their arrival, they can give credit to
the Continental currency, we shall be subjected to
many inconveniences. I am not at present able to
make out a perfect return of the troops here, but
shall as soon as in my power.

From this situation of things, your Excellency will
judge, whether double the number of troops, mentioned above, will be more than sufficient for the
defence of this Province, should there be a reënforcement of the Ministerial troops; as there is the utmost

reason to suppose there will be, as soon as the navigation of the river will permit, especially considering the little dependence that is to be made on the Canadians.

I should have been happy, could I, consistently with truth, have given a more pleasing account of the state of our affairs in Canada; but it is my duty to represent facts as they are. I am, Sir, with the greatest respect,

> Your most obedient, humble servant,
>
> JOHN THOMAS.

FROM MAJOR-GENERAL WARD.

Boston, 4 May, 1776.

SIR,

Your letter of the 29th of April is just come to hand. Agreeably to your desire, I shall give an account of what has been done towards fortifying the harbour. The forts on Fort Hill in Boston, Charlestown Point, and Castle Point, are almost completed, with a number of heavy cannon mounted in each. A work is in good forwardness on Noddle's Island, and a detachment of the army is at work at Castle Island, repairing the batteries there. A number of hulks are preparing to sink in the channel. I have employed the troops here to the greatest advantage in my power; have ordered all the men, not on actual duty, to turn out upon fatigue every day, not allowing any superfluous cooks nor waiters; and, upon receiving intelligence of the British fleet being on its passage this way, I directed all the officers to turn out with their men upon the works, which they cheerfully complied with, and are instantly upon fatigue with their men. I have set every wheel in motion, which I could move to advantage, and shall neglect nothing in my power in order to give the enemy a proper reception, if they should pay us a visit.

I have inclosed a return of this division of the army.

I am to inform your Excellency, that I have just received a letter from the President of the Congress, by which I am informed the Congress has accepted my resignation. The sooner I am relieved, the more agreeable it will be to me, as my health has declined much this spring. I am

Your Excellency's obedient, humble servant,

ARTEMAS WARD.

FROM GOVERNOR COOKE.

Providence, 6 May, 1776.

SIR,

Your Excellency's favor, in which you assure me you will recommend this unhappy Colony to the Continental Congress, hath been laid before the General Assembly, to whom it gave great satisfaction.

I inclose you a copy of Colonel Babcock's dismission. The office of Brigadier-General is still kept vacant, in hopes that the brigade will be put upon the Continental establishment, and that a Commander-in-chief will be appointed by Congress.

I also inclose a copy of an act, discharging the inhabitants of this Colony from allegiance to the King of Great Britain, which was carried in the House of Deputies, after a debate, with but six dissentient voices, there being upwards of sixty members present. I may also inform your Excellency, that the Delegates from this Colony are instructed and authorized to join with the major part of the Delegates in entering into a treaty with any Prince, State, or Potentate for the security of the Colonies, and to adopt any other measures that may be thought prudent and effectual. This instruction passed *nem. con.*

The Lower House afterwards passed a vote for taking the sense of the inhabitants at large, upon the question of Independence; but the Upper House having represented to them, that it would probably be discussed in Congress before the sense of the inhabitants could be taken, and transmitted to the Delegates, in which case the Colony would lose their voice, as the Delegates would be laid under the necessity of waiting for instructions from their constituents, and further observed that the Delegates, when they should receive a copy of the vote, renouncing allegiance to the British King, and their instructions, could not possibly be at a loss to know the sentiments of the General Assembly, upon this the matter was dropped.

I have also the satisfaction to inform your Excellency that, at a very full town-meeting of the inhabitants of Newport, held last Monday, it was unanimously voted to enter into the defence of the town; and last Thursday a considerable body of them began to work upon the fort to be erected upon Brenton's Point. This happy event, I have great hopes, will make us an united people, and root up every seed of disaffection in the Colony.

I take the liberty, once more, to press your Excellency in behalf of the Colony, the defence of which must be abandoned unless we receive assistance from the Congress. I am, with great respect, Sir, your

Most obedient and most humble servant,

NICHOLAS COOKE.

P. S. By this day's post I have forwarded to Mr. Hopkins an instruction from the General Assembly, directing him to make immediate application to Congress to put our troops upon the Continental establishment.

FROM BRIGADIER-GENERAL ARNOLD.

Montreal, 8 May, 1776.

DEAR GENERAL,

Your favor of the 3d of April I received a few days since, and I should have answered by the last post, but was obliged to go to Chamblee to give directions about some gondolas building there. I heartily congratulate you on the success of your arms against Boston, and am sorry it is not in my power to give you a more pleasing account of our affairs in this country, which wear no very favorable aspect at present. General Thomas arrived here about ten days since, and has joined the army before Quebec. General Wooster is disgusted, and expected here daily. Our army consists of few more than two thousand effective men, and twelve hundred sick and unfit for duty, chiefly with smallpox, which is universal in the country. We have very little provisions, no cash, and less credit; and, until the arrival of the heavy cannon and two mortars from Cambridge, our artillery has been trifling. The mortars I expect will reach the camp to-morrow, and shells can be supplied from Three Rivers. I hope they will have the desired effect; the want of cash has greatly retarded our operations in this country. We are fortifying two very important posts, which command the river at Richelieu, fifteen leagues above, and at Jacques Cartier, which commands a pass between two mountains, eleven leagues above Quebec. If succours should arrive before we can possess ourselves of Quebec, I hope we shall be able to maintain these two posts until a reënforcement arrives to our assistance, which we are told are on their way here. These are the only posts that secure the river, until you approach near Montreal; and of so much consequence, that nothing but superior numbers will oblige us to abandon them.

I have mounted three twenty-four-pounders on a gondola, and armed several bateaux, which go down the river to-morrow; these, with a schooner mounting ten guns, and a gondola mounting one twelve-pounder, are all the force we have in the river. Four other gondolas are building at Chamblee, calculated to mount three heavy pieces of cannon, but will not be completed these two weeks. To-morrow I set off to the army with no very agreeable prospect before me. Should the enemy receive any considerable reenforcement soon, I make no doubt we shall have our hands full. At any rate, we will do all that can be expected from raw troops, badly clothed and fed, and worse paid, and without discipline. I trust the event to Providence.

We have received advice that the eighth regiment, of about four hundred men, with a number of savages, are coming down from the upper countries. I have posted five hundred men at the Cedars, a narrow pass fifteen leagues above this place. They have two pieces of cannon, and well intrenched, by which they must pass.

I have only time to beg you will accept my best wishes and respectful compliments, and make the same to the gentlemen of your family. I am, most respectfully, dear General,

Your obedient and very humble servant,

BENEDICT ARNOLD.

FROM MAJOR-GENERAL THOMAS.

Head-Quarters, Point Dechambeau, 8 May, 1776.

SIR,

Immediately on my arrival at the camp before Quebec, which was on the 1st instant, I examined into the state of the army, and found, by the returns, there were nineteen hundred men. Of this number only one thousand were fit for duty, officers included; the remainder were invalids, chiefly confined with the smallpox. Three hundred of the effective were soldiers whose enlistments expired on the 15th ultimo, many of whom peremptorily refused duty, and all were very importunate to return home; and two hundred others, engaged for the year, had received the infection of the smallpox by inoculation, and would, in a short time, be in the hospitals. Several posts were necessary to be supported by the small number able to do duty, at such distances from each other, that by means of rivers and other obstructions, not more than three hundred men could be rallied to the support of any one post, should it be attacked by the whole force of the enemy. In all our magazines there were but one hundred and fifty pounds of pow-

der, nor more than six days' provision; the French
inhabitants (as I hinted in my last) much disaffected, so that supplies of any kind were obtained with
great difficulty from them.

Considering these and many other disagreeable circumstances, I thought it expedient to call a Council
of War; and the Council, consisting of Brigadier-General Wooster, and all the field-officers in camp, after
mature deliberation, were unanimously of the opinion
that, as, upon the first arrival of any reënforcement
to the enemy, all communication by the river would
inevitably be cut off by their armed vessels, it was
absolutely necessary, for the safety of the invalids,
immediately to remove them to Three Rivers, and to
collect the artillery and other stores, in order to
move them and the army further up the river, as
soon as it could conveniently be done, to secure some
posts where there would be a prospect of resisting
with success. This was on the 5th instant, and, in
the evening of the same day, I received certain intelligence of fifteen ships being forty leagues below
Quebec. Early next morning, five of them appeared
in sight, and the wind and tide being favorable, they
soon arrived before the city. We were at this time
employed in carrying the sick on board the bateaux,
removing the artillery, &c.; the enemy, in landing
their troops, and, as the event shows, in preparing to
make a sally. Our movements were retarded by the
change the arrival of these vessels produced in the
inhabitants; for they would neither furnish us with
teams, nor afford us the least assistance, but kept
themselves concealed.

About one o'clock, a considerable body of the enemy attacked our sentries and main guard, in consequence of which I instantly ordered the troops under

17 *

arms, and detached a party to support the main guard, which was now coming off in good order. By the best judgment I could make, the enemy were a thousand strong, formed into two divisions, in columns six deep.

The most that we could collect at this time, on the Plains, did not exceed a quarter of that number, with one field-piece, whereas the enemy were supported with a train of six pieces of cannon.

No intrenchments had been thrown up, nor any lines formed, which would serve for a cover. We had no place of retreat, if we had been overpowered with numbers; a defeat would have been decisive against the whole army in this encampment, and victory would have given us no considerable advantages, as the enemy might securely have retreated to their garrison, and their shipping entirely commanded the river.

This being our situation, rather than contend on so unequal ground, with so little probability of reaping emolument by the contest, by advice of the field-officers present, I gave orders for the army to march up the river, as far as this place, where the greater part came up yesterday. On my arrival, I without delay called a Council of War, a copy of the determinations of which I have inclosed, as I have of that held in the camp before Quebec. The result of the council was, as your Excellency will see, to advance still further up the river, and was founded on several reasons, some of which I will suggest. The ships of war were hastening forward with all possible despatch, and had already got up to Jacques Cartier, between two and three leagues distant from hence; we had no cannon to prevent their passing the falls of Richelieu (the only advantageous post to fortify for this purpose); our provision would not more than subsist the army for two or three days. We should, therefore, labor under the same disadvantages at Dechambeau as before Quebec; the men-of-war would run up the river, intercept all our resources, and soon oblige us to decamp.

I shall, however, send the invalids forward, and remain here myself, with about five hundred men, until I receive advices from Montreal, whether such supplies can be despatched immediately, as will enable me to defend this post.

The cannon in the bateaux were taken; and near two tons of powder, which General Schuyler had forwarded by Lieutenant-Colonel Allen, were unfortunately intercepted by a frigate, before it reached the camp.

I hope my conduct, in these transactions, will meet with your Excellency's approbation. I have kept the importance of the cause in view, and acted according to the best of my understanding. I do not mean to reflect on any gentleman, who has had the command in this department; but, in my ideas of war, as there was nothing which promised success in the issue, it would have been highly proper to have made this movement some weeks past. I am, with great respect, your Excellency's

Most obedient, humble servant,
JOHN THOMAS.

Boston, 9 May, 1776.

SIR,

By Mr. Harrison's letter, of the 2d instant, I am acquainted that you have been informed "the regiments stationed on Dorchester Heights and Bunker's Hill have not been employed in carrying on the works for the defence of Boston," which representation is an injurious falsehood; and I beg to be informed who made it. I have paid the strictest attention to your instructions, and constantly employed the men, to the greatest advantage, in forwarding the works for the defence of the town and harbour of Boston, that I could. Six companies of Colonel Sargent's regiment have been employed in demolishing the enemy's works on Bunker's Hill, and building the fort on Charlestown Point, until these were nearly completed. Since, the greatest part of them have been at work on Noddle's Island. Colonel Hutchinson's regiment has been employed in the works on Dorchester Point, next to Castle Island, until that fort was nearly finished, and then I ordered part of the regiment to work on Castle Island in repairing the batteries there. I believe I can truly affirm that more work has never been done in the American army by an equal number of troops, than has been performed by the troops which are stationed here, in the same space of time; but, because fifteen hundred men could not throw up works as fast as six or seven thousand had done in time past, there appeared to some people an unaccountable delay.

I have the pleasure to inform your Excellency that, on the 7th instant, Captain Tucker, commander of the armed schooner Hancock, took two brigs in the Bay (within sight of the men-of-war), and carried them into Lynn.   One of them was from Cork, ninety tons burden, laden with beef, pork, butter, and coal; the other was from the Western Islands, laden with wine and fruit, about one hundred tons burden. Neither of them gave any important intelligence; they brought no papers nor letters that had any relation to public affairs.   The master of the Irish vessel says he sailed from Cork the 1st of April; that five regiments lay there ready to embark for America; that he heard that Hessians and Hanoverians were coming to America; but had not heard of any troops having sailed from Great Britain or Ireland for America this spring.   I am

Your Excellency's obedient, humble servant,

ARTEMAS WARD.

FROM MAJOR-GENERAL LEE.

Williamsburg, 10 May, 1776.

MY DEAR GENERAL,

The most compendious method to give you an idea of the state of your Province, is to inclose to you the result of a Council of Officers, every article of which is approved by your Convention.   We have just received an express from North Carolina, informing us of the arrival of eight large transports in Cape Fear River, in the whole containing, as it is supposed, about two thousand men.   I had before, on a suspicion of their arrival, detached a battalion of riflemen, and shall set out myself the day after to-morrow.

The Convention has ordered twelve hundred militia or minute-men to that Province. My command, as you may easily conceive, is extremely perplexing from the consideration of the vast extent of the valuable parts of this country, intersected by such a variety of navigable waters, and the expedition with which the enemy, furnished with canvas wings, can fly from one spot to another. Had we arms for the minute-men, and half a dozen good field engineers, we might laugh at their efforts; but in this article (like the rest of the Continent) we are miserably deficient. Engineers we have but two; and they threaten to resign, as it is impossible that they should subsist on a more wretched pittance than common carpenters or bricklayers can earn. I have written to the Congress, entreating them to augment the pay. A word from you would, I make no doubt, effect it.

I wish, my dear General, you would send me Captain Smith, on condition Congress make it worth his while; otherwise, I have not the conscience to propose it. I am well pleased with your officers in general, and the men are good, some Irish rascals excepted. I have formed two companies of grenadiers to each regiment, and with spears of thirteen feet long. Their rifles (for they are all riflemen) sling over their shoulders; their appearance is formidable, and the men are conciliated to the weapon. I am likewise furnishing myself with four-ounced rifle-amusettes, which will carry an infernal distance; the two-ounced hit a half sheet of paper five hundred yards distant. So much for military.

A noble spirit possesses the Convention. They are almost unanimous for independence, but differ in their sentiments about the mode; two days will decide it. I have the pleasure to inform you that I am extremely well in the opinion of the senatorial part, as well as of the people at large. God send me grace to preserve it! But their neighbours of Maryland (I mean their Council of Safety) make a most damnable clamor (as I am informed) on the subject of a letter I wrote to the Chairman of the Committee of Baltimore, to seize the person and papers of Mr. Eden, upon the discovery which was communicated to me of his treacherous correspondence with the Secretary of State. It was a measure not only justifiable in the eyes of God and men, but absolutely necessary. The Committee of Safety here are indeed as deep in the scrape as myself. The Congress must, and will, I dare say, support and vindicate the measure.

Captain Green and his party are upon their march, as you ordered. I was a d—d blockhead for bringing them so far, as their accounts will be intricate; but I hope not so intricate as not to be unriddled. I send you an account of the money I advanced to the different officers, to Captains Smith, Lunt, and Green. I have taken the liberty to appoint a Sergeant Denmark, of the Rifle battalion, to do duty as Ensign. He is a man of worth, and I beg you will confirm his commission. Another Sergeant, of the same battalion, I have promoted to the rank of second Lieutenant in the Artillery of this Province. He is a German, his name Holmer, and very deserving. If little Eustace cannot be provided for with you, I could wish, if there is a cheap method of doing it, you would send him to me, as I have it in my power to please him, and quite doat upon him.

My love to Mrs. Washington, Gates, and her bad half, to Moylan; but Palfrey is a scoundrel for not writing. Adieu, my dear General.

Yours, most entirely,

CHARLES LEE.

FROM MAJOR-GENERAL WARD.

Boston, 20 May, 1776.

Sir,

I am to inform your Excellency that yesterday afternoon, Captain Mugford, in the armed schooner Franklin, fell down in order to go out on a cruise, but got aground near Point Shirley in the evening. Major Frazer's little armed schooner went down at the same time with the Franklin, and anchored not far from her. About midnight, a number of sail and other boats from the men-of-war attacked the two armed schooners. The people on board Major Frazer's cut their cable and came up. Captain Mugford was very fiercely attacked by twelve or thirteen boats, full of men; but he and his men exerted themselves with remarkable bravery, beat off the enemy, sunk several of their boats, and killed a number of their men; it is supposed they lost sixty or seventy. The intrepid Captain Mugford fell a little before the enemy left his schooner; he was run through with a lance, while he was cutting off the hands of the pirates as they were attempting to board him; and it is said that with his own hand he cut off five pairs of theirs. No other man was either killed or wounded on board the Franklin.

These are all the particulars I have been able to collect, as but one man has yet come up from the schooner this morning.

I am your Excellency's obedient, humble servant,

ARTEMAS WARD.

P. S. Mr. Mugford was not commissioned Captain of the Franklin, but master; and, as the other officers had left the schooner, he took the command.

Philadelphia, 21 May, 1776.

SIR,

As I imagine this will meet you on the road to this place, I waive making any mention of public matters, except that it is the wish of Congress you would, if consistent with the good of the service, order one battalion from New York to be posted at Amboy, in the Jerseys, agreeably to the inclosed resolve.

General Gates arrived this morning; soon after which I was honored with your favor by post, which I laid before Congress; and, as they expect you so soon here, I imagine they will defer consulting General Gates, and wait your arrival.

Your favor of the 20th instant I received this morning, and cannot help expressing the very great pleasure it would afford both Mrs. Hancock and myself to have the happiness of accommodating you during your stay in this city. As the house I live in is large and roomy, it will be entirely in your power to live in that manner you should wish. Mrs. Washington may be as retired as she pleases while under inoculation, and Mrs. Hancock will esteem it an honor to have Mrs. Washington inoculated in her house; and, as I am informed Mr. Randolph has not any lady about his house to take the necessary care of Mrs. Washington, I flatter myself she will be as well attended in my family. In short, Sir, I must take the freedom to repeat my wish, that you would be pleased to condescend to dwell under my roof. I assure you, Sir, I will do all in my power to render your stay agreeable, and my house shall be entirely at your disposal. I must, however, submit this to your determination, and only add that you will peculiarly gratify Mrs. Hancock and myself in affording me an opportunity of convincing you of this truth, that I am, with every sentiment of regard for you and your connections, and with much esteem, dear Sir, your faithful and most obedient and humble servant,

JOHN HANCOCK.

P. S. Fessenden is complaining for the want of money; I have advanced him sixteen dollars, which you will please to order him to account for.

FROM BRIGADIER-GENERAL GREENE.

Long Island, 21 May, 1776.

DEAR SIR,

From the last accounts from Great Britain, it appears absolutely necessary that there should be an augmentation of the American forces, in consequence of which I suppose there will be several promotions. As I have no desire of quitting the service, I hope the Congress will take no measure that will lay me under the disagreeable necessity of doing it. I have ever found myself exceeding happy under your Excellency's command. I wish my ability to deserve was equal to my inclination to merit. How far I have succeeded in my endeavours, I submit to your Excellency's better judgment. I hope I shall never be more fond of promotion than studious to merit it. Modesty will ever forbid me to apply to that House for any favors. I consider myself immediately under your Excellency's protection, and look up to you for justice. Every man feels himself wounded, where he finds himself neglected, and that in proportion as he is conscious of endeavouring to merit attention. I shall be satisfied with any measure that the Congress shall take, that has not a direct tendency to degrade me in the public estimation. A measure of that sort would sink me in my own esteem, and render me spiritless and uneasy in my situation, and consequently unfit for the service.

I wish for nothing more than justice, either upon principle of merit or rank, and will at all times rest satisfied when your Excellency tells me I ought to be. I feel myself strongly attached to the cause, to the Continental Congress, and to your Excellency's person; and I should consider it a great misfortune to be deprived of an opportunity of taking an active part in the support of the one, and the promotion of the other.

But should any thing take place contrary to my wishes, which might furnish me with sufficient reason of quitting the service, yet I will not do it, until the danger and difficulties appear less than at present. Believe me to be, with the highest respect, your Excellency's

> Most obedient and humble servant,
> NATHANAEL GREENE.

FROM BRIGADIER-GENERAL THOMPSON.

> Camp at Sorel, 2 June, 1776.

DEAR GENERAL,

The news of this country you will hear from the Honorable Commissioners of Congress. The prospect is rather unfavorable on our side at present, but I hope will clear up.

On the night of the 31st ultimo, I received an account of General Carleton's having passed the Rapids of Richelieu, whilst I was at Chamblee, attending a Council of War. I made no delay in setting out for this place, and arrived in time to prevent any bad consequences following the intelligence here.

Having received information, that Colonel McLean, with about eight hundred regulars and Canadians, had advanced as far up as the Three Rivers, I have sent off Colonel St. Clair, with between six and seven hundred men, to attack his camp, if it can be done with the least probability of success. This may be a means to prevent the Canadians and savages from taking up arms against us, which they begin already to do, and might otherwise, in a little time, increase the number of the enemy to a very formidable force. Colonel St. Clair is an officer of great experience, and I make no doubt he will acquit himself well of his command.

I have wrote to General Arnold, at Montreal, to send the Pennsylvania troops, in number about three hundred, from thence to join me here; and likewise to the Baron,* to send from St. John's the first regiment that arrives there. With those troops I may be able to make the most advantage of Colonel St. Clair's success, if he should prove fortunate, or support a retreat, if driven to that necessity.

Had I arrived in this country two weeks sooner, with my reënforcement, I think we could have prevented General Carleton's passing Dechambeau this

---

* Baron de Woedtke, a Brigadier-General in the American service.

summer. Three thousand men could have defended Canada at that place, better than ten thousand can now we are out of possession of it. I now begin to entertain doubt of our ability to keep the Province. Our artillery is lost; and the New England troops are so much infected with, or afraid of, the small-pox, as to almost prevent their doing duty. Could I have the command of the Jersey and Pennsylvania regiments, I still believe, if I could not keep the country, it would require at least five thousand men to oblige me to evacuate it, and that we could be easing the southern Colonies of so many enemies during the course of the campaign, and perhaps re-cover a little of the honor we have lately so lavishly thrown away.

Mr. Chase is of opinion we may with safety break the capitulation made with General Arnold. 'T is extremely hard to give up all the fruits of the last year's campaign in Canada, which cost so much, and, what was still a greater loss to us, the life of Gene-ral Montgomery, without even releasing our distressed friends in Quebec. But, if engagements of this deli-cate nature are broken, without the fullest testimony to support us, we shall be forever undone.

I have sent off the sick and heavy baggage from hence, that, if I am reduced to the necessity of re-treating, I can do it with little loss.

Including the men that went with Colonel St. Clair, those employed in rowing his boats and gone to remove the sick, with fifty stationed on the oppo-site side of the St. Lawrence, the number of troops here is reduced to about two hundred. In a few days I shall be joined by Colonel Dehaas with his detachment.

My greatest distress, at present, is on account of

18 *

the unhappy situation of the Canadians, who have taken an active part with us, as I know not whether I shall long have it in my power to protect them from the vengeance of General Carleton, with which they are threatened. They apprehend the worst, and are truly objects of compassion. I am, my dear General,

Your affectionate, humble servant,

WILLIAM THOMPSON.

FROM BRIGADIER-GENERAL SULLIVAN.*

Chamblee, 3 June, 1776.

MY DEAR GENERAL,

I had wrote a letter to Congress, and expected to have the honor of writing one to you before the Commissioners departed; but, as I found them going off before I could possibly finish one to you, I sealed that, and begged Mr. Chase to desire your Excellency to open and read it, which contained the purport of what I intended to write your Excellency. I have, since that, been to Montreal, and find almost every person agreed to depart, without even seeing the enemy.

General Thompson writes, that about eight hundred of the enemy had arrived at Three Rivers, forty-five miles below Sorel, where he is. This he has by report only. I find that all the heavy baggage is sent

---

* Six regiments had been detached from the main army in New York, commanded by General Sullivan, to join the army in Canada. General Thomas, who had the chief command in Canada, died of the smallpox, on the 2d of June, at Sorel, and the command devolved on General Sullivan.

away, with the intrenching tools, &c. On that account I have ordered them back, and am this moment embarking for Sorel, where I hope to arrive by daybreak, and meet them with all the force I can make. I am far from fearing eight hundred men against such a force as I can muster. I have desired all the general officers to be with me there, who seem well satisfied to go on. Want of time prevents my writing more fully on the state of affairs here at present, which I shall not forget to do as soon as possible. In the interim, I am, dear General, with great respect,

Your most obedient servant,
JOHN SULLIVAN.

<hr>

FROM BRIGADIER-GENERAL SULLIVAN.

Sorel, 5 June, 1776.

DEAR GENERAL,

I have the pleasure to inform you, that I arrived here at a very critical moment with my brigade. General Thompson was left but with very few men to defend this important post, the troops being scattered about in a most shocking manner. I had issued orders for all the well men to follow me, as, upon departure of General Wooster and the death of General Thomas, the command devolved upon me.

Having given these orders, I proceeded, with the troops I brought with me, to join General Thompson, who was in the greatest distress. As General Carleton's fleet had passed the Sorel, and was coming up the river with a fair wind (as was reported in all quarters), a retreat seemed in all parts to be agreed upon; and the heavy baggage and most of the artillery were removed to St. John's and Chamblee. This caused the Frenchmen to curse our cowardice, and lament their folly in favoring a cause which we had so poorly defended; but, upon my coming with a large force, ordering all the troops to follow, and the cannon to be returned, I found joy in every countenance, except some very few Tories. It really was affecting to see the banks of the Sorel lined with men, women, and children, leaping and clapping their hands for joy to see me arrive; it gave no less joy to General Thompson, who seemed to be wholly forsaken, and left to fight against an unequal force, or retreat before them.

Upon my arrival I was surprised to hear that, notwithstanding all we have read about the Sorel, our people had not thrown up as much work as I could do with a hundred men in two days, and that extremely ill done. There were three cannon, and three only, mounted in all the works. I set all the men at work, and have this day almost inclosed the encampment, and completed a battery on the north side of the river, with three cannon. General Thompson says, and I believe with great truth, that more work was done here this day than has been done in Canada since the surrender of St. John's.

June 6th. This morning two expresses arrived from Three Rivers, which were sent to observe the motions of the enemy; one of them was a friendly Canadian, who lived at Three Rivers, and passed among the fleet, the other one of our officers. They agree that the number of vessels are as follows, namely, one ship, one brig, and eight sloops and schooners. They both say that the troops there amount to no more than three hundred, who are intrenching themselves at the

Three Rivers. I have detached General Thompson, with about two thousand of your best troops, to attack them. A copy of his orders is inclosed, which I hope will be approved by your Excellency.

Our affairs here have taken a strange turn since our arrival. The Canadians are flocking by hundreds to take a part with us. I am giving them commissions, agreeable to the inclosed form, which I hope will not be thought an unnecessary assumption of power. I really find most of them exceedingly friendly. I have sent out for carts and teams, &c. They have come in with the greatest cheerfulness; and, what gives still greater evidence of their friendship is, that they have voluntarily offered to supply us with what wheat, flour, &c., we want, and ask nothing in return but certificates. They begin to complain against their priests, and wish them to be secured; I shall, however, touch this string with great tenderness at present, as I know their sacerdotal influence.

I really find, by the present behaviour of the Canadians, that the only reason of their disaffection was because our exertions were so feeble that they doubted much of our success, and even of our ability to protect them; but the face of our affairs seems to be changed; and, in the midst of our pleasing prospects, an express arrives from General Schuyler, with sixteen hundred and sixty-two pounds one shilling and three pence, Pennsylvania currency, in specie, with the spirited resolves of Congress. This gives new life to our Canadian friends, and added spirit to our troops.

I was extremely happy to find, that I had anticipated the wishes of Congress, and had, through every embarrassment, pressed downward toward the important posts they wished; for it was my fixed determination to gain post at Dechambeau, which I mean to fortify so as to make it inaccessible. This commands the channel, secures the country, destroys the communication, and affords a safe retreat, if we are obliged to make one. General Thompson was embarking for that purpose, when the resolves arrived. The ships are now above that place; but if General Thompson succeeds at Three Rivers, I will soon remove the ships below Richelieu Falls, and after that approach towards Quebec as fast as possible; and, according to the present appearance of affairs, may exceed in number the Hanoverians, &c., which we are threatened with. I have no doubt of the general attachment of the Canadians, though I suppose some unprincipled wretches among them will always appear against us; but a vast majority will be for us, and perhaps as many, according to their numbers, are really in our favor as in some other Colonies upon the Continent. Many of them are with General Thompson in this expedition, and great numbers are here, ready equipped, waiting my orders.

I may venture to assure you and the Congress that I can, in a few days, reduce the army to order; and, with the assistance of a kind Providence, put a new face to our affairs here, which a few days since seemed almost impossible. General Thompson and the Baron de Woedtke have done every thing in their power to assist me. General Arnold has not joined me, being, as you may see by his letter, which I inclose to you, much engaged at Montreal, upon affairs of importance. The post at La Chine, which he mentions, I can by no means consent to afford such a large body of men to defend against a petty number of savages, little else than a mob. I have, therefore, ordered a small fortification to be thrown up by Colonel Dehaas's party, consisting of about nine hundred men, and made inaccessible, at least to savages, and garrisoned it with two hundred men; the rest to return to me, as all our operations ought to be down the river, where, if we are successful, the insurrection there will die, of course. I have ordered a month's provision to be lodged there, lest an excuse of surrendering, for want of provision, before we can relieve it, should take place, as at the Cedars. I do not think it a post of great importance, or, indeed, any in our rear, except St. John's and Chamblee, which will ever secure a retreat, and to these I will pay particular attention.

I hope, dear General, to give you, in a few days, some agreeable intelligence; while I remain, with the most profound respect,

Your Excellency's obedient servant,
JOHN SULLIVAN.

P. S. I shall soon obtain proper returns of our scattered army, and will forward them, with return of stores, &c.; after which you may expect them weekly. I have, for your diversion, inclosed to you one which is similar to what the other Colonels must make, if called upon. I inclose to your Excellency a letter from Colonel Duggan. I have appointed a Court of Inquiry into the accusation against him. I am informed, by General Thompson, Mr. Bromfield, and others, that the accusation is false, and that he is a very useful man. He has, at my request, since he wrote the above letter, raised and armed upwards of two hundred men for us.

I have the honor to be your Excellency's most obedient servant,   JOHN SULLIVAN.

As I have not time to write the Congress, I beg your Excellency to forward to them a copy of this.

FROM BRIGADIER-GENERAL SULLIVAN.

Sorel, 8 June, 1776.

DEAR GENERAL,

At three quarters after eleven o'clock this forenoon, I received a letter from General Thompson, of
which the inclosed is a copy. I find that he has
proceeded in the manner proposed, and made his attack on the troops at Three Rivers, at daylight; for
at that time a very heavy cannonading began, which
lasted, with some intervals, to twelve o'clock. It is
now near one, P. M.; the firing has ceased, except
some irregular firing with cannon, at a considerable
distance of time one from the other. At eight o'clock,
a very heavy firing of smallarms was heard, even
here, at the distance of forty-five miles. The distance
might have rendered it doubtful, had not the boats
down the bay, which have since arrived, confirmed it,
and declared that they distinctly heard the smallarms
for a long time. I am almost certain that victory
has declared in our favor, as the irregular firing of
the cannon for such a length of time after the smallarms ceased, shows that our men are in possession of
the ground.

I should immediately set off to join General
Thompson, with Colonel Dehaas's detachment; but,
by some strange kind of conduct in General Arnold,
directly contrary to repeated orders, he has kept that
detachment dancing between this and Montreal ever
since my arrival. Some of the officers, this moment
arrived, inform me that he let them come within
eighteen miles of this place, and ordered them back
again. He has now permitted them to pass to Chamblee, and I expect them here this evening, when I

shall immediately set off with them to join General Thompson. I am now informed, by Mr. McCarty, that General Arnold has abandoned Montreal, and gone to Chamblee, with all the troops. I hope this report is not just, as the step must, in every light, be imprudent and injudicious; it leaves that quarter entirely without a check, and gives our enemies liberty to assemble and form any mischievous designs they please, without interruption.

I hear that the report at Montreal, yesterday, was, that the enemy had passed us at Sorel, and were passing up the river. This gave them the alarm, and caused them to abandon the city. I wish it may not prove true; but, as it is so much of a piece with former conduct, I cannot help giving it some degree of credit. Notwithstanding the weakness of this post, occasioned by the strange delay of Colonel Dehaas, I have sent Colonel Winds, with his regiment, to reënforce General Thompson. This I did this morning, at eight o'clock. They have joined him before now, I trust. I hope soon to follow, with more force, to maintain the ground which, I dare say, our troops have won. We hear no firing now, except a few cannon at a great distance of time between, sometimes half an hour's space at least. This, with many other circumstances, induces me to believe our troops are victorious. I am anxious to know the event, which God grant may be fortunate. However, if our party have been, or should be, defeated, I am determined not to leave Canada, but to make vigilance and industry supply the want of numbers. I am determined to fortify and secure the most important posts, and hold them as long as one stone is left upon another.

It is a serious truth that our army is extremely

weak. Colonel Greaton is with me, without a single
man, all under inoculation; Colonel Bond, with all
his regiment, in the same situation; Colonel Patterson has six only; Colonel Stark, about forty; Colonel
Reed's and Colonel Poor's nearly in the same situation. Poor is at St. John's; Reed at Chamblee. Colonel Burrell's return I sent in my last, and the other
regiments are most of them in the same situation;
for this Colony, it seems, has of late been considered
the general hospital of America. The party with
General Thompson, and that with Colonel Dehaas,
contain the flower of our army at present. Some
regiments are nearly out of the smallpox, and will
be fit for duty in a few days. Our numbers will be
daily increasing. I should rejoice, however, to see
General Greene here, with his brigade, if he can be
spared from New York.

June 12, 1776. I could not close the foregoing
letter, till I could get some certain intelligence of
General Thompson and his party, most of which,
after being unfortunately repulsed, are now returned;
but the General himself, with Colonel Irvine, Dr.
McKenzie, Mr. Currie, Mr. Bird, Mr. Edy, and Parson
Colley, are unluckily fallen into the hands of our
enemies. A flag has arrived this night for their baggage, by which he writes that he and the other gentlemen are treated with the greatest politeness by
General Burgoyne, who commands at Three Rivers.
The officers suppose they had about twenty-five killed, and we find missing in the whole about a hundred and fifty, some of which we expect in yet, as
some have arrived this evening, and say more will
be in. The General was taken, after the retreat, by
some Canadian militia, summoned in by Carleton. I
have also a number, which I have summoned in to

take part with us, under the Baron de Woedtke. Our people say that the Canadians were, in general, very kind to them upon their retreat, and gave them every assistance in their power.

The unfortunate defeat of General Thompson and his detachment happened in this manner; namely, the repeated accounts from Three Rivers of the smallness of their numbers induced General Thompson to detach Colonel St. Clair to attack them with seven hundred men, before my arrival. This not being put in execution, and St. Clair remaining at Nicolet, and the account of their weakness being confirmed, the General solicited the liberty of attacking them, which I granted, giving the orders which I inclosed in my last. He crossed from Nicolet to Three Rivers in the night, but being led into a morass by his guides, was obliged to return back near two miles; in which time the day broke, he was discovered, the ships began to cannonade, and continued while he marched through a swamp, which took near an hour and a half. The people came up to the attack, but, unluckily for them, twenty-five vessels had arrived that evening with troops, which they landed, while he marched on, and, being well prepared, gave them so warm a reception that the troops soon broke and quitted the ground. The cannonading and all the firing after that was a mere random firing, which answered very little purpose. When they found our troops began to give way, they detached a party of six hundred by the side of the river, to attack them in flank, and secure our bateaux. The bateaux were preserved by Major Woods, who brought them off. One bateau only was taken, with four barrels of powder, and nothing else on board; the men escaped.

This, dear General, is a state of this unfortunate

enterprise. What you will hear next, I cannot say. I am every moment informed of the vast number of the enemy which have arrived. Some, indeed, say that great numbers have arrived from England, and all the troops from Halifax. This I do not believe; but I apprehend their numbers now are very great. I have here only two thousand five hundred and thirty-three, rank and file. Most of the officers seem discouraged, and, of course, their men. I am employed, day and night, in fortifying and securing my camp, and am determined to hold it as long as a person will stick by me. I have heard nothing of Colonel Dayton's, or the residue of Colonel Wayne's regiment, or of the others ordered here. Sure I am that they are much wanted. There are some regiments all down with the smallpox; not a single man fit for duty. This will be remedied in time, unless the enemy make a sudden push, which, indeed, we expect every hour. If so, we must, with the numbers we have, sustain their efforts, and I hope repulse them.

Dear General, I am, with much regard, your most devoted, humble servant,

JOHN SULLIVAN.

P. S. Our old friend Colonel Louis, of the Caghnawagas, has this moment arrived express from that tribe. He says all the Indians have made peace, even the Canasadagas, and those tribes which joined Captain Forster at the Cedars, except the Roundorks. These have refused in council, and say they will take arms for the King, and have sent to General Carleton to let him know it. This tribe consists of fifty warriors only. The Caghnawagas and other tribes desire we should send up some other tribes, which they will join with, to extirpate them. This they would do themselves, but are apprehensive that some few French, through the influence of their priests, will join them. Indeed I can but illy spare the force; but it is a matter of too much importance to be neglected. I must, therefore, send some force under the command of an experienced officer.

I have the honor to be, your Excellency's most obedient servant,

JOHN SULLIVAN.

FROM THE PRESIDENT OF CONGRESS.

Philadelphia, 11 June, 1776.

SIR,

I am honored with your letters of the 7th, 8th, and 9th instant. The two first I have read in Congress. We have been two days in a Committee of the Whole, deliberating on three capital matters, the most important in their nature of any that have yet been before us, and have sat till seven o'clock in the evening, each day. That not being finished, I judge best to return the express. I shall press Congress as soon as possible to determine upon the several matters you wish to be ascertained, and immediately transmit you the result.

The Congress have agreed to settle the mode of paying the troops in the Eastern Department this morning, and to proceed to the appointment of a Deputy Paymaster-General.

The particular mode of establishing expresses is now under the consideration of a Committee, and as soon as agreed, you shall know the issue.

Although Congress have not acted upon your que-

19*

ries respecting the Indians, yet I will venture to give my opinion that Congress intended the resolution of May 25th should be general, and extend to the several departments; and that the resolution of the 3d of June goes only to the number which the General shall be empowered to employ in Canada. But I hope soon to give you a full answer to all your queries; and in future I will exert myself in Congress, that your applications may be considered as soon as received, and keep you punctually and regularly informed of the result.

Inclosed you have a resolve, whereby you will see that all the troops in the Middle Department are put upon the same pay, six and two thirds dollars, as the troops in the Eastern Department.

I have sent you four bundles of commissions, and will forward you more by next opportunity.

The inclosed, from Mrs. Washington, I wish safe to hand. I have the pleasure to acquaint you she is in fine spirits, and proposes paying you a visit next week. I sent her your letter by the express; and when you write, if you will please to put the letter under my cover, I will immediately deliver it. I have the honor to be, with every sentiment that respect and esteem inspire,

Sir, your very humble servant,

JOHN HANCOCK, *President.*

Albany, 12 June, 1776; 4 o'clock, P. M.

DEAR SIR,

The letter, which I had the honor to write you yesterday, I delivered to General Wooster, who sailed this day.

I have, within this half hour, received a letter from General Arnold, of which the inclosed is a copy. I fear the next will announce the evacuation of Canada by our troops, probably with loss, as I fear that not a sufficient attention has been paid to a recommendation of mine, to bring all the bateaux, that could possibly be spared from Sorel, to St. John's. I shall immediately despatch an express to Fort George to send bateaux to St. John's; but, after all, the number will be very small, for want of men to navigate them. I suppose one hundred and twenty, at least, are at Lake George.

I am not under the least apprehension that the enemy will be able to cross Lake Champlain, provided that our army is able to retreat into that Lake, that ammunition is speedily sent up, and a further supply of pork forwarded, without delay, to this place.

Your Excellency will perceive that General Arnold informs me, that the enemy have the frames, &c., for gondolas on board. We should therefore build a number of these vessels, with all possible despatch; one is now on the stocks, but we want people that understand the construction of them. I have some time ago begged Congress to send one, express; let me entreat that some more capable persons may be sent up, and twenty shipwrights with them.

As I fear the saw-mills will not be able to saw a sufficient number of plank, I wish to have a dozen of whipsaws and files sent up with all possible despatch.

I shall order all the bateaux that do not go to St. John's out of Lake George, to Ticonderoga, that they may be ready, at that place, to be sent to Skenesborough, to convey the militia, should they be sent up. I am, with every respectful sentiment, your Excellency's

Most obedient, humble servant,

PHILIP SCHUYLER.

FROM RICHARD HENRY LEE.

Philadelphia, 13 June, 1776.

DEAR SIR,

I am informed that a certain Mr. Eustace, now in New York, but some time ago with Lord Dunmore, is acquainted with a practice that prevailed, of taking letters out of the post-office in Virginia, and carrying them to Dunmore for his perusal, and then returning them to the office again. As it is of the greatest consequence that this nefarious practice be stopped immediately, I shall be exceedingly obliged to you, Sir, for getting Mr. Eustace to give, in writing, all that he knows about this business, and inclose the same to me at Williamsburg. I wish to know, particularly, what post-offices the letters were taken from, by whom, and who carried them to Lord Dunmore.

This day I set off for Virginia, where, if I can be

of any service to you, it will oblige to command me.
It is more than probable that Congress will order our
friend Gates to Canada.   His great abilities and virtue will be absolutely necessary to restore things
there, and his recommendations will always be readily
complied with.   You will find that great powers are
given to the commander in that distant department.
The system for Canada, adopted since the arrival of
the Commissioners here, will, I hope, be of essential
service to our affairs.

All good men pray most heartily for your health,
happiness, and success, and none more than, dear Sir,

Your affectionate friend and obedient servant,

RICHARD HENRY LEE.

FROM THE PRESIDENT OF CONGRESS.

Philadelphia, 18 June, 1776.

SIR,

You will see, from the inclosed resolves, which I do
myself the pleasure of forwarding, in obedience to
the commands of Congress, that they have bent their
whole attention to our affairs in Canada, and have
adopted such measures, as, in their opinion, are calculated to place them on a better and more repu-
table footing for the future.

The most unfortunate death of General Thomas
having made a vacancy in that department, and the
service requiring an officer of experience and distinction, the Congress have thought proper to appoint
General Gates to succeed him.   And I am to request
you will send him into that Province, to take the
command of the forces there, as soon as possible; and

that you direct him to view Point-au-Fer, and to order a fortress to be erected there, if he shall think proper.

My opinion on the resolve of the 25th May was well founded; Congress having since determined, as you will find by a resolve herewith transmitted, that you are to employ the Indians wherever you think their services will contribute most to the public good.

I shall write to the Colonies of New York, New Jersey, and Connecticut, to request them to authorize you to call on their militia, if necessary. My time will not permit me to do it now, as the post will set out directly, and the inclosed resolves were not passed till late yesterday evening.

I have the honor to be, Sir, your most obedient and very humble servant,

JOHN HANCOCK, *President.*

P. S. A Mustermaster-General, in the room of Mr. Moylan, will be appointed this day or to-morrow, and a Deputy will afterwards be sent into Canada.

I beg you will think of the Eastern Department, with respect to General Officers, when your very important concerns will admit.

FROM MAJOR-GENERAL WARD.

Boston, 20 June, 1776.

SIR,

I have to inform you that the Continental privateers brought into this port, the 18th instant, another Scotch transport, with a Highland company of grenadiers on board, consisting of upwards of an hundred, with their officers, with a few arms more than what belonged to the company. Each transport brings a considerable quantity of provisions for the troops. The prisoners are going into the country towns, agreeably to the order of Congress.

The Colonel, mentioned in my last, is Lieutenant-Colonel Campbell, commander of one of General Frazer's battalions of Highlanders. He is a member of Parliament, and a gentleman of fortune.

I must repeat my earnest request to be relieved immediately, as I have been so very ill for some time past as to be confined to my chamber, and have no prospect of recovering my health until I have a relaxation from business. I am,

Your Excellency's obedient, humble servant,

ARTEMAS WARD.

FROM THE PRESIDENT OF CONGRESS.

Philadelphia, 21 June, 1776.

SIR,

The Congress, having the greatest reason to believe there has been very gross misconduct in the management of our affairs in Canada, have come to a resolution to have a general inquiry made into the behaviour of the officers employed on that expedition. The honor of the United Colonies, and a regard for the public good, call loudly for such an inquiry to be set on foot. I am, therefore, directed to request, after having made the inquiry agreeably to the inclosed resolve, you will transmit the result, together with the proofs, to Congress.*

The opinion that an officer cannot be tried by a court-martial after his resignation, for offences while he held a commission, so dangerous to the service, and particularly destructive in our army, where the short enlistment of the troops might furnish temptation to crimes from the prospect of impunity, has been this day reprobated by Congress.

I have written to the Convention of New York on the subject of the inclosed resolve respecting another regiment to be raised in that Colony. The terms on which the commissions are to be granted are extremely well calculated to excite the officers to exert themselves to fill up their companies.

I have likewise written to the respective Colonies, and have sent copies of the inclosed resolve recommending to them to provide clothes for the troops of their Colonies. These, or such articles of them as you shall want, the Congress have empowered you to draw for on the Assemblies and Conventions, from time to time, as you shall judge necessary. I have

---

* *In Congress, June 21st.* "Resolved, That General Washington be directed to order an inquiry to be made into the conduct of the officers heretofore employed in the Canada Department; that the said inquiry be made at such times and places as, in his judgment, shall be most likely to do justice, as well to the public as to the individuals; and that the result of the said inquiry, together with the testimonies upon the subject, be transmitted to Congress; that, moreover, all officers accused of cowardice, plundering, embezzlement of public moneys, and other misdemeanours, be immediately brought to trial. And whereas Congress is informed that an opinion has prevailed that officers resigning their commissions are not subject to trial by court-martial for offences committed previous to such resignation, whereby some have evaded the punishments to which they were liable, it is hereby declared that such opinion is not just."

represented to them that it is totally impossible that the American army should ever be on a respectable footing, or that they should render such essential services to their country as we expect and desire, unless the United Colonies will, on their part, take care that they are well appointed and equipped with every thing necessary for an army.

General Wooster, it is the order of Congress, should be permitted to return to his family.

I have delivered Mr. Visscher his commission as Lieutenant-Colonel in the regiment commanded by Colonel Nicholson, and directed him to wait on you, upon his arrival at New York.

Apprehending that such of the resolves of Congress as respect the conduct of the army, are executed in consequence of orders issued by you, I have omitted sending to General Schuyler such as respect him, concluding that the directions would go from you; but if it will be any way a relief to you, I will continue to forward them. I have the honor to be, with much esteem, Sir,

Your most obedient, humble servant,
JOHN HANCOCK, President.

22d. Your letter of the 20th this moment came to hand, and shall be laid before Congress on Monday.

FROM JOSEPH HAWLEY.

Watertown, 21 June, 1776.

GENERAL WASHINGTON,

The most important matters are soon to be decided by arms. Unhappy it is, for the Massachusetts, and

I fear for the whole Continent, that, at this season, we have a large and numerous Assembly. More than one half of the House are new members. Their decisions are most afflictingly slow, when every thing calls for the utmost ardor and despatch. The Lord have mercy on us! This Colony, I imagine, will raise the men required by Congress before snow falls, but in no season for the relief of either New York or Canada.

Pray, Sir, consider what there is to be done. It is my clear opinion that there will not be a single company move in this Colony, for either of those places, these three weeks. I know, Sir, it will vex you; but your Excellency will not be alone in the vexation. My soul, at times, is ready to die within me at the delays; at others, my blood to press out at the pores of my body. But what shall be the expedients? I never was good at them, but will venture to propose again the same I mentioned in my last; namely, that some, or all, of the five Continental regiments here be ordered to march, without one moment's delay, to Canada or New York, as the exigencies require. In such case they must be paid up their arrears, or nearly. In that way you will, in effect, get succours for New York or Canada, or both, from this Colony. Our people are so jealous for their own safety (though you know, Sir, that I judge them at present in very little danger), that they will raise the militia for their own defence.

I beg your Excellency to advert to the proposal a moment. Our own militia are as good, for all the intents answered, or to be answered here, by those regiments, as they are. They are much better for Canada or New York than the militia. They are officered and organized, and well armed; the militia to be officered, armed and equipped. The differences are too many to be enumerated. If I may say it, I am astonished at the policy of Congress in ordering more regiments here, instead of ordering those which are here to parts where they are infinitely more needed. But my opinion is of little worth; but, such as it is, I have given it. It may serve as a suggestion.

I am, may it please your Excellency, most sincerely yours,

JOSEPH HAWLEY.

FROM BRIGADIER-GENERAL SULLIVAN.

Isle-aux-Noix, 24 June, 1776.

MY DEAR GENERAL,

It is with the greatest pain I inform you, that, after our retreat from Canada to this place, of which I have given your Excellency an account through General Schuyler, and after I had determined to make a stand here till I received your Excellency's order, I find myself under an absolute necessity of quitting this Island for a place more healthy; otherwise the army will never be able to return, as one fortnight longer in this place will not leave us well men enough to carry off the sick, exclusive of the public stores, which I have preserved thus far. The raging of the smallpox deprives us of whole regiments in the course of a few days, by their being taken down with that cruel disorder. But this is not all. The camp disorder rages to such a degree that, of the regiments remaining, from twenty to sixty in each are taken down in a day, and we have nothing to give them but salt pork, flour, and the poisonous waters of this Lake. I have, therefore, determined, with the unanimous voice of the officers, to remove to Isle-la-Motte, a place much more healthy than this, where I have some hope we shall preserve the health of the few men we have, till some order is taken respecting our future movements.

I think it would be by far the best to remove to Crown Point, fortify that, build row-galleys to command the Lake, and by scouting parties to defend our frontiers, as the savages have already begun upon us. They have made two attacks upon our men, killed and taken near twenty, among whom are some officers. These officers went on shore unarmed, when I was gone to reconnoitre Point-au-Fer. The other party went on shore at river Lecot to buy milk. They were in boats loaded with flour, which they brought off, but had some men killed. The whole of our loss, in killed and taken, amounts to about twenty. This happened in both cases for want of that care which should ever be taken in an enemy's country. I hope it will be a warning to our people in future.

I hear, from all quarters, that the enemy are very numerous in Canada. Their shipping is also numerous, and it cannot be doubted that all the Canadians and all the Indians in this quarter will be compelled to bear arms against us. This I know they would gladly have avoided; but, finding that we are not able to afford them that protection we promised, they are obliged to make their peace, in the best manner they can. I think it is now past a doubt, that the neglect and inattention to this department has not only lost us Canada, but involved us in a war with all the blacks and whites in this quarter; and to check their progress I know of no better method than to secure the important posts of Ticonderoga and Crown Point, and, by building a number of armed vessels, command the Lakes; otherwise the forces now in Canada will be brought down upon us as quick as possible, having nothing now to oppose them in that Colony.

They have a number of bateaux framed, which they brought from Three Rivers. They will doubtless construct some armed vessels, and then endeavour to penetrate the country toward New York. This, I am persuaded, they will attempt, but am sure they can never effect, unless we neglect to secure the important posts now in our power. I have written to General Schuyler, and wait with impatience for his answer, as I know that no time ought to be lost in fortifying this place or Crown Point. If I attempt to fortify here, and afterwards am ordered to leave it, I shall strengthen the enemy, by preparing a work for them, which I would not willingly do. If I am to tarry and fortify here, I should be glad to know it as soon as possible, that I may put the order in execution; but I must say that, unless our men grow much more healthy, our army here will be no kind of check upon the enemy after remaining in this low marsh for a few weeks longer.

I inclose your Excellency a general return, drawn from the returns made the day before yesterday; since which I suppose a quarter part have been taken down with the camp disorder. This, however incredible it may seem, is a real fact. For instance, Colonel Wayne has sixty, out of one hundred and thirty-eight, taken down since. Colonel Dehaas and all his field-officers, with a number of his men, are since taken down. This seems to run through the whole,

20 *

no corps being exempt from it. I am shocked to relate, but much more to see, this dreadful havoc among the troops.

I inclose your Excellency a return of the ordnance and stores at St. John's on the 12th instant. The whole could not, in our confused state, be procured. As to the provisions, some are on board the armed vessels, some at this place, and some at Isle-la-Motte, which were never brought further down. I can make no accurate return at present. I will have one made as soon as possible and forward it, and send regular returns in future. I do not despair of getting this army yet into some kind of order and regulation; but I must confess that it is a work of time and trouble, as order and regularity seem to have been strangers in this northern army.

I received your Excellency's favor of the 13th instant. I am extremely sorry it was not in my power to fulfil your Excellency's wishes, by leading on our troops to victory. The reasons for my not being able have doubtless long since reached you in my letters giving an account of the strength of the enemy, the weakness of our army, and the unhappy defeat of General Thompson at Three Rivers, as also the result of our Council of War in Canada. I think we shall secure all the public stores and baggage of the army, and secure our retreat, with very little loss. Whether we shall have well men enough to carry them on, I much doubt, if we don't remove quickly, unless Heaven is pleased to restore health to this wretched army, now, perhaps, the most pitiful one that ever was formed.

There is no return of Colonel Patterson's regiment, as he has but five men here fit for duty, whom I this day ordered to Crown Point to join the rest of the regiment, who are all sick there. You may assure yourself, my dear General, that nothing shall be wanting, on my part, to restore order among the troops here and to recover their health, as also to throw every stumblingblock in the way of the enemy, that lies in the power of your Excellency's

Most affectionate, humble servant,

JOHN SULLIVAN.

FROM THE PRESIDENT OF CONGRESS.

Philadelphia, 25 June, 1776.

SIR,

Your letter of the 21st instant, by Mr. Bennett, with the inclosure, was duly received and laid before Congress, as you will perceive by the inclosed resolves, to which I beg leave to request your attention.

Although the Commissioners have undoubtedly mistaken the intention of Congress, yet the terms in which the resolve is conceived, namely, "That the General be empowered to employ in Canada a number of Indians, not exceeding two thousand," may, at first view, seem to confine their employment to the limits of that Province, and to give a latitude of construction as to the place in which they are to be raised; and in this sense they must have been understood by General Schuyler and the other Commissioners. I am, however, to request you will give orders to have a stop put to raising the Mohegan and Stockbridge Indians, as soon as possible. I shall write Governor Trumbull to the same purpose.

The conduct of the Quartermaster-General, in detaining the tents sent from this place to Massachusetts Bay, is a stretch of office which, though it may be well meant, is certainly a very extraordinary one. You will, therefore, be pleased to order them to be delivered up, and forwarded to the Massachusetts Bay as soon as possible.

The other resolves, herewith transmitted, calculated to suppress insurrections and to promote good order and obedience to laws in the United Colonies, are so full and explicit that I need not enlarge. It is sufficient to observe, that internal convulsions do always extremely weaken the force and springs of Government, and must necessarily render its operations against foreign enemies less vigorous and decisive.*

Application having been made to Congress with regard to victualling the Flying Camp, I am directed to request you will inform them what is the cost of a ration, as furnished by the Commissary-General.

The several matters in your letters are before a

---

* *In Congress, June 24th,* "Resolved, that all persons abiding within any of the United Colonies, and deriving protection from the laws of the same, owe allegiance to the said laws, and are members of such Colony; and that all persons passing through, visiting, or making a temporary stay in any of the said Colonies, being entitled to the protection of the laws during the time of such passage, visitation, or temporary stay, owe, during the same, allegiance thereto;

"That all persons, members of, or owing allegiance to any of the United Colonies, as before described, who shall levy war against any of the said Colonies within the same, or be adherent to the King of Great Britain, or other enemies of the said Colonies, or any of them, within the same, giving to him or them aid and comfort, are guilty of treason against such Colony;

"That it be recommended to the Legislatures of the several United Colonies, to pass laws for punishing, in such manner as to them shall seem fit, such persons before described, as shall be provably attainted of open deed, by people of their condition, of any of the treasons before described."

Committee. The proposal respecting a troop of horse is liked; and as soon as the Committee bring in their report, and it is considered, you shall be made acquainted with the result.

I have the honor to be, Sir, your most obedient and very humble servant,

JOHN HANCOCK, *President.*

FROM BRIGADIER-GENERAL ARNOLD.

Albany, 25 June, 1776.

DEAR GENERAL,

By this express you will receive advice from General Schuyler of our evacuating Canada, an event which I make no doubt (from our distressed situation) you have some time expected. The particulars of General Thompson's repulse and captivity, as nearly as could be ascertained, have been transmitted you. On advice of which, [with] very direct intelligence that the enemy were greatly superior to us in numbers, I advised General Sullivan to secure his retreat by retiring to St. John's. He was determined to keep his post at Sorel, if possible, and did not retire until the 14th instant, at which time the enemy were as high up with their ships as the Sorel.

On the 15th, at night, when the enemy were at twelve miles' distance from me, I quitted Montreal with my little garrison of three hundred men. The whole army, with their baggage and cannon (except three heavy pieces left at Chamblee), arrived at St. John's the 17th, and at the Isle-aux-Noix the 18th; previous to which it was determined, by a Council of War at St. John's, that in our distressed situation, (one half of the army sick, and almost the whole destitute of clothing and every necessary of life, except salt pork and flour), it was not only imprudent, but impracticable, to keep possession of St. John's.

Crown Point was judged the only place of health and safety, to which the army could retire and oppose the enemy. It was found necessary to remain at the Isle-aux-Noix for some few days, until the sick, heavy cannon, &c., could be removed. General Sullivan did not choose to leave the Isle-aux-Noix until he received positive orders for that purpose, and thought it necessary for me to repair to this place, and wait on General Schuyler. I arrived here last night, and am happy to find him of our sentiments in quitting the Isle-aux-Noix, which, from its low situation, is rendered very unhealthy, and from the narrow channel leading to it from the north part of Lake Champlain, of six miles in length and from three to eight hundred yards in breadth, is rendered very insecure, as the enemy, by light pieces of cannon and smallarms, might render all access to it dangerous, if not impracticable.

It now appears to me of the utmost importance, that the Lakes be immediately secured by a large number of (at least twenty or thirty) gondolas, rowgalleys, and floating batteries. The enemy, from undoubted intelligence, have brought over a large number (it is said one hundred) frames for flat-bottomed boats, designed to be made use of on Lake Champlain; and, from their industry and strength, will doubtless become masters of the Lake, unless every nerve on our part is strained to exceed them in a naval armament. I think it absolutely necessary, that at least three hundred carpenters be immediately employed. Fifty sent from Philadelphia, who are acquainted with building that kind of craft, would greatly facilitate the matter.

A particular return of the army could not be obtained, in our hurry and confusion. It will be transmitted to you in a few days. I believe the whole about seven thousand, and at least one half of them sick and unfit for duty, but daily recovering. Upwards of one thousand more are yet to have the smallpox. The enemy, from the best intelligence that can be obtained, are near ten thousand, exclusive of Canadians and savages. Few of the latter have joined them as yet.

I make no doubt it will be thought necessary to repair Crown Point, or build a new fort near that place. The former, from the advantage of its situation, and the fine barracks nearly completed, will, I believe, be thought most proper. I make no doubt but General Gates, who I am happy to hear is on his way here, will pay immediate attention to it.

I flatter myself our arms, under your immediate direction, will meet with more success than they have done in this quarter. I make not the least doubt our struggles will be crowned with success. I am, with every friendly wish, most respectfully, dear General, your affectionate and

Obedient, humble servant,
BENEDICT ARNOLD.

FROM MAJOR-GENERAL SCHUYLER.

Albany, 25 June, 1776; 1 o'clock, A. M.

DEAR GENERAL,

About an hour ago General Arnold, who is arrived here from Canada, sent me a letter from General

Sullivan, inclosing one from General Arnold to him, another from Colonel Hazen, and a third from Lieutenant-Colonel Antill, copies of all which I do myself the honor to inclose. The grief I feel on the evacuation of Canada by our troops, is greatly alleviated by the little loss sustained in the retreat, and the hope I have, that we shall maintain a superiority on the Lakes.

Your Excellency will observe that General Sullivan intimates that further than the Isle-aux-Noix he could not retreat, without your Excellency's or my orders, previous to which he observes, that the Council of War were unanimous for coming to Crown Point. I do not hesitate to say, that I wish he had retreated, at least as far south as Point-au-Fer, or Isle-la-Motte, as I am afraid that the enemy will throw themselves between him and the broad part of Lake Champlain, and render it extremely difficult, if not impossible, to send on a supply of provisions, as they can with light cannon and even wall-pieces command the waters from shore to shore in most places, for six miles south of Isle-aux-Noix, and in many even with musketry.

Did not the danger of remaining there, especially with an army broken and spiritless, and who wish so much to come further south, that the officers, as General Arnold informs me, have already, in a body, entreated him to come away, appear to me too great to admit of the delay of waiting your Excellency's orders, I should not send mine for a further retreat, until your pleasure could be known; but I trust I shall be justified in doing it, and yet I believe the order will meet the army on this side of Isle-aux-Noix.

Be pleased to order up six anchors and cables for the gondolas that are constructing, of the size of what is called the small anchor and cable of an Albany sloop.

I shall immediately write to Governor Trumbull to provide fifty ship-carpenters, if he can, and send for a like number to the Massachusetts Bay.

If any Dutch mill-saws can be procured at New York, be pleased to order up four dozen, with six dozen of files for them.

Having learned that General Gates is upon his way up, I have ordered a boat down to meet him. I am, dear General, with every sentiment of esteem and respect, your Excellency's

Most obedient, humble servant,

PHILIP SCHUYLER.

FROM BRIGADIER-GENERAL SULLIVAN.

25 June, 1776.

DEAR GENERAL,

This morning at daybreak, I received your Excellency's favor of the 16th instant; am extremely mortified to find that every thing here has turned out contrary to my expectations, and your Excellency's wishes. This was not owing to my being deceived with respect to the enemy on the ground at the time I wrote, but to the sudden arrival of such a number under General Burgoyne, the night before the battle of Three Rivers, of which I have given a full and perfect account in former letters. I am conscious of having done every thing in my power to gain the ground our troops had lost, and to secure the retreat of the army, when I found our point could not be carried. I imagine that General Schuyler forgot to inclose the return, as I think it went from me at the time; but I am not clear whether it did not go in a separate letter. I dare say it has reached you before this. I now inclose another which I wish safe to hand, and hope to have a more complete and perfect one in a few days, which I shall forward to your Excellency.

I am well convinced of the necessity of a good understanding being kept up among the officers of the army. This has been remarkably the case since my arrival. I have not seen an instance to the contrary, except some few reflections which seemed to take place between the northern and southern troops, which I hope I have sufficiently cured by calling upon the officers of every corps, and requesting them to suppress a thing, which, if continued, must weaken, if not destroy, the army. They all agreed to join heartily in putting an end to this dangerous behaviour among the troops, which I am convinced they did, as I have heard nothing of it since, and find that harmony takes place among the troops in a surprising manner. In all our difficulties there seemed a unanimity of sentiment among all the officers. Indeed, I have not known the least dispute among them. The unfortunate General Thompson, the Baron de Woedtke, and myself were at Sorel. Never did greater harmony and friendship exist. General Arnold was at Montreal, and kept up the most friendly intercourse and correspondence with us, and we with him. It is true, I thought the keeping Colonel Dehaas from Sorel was wrong, but only supposed it an error in judgment, as I did that of his keeping the forces in too great numbers at the posts up the country. This I communicated to him in the most friendly manner, which he accounted for in a way that convinced me that he acted not without some foundation; though I think it would have been better had it not been done. Assure yourself, my dear General, that I will exert myself in cultivating harmony and friendship among both officers and soldiers in the army, and that I am, with the most profound respect, your Excellency's

Most devoted, humble servant,
JOHN SULLIVAN.

P. S. The Brigade-Major and Adjutant of the day have this moment informed me, that, while they were parading the main guard, four men dropped down under arms, and appear like dead men. I am almost distracted with the thought of losing so many men as daily go off by sickness. I shall, to-day, remove from this infectious place to Isle-la-Motte, which I should have done before now, had not too many of our bateaux gone forward with the sick to Crown Point.

FROM MAJOR-GENERAL LEE.

Charleston, 1 July, 1776.

MY DEAR GENERAL,

I have the happiness to congratulate you on a very signal success (if I may not call it a victory), which we have gained over the mercenary instruments of the British tyrant. I shall not trouble you with a detail of their manœuvres or delays, but defer it to another time, when I have more leisure to write, and you to attend. Let it suffice, that having lost an opportunity (such as I hope will never again present itself) of taking the town, which, on my arrival, was utterly defenceless, the Commodore thought proper, on Friday last, with his whole squadron, consisting of two fifties, six frigates, and a bomb (the rates of which you will see in the inclosed list), to attack our fort on Sullivan's Island.

They dropped their anchors about eleven in the forenoon, at the distance of three or four yards before the front battery. I was myself, at this time, in a boat, endeavouring to make the Island; but the wind and tide being violently against us, drove us on the main. They immediately commenced the most furious fire I ever heard or saw. I confess I was in pain, from the little confidence I reposed in our troops; the officers being all boys, and the men raw recruits. What augmented my anxiety was, that we had no bridge finished for retreat, or communication; and the creek, or cove, which separates it from the continent, is near a mile wide. I had received, likewise, intelligence that their land troops intended at the same time to land and assault. I never in my life felt myself so uneasy; and what added to my uneasiness was, that I knew our stock of ammunition was miserably low. I had once thoughts of ordering the commanding officer to spike his guns, and, when his ammunition was spent, to retreat with as little loss as possible. However, I thought proper previously to send to town for a fresh supply, if it could possibly be procured, and ordered my Aid-de-camp, Mr. Byrd, (who is a lad of magnanimous courage) to pass over in a small canoe, and report the state of the spirit of the garrison. If it had been low, I should have abandoned all thoughts of defence. His report was flattering. I then determined to maintain the post at all risks, and passed the creek or cove, in a small boat, in order to animate the garrison *in propriâ personâ;* but I found they had no occasion for such encouragement.

They were pleased with my visit, and assured me they never would abandon the post but with their lives. The cool courage they displayed astonished and enraptured me, for I do assure you, my dear General, I never experienced a hotter fire. Twelve full hours it was continued without intermission. The noble fellows, who were mortally wounded, conjured their brethren never to abandon the standard of liberty. Those who lost their limbs deserted not their posts. Upon the whole, they acted like Romans in the third century. However, our works were so good and solid, that we lost but few; only ten killed on the spot, and twenty-two wounded, seven of whom lost their legs or arms. The loss of the enemy, as you will perceive by the inclosed list, was very great. As I send a detail to the Congress, I shall not trouble you with a duplicate; but, before I finish, you must suffer me to recommend to your esteem, friendship, and patronage my (though young) Aids-de-camp, Byrd and Morris, whose good sense, integrity, activity, and valor, promise to their country a most fruitful crop of essential services. Mr. Jenifer, of Maryland, a gentleman of fortune, and not of the age when the blood of men flows heroically, has shown not less spirit than these youngsters. I may venture to recommend in these high terms, because the trial was severe.

Colonel Moultrie, who commanded the garrison, deserves the highest honors. The manifest intention of the enemy was to land, at the same time the ships began to fire, their whole regulars on the east end of the Island. Twice they attempted it, and twice were repulsed by a Colonel Thompson, of the South Carolina Rangers, in conjunction with a body of North Carolina regulars. Upon the whole, the South and North Carolina troops and Virginia Rifle battalion we have here, are admirable soldiers. The enemy is now returned to their old station on this side the bar. What their intention is, I cannot divine. One of the five deserters, who came over to us this day, is the most intelligent fellow I ever met with. The accounts of their particular loss and situation are his, and I think they may be depended upon.

For God's sake, my dear General, urge the Congress to furnish me with a thousand cavalry. With a thousand cavalry I could insure the safety of these Southern Provinces; and without cavalry, I can answer for nothing. I proposed a scheme in Virginia for raising a body almost without any expense. The scheme was relished by the gentlemen of Virginia, but I am told the project was censured by some members of the Congress, on the principle that a military servant should not take the liberty to propose any thing. This opinion I sincerely subscribe to, when our distance from the sovereign is so small, and the danger so remote, as to admit of proposing, deliberating, resolving, and approving; but when a General is at a vast distance, and the enemy close to him, I humbly conceive that it is his duty to propose and adopt any thing, without other authority than the public safety. From want of this species of troops, we had infallibly lost this Capital, but the dilatoriness and stupidity of the enemy saved us.

I this instant learn that the Commodore is fixing buoys on the bar, which indicates an intention of quitting the place. It is probable that they will bend their course to Hampton, or Chesapeake Bay.

I am extremely happy, dear General, that you are at Philadelphia, for their counsels sometimes lack a little military electricity.

I have ordered the Adjutant-General to send you a return; I mean only a return of the strength of this place. I suppose it will be imperfect, for it is an Herculean labor, to a South Carolina officer, to make any detail. God bless you, my dear General, and crown you with success, as I am,

> Most entirely and affectionately, yours,
>
> CHARLES LEE.

P. S. I am made quite happy by the resolution of Congress to keep Canada. Had it been relinquished, all would have been lost.

FROM MAJOR-GENERAL SCHUYLER.

Albany, 1 July, 1776.

DEAR GENERAL,

On Friday evening I received a line from General Sullivan, a copy whereof I have the honor to inclose. By the contents your Excellency will perceive, that we have reasons to believe his next will announce his arrival at Crown Point.

Yesterday morning General Gates introduced a Mr. Avery to me, who applied to me for money to carry on the Commissary-General's department here. I asked if Mr. Livingston was superseded, and begged to see how he (Avery) was authorized to act here. He showed me a commission from Mr. Trumbull, the Commissary-General, with instructions annexed, appointing him Deputy-Commissary in Canada, and the instructions were correspondent to such appointment. I told him his commission did not, by any means, supersede Mr. Livingston's, and until that was done, I must consider Mr. Livingston as the Deputy-Commissary-General here, and that all warrants for money to carry on that department here must be drawn in his favor, unless Mr. Trumbull himself was present.

He assured me that it was Mr. Trumbull's intention that he (Avery) should have the sole management, and that Mr. Livingston was only to be considered as a contractor. I sent for Mr. Livingston, who produced a letter of the 25th instant from Mr. Trumbull, directly contradictory to what Mr. Avery had asserted; upon which he declared that Mr. Trumbull had informed him, that Congress had given him full power to make any arrangement he thought proper, and displace whom he pleased, and that it was his intention, by giving him (Avery) that commission, to supersede Mr. Livingston. To which Mr. Livingston answered, that, although Mr. Trumbull had no power to remove him unless authorized so to do by Congress, as he held his commission immediately from that body, yet, if Mr. Trumbull had expressed any such intention, he would immediately resign, and he would put the question to Mr. Trumbull. I observed to Mr. Avery that nothing in his commission, or the instructions annexed, authorized him to say what he did; that Mr. Trumbull's letter to Mr. Livingston flatly contradicted it; that if he remained with the army, provided it was not in Canada, he must be subordinate to Mr. Livingston, and obey his orders, which he chose not to do, and is now going down.

I advised him to remain until the affair was determined, and candidly told him that I should try to keep Mr. Livingston in the employment if he chose it, because, admitting that their abilities and integrity were perfectly equal, Mr. Livingston's conduct had met my approbation, and that his great family connections in this county had enabled him to carry on the service, when others could not have done it, of which I gave instances. General Gates was present, and acquiesced in the propriety of what I observed. I was, therefore, greatly surprised to be informed, that he should tell Mr. Avery that he had nothing to say here, but that as soon as he came to the army he would employ him. I say I was greatly surprised, because General Gates knew that the army was no longer in Canada, and because I did not know that he then claimed a right to control my orders with respect to the army, even if it should be at Crown Point; nor could I imagine he thought so, as your Excellency's instructions to him gave, as I conceive, not the least color for it. Your last letter to me holds up a contrary idea, and so does every resolution of Congress hitherto transmitted to me; but that General Gates conceived, and still does, that the army is immediately under his command, I had, a very few hours after, the most convincing proof of, as your Excellency will observe from the inclosed paper, which I hastily drew up immediately after the discourse, and which I desired General Gates to read, that no misunderstanding might arise for want of recollecting what had been said, and which he acknowledges contains the substance of what passed between us.

By your Excellency's instructions to General Gates, he is empowered to appoint a Quartermaster-General in Canada. I observed, this morning, that I believed it was founded on a supposition that Colonel Campbell was then about quitting Canada, for that I could not imagine that an officer being "ordered to Congress to settle his accounts" deprived him of his employments; that Colonel Campbell was originally appointed to this department, and that Canada now being made a separate one, and the command of it given to General Gates, he could, under the powers he had, appoint whom he pleased to act there; but that, unfortunately for us, the evacuation of that country by our troops had taken place, and that I must and should consider Colonel Campbell as the Deputy Quartermaster-General on this side of Canada.

If Congress intended that General Gates should command the Northern army, wherever it may be, as he assures me they did, it ought to have been signified to me, and I should then have immediately resigned the command to him; but until such intention is properly conveyed to me, I never can. I must, therefore, entreat your Excellency to lay this letter before Congress, that they may clearly and explicitly signify their intentions, to avert the dangers and evils that may arise from a disputed command; for, after what General Gates has said, the line must be clearly drawn, as I shall, until then, stand upon punctilios with General Gates, that I would otherwise with pleasure waive; but that the service may not be retarded, nor suffer the least from a difference of opinion between General Gates and me, I have determined to remain here, although I had, before this affair came to light, mentioned to him my intentions of going up with him.

As both General Gates and myself mean to be candid, and wish to have the matter settled without any of that chicane which would disgrace us as officers and men, we have agreed to speak plain, and to show each other what we have written to you upon the occasion; and he has accordingly read the whole of what I have above said.

Since writing the above, General Gates has shown me the resolutions of Congress of the 17th ultimo, which confirm me in the opinion I have entertained, that he was only to command the army in Canada, and that I had no control upon him when there.*

Your Excellency may be assured of my best exertions to prevent the enemy from penetrating into these Colonies. General Gates is in sentiment with me on the mode; that of increasing our naval strength, and fortifying some advantageous spot on the east side of Lake Champlain, either opposite to Ticonderoga, or between that and Crown Point.

Part of the militia from this Colony is marched up; none of the others are yet moved. Their tardiness will greatly distress us, as we have much, very much, to do, and few men to do it with.

The cannon sent by Colonel Knox arrived yesterday; and, although the Indians have deferred the treaty to the middle of this month, yet I have

---

* *In Congress, June 17th.* "Resolved, That an experienced General be immediately sent into Canada, with power to appoint a Deputy Adjutant-General, a Deputy Mustermaster-General, and such other officers as he shall find necessary for the good of the service, and to fill up vacancies in the army in Canada, and notify the same to Congress for their approbation; and he also have power to suspend any officer there, till the pleasure of Congress be known, he giving his reasons for so doing in the orders of suspension, and transmitting to Congress, as soon as possible, the charge against such officer; provided, that this power of suspending officers and filling up vacancies shall not be continued beyond the first day of October next;

"That General Washington be directed to send Major-General Gates into Canada, to take command of the forces in that Province."

thought it advisable to take post at Fort Stanwix; and all the stores are moving from here to-day, and will, I hope, leave Schenectady on Wednesday morning. The Commissioners of Indian Affairs have prepared a message to the Six Nations, giving the reasons why we take post at Fort Stanwix. This will, however, not be sent until every thing is so far advanced that there may be no danger in communicating to them my intentions.

Should the enemy advance, and we be under the necessity of calling forth the militia nearest to us, we shall be at a loss for ball and buckshot. I wish, therefore, to have twenty-five rounds a-piece for ten thousand men sent up the soonest possible, if it can anywhere be procured, with a proportionate quantity of cartridge-paper, and two tons of oakum.

If any cutlasses, stinkpots, and handgrenades can be got, I beg they may also be sent for the use of our armed vessels.

One hundred thousand of the dollars brought up by General Gates are ordered to the army; better than half of the other are already expended, nor will any be left in two or three days.

Mr. Duane informed me, and gave me leave to make use of his name, that the five hundred thousand voted by Congress the 22d of May for this department, were actually charged, and he fears that they may have met with some accident on the way up.

I have ordered the silver to be kept in chests, except about three thousand pounds, which we borrowed here, and must now be repaid.

Four o'clock, P. M. I am this moment favored with your Excellency's letter of the 27th ultimo, inclosing a copy of a resolution of Congress of the 24th. I have immediately an opportunity of forwarding copies thereof to Governor Trumbull and Mr. Edwards. The latter has already received one month's advance wages for the Stockbridge company, which, I suppose, is by this time paid to them, as he informed me that they were to be here on Wednesday or Thursday next. I am afraid it will give great umbrage, if they are immediately discharged; but, as the order is positive, I dare not presume to defer complying with it. I shall, however, request Mr. Edwards to do it in a manner that will give the least offence.

I wish Colonel Francis and Colonel Wolcott were immediately ordered up to attend the conference at the German Flats on the 15th instant, as I propose going to Crown Point to-morrow, having, upon further consultation with General Gates and General Arnold since writing the foregoing, determined upon it; and this journey may detain me so long as to prevent my attendance, in which case there will be only two Commissioners present.

I am, dear General, most respectfully, your obedient, humble servant,

PHILIP SCHUYLER.*

FROM GOVERNOR TRUMBULL.

Lebanon, 4 July, 1776.

SIR,

The retreat of the Northern army, and its present situation, have spread a general alarm. By intelli-

---

* See the answer to this letter in Washington's Writings, Vol. III. p. 462.

gence from Major-General Schuyler, received last evening, I have reason to conclude that they are now at Crown Point and Ticonderoga, in a weak state, and under the necessity of an immediate re-enforcement, to enable them to make a stand, and prevent the enemy from passing the Lake and penetrating into the country. The prevalence of the smallpox among them is every way unhappy. Our people, in general, have not had that distemper. Fear of the infection operates strongly to prevent soldiers from engaging in the service, and the battalions ordered to be raised in this Colony fill up slowly; and though no measures be taken to remove the impediment, may not the army be soon freed from that infection? Can the reënforcements be kept separate from the infected? Or may not a detachment be made from the troops under your command and the militia raising in the several Colonies and ordered to New York, of such men as have had the smallpox, to be replaced by the troops raising for the Northern Department? Could any expedient be fallen upon, that would afford probable hopes that this infection may be avoided, I believe our battalions would soon join the Northern army. I shall omit nothing in my power to expedite them.

The retreat of the army from Canada exposes the Northern frontiers of New York and New Hampshire to the ravages of the Indians, who will doubtless be spirited up to fall upon them. Some of the settlements on Onion River, I am informed, are breaking up and removing, and the whole filled with the most disquieting apprehensions. Some powder and lead, upon application, have been supplied them from this Colony; but the settlers there, from their infant state, and consequent poverty, are unable to devote themselves to the defence of the frontiers, unless they should be enabled to hire laborers to carry on the business of their farms in their absence. I could therefore wish, that your Excellency might think proper to recommend it to the Continental Congress, to order a battalion to be raised and stationed there, for the defence of those settlements. It would, I trust, be immediately filled up with a hardy race of men in that quarter, well adapted to repel the attacks of the savages, and ready to join and support the Northern army, upon occasion, and at all times may scour the woods, and furnish intelligence of the enemy's motions.

If those settlers are driven back, besides the loss of their property, a much heavier expense will fall upon some of the Colonies for the support of their families, than the charges arising from the raising and maintaining a battalion of Continental troops; and we shall still have a frontier to defend.

The anxiety of the friends and relations of many, if not most, of those settlers who emigrated from this Colony, and the importance of the matter, will, I trust, be my sufficient apology for wishing to engage your influence with Congress, to support the motion I judge advisable and shall make, to have a battalion raised out of, and stationed on, those frontiers.

By a letter from General Schuyler, of the 1st instant, received last evening, I am advised that Generals Schuyler, Gates, and Arnold, were to set out on Tuesday morning. I trust they are by this time at the end of their journey, and hope their presence may have a happy effect towards retrieving affairs in that quarter. I am, with great truth and regard, Sir,

Your most obedient, humble servant,

JONATHAN TRUMBULL.

FROM THE PRESIDENT OF CONGRESS.

Philadelphia, 6 July, 1776.

Sir,

The Congress, for some time past, have had their attention occupied by one of the most interesting and important subjects, that could possibly come before them or any other assembly of men.

Although it is not possible to foresee the consequences of human actions, yet it is, nevertheless, a duty we owe ourselves and posterity, in all our public councils, to decide in the best manner we are able, and to leave the event to that Being who controls both causes and events, to bring about his own determinations.

Impressed with this sentiment, and at the same time fully convinced that our affairs may take a more favorable turn, the Congress have judged it necessary to dissolve the connection between Great Britain and the American Colonies, and to declare them free and independent States, as you will perceive by the inclosed DECLARATION, which I am directed by Congress to transmit to you, and to request you will have it proclaimed at the head of the army in the way you shall think most proper.*

Agreeably to the request of Congress, the Committee of Safety of this Colony have forwarded to you ten thousand flints, and the flints at Rhode Island are ordered to be sent to you immediately.

---

* *In Congress, July 4th.* "Resolved, That copies of the Declaration be sent to the several Assemblies, Conventions, and Committees or Councils of Safety, and to the several commanding officers of the Continental troops, that it be proclaimed in each of the United States, and at the head of the army."

It is with great pleasure I inform you, that the militia of this Colony, of Delaware Government, and Maryland, are, and will be every day in motion, to form the Flying Camp, and that all the militia of this Colony will soon be in the Jerseys, ready to receive such orders as you shall please to give them.

I have written to Governor Cooke, to engage immediately, and send forward as fast as possible, fifty ship-carpenters to General Schuyler, for the purpose of building vessels on the Lakes. Fifty have already gone from hence on that business.

The Congress having directed the arms, taken on board the Scotch transports, to be sent to you. I have written to the agents in Rhode Island and Massachusetts Bay, to forward them immediately.

The inclosed copy of a letter from Mr. Green, I am directed to forward, by Congress, with a request that you will order such parts of the stores, therein mentioned, to New York, as you shall judge proper.

I have the honor to be, Sir, with perfect esteem, your most obedient and very humble servant,

JOHN HANCOCK, *President.*

FROM THE PRESIDENT OF CONGRESS.

Philadelphia, 13 July, 1776.

SIR,

I am to acknowledge the receipt of your favor of the 10th instant, and to acquaint you that it is now under the consideration of Congress.

The inclosed resolves I do myself the honor to transmit, as necessary for your information. I have

22 *

written to General Schuyler, and the Commissioners for Indian Affairs, respecting the same.

In obedience to the commands of Congress, I have inclosed you two copies of sundry resolves they have passed relative to the treatment of our prisoners by Captain Forster, in Canada. I am to request you will take the proper steps to send one of them to General Howe, and the other to General Burgoyne. I transmit, also, a third copy for your own use.*

Should the United States of America give their sanction to the Jesuitical and villanous distinction

---

* A Committee had reported the facts relating to the transactions at the Cedars, in Canada, and, after taking the report into consideration, the Congress adopted the following resolutions ;

"Resolved, That all acts contrary to good faith, the laws of nature, or the customs of civilized nations, done by the officers or soldiers of his Britannic Majesty, or by foreigners or savages taken into his service, are to be considered as done by his orders, unless indemnification be made, in cases which admit indemnification, and in all other cases, unless immediate and effective measures be taken by him, or by his officers, for bringing to condign punishment the authors, abettors, and perpetrators of the act;

"That the plundering the baggage of the garrison at the Cedars, stripping them of their clothes, and delivering them into the hands of the savages, was a breach of the capitulation on the part of the enemy, for which indemnification ought to be demanded;

"That the murder of the prisoners of war, was a gross and inhuman violation of the laws of nature and nations ; that condign punishment should be inflicted on the authors, abettors, and perpetrators of the same ; and that, for this purpose, it be required that they be delivered into our hands;

"That the agreement entered into by General Arnold, was a mere sponsion on his part, he not being invested with powers for the disposal of prisoners not in his possession, nor under his direction; and that therefore, it is subject to be ratified or annulled at the discretion of this House ;

"That the shameful surrender of the post at the Cedars, is chargeable on the commanding officer; that such other of the prisoners as were taken there, showed a willingness and desire to fight the enemy and that Major Sherburne, and the prisoners taken with him, though their disparity of numbers was great, fought the enemy bravely for a

which Captain Forster adopts to justify his conduct, there would be no end to butchering our prisoners. They have, therefore, very properly reprobated it; and, in the genuine spirit of freedom, resolved, that such cruelty as shall be inflicted on prisoners in their possession, by savages or foreigners taken into pay by the King of Great Britain, shall be considered as done by his orders, and recourse be immediately had to retaliation.   It is to be hoped their determination will have the desired effect, and that for the future, such barbarous scenes will never be acted under the eye and approbation of a British officer; for there is the greatest reason to believe, that Captain Forster engaged the Indians to join him, on the express condition of giving up to them all such prisoners as might fall into his hands.   His subsequent conduct, indeed, renders this conjecture more than probable.

---

considerable time, and surrendered at last, but on absolute necessity; on which consideration, and on which alone, it is resolved, that the said sponsion be ratified; and that an equal number of captives from the enemy, of the same rank and condition, be restored to them, as stipulated by the said sponsion;

"That, previous to the delivery of the prisoners to be returned on our part, the British commander in Canada be required to deliver into our hands the authors, abettors, and perpetrators of the horrid murder committed on the prisoners, to suffer such punishment as their crime deserves; and also, to make indemnification for the plunder at the Cedars, taken contrary to the faith of the capitulation; and that, until such delivery and indemnification be made, the said prisoners be not delivered;

"That if the enemy shall commit any further violences, by putting to death, torturing, or otherwise ill treating the prisoners retained by them, or any of the hostages put into their hands, recourse be had to retaliation, as the sole means of stopping the progress of human butchery; and that, for that purpose, punishments of the same kind and degree be inflicted on an equal number of the captives from them in our possession, till they shall be taught to respect the violated rights of nations;

"That a copy of the above report and resolutions be transmitted to the Commander-in-chief of the Continental forces, to be by him sent to Generals Howe and Burgoyne." *Journals of Congress, July* 10*th*.

I have the honor to be, with perfect esteem, Sir, your most obedient and very humble servant,

JOHN HANCOCK, President.

One o'clock, P. M. This moment your favor, per post of the 11th instant, came to hand. I shall lay it before Congress on Monday evening.

FROM BRIGADIER-GENERAL GEORGE CLINTON.*

Fort Montgomery, 15 July, 1776.

SIR,

I received your favor of the 12th instant yesterday, at this place; previous to which, about nine o'clock Saturday morning, the signal at Fort Constitution being given, and the masters of two sloops, which about the same time came to, opposite my house, having informed me that the enemy had attacked New York the evening before, and that they judged, by the report of the cannon, that their shipping had passed by, and were up the river as far as King's Bridge, I thought it my duty to put the neighbouring militia

---

* At this time commanding the New York militia. On the 5th of August he was appointed, by the Convention of the State of New York, to take command of the levies recently raised for immediate service. Nathaniel Woodhull, the President of the Convention, wrote to him as follows; —

"The accounts received from General Washington are of a very alarming nature. You are therefore to send expresses to Dutchess, Ulster, Orange, and Westchester counties, and order the new levies to march with the utmost expedition to the post erected on the north side of King's Bridge, since it is of the utmost importance to prevent the enemy's occupying that post, and cutting off the communication between the army in town and the country." August 5th.

in motion; and accordingly issued orders to three regiments, one immediately to march into these works, another into Fort Constitution, and the third to rendezvous at Newburg, on the bank of the river, about nine miles above Fort Constitution, with orders to march and reënforce that garrison, upon the next signal given.

At the same time I issued orders to all the regiments in my brigade, to stand ready to march on a moment's warning, and despatched expresses to all owners of sloops and boats twenty miles up the west side of the river, to haul them off so as to prevent their grounding; that as many of them as were necessary might be ready to carry down the militia to the forts. The residue I ordered down to Fort Constitution, as I believe by drawing a chain of them across the narrowest part of the river, and fixing them properly to be set on fire, should the enemy's shipping attempt passing by, they would answer a most valuable purpose. Early in the afternoon of that day, I marched into Fort Constitution with about forty of my neighbours, and in the evening came to this fort, being nearer the enemy and better situated to discover their motions. Yesterday evening I was joined by Colonel Woodhull, with between two and three hundred of his regiment; this morning early, by Lieutenant-Colonel McClaghry, with upwards of five hundred of his; and I hourly expect parts of two other regiments. When these join me, I will draft, out of the four, six hundred men, and employ them as your Excellency has directed. I have ordered the Colonels I have called in, to leave the frontier companies at home to protect the country against the Indians, should they be troublesome, and as many men out of each company as will be sufficient to guard against any attempts that might be made by internal enemies.

The men turn out of their harvest fields, to defend their country, with surprising alacrity. The absence of so many of them, however, at this time, when their harvests are perishing for want of the sickle, will greatly distress the country. I could wish, therefore, a less number might answer the purpose. I would fain hope the enemy mean, by their shipping in our bays, at present only to cut off the communication between the country and city, and prevent our obstructing the channel. Many of the militia may be called in in eight hours; some in a much less time, should there be occasion for them.

Since writing the above, I received a letter from Colonel Hay, of Haverstraw, a copy of which is inclosed. I will send a small party down there this evening, or in the morning, but don't believe I shall be able to continue them long, as the militia here will think hard to be carried there. The bearer, Mr. Boyd, who is well acquainted with this country, the fortifications here, and may be confided in, will be able to give your Excellency any further information. I am, with great esteem,

Your Excellency's most obedient servant,

GEORGE CLINTON.

P. S. I should be glad to know whether it is best to keep the sloops, &c., ordered down to Fort Constitution, there, as it may be attended with considerable expense, which, however, if they can be made to answer a good purpose, ought not, in my opinion, to be regarded.

FROM BENJAMIN FRANKLIN.

Philadelphia, 22 July, 1776.

Sir,

The bearer, Mr. Joseph Belton, some time since petitioned the Congress for encouragement to destroy the enemy's ships of war by some contrivances of his invention. They came to no resolution on his petition; and, as they appear to have no great opinion of such proposals, it is not easy, in the multiplicity of business before them, to get them to bestow any part of their attention on his request. He is now desirous of trying his hand on the ships that are gone up the North River; and, as he proposes to work entirely at his own expense, and only desires your countenance and permission, I could not refuse his desire of a line of introduction to you, the trouble of which I beg you to excuse. As he appears to be a very ingenious man, I hope his project may be attended with success.

With sincerest esteem and respect, I have the honor to be, &c.

BENJAMIN FRANKLIN.

FROM BRIGADIER-GENERAL GREENE.

amp on Long Island, 25 July, 1776.

Sir,

I have just completed a brigade return for the vacancies in the different regiments. My brigade is so dispersed that it is difficult getting returns seasonably. I should have made this return yesterday, but could not get Colonel Hand's until last evening.

The outguards report nothing worthy your Excellency's notice this morning.

I am so confined, writing passes, &c., that it is impossible for me to attend to the duties of the day, which, in many instances, prejudices the service. Such a confined situation leaves one no opportunity of viewing things for themselves. It is recommended, by one of the greatest Generals of the age, not only to issue orders, but to see to the execution; for the army being composed of men of indolence, if the commander is not attentive to every individual in the different departments, the machine becomes dislocated, and the progress of business retarded.

The science or art of war requires a freedom of thought, and leisure to reflect upon the various incidents that daily occur, which cannot be had where the whole of one's time is engrossed in clerical employments. The time devoted to this employment is not the only injury I feel; but it confines my thoughts as well as engrosses my time. It is like a merchandise of small wares.

I must beg leave to recommend to your Excellency's consideration the appointing an officer to write and sign the necessary passes. The person I should wish to be appointed is Lieutenant Blodget. If it was put in general orders, that passes signed by him should be deemed authentic, as if signed by me, it would leave me at liberty to pursue the more important employments of my station.

I hope your Excellency will not think this application results from a lazy habit, or a desire to free myself from business. Far from it. I am never more happy than when I am honorably or usefully employed. If your Excellency thinks I can promote the service as much in this employment as in any other,

I shall cheerfully execute the business, without the least murmur.

I am, with all due respect, your Excellency's most obedient, humble servant,

NATHANAEL GREENE.

Middletown, 25 July, 1776.

SIR,

I arrived here the 22d instant, after a tedious passage of sixty-six days from Quebec, on my parole of honor, to return when called for, a copy of which, together with my pass from General Carleton, is inclosed. The original is in the hands of General Howe. I am to represent to your Excellency the situation of the unfortunate detachment that were made prisoners on the 31st December last.

The number now in Quebec is about three hundred, including officers. The officers were confined in the Seminary, the soldiers in the Jesuits' College, and were served with the same rations that were served to the garrison after the siege was raised. The officers had liberty to walk in a large garden that is adjoining the Seminary. The officers and privates are in great want of money, as they cannot procure clothing without it, of which they are in great want. The officers are now considerably in debt for necessaries, exclusive of the garrison allowance. Generals Carle-

----

* Major Meigs was in the expedition under Arnold through the wilderness to Quebec, and was made prisoner in the assault upon that city by General Montgomery.

ton and Howe have given their word for the protection of any private gentleman that may be sent with money, but will not admit that an officer of the army be sent.

The prisoners bear their confinement with becoming fortitude, but are anxious for an exchange of prisoners, if it can be obtained consistent with the interest of their country. I am informed that Lieutenant-Colonel Campbell, of the Highlanders, has applied to General Howe for a cartel, and that Major French and others are anxious for an exchange. In February last, the officers, prisoners at Quebec, petitioned General Carleton for an exchange of prisoners, provided our country should approve it. The General received the petition, read it, and told the officer that presented it, that he would consider of it, but returned no other answer.

I intended to have waited on your Excellency myself, but was advised, by the gentlemen in Hartford and this town, not to do it without your Excellency's advice, as it would be undoubtedly known to General Howe, and perhaps even represented that I had joined the army, or was giving intelligence, for which he might immediately demand me. When I gave my parole to General Carleton, he told me Major Skene, son to Governor Skene, had arrived at Quebec two days before, and that he should not employ him till he had the advice of the King of England.

I have sent by the bearer a number of unsealed letters, which I brought from the prisoners at Quebec. I have the honor to be, with the greatest respect, your Excellency's

Most obedient and most humble servant,
RETURN J. MEIGS.

FROM THE PRESIDENT OF CONGRESS.

Philadelphia, 2 August, 1776.

SIR,

I am particularly instructed, by Congress, to answer that part of your letter of 29th ultimo, directed to the Board of War, which relates to the filling up vacancies in the army. The Congress are concerned to find, that an opinion is entertained that greater confidence has been placed in, and larger powers given to other commanders in that respect, than to yourself.

They have, in no instance, except in the late appointment of General Gates to the command in Canada, parted with the power of filling up vacancies. The great confusion and many disorders prevalent in that army, and its distance, induced Congress to lodge such a power in that General, for the limited space of three months, and only during his continuance in Canada. Should Congress ever empower its Generals to fill up the vacancies in the army, they know of no one in whom they would so soon repose a trust of such importance as in yourself; but future Generals may make a bad use of it. The danger of the precedent, not any suspicion of their present Commander-in-chief, prompts them to retain a power that, by you, Sir, might be exercised with the greatest public advantage.

I do myself the honor to inclose sundry resolves, and to request your attention to them. They relate principally, as you will perceive, to some new regulations with regard to Paymasters, Commissaries, and Quartermasters in the American army, and are intended to prevent confusion and disorder in those several departments.

The Congress approve of your employing, in the service of the States, the Stockbridge Indians, if you think proper.

The inclosed resolve, for taking into the pay of the States such of the seamen as may fall into our hands on board of prizes, will, I trust, be attended with the good effects Congress had in view when they passed it.

I have the honor to be, with perfect respect and esteem, Sir, your most obedient and very humble servant,

JOHN HANCOCK, *President.*

N. B. Your favor of 5th instant, just come to hand, will be replied to by to-morrow's post.

FROM GOVERNOR TRUMBULL.

Lebanon, 5 August, 1776.

SIR,

I have received your two favors of the 24th and 25th of July last. I have put Colonel Ward's regiment under marching orders, to proceed without loss of time, whatever way Congress shall direct. The troops from this State, destined to the northward, are marched to Bennington, and from thence to Skenesborough. At the request of General Schuyler for one thousand felling axes, I have sent eight hundred, ground and with helves, to go the same route. They went from hence the 29th last. The residue will go with clothing, preparing for that army, next Monday. I thought it not best to wait for orders, as we were very well assured of their necessity.

Notwithstanding our enemies are so numerous and powerful, and have hired mercenaries into their service, yet, knowing our cause righteous, and trusting Heaven will support and defend us, I do not greatly dread what they can do against us. Our internal malignants may be permitted to do many injurious and insidious things. They are, therefore, to be watched with care and diligence, to prevent such hypocritical and designing men carrying on and perpetrating their wicked purposes. No doubt there are many such, the persons and characters unknown to me; and not convenient to mention in a letter the notices given me of any.

Last week I sent circular letters addressed to the civil authority, Selectmen, Committees of Inspection, and Military Officers, in all the towns in this State, to promote and facilitate the filling the several battalions ordered to be raised here, and to send them forward to the places of their destination. Recruiting officers for the companies not filled are necessary, and I conclude are left for the purpose. The people have, in some measure, got through the hurry of harvest, &c. Hope that they will now cheerfully enlist and go on.

Colonel Dyer and Richard Law, Esq., are directed to repair to New York to confer with your Excellency on every subject needful for our direction, and for your information. You know our readiness to afford every assistance for our common defence. I am, with great esteem and regard, Sir,

Your most obedient, humble servant,
JONATHAN TRUMBULL.

23*

P. S. *6th, 8 o'clock, A. M.* Just received your
two favors of the 1st instant. Orders are gone to
Colonel Elmore, and express to carry those to Colonel Ward expected in soon. The orders are ready.

FROM BRIGADIER-GENERAL MIFFLIN.

Mount Washington, 6 August, 1776.

DEAR GENERAL,

Agreeably to your order, by Colonel Reed's letter,
I have directed Colonel Holden to march with his
three companies this evening to King's Bridge.

I shall, in consequence of that order, be under the
necessity of totally neglecting the Point Battery, until men are sent up to work on it; our two battalions being employed in raising part of our parapet,
covering the large magazine, cutting and forming the
abatis, digging wells, &c. That magazine will be prepared to receive the powder this evening. The magazine within the fort will be completed in two days.

We have so many sick and on guard, that I have
been obliged to give up the outworks for the present.

As I had no orders respecting the *chevaux-de-frise*,
and as the artists appeared willing to take their own
way, I did not presume to interfere.

In future I will watch and direct their movements.
But, as Colonel Putnam is absent with the soundings,
and as the vessels are sent up without persons who
are acquainted with the depth of water for which
they were calculated, I shall be at a loss to sink
them. The sloops which came up this morning,

being small, must, in my opinion, be sunk to the westward of the brigs. If Colonel Putnam had another destination for them, I beg to be favored with directions where to place them.

In future it will be best to send up single vessels, it being the most abstruse problem in hydraulics to determine of what size the several ports, or holes, would be, in vessels of different tonnage and construction, in order to their sinking at the same time. If one sinks before the other, we risk, as yesterday.

I believe that vessels above ninety tons, without iron work, will answer very well. No ship will attempt to pass over them, even if they were eighteen feet below the surface. If five or six vessels, of one hundred tons each, could be sent up, I shall apprehend no danger of ships of war passing them. It will be the most expeditious and the most frugal scheme. The Colossus is now at anchor, a little to the westward of her post. The buoy, fixed by Colonel Putnam, appears to be too distant from the shore. Possibly it may have been carried there by the wind and current. It shall be removed this night, if possible; the brigs, this afternoon.

The enemy may possibly attempt to weigh some of the vessels. It will, therefore, be necessary to fix some guns at the battery. If I can obtain no heavy guns, I will send down our four twelve-pounders and the howitzer, and fight them. I am, with zeal and attachment,

Your Excellency's, &c.

THOMAS MIFFLIN.

FROM ROBERT R. LIVINGSTON.*

Haerlem, 9 August, 1776.

SIR,

It is with peculiar pleasure that I acknowledge the receipt of your Excellency's favor of yesterday, since I cannot but consider it as an additional mark of that confidence with which your Excellency has hitherto honored me. I have made the proper use of it, and imparted it, in confidence, to the members of the Convention, on whose secrecy I thought I could most safely rely, and from whose influence I hoped to draw the most effectual assistance.

I early foresaw what has since happened, and therefore made it my endeavour to enforce the drawing out as much of the strength of this State as could possibly be collected. I cannot but hope that the good effect of this measure will very shortly appear. A considerable body of troops will, as we suppose, begin their march for King's Bridge to-morrow, and I flatter myself that in five or six days their number will be increased to sixteen or eighteen hundred men. Such is my idea of the importance of this post, that I could wish your Excellency to count as little as possible upon the raw troops we send there, but to send thither all you originally designed for that station. Your Excellency is best able to judge whether it can be rendered tenable without some cannon, gunners, and matrosses; and how far it

---

* A member of the Continental Congress, now attending the New York Convention, and acting as one of a Secret Committee for facilitating the military operations on Hudson's River.

is prudent to supply that want under which it now labors, by sending them from some other place.

Since I am upon this subject, I will take the liberty to hint what may possibly have escaped your Excellency's attention, in the multiplicity of business in which you are involved; I mean the possibility of the enemy's destroying the bridge (if their fleet should get above the town) by means of a body of troops sent up the creek in boats, before any assistance could come in, unless some small work was thrown up there for its defence, which the situation renders very practicable.

The troops raised on Long Island, and which we have subjected to your Excellency's command, and ordered to join General Greene's brigade, may amount to about eight hundred men; but as part of them are very remote, they may possibly not all arrive at their stations in less than eight days.

We shall, this morning, endeavour to raise some more of our militia, to occupy the passes in the Highlands, and that of the northern counties, which we have hitherto reserved in case of any misfortunes happening to the army at Ticonderoga. I fear they will not come in time to assist your Excellency at New York, if the enemy should be speedy in their attack, as they are very remote and ill armed. Perhaps we may be able to send some of the neighbouring militia to General Greene, to be dismissed when the Long Island levies are all come in.

Your Excellency may be assured that the little influence I have shall be exerted to forward any operations which your Excellency may form, since I am fully satisfied that they will always be directed by that spirit of patriotism which has so deservedly secured to you the esteem of this Continent; and shall therefore think it a happiness to be honored with your commands. I have the honor to be, with the greatest esteem and respect, your Excellency's

Most obedient, humble servant,

ROBERT R. LIVINGSTON.

FROM BRIGADIER-GENERAL LIVINGSTON.*

Elizabethtown, 12 August, 1776.

MAY IT PLEASE YOUR EXCELLENCY,

Your letter of the 8th instant, I received on a journey to Brunswick, on Friday last, where I had an opportunity of conferring with our Convention, and urging your Excellency's requisition relating to the militia, the propriety of which is so obvious. I returned on Saturday evening, and delayed answering your favor, in hopes of receiving the resolution of the Convention thereon. I have just been favored with a rough draught of their ordinance, which I shall send you as soon as I get a correct copy.

The outlines are, that the one half of the whole militia, without exception, be immediately called out, and join the Flying Camp; that every person refusing his attendance be fined three pounds; that they be formed into thirteen battalions, and to remain on service one month, and then to be relieved by the other half.

---

* William Livingston had been a member of the Continental Congress, and was now in command of the New Jersey militia, acting in concert with the Continental Army. He was soon afterwards chosen Governor of that State, which office he held during the war.

There being no mention made of any number to be forwarded to New York, I take it for granted the whole are to be under your Excellency's direction as to their station, &c.

The two thousand men for the Flying Camp, under General Dickinson, are in great forwardness, and (although very little acquainted with their duty) might answer a valuable purpose in New York, on the present emergency, especially as their places will be so soon filled by the half of the militia now to be raised.   A considerable body of the militia must be kept here to supply the place of the Pennsylvania Associators, who are deserting their post in considerable numbers, notwithstanding the most spirited exertions of their officers, and particularly their Colonel, whose behaviour does honor to his Province in particular, and America in general.

We have taken such measures as I hope will put a stop to any further behaviour of this kind.   This corps, since our militia were dismissed, have not carried on any of the works at the Point, which, as soon as they are relieved by any men under my command, I shall order to be prosecuted with all possible vigor; as, it is more than probable, the enemy will attempt an incursion into this Province, to which its present defenceless state, in this part, seems strongly to invite them.   I am, with much truth and regard, your Excellency's

Most obedient and humble servant,

WILLIAM LIVINGSTON.

FROM MAJOR-GENERAL HEATH.

King's Bridge, 17 August, 1776.

DEAR GENERAL,

The last night the fire-ships and row-galleys made an attempt upon the enemy's ships, which lay at anchor up the river. The fire-ships were well conducted; the armed schooner was grappled and burnt; the Phœnix was grappled for about ten minutes, but got herself clear. The Lady Washington galley and Independence, were conducted with great judgment and bravery. I wish I could say that the other galleys did any thing at all. The Phœnix either slipt or cut her cable; the Rose was left alone, and it is thought might have been taken. I was an eye-witness to the whole; and, from the confusion which was apparent, I am confident that if an attempt should be made on the fleet below, and but one or two ships set on fire, their confusion would be beyond description.*

I have the pleasure to acquaint your Excellency, that General Mifflin has about five hundred men at a moment's notice, to aid you in case of need. They were the last evening drawn out, when I reviewed them. They are of Colonels Shee's and Magaw's regiments, and the best disciplined of any troops that I have yet seen in the army. I shall, this evening, or to-morrow, send a return of the troops at this post. We are pushing our works with all diligence. I have the honor to be, with great respect,

Your Excellency's humble servant,

WILLIAM HEATH.

---

* For a more extended account of this adventure, see Heath's Memoirs, p. 53.

King's Bridge, 18 August, 1776.

DEAR GENERAL,

Early this morning, the Phœnix man-of-war, Rose frigate, and the two tenders, came to sail, and stood down the river, keeping close under the east shore, in order to avoid the fire of our cannon. But, notwithstanding this precaution, the Phœnix was thrice hulled, by our shot from Mount Washington, and one of the tenders once. The Rose was hulled once by a shot from Burdett's Ferry. They kept their men close, otherwise some of them would have been picked down by a party of riflemen, who were posted on the bank. They fired grape-shot as they passed, but did no damage save to one tent. We hope to hear that your batteries have done the work for some of them.

We shall recover some swivel-guns, gun-barrels, shot, &c., out of the wreck of the tender, which was burnt the other night, the particulars of which shall be transmitted to your Excellency as soon as I can obtain them. General Clinton has about fourteen hundred men already come in, but their quarters are so scattered, that it will be almost impossible to collect them suddenly, if occasion should require it. If there are any spare tents, I earnestly beg for them, if it were but for one regiment. General Clinton has orders from the Convention of the State of New York to purchase ten thousand feet of boards, for erecting sheds, &c., but it is uncertain when we shall have them. I shall, to-morrow, send for six or seven hundred of tools, being able to employ that number more than we have at present. The more I view this post, the more I am convinced of its importance.

The ships have now tried the practicability of passing our works. They have explored every part of the shore, as far as they have gone up the river, and sounded the river in almost every place. Should the ships rejoin the fleet without receiving much damage, I think Howe will be emboldened to attempt an attack somewhere above this place, thinking that there may be a greater probability of succeeding here, than in the face of so many and strong works as have been erected in and around the city. However, should his inclination lead him this way, nature has done much for us, and we shall, as fast as possible, add the strength of art. Our men are in good health and spirits, and I dare say will give them a warm reception.

I should be glad to have the carriages for the four-pounders sent forward the moment they are done, as we have not as yet a single cannon mounted beyond Mount Washington. I have just now received your Excellency's commands to inquire into the cause of the inactivity of some of the row-galleys, in the late attack on the enemy's ships; but as the galleys have all left this post, and fallen down to the city, I must beg your Excellency to excuse me from that service. I have the honor to be, with the greatest respect,

Your Excellency's most humble servant,

WILLIAM HEATH.

FROM MAJOR-GENERAL GATES.

Ticonderoga, 28 August, 1776.

Sir,

Yesterday I had the honor to receive your Excellency's letter of the 14th instant, which is all I have been favored with since that of the 19th July. I have at length the satisfaction to send a pretty correct general return of the army in this part of the northern district of America. A copy of my last letter to General Schuyler, which is in the packet, will explain the return to your Excellency. I also inclose my orders and instructions to Lieutenant Whitcomb, who went from hence the 20th instant upon a scout towards St. John's, Chamblee, &c. The report of his last scout, which General Sullivan sent him upon, has already been sent to General Schuyler, who has doubtless transmitted it to your Excellency.

As the smallpox is now perfectly removed from the army, I shall, in consequence of the intelligence received of the motions of the enemy, immediately assemble my principal strength to maintain this important pass; and hope General Waterbury, in a week, at farthest, will be able to come with the three row-galleys to Ticonderoga, and proceed, the instant they arrive and are fitted, to join General Arnold upon the Lake. In the mean time, we are exerting our utmost industry to fortify this post, a plan of which is inclosed. The weather of late has been so uncommonly wet and stormy for the season, that we are much retarded in our works. As the enemy feel alike the inclemency of the season, I hope we shall be prepared for them when they come.

My orders to Brigadier-General Arnold your Excellency will find in the packet. He read and entirely approved them before he left Ticonderoga. I hope they are the sentiments of your Excellency, and the most Honorable the Congress, upon that momentous command.

As the New Hampshire and Connecticut militia have come without tents, much time is lost, by those regiments, in covering themselves. It happens, very fortunately, that Mount Independence affords an ample supply of huts; otherwise those corps must soon have felt great distress. The Massachusetts militia are arrived, well supplied with excellent tents, and a sufficiency of good camp utensils. This, in our present circumstances, is a great help to us, and does that Province much honor.

Governor Trumbull acquaints me he has forwarded one thousand felling-axes and two loads of clothing. His Excellency has, from the beginning of the misfortunes of this army, done every thing in his power to establish it in health and power. Too much cannot be said in his praise. Your Excellency must, long ere this, have received from General Schuyler the report of Major Bigelow, who returned with the flag of truce from Isle-aux-Noix. As I constantly report every extraordinary occurrence to General Schuyler, I take it for granted there is no delay with him in forwarding them to your Excellency and the Congress. I have ordered Commissary Avery to forward to Colonel Trumbull the returns and reports that are proper to be made in his department, and Dr. Morgan has, before this, shown your Excellency my letter to him of the 22d instant.

I am pleased at the account General Schuyler gives me, of five hundred and thirteen thousand dollars being arrived at Albany from Philadelphia. It is much wanted both there and here, as the militia were promised their mileage and billeting-money at Number Four; but no money was sent there to pay them. This neglect caused much murmuring amongst them, and was very near stopping their march from thence. I wish good care was taken not to make any promises to troops but such as are punctually performed. I apprehend this promise was made by the Legislature at Watertown. I have the honor to be, your Excellency's

Most obedient, humble servant,
HORATIO GATES.

FROM GOVERNOR TRUMBULL.

Lebanon, 31 August, 1776.

SIR,

Adjutant-General Reed's letter, of the 24th instant, came to hand Tuesday morning, the 27th; yours, of the same date, yesterday.

On receiving the former, I advised with my Council. We concluded to send Benjamin Huntington, Esq., one of my Council, with direction to take with him Major Ely, at New London, an officer there well acquainted with the people on Long Island, to proceed there and consult and agree with some of the sure friends of our cause, with secrecy, as far as the circumstances would admit, for a number of their men, assured friends, and well acquainted on the Island, to join with a body from this State, if possible to accomplish your wishes, to cause a diversion to the enemy, to harass them on their rear, and to prevent

24 *

their excursions in pursuit of the provisions the Island affords. I hear they sailed for the Island yesterday. His return is expected the beginning of next week.

If he succeeds according to our hopes, no exertions of this State, I trust, will be wanting, at this critical conjuncture, to harass and keep the enemy at bay, to gain time and every advantage the case may admit. I shall give the earliest intelligence of our proceedings, that you may coöperate with our designs. The race is not to the swift, nor the battle to the strong. It is nothing with God to help, whether many, or with those that have no power. He hath so ordered things, in the administration of the affairs of the world, as to encourage the use of means; and yet, so as to keep men in continual dependence upon him for the efficacy and success of them; to make kings and all men to know the reins of the world are not in their hands, but that there is One above who sways and governs all things here below.

I am closing. A post comes in, and brings the letters, copies of which are inclosed. I now expect Mr. Huntington's speedy return. Have sent for my Council. My own thoughts, and such as come to me, are to send forward four or five of the companies now stationed at New London, with four field-pieces, I hope six pieces, to join those men which may be ready for the service on Long Island; four or five companies to follow from New London as soon as they can be marched down; and also to order on other companies to take the places of such as are removed from thence.

I am inclined to think we shall fall upon some measure similar to what is mentioned. No delay can be admitted at this critical moment. Please to give me the earliest intelligence how we may best serve agreeably to your desires.

Shall send in the morning this intelligence to Governor Cooke, of Providence, and ask his assistance in the best way he shall think the circumstances of that State will admit.

September 1*st.* Inclosed is a copy of another letter, dated yesterday, from Southold, that you may observe the contents. I hope to pursue our measures so as to stop the enemy getting into Suffolk county. I am, with esteem and regard, your Excellency's

Most obedient, humble servant,

JONATHAN TRUMBULL.

FROM GOVERNOR COOKE.

Providence, 6 September, 1776.

SIR,

The necessity, which caused the unexpected evacuation of Long Island, hath alarmed the General Assembly of this State, as it seems that communications cannot be kept open with an island where the enemy's ships can approach. This hath filled us with apprehensions for the town of Newport and the Island of Rhode Island, which are of so great importance to this and the other United States. Upon which the Assembly have thought proper to appoint John Collins, Joshua Babcock, and Joseph Stanton, Esqs., a Committee to wait upon your Excellency, to acquaint you with the state of this Government, and to confer with you upon the best measures to be taken for its defence, and with respect to the Island of Rhode Island. I beg the favor of your Excellency to treat them with the most entire confidence; and have no doubt but that the same disposition which hath always induced you to manifest your regard to this State, will induce you to give us your best advice and assistance.

Upon receiving information of the landing of the enemy upon Long Island, and a letter from Governor Trumbull, acquainting us with your request that a body of men might be thrown upon the east end of that Island, this State ordered the whole brigade, with the two galleys, and a sufficient quantity of provisions and ammunition, to proceed to that Island, and ordered them to be replaced by the militia of the State. We exerted ourselves to get them in readiness; and some of them were under orders to proceed, when we received the most uncertain and aggravated accounts of the evacuation of Long Island, which occasioned us to stop the men until we could receive intelligence to be depended upon; which we did not gain until the last evening. I beg leave to observe to your Excellency 'the advantages that may accrue to the common cause from the several States having early and authentic intelligence of all matters of importance that shall happen, and to request your Excellency to favor us with accounts of every thing material. I have the honor to be, with every sentiment of esteem and respect, Sir, your Excellency's

Most obedient, humble servant,

NICHOLAS COOKE.

FROM BRIGADIER-GENERAL MERCER.

Amboy, 8 o'clock, A. M., 7 September, 1776.

SIR,

I have been confined two days by a fever, which has not yet left me; it is a great mortification that I have it not in my power to attend at head-quarters. It would, however, have been impossible for any officers from this place to be in time at New York. By some neglect of the messenger, your letter was not delivered till seven this morning. General Roberdeau waits on your Excellency to know the result of your determinations, and to inform you of the state of the troops in New Jersey.

My ideas of the operations for this campaign are to prevent the enemy from executing their plan of a junction between the armies of Howe and Burgoyne, on which the expectations of the King and Ministry are fixed. We should keep New York, if possible, as the acquiring of that will give *éclat* to the arms· of Britain, afford the soldiers good quarters, and furnish a safe harbour for the fleet. If it even could be retained a month or two, keeping the field so long in this climate may be supposed to affect the health of European troops very much. On the other hand, a free and safe communication with the countries, from whence supplies of men and provisions can come to your army, is a consideration of superior moment to any other.

How far both those objects may be within the compass of your Excellency's force, I cannot pretend to judge, having a very inadequate knowledge of the particulars necessary to found an opinion upon. I have not seen Colonel Clark, but gave general orders at all the posts along the Jersey shore, that the troops from Maryland should proceed immediately to New York. I hope to be able, very soon, to effect some enterprise on Staten Island, when we have a sufficient number of men for the Flying Camp to dispose along the different posts; but the militia are not the men for such a purpose. Four Colonels were with me some nights ago, to inform that their men would fight the enemy on this side, but would not go over to Staten Island. I have the honor to be, Sir,

Your Excellency's most obedient servant,
HUGH MERCER.

FROM MAJOR-GENERAL SCHUYLER.

Albany, 9 September, 1776.

DEAR SIR,

At half after ten, this morning, I received a letter from General Gates, copy whereof I inclose your Excellency.

As it is most probable the enemy are attempting to cross the Lake, I have therefore thought it necessary to apply to the neighbouring counties of the New England States, and those of Ulster and Duchess in this, to order their militia to march up. As soon as they arrive, I shall either move with what part may go to the northward, or with those to the westward, as may be most necessary. This can, however, only be determined by farther intelligence from General Gates and Colonel Dayton, which I momently expect to receive.

The cartridge-paper arrived here on the 2d instant,

was sent forward on the 3d, and arrived at Fort George on the 5th, at night, and was probably forwarded from thence on the 6th.

I am informed that the army is in the greatest distress for medicines. As every misfortune and want they labor under is imputed to me, so is this. I am heartily tired of abuse, and was in hopes that Congress would have ordered an inquiry into my conduct. I requested it, most earnestly, on the 16th of last month, but have not yet been honored with an answer. I will no longer suffer the public odium, since I have it most amply in my power to justify myself, and shall therefore resign my commission as soon as I return from Ticonderoga, or Tryon county. Of this I shall advise Congress, that orders may be given for a General Officer to reside in this place, without which the service will suffer. But, in doing this, I shall never forget the duty I owe to my country; and if I can, by advice or any other means, promote the weal of it, none will do it with more alacrity. I am, dear Sir, with every sentiment of esteem and respect, your Excellency's

Most obedient, humble servant,

PHILIP SCHUYLER.

FROM EDWARD RUTLEDGE.*

Brunswick, Wednesday Evening 10 o'clock,
11 September, 1776.

MY DEAR SIR,

Your favor of this morning is just put into my hands. In answer I must beg leave to inform you,

---

* Lord Howe and General Howe had been appointed Commissioners by the King, in conformity with an Act of Parliament, to endeavour to

that our conference with Lord Howe has been attended which no immediate advantages. He declared that he had no powers to consider us as independent States; and we easily discovered that, were we still dependent, we should have nothing to expect from those with which he is vested. He talked altogether in generals;—that he came out here to consult, advise, and confer with gentlemen of the greatest influence in the Colonies, about their complaints; that the King would revise the Act of Parliament, and royal instructions, upon such reports as should be made; and appeared to fix our redress upon his Majesty's good will and pleasure. This kind of conversation lasted for several hours, and, as I have already said, without any effect.

Our reliance continues, therefore, to be, under God, on your wisdom and fortitude, and that of your forces; that you may be as successful as I know you are worthy, is my most sincere wish.

I saw Mrs. Washington the evening before I left Philadelphia. She was well. I gave Mr. Griffin a letter from her for you. The gentlemen beg their respects. God bless you, my dear Sir.

Your most affectionate friend,

EDWARD RUTLEDGE.

---

bring about a reconciliation between Great Britain and the Colonies. Congress had appointed Dr. Franklin, John Adams, and Edward Rutledge, to meet Lord Howe, and consult on this subject. The interview took place on Staten Island, on the 11th of September, and the American Commissioners returned the same evening to Amboy. See the particulars of this negotiation in Sparks's edition of Franklin's Works, Vol. I. p. 412; Vol. V. p. 97.

FROM SIR WILLIAM HOWE.

Head-Quarters, York Island, 21 September, 1776.

Sir,

I have the favor of your letters of the 6th and 19th current. In consequence of the latter, directions are given for Major-General Sullivan being conveyed to Elizabethtown on the earliest day, and I conclude Major-General Prescott will return in the same boat.

The exchange you propose, of Brigadier-General Alexander, commonly called Lord Stirling, for Mr. McDonald, cannot take place, as he has only the rank of Major by my commission; but I shall readily send any Major in the inclosed lists of prisoners, that you will be pleased to name, in exchange for him; and, that Lord Stirling may not be detained, I would propose to exchange him for Governor Montfort Brown, although the latter is no longer in the military line.*

Inclosed you have a list of the officers belonging to the army under my command, who are your prisoners. It is not so correct as I could wish, having received no regular return of the officers of the forty-second and seventy-first regiments, taken this year; but beg leave to refer you to Lieutenant-Colonel Campbell, of the seventy-first, to rectify any omissions that may be; and I am to desire you will put, opposite to their names, such of your officers, of equal rank, as you would have in exchange for them. The

---

* Montfort Brown, Governor of Providence Island, in the West Indies, had been captured by Commodore Hopkins. See Washington's Writings, Vol. III. p. 352.

names of the non-commissioned officers and privates,
prisoners with you, are not sent, being unnecessary;
but the return, herewith inclosed, specifies the number, and I shall redeem them by a like number of
those in my possession; for which purpose I shall
send Mr. Joshua Loring, my Commissary, to Elizabethtown, as a proper place for the exchange of prisoners, on any day you may appoint, wishing it to
be an early one, wherein I presume you will concur.
as it is proposed for the more speedy relief of the
distressed.

As it may be some time before Mr. Lovell arrives
here from Halifax, though I took the first opportunity
of sending for him after your agreement to exchange
him for Governor Skene, I am willing to believe
upon my assurances of Mr. Lovell's being sent to
you immediately on his arrival, that you will no
have any objections to granting the Governor hi
liberty, without delay; and am induced to make th
proposal for your compliance, neither of the person
being connected with military service.

General Carleton has sent from Canada a numbe
of officers and privates, as per return inclosed, t
whom he has given liberty upon their paroles; an
in pursuance of his desire and their engagements t
him, I shall send them to Elizabethtown on th
earliest day. It is, nevertheless, the General's expec
ation, that the exchange of prisoners, as settled b
Captain Forster, in Canada, will be duly complie
with; and I presume you are sufficiently sensible c
the sacred regard that is ever paid to engagemen
of this kind, [not] to suffer any infringement upc
the plighted faith of Colonel Arnold.

It is with much concern, that I cannot close th
letter without representing the ill treatment which,

am too well informed, the King's officers now suffer in common jails, throughout the Province of New England. I apply to your feelings alone for redress, having no idea of committing myself by an act of retaliation upon those in my power.

My Aid-de-camp, charged with the delivery of this letter, will present you with a ball cut and fixed to the end of a nail, taken from a number of the same kind found in the encampments quitted by your troops on the 15th instant. I do not make any comment upon such unwarrantable and malicious practices, being well assured the contrivance has not come to your knowledge. I am, with due regard, Sir,

Your most obedient servant,
WILLIAM HOWE.*

FROM GOVERNOR TRUMBULL.

New Haven, 11 October, 1776.

SIR,

In consequence of your favor, proposing a descent on Long Island, although I was so unhappy as not to be able to meet Generals Clinton and Lincoln at this place, as requested, I applied to the State of Rhode Island, and obtained their consent and orders, that Colonel Richmond, and such part of his battalion as shall not enlist on board the Continental vessels, should assist in the enterprise. Colonel Richmond will accordingly begin his march this day for New

---

* See the answer to this letter, in Washington's Writings, Vol. IV. p. 105.

London, and bring with him the whaleboats collected in Massachusetts Bay and Rhode Island, to the number of between eighty and ninety, which, it is apprehended, will be of great use to the troops ordered on this service, especially to secure and assist their retreat, should it be attempted to be cut off. When Colonel Richmond arrives at New London, he has orders to put himself under the command of such General Officer as your Excellency shall appoint.

I have this day conferred with Colonels McIntosh and Livingston on the subject. They inform me they are supplied with provisions and ammunition for their purpose, and only want such a number of water-craft, as, with the whaleboats divided into three parts, in the whole may be sufficient to transport twelve hundred men; as he means each division to be so placed at the inlets to the Island, as, if cut off from one, he may resort to the other to make his retreat sure, if necessary. These I have ordered for him, and they will be provided and ready without delay.

The number of men he proposes to set out with will doubtless be sufficient for his first attempts. But what reënforcements will be necessary soon to follow, to answer every purpose, your Excellency will judge. They may be thrown over from Stamford or Norwalk very soon, if placed there. I am apprehensive lest some difficulties may arise with regard to the command of this detachment. Colonel McIntosh is a superior officer to Lieutenant-Colonel Livingston; and Richmond is superior in rank to both. Colonel Livingston appears to be a young gentleman of real spirit and abilities, and has every advantage in his knowledge of the Island, and the people there. The other gentlemen have also their merit. May not a difficulty arise as to the command? I hope there will not. As the gentlemen are all well disposed, I hope they will coöperate to the best advantage in the whole. What is further necessary to render their operations effectual, you will please to consider and direct.

Our naval expedition against the ships of the enemy in the Sound is still in contemplation, and preparations are making for the same as fast as we can. Commodore Hopkins writes me, the 5th instant, that the Alfred and Hampden are ready, and that the two new frigates there would be ready in about a week, if they can be manned, neither of them having more than half their complement at that time. Our ship and brig will, we trust, be ready to join them, and when they are equipped it is proposed that they first attack the two frigates that infest the coast and Sound, if they, or either of them, shall appear in their way; otherwise they will proceed directly up the Sound, and give the best account they can of the ships this side Hell Gate, which is the principal object. I am now informed that the two frigates and the Alfred are manned from Colonel Richmond's regiment, which I hope will prove true; but, if not, am in hopes they may be completed by volunteers from Rhode Island and New London; but if they should still fall short of their full complement, I beg leave to suggest to your Excellency whether they could not, without inconveniency, be filled up from some parts of your army, unless the row-galley men, by the enemy's ships passing up the North River, are rendered useless, in which case they may be ordered to some proper place along the Sound, for Commodore Hopkins to take them in.

I have given Commodore Hopkins the utmost assurance to give him all possible intelligence, from

25*

time to time, of the enemy's ships of force this side
Hell Gate, that he may be apprised what he has to
encounter. To that purpose I beg leave to suggest
to your Excellency to give orders to such commanders of the guards, or posts, in sight of the enemy's
ships, to give me intelligence of their force, situation,
and motions, or whether and when joined by any
other of the enemy's ships through Hell Gate.

I have heard that one twenty-four gunship of the
enemy has already passed through to them. Since
my last from Commodore Hopkins, am informed that
the Columbus, Captain Whipple, has arrived in port
at Rhode Island. I have wrote to him to take her
with him, which will make considerable addition to
his force. Please to afford me your advice and fullest
information. I cannot but flatter myself with strong
hopes of advantages to be derived from this adventure of our ships, as well as the expedition to Long
Island. Secrecy in both is of utmost importance. I
am, with great esteem and regard, Sir,

Your most obedient, humble servant,
JONATHAN TRUMBULL.

FROM ROBERT R. LIVINGSTON.

Fishkill, 12 October, 1776.

DEAR SIR,

I should do great injustice to the polite attention
with which your Excellency has listened to the un-
digested opinions which I have sometimes offered, if
I did not, without any apology, give my sentiments
freely on the present alarming condition of this Colony, and submit to your Excellency's better judgment

such measures as will, in my idea, be most likely to insure success.

Since, upon experiment (contrary to the general sentiment), it appears that the passage of the river is not effectually obstructed, the present situation of the army, though not exactly similar, bears some resemblance to that in which it was at New York. The enemy may land above and reduce your Excellency to the necessity of attacking them at their landing, or of suffering them to seize upon passes from which it will be impossible to dislodge them; nor (such is the peculiar situation of the country and the vicinity of the Sound) will it be very difficult so to station themselves as to render every supply going to our camp extremely precarious. This, too, may be done with a part of their forces, while the remainder, having their retreat secured, may, at their leisure, ravage the open country beyond the Highlands, encourage the disaffected, and, by their assistance, carry their arms to Albany, which would, while it distressed the troops in your Excellency's camp, inevitably destroy the Northern army.

To stay at Ticonderoga, without daily supplies, would be impossible; a march to Albany would be equally so, without carriages or horses to carry their provisions or stores, or a sufficient number of boats to transport them in time across Lake George. No other means would be left them but to retreat into New England, without stores, artillery, or provisions, in which case their strength would soon be dissipated by desertions, or the whole body separated through want of necessaries.

These fears may appear ideal to those who do not reflect, that the distance from the Highlands to Albany is but one hundred miles; that the road from

Ticonderoga to Albany is equally distant, through a broken and almost uninhabited country; that most of the militia of this State that can be armed, or depended on, are in your Excellency's camp; and that all the men which we have at present ventured to call upon, in addition to those in service, do not exceed three hundred, and even these we have little reason to expect that we shall obtain. Add to this, that bodies of men are already enlisted throughout this State, and, we have reason to fear, are already collecting under the direction of disguised officers in the Highlands.

Those evils might, in my humble opinion, be fully guarded against by sending a single regiment with a good engineer, to take possession of the passes in the Highlands, and by forming two camps, the one to secure the passes into Connecticut (which might be done by the militia of the New England States), the other at or near the place where the ships now lie in the North River, which would reduce the enemy to the necessity of attacking the lines in front, or expose them, if they landed above, to the danger of being surrounded. The very reputation of such camp being formed, will prevent their making any such attempts, and, in case of any misfortune at New York, will afford a secure retreat, and effectually prevent the enemy from pushing their advantage, more especially if all stores, which are not absolutely necessary for the army, are removed to this place.

Your Excellency has, I dare say, seen the necessity of laying up magazines of provisions, and collecting materials for barracks, at or near this place, that the want of them should not, in case of a defeat, oblige the army to separate. Were not the treasury of this State exhausted by the uncommon expense to which we have been put by the disaffection of our own people, the debt due from the Continent, and the disappointment we have met with in striking money, the Convention of this State would have done something therein at their own risk. Mr. Hubbard promised to give your Excellency some information relative to the forts in the Highlands, and the General that commands. The subject is too delicate for a letter.

Your Excellency sees the opinion I have of your patience and good nature, by my venturing to obtrude upon them these crude and hasty remarks, which I have not even leisure to copy. Perhaps I might find some excuse for them in my anxiety for the great cause your Excellency supports, and my knowledge of a country which you have had no opportunity to explore. I have the honor to be, with the greatest respect, your Excellency's

Most obedient, humble servant,

ROBERT R. LIVINGSTON.

FROM MAJOR-GENERAL GREENE.

Fort Lee, 24 October, 1776.

DEAR SIR,

Inclosed you have a copy of the letter, in answer to mine to Congress, relative to cartridges. As soon as the cartridges come up, they shall be forwarded. Colonel Biddle has wrote to Amboy for ninety thousand that are at that post.

We have collected all the wagons in our power, and sent over. Our people have had extreme hard duty; the common guards, common fatigue, and the extraordinary guards and extraordinary fatigue, for the removal of the stores, and forwarding the provisions, have kept every man on duty.

General Putnam requested a party of men to re-enforce them at Mount Washington. I sent between two and three hundred of Colonel Durkee's regiment. Please to inform me whether your Excellency approves thereof.

We shall get a sufficient quantity of provisions over to-day for the garrison at Fort Washington. General Mifflin thinks it not advisable to pull the barracks down yet. He has hopes of our army returning to that ground for winter-quarters. I think this would be running too great a risk to leave them standing in expectation of such an event. There being several strong fortifications in and about King's Bridge, if the enemy should throw in a thousand or fifteen hundred men, they could cut off our communication effectually; and, as the state of the barracks is, they would find exceeding good cover for the men. But if we were to take the barracks down, if the boards were not removed, it would, in a great measure, deprive them of that advantage. However, I have not had it in my power to do either as yet.

I have directed all the wagons that are on the other side to be employed in picking up the scattered boards about the encampments. I believe, from what I saw yesterday in riding over the grounds, they will amount to several thousands. As soon as we have got these together, I purpose to begin upon the barracks. In the mean time, I should be glad to know if your Excellency has any other orders to give respecting the business.

I have directed the Commissary and Quartermaster-General of this department to lay in provisions and provender, upon the back road to Philadelphia, for twenty thousand men for three months. The principal magazine will be at Aquackanock. I shall fortify it as soon as possible, and secure that post and the pass at the bridge, which is now repaired and fit for an army to pass over, with the baggage and artillery.

I rejoice to hear of the defeat of that vile traitor, Major Rogers, and his party of Tories, though I am exceeding sorry to hear it cost us so brave an officer as Major Greene. I am, with great respect,

Your Excellency's obedient servant,
NATHANAEL GREENE.

FROM MAJOR-GENERAL GREENE.

Fort Lee, 31 October, 1776.

DEAR SIR,

The enemy have possession of Fort Independence, on the heights above King's Bridge. They made their appearance the night before last. We had got every thing of value away. The bridges are cut down, and I gave Colonel Magaw orders to stop the road between the mountains.

I should be glad to know your Excellency's mind about holding all the ground from King's Bridge to the lower lines. If we attempt to hold the ground, the garrison must still be reënforced; but if the garrison is to draw into Mount Washington, and only keep that, the number of troops on the Island is too large.

We are not able to determine, with any certainty, whether those troops, that have taken post above King's Bridge, are the same troops or not that were in or about Haerlem. Several days past they disappeared from below, all at once, and some little time after about fifty boats, full of men, were seen going up towards Hunt's Point, and that evening the enemy were discovered at Fort Independence. We suspect them to be the same troops that were engaged in the Sunday skirmish.

Six officers, belonging to privateers that were taken by the enemy, made their escape last night. They inform me they were taken by the last fleet that came in. They had about six thousand foreign troops on board, one quarter of which had the black scurvy, and died very fast.

Seventy sail of transports and ships fell down to Red Hook. They were bound for Rhode Island, and had on board about three thousand troops. They also inform, that after the Sunday action an officer of distinction was brought into the city, badly wounded.

The ships have come up the river to their station again, a little below their lines. Several deserters from Paulus Hook have come over. They all report that General Howe is wounded, as did those from the fleet. It appears to be a prevailing opinion in the land and sea service.

I forwarded your Excellency a return of troops at this post, and a copy of a plan for establishing magazines. I could wish to know your pleasure as to the magazines, as soon as possible.

I shall reënforce Colonel Magaw with Colonel Rawlings's regiment, until I hear from your Excellency respecting the matter.

The motions of the Grand Army will best determine the propriety of endeavouring to hold all the ground from King's Bridge to the lower lines. I shall be as much on the Island of York as possible, so as not to neglect the duties of my own department.

I can learn no satisfactory account of the action the other day. I am, with great respect,
Your Excellency's obedient servant,
NATHANAEL GREENE.

FROM MAJOR-GENERAL GREENE.

Fort Lee, 7 November, 1776.

DEAR SIR,

By an express from Major Clark, stationed at Dobbs's Ferry, I find the enemy are encamped right opposite, to the number of between three and four thousand; and the Major adds, from their disposition and search after boats, they design to cross the river. A frigate and two transports or provision-ships passed the *chevaux-de-frise* night before last. They were prodigiously shattered, from the fire of our cannon. The same evening, Colonel Tupper attempted passing the ships with the petiaugres, loaded with flour. The enemy manned several barges, two tenders, and a row-galley, and attacked them. Our people ran the petiaugres ashore, and landed and defended them. The enemy attempted to land several times, but were repulsed. The fire lasted about an hour and a half, and the enemy moved off. Colonel Tupper still thinks he can transport the provision in flat-bottomed boats. A second attempt shall be speedily made. We lost one man, mortally wounded.

General Mercer writes me the Virginia troops are coming on. They are now at Trenton. He proposes an attack on Staten Island; but the motions of the enemy are such I think it necessary for them to come forward as fast as possible. On York Island, the enemy have taken possession of the hill, next to Spiten Devil. I think they will not be able to penetrate any farther. There appears to be about fifteen hundred of them. From the enemy's motions, I should be apt to suspect they were retreating from your army, or at least altering their operations. Mr. Lovell, who is at last enlarged from his confinement, reports that Colonel Allen, his fellow prisoner, was informed that transports were getting in readiness to sail, at a moment's warning, sufficient to transport fifteen thousand men.

The officers of Colonel Hand's regiment are here, with enlisting orders. The officers of the Pennsylvania regiments think it a grievance (such of them as are commissioned for the new establishment), that officers of other regiments should have the privilege of enlisting their men before they get orders. I have stopped it until I learn your Excellency's pleasure. Governor Ewing is very much opposed to it. You will please to favor me with a line on the subject. I am, with the greatest respect,

Your Excellency's obedient servant,
NATHANAEL GREENE.

FROM MAJOR-GENERAL GREENE.

Fort Lee, 9 November, 1776.

DEAR SIR,

Your Excellency's letter of the 8th, this moment came to hand. I shall forward the letter to General Stevens by express. The stores at Dobbs's Ferry I had just given orders to the Quartermaster to prepare wagons to remove. I think the enemy will meet with some difficulty in crossing the river at Dobbs's Ferry. However, it is not best to trust too much to the expected difficulties they may meet there.

By the letter that will accompany this, and was to have gone last night by Major Mifflin, your Excellency will see what measures I took before your favor came to hand. The passing of the ships up the river is, to be sure, a full proof of the insufficiency of the obstructions in the river to stop the ships from going up; but that garrison employs double the number of men to invest it that we have to occupy it. They must keep troops at King's Bridge, to prevent a communication with the country; and they dare not leave a very small number, for fear our people should attack them.

Upon the whole, I cannot help thinking the garrison is of advantage; and I cannot conceive the garrison to be in any great danger. The men can be brought off at any time, but the stores may not be so easily removed; yet I think they can be got off, in spite of them, if matters grow desperate. This post is of no importance only in conjunction with Mount Washington. I was over there last evening. The enemy seem to be disposing matters to besiege the place; but Colonel Morgan thinks it will take them till December expires before they can carry it. If the enemy do not find it an object of importance, they will not trouble themselves about it; if they do, it is open proof they feel an injury from our possessing it. Our giving it up will open a free communication with the country, by the way of King's Bridge, that must be a great advantage to them and injury to us.

If the enemy cross the river, I shall follow your Excellency's advice respecting the cattle and forage. Those measures, however cruel in appearance, were ever my maxims of war, in the defence of a country; in attacking, they would be very improper.

By this express, several packets from Congress are forwarded to you.

I shall collect our whole strength, and watch the motions of the enemy; and pursue such measures, for the future, as circumstances render necessary.

As I have your Excellency's permission, I shall order General Stephen on as far as Aquackanock, at least. That is an important pass. I am fortifying it as fast as possible.

I am, dear Sir, your most obedient,
And very humble servant,
NATHANAEL GREENE.

FROM MAJOR-GENERAL LEE.*

Camp at Philipsburg, 12 November, 1776;
9 o'clock, P. M.

DEAR GENERAL,

This instant came express, from Colonel Tupper, (stationed opposite to Dobbs's Ferry), one David Keech. The substance of his intelligence is as follows. That the enemy began their march at nine this morning, down the river, with their baggage, artillery, &c.; that the man-of-war and two store-ships had just set sail, and were making down (I mean those which came up last); that three ships still lie

------

* General Lee returned from the Southern Department and joined the army under Washington on the 14th of October.

off Tarrytown and Sing Sing, two at the former, and one at the latter. Keech says the whole army have quitted Dobbs's Ferry, and imagines the rear have by this time reached King's Bridge.

I am far from being satisfied with the conduct of our scouts. I do not think they venture far enough, for they generally bring back very lame, imperfect accounts. But I have projected a plan for breaking in, at least, upon Rogers's party, and believe I shall succeed. The sentence on Austin is, that he should be reprimanded; but I have ordered a new court-martial, with a charge of wanton, barbarous conduct, unbecoming, not only an officer, but a human creature.

General Lincoln and the Massachusetts Committee are using their efforts to detain the militia; whether they will succeed, heaven only knows. Hitchcock and Varnum do not recollect the recommendation of General Greene, but I have ordered them to give me a list of those who they think ought to be recommended; for it is now too late to refer to Greene, as the Commissioners are expected every hour. I wish to God you were here, as I am in a manner a stranger to their respective merits. When the list is made out, I shall inform myself, as well as I can, if their recommendation is impartial, and proceed accordingly. I am, dear General,

Yours, most sincerely,

CHARLES LEE.

26 *

Camp, 19 November, 1776.

DEAR GENERAL,

The recommendation of General Greene, which you transmitted to me, threw the officers to whom I communicated it into so great a flame of discontent, that I ventured, notwithstanding your orders, to hesitate. They accused him of partiality to his connections and townsmen, to the prejudice of men of manifestly superior merit. Indeed, it appears, from the concurrent testimony of unbiased persons, that some of the subjects he recommended were wretched. In short, I was so stunned with their clamor, that I delayed till the arrival of the Committee, for which I ought to ask your pardon. But, at the same time, I think the delay has been salutary.

My objections to moving from our present post are, as I observed before, that it would give us the air of being frightened; it would expose a fine fertile country to their ravages; and I must add, that we are as secure as we could be in any position whatever. We are pretty well disencumbered of our impediments, which I propose depositing in or about Crompond, which (though I confess I have not reconnoitred the place), from its situation, must be full and safe, and is much more centrical than Peekskill. If on further examination, it has any material disadvantages, we can easily move from thence.

As to ourselves, light as we are, several retreats present themselves. In short, if we keep a good look out, we are in no danger; but I must entreat your Excellency to enjoin the officers posted at Fort Lee to give us the quickest intelligence, if they ob serve any embarkations of troops in the North River. Our scouts are of late grown more vigilant, and make prisoners. The militia, according to their laudable custom, would not stay a moment beyond their usual time. Oh, General, why would you be overpersuaded by men of inferior judgment to your own? It was a cursed affair.

Yours, most affectionately,
CHARLES LEE.

P. S. The returns of the soldiers of the different regiments now in the hands of the enemy, according to the mode you require, are not yet made out, but will soon, and shall be sent.

FROM MAJOR-GENERAL LEE.

Camp, Philipsburg, 26 November, 1776.

DEAR GENERAL,

It never was my idea to leave the Highlands unguarded, but only for expedition's sake that Heath should detach two thousand of his corps immediately over the river, and to replace these two thousand by the same number, the most lightly accoutred, from this body here, till the main body, with their baggage, cannon, &c., could move. I conceived this movement could be attended with no risk, as he has now nothing to guard but the western passages; for there is no possibility of their approaching by the eastern, having, as I can learn, no vessels on the eastern river to transport their cannon, and the road from King's Bridge by land is now almost impracticable.*

---

* General Heath was stationed at Peekskill for the defence of the country in the neighbourhood of the Highlands. A full account of the

The want of carriages, and this disappointment with respect to Heath, but above all, the alarms we have been thrown into by the activity of the Tories, and the important consideration of leaving this country in a tolerable state of security on my departure, have still detained me here. The enemy kept a very considerable part of their force on this side of King's Bridge till yesterday, so considerable, indeed, that from what we saw we conceived the numbers transported to the Jerseys not near so great as you were taught to think. This, and the apprehension of their gleaning all the forage of this district, contributed to the other considerations I have mentioned, have detained me so much longer than I could have wished.

Yesterday they drew themselves in, and we made a sweep of the country from Phillips's house. Part of the army have moved on. I set out to-morrow. No militia are come in to cover the country. I have wrote most pressing letters on this subject to Trumbull, and hope they will have effect. I have been equally urgent with Mr. Bowdoin for blankets, shoes, &c. Indeed, our soldiers are not in a moving condition, but seem well disposed, and engage themselves beyond expectation. But we are in great want of money for bounty. I have been under the necessity, without authority, to draw for this purpose. Several deserters, come out to-day, inform us that a considerable embarkation is made for Amboy.

I shall take care to obey your Excellency's order, in regard to my march, as exactly as possible; and am,

Dear General, yours,

CHARLES LEE.

---

particulars here alluded to may be found in Heath's Memoirs, p. 88. Other letters from General Lee at this time are contained in Washington's Writings, Vol. IV. Appendix, p. 530.

FROM GENERAL CADWALADER.*

Bristol, 26 December, 1776.

SIR,

The river was so full of ice that it was impossible
to pass above Bristol, where I intended, and therefore concluded to make an attempt at Dunks's Ferry.
As soon as it was dark, I sent down all the boats I
could muster, and marched down about eight o'clock.
I embarked a few men to line the river, and prevent any person escaping to give intelligence to the
enemy; and these were followed by a part of the
first battalion of militia, then two field-pieces, with
which I went over to see if it was practicable to
land them, and, upon examination, found it was impossible, the ice being very thick.   Upon reporting
this to the field-officers, they were all of opinion
that it would not be proper to proceed without cannon.   During this time the third battalion was landed.   We concluded to withdraw the troops that had
passed, but could not effect it till near four o'clock
this morning.   The whole then were ordered to march
for Bristol.

I imagine the badness of the night must have prevented you from passing, as you intended.†   Our
men turned out cheerfully.   We had about eighteen
hundred rank and file, including artillery.   It will be
impossible for the enemy to pass the river till the
ice will bear.   Would it not be proper to attempt to

---

* Commanding the Pennsylvania militia.

† Notwithstanding the badness of the weather, Washington had crossed
the Delaware with his army the night before, and captured the Hessians
at Trenton. See Washington's Writings, Vol. IV. p. 541.

cross below, and join General Putnam, who was to go over from Philadelphia to-day, with five hundred men, which number, added to the four hundred Jersey militia which Colonel Griffin left there, would make a formidable body. This would cause a diversion, that would favor any attempt you may design in future, and would expose their baggage and stores, if they attempt to cross. It is impossible, in our present situation, to coöperate with General Putnam. The militia will be easier kept together by being in motion. We shall have some service from Colonel Hitchcock's brigade, whose time of enlistment will be up in a few days. We have procured a considerable number of shoes, stockings, and breeches for them. They are in good spirits, and enlist very fast. I am, Sir, with great respect,

Your most obedient, humble servant,
JOHN CADWALADER.

FROM ROBERT MORRIS.

Philadelphia, 26 December, 1776.
DEAR SIR,

I have just received yours of yesterday, and will duly attend to those things you recommend to my consideration. At present I have to inclose you a letter from Congress, which I suppose contains their resolves of the 20th instant; but as the President does not say, in his letter to me, that they are inclosed to you, and as it is necessary you should have them, I take the liberty to send herewith a copy of them.*

---

* On the 20th of December, Congress "Resolved, That the President write to General Washington, and desire him to send a flag to General

I am well pleased to see the attention they pay General Lee; and I shall make it a point to collect and send your Excellency, soon as possible, the one hundred half johannes they order.* You will observe Mr. Clymer, Mr. Walton, and myself are appointed a Committee to transact the Continental business here, that may be necessary and proper; and I apprehend that it will frequently be necessary that we should know the substance of your correspondence with Congress.† Your letters to the President, if sent open under our cover, shall always meet despatch, and their contents kept secret; and when you think it improper we should see them before the Congress, seal them, and they shall go forward untouched; and, if you do not approve of submitting them to our inspection at all, write us freely, and your wishes in that respect shall be complied with.

We have just heard of your success at Trenton. The account is but imperfect; but we learn you are master of that place, and all the baggage and stores our enemy had there, and of three hundred prisoners,‡ and that your troops were still in pursuit of the

---

Howe, and inquire in what manner General Lee, who has been taken prisoner, is treated; and, if he finds that he is not treated agreeably to his rank and character, to send a remonstrance to General Howe on the subject; and further to inquire of General Howe, whether he will grant permission to send General Lee such supplies of money as may be necessary to support him, during his confinement, in a manner suitable to his rank in the service of the United States."

* General Lee had been captured by the enemy at Baskingridge, on the 13th of December, and was taken to New York. See Sparks's Life of Charles Lee, in the *Library of American Biography*, second series, Vol. VIII. p. 143.

† The Congress had recently removed to Baltimore, and left this Committee in Philadelphia.

‡ This number is erroneous. Washington reported to Congress the number of prisoners to be "twenty-three field-officers, and eight hundred and eighty-six men."

flying enemy. I have just wrote to Congress, and told them thus much, as the substance of an account just come down; and I told them further, I had been informed that you had executed in this matter your part of a well-concerted plan; that General Heath, at Hackensack, had orders from you, and that General Ewing and Colonel Cadwalader, also, had orders to cross the Delaware at the same time you did, but had been prevented by driving ice.

Good news sets all the animal spirits to work. The imagination is heated, and I could not help adding, that I expected General Heath was to continue his march towards Brunswick, which would draw the attention of any troops posted there and at Princeton, while you would pursue the flying heroes to Bordentown and Burlington, where Ewing and Cadwalader would stop them, and cut off their communication with the two thousand Hessians and Highlanders, that came after Griffin; nay, I almost promised them that you should, by following up this first blow, finish the campaign of 1776 with that *éclat* that your numerous friends and admirers have long wished for. I congratulate you most heartily on what is done; and am, with perfect esteem, dear Sir,

Your Excellency's most obedient servant,

ROBERT MORRIS.

FROM GENERAL CADWALADER.

Burlington, 10 o'clock, 27 December, 1776.

SIR,

As I did not hear from you this morning, and being prepared to embark, I concluded you were still on this side, and therefore embarked, and landed about fifteen hundred men about two miles above Bristol. After a considerable number were landed, I had information from the Paymaster of Colonel Hitchcock's brigade, that you had crossed over from Trenton. This defeated the scheme of joining your army. We were much embarrassed which way to proceed. I thought it most prudent to retreat; but Colonel Reed was of opinion that we might safely proceed to Burlington, and recommended it warmly, lest it should have a bad effect on the militia, who were twice disappointed. The landing in open daylight must have alarmed the enemy, and we might have been cut off by all their force collected to this place. We had intelligence, immediately afterward, that the enemy had left the Black Horse and Mount Holley. Upon this we determined to proceed to Burlington.

Colonel Reed and two other officers went on, from one point to another, till they came to Bordentown, where they found the coast clear. Colonel Reed and Colonel Coxe are now there, and we shall march, at four to-morrow morning, for that place. This information has induced me to proceed, though not quite conformable to your orders, which I received on the march this afternoon. If you should think proper to cross over, it may be easily effected at the place where we passed. A pursuit would keep up the panic.

They went off with great precipitation, and pressed all the wagons in their reach. I am told many of them are gone to South Amboy. If we can drive them from West Jersey, the success will raise an army by next spring, and establish the credit of the Continental money to support it. I shall write to-morrow, I hope, from Trenton. I am, Sir,

        Your most obedient, very humble servant,
                  JOHN CADWALADER.

P. S. I have two six-pounders, brass, and two three-pounders, iron.

FROM BRIGADIER-GENERAL MIFFLIN.

        Bristol, Saturday evening, 8 o'clock,
              28 December, 1776.

DEAR GENERAL,

The inclosed I have this minute received from an express sent by my order to General Cadwalader. The General, not knowing that I was here, did not write to me, and as I supposed the contents of importance in my movements, I took the liberty to open the letter, for which I must plead only the occasion in excuse.

I came here at four o'clock this afternoon. Five hundred men, sent from Philadelphia yesterday, crossed to Burlington this morning. This evening I sent over near three hundred more. To-morrow seven or eight hundred shall follow. I will cross in the morning, and endeavour to form them into regiments, and a brigade. They consist of many different corps, and want much regulation.

If your Excellency has any orders for me, other

than to join General Cadwalader as soon as possible, please to favor me with such as are necessary, and I will punctually obey them. Pennsylvania is at length roused, and coming in great numbers to your Excellency's aid. Mr. Hall will return with your orders. I am informed that we cannot cross at Bordentown, nor at any place between that place and this. I have no doubt of effecting it here, having sent from Philadelphia in the morning several fine boats, which are now here.

I most heartily congratulate your Excellency on your late capital stroke, and wish most ardently a repetition. I am, with great affection and attachment,

Your Excellency's obedient servant,

THOMAS MIFFLIN.

FROM ROBERT MORRIS.

Philadelphia, 30 December, 1776.

SIR,

I have just received your favor of this day, and sent to General Putnam to detain the express until I collect the hard money you want, which you may depend shall be sent, in one specie or other, with this letter, and a list thereof shall be inclosed herein.

I had long since parted with very considerable sums of hard money to Congress; therefore must collect from others, and, as matters now stand, it is no easy matter. I mean to borrow silver, and promise payment in gold, and will then collect the gold in the best manner I can. Whilst on this subject, let me inform you that there are upwards of twenty thousand dollars in silver at Ticonderoga. They have no particular use for it, and I think you might as well send a party to bring it away, and lodge it in a safe place convenient for any purposes for which it may hereafter be wanted.

I gave Mr. Commissary Wharton an order for forty thousand dollars this morning, and pressed him to attend most diligently to your supplies. I will send for him again, know what is done, and add springs to his movements, if I can. I wish he was more silent, prudent, &c.; but I fancy he is active. Whatever I can do shall be done for the good of the service. I ever am, dear Sir,

Your Excellency's obedient, humble servant,

ROBERT MORRIS.

P. S. Hearing that you are in want of a quarter cask of wine, I have procured a good one, which Mr. Commissary Wharton will send up.

FROM ROBERT MORRIS.

Philadelphia, 1 January, 1777.

SIR,

I was honored with your favor of yesterday by Mr. Howell, late last night, and, ever solicitous to comply with your requisitions, I am up very early this morning to despatch a supply of fifty thousand dollars to your Excellency. You will receive that sum with this letter; but it will not be got away so early as I could wish, for none concerned in this movement, except myself, are up. I shall rouse them immediately. It gives me great pleasure that you have engaged the troops to continue, and if further occasional supplies of money are necessary, you may depend on my exertions either in a public or private capacity.

The year 1776 is over. I am heartily glad of it, and hope you nor America will ever be plagued with such another. Let us accept the success at Trenton as a presage of future fortunate events; and under that impression, I do most sincerely wish you a successful campaign in 1777, to crown you with immortal honors, in reward of the dangers and fatigues of war; and that you may, for many, many years after, enjoy the sweets of peace and domestic happiness, in reward of your social virtues. With sincere esteem and regard, I ever am, Sir,

Your obedient servant,
ROBERT MORRIS.

FROM THE PRESIDENT OF CONGRESS.

Baltimore, 1 January, 1777.

SIR,

I am to acknowledge the receipt of your several favors, to the 27th ultimo. Your letter of that date, containing the very agreeable intelligence of the success of the Continental arms under your command, was last night delivered to me by your Aid-de-camp, Colonel Baylor, together with the Hessian standard. I entertain the most pleasing expectation that our affairs will henceforth assume a better complexion. Your account of the behaviour and spirit of the troops, gave the highest satisfaction to Congress; and

27*

manifests a disposition which may prove the forerunner of future success.

Considering the unfavorable temper of the men, broken by fatigue and ill fortune, the happy event of the expedition appears the more extraordinary. But troops properly inspired, and animated by a just confidence in their leader, will often exceed expectation, or the limits of probability. As it is entirely to your wisdom and conduct the United States are indebted for the late success of their arms, the pleasure you must naturally feel on the occasion will be pure and unmixed. May you still proceed in the same manner to acquire that glory, which, by your disinterested and magnanimous behaviour, you so highly merit.

I inclose to you a copy of resolves transmitted to General Schuyler, relative to the Northern Department, and also sundry other resolves relative to your own immediate department, which are all the Congress have come into since I wrote you last. I have forwarded to all the States copies of the resolves, vesting you with the powers which I had the pleasure of transmitting in my last, accompanied with letters explaining the reasons on which Congress acted in that particular.*

From the inclosed resolve, you will perceive Congress have determined, that a horse, properly caparisoned, be presented to your Aid-de-camp, Colonel Baylor, and to recommend it to you to promote him to be a Colonel of a regiment of Light Horse. As the Congress have been pleased to intrust me with

* See the letter and resolves, here alluded to, in Washington's Writings, Vol. IV. p. 550.

the execution of this resolve, I must beg you will do me the favor to give directions to the Quartermaster, or other proper person, to purchase as handsome a horse, for this purpose, as can be found. The reason of my making this application, is an information I had received, that some Light Horse were taken at Trenton, and are to be publicly sold for the benefit of the soldiery. Should this be the case, I must further ask the favor of you to give directions at the same time to purchase one or two for my own use. The money shall be immediately remitted, whatever it may be. I should be glad to know what kind of horse furniture you think the most proper, as I would, by all means, wish to procure the best; but, without your advice and assistance, I am apprehensive I shall not succeed. If the horses are to be had, be pleased to order them to be sent to me, and every expense shall be paid arising thereon.

This recommendation of Colonel Baylor, I doubt not, will meet with your approbation, and that, on his return from Virginia, you will give him a commission, with such pay as you shall think suitable and adequate.

Wishing you, very sincerely, the compliments of the season, I have the honor to be, with every sentiment of esteem and regard, Sir,

Your most obedient and very humble servant,

JOHN HANCOCK, *President*.

P. S. I shall send you the letter-books by the first safe hand. By this opportunity, I send you four bundles, containing two hundred commissions; the rest shall immediately follow.

FROM MAJOR-GENERAL LINCOLN.*

Peekskill, 4 January, 1777.

DEAR GENERAL,

I have just arrived here; find only part of two regiments of the militia, from the Massachusetts. The badness of the roads hath much retarded the troops. I have left some of our best officers at different posts to forward them, and provide every necessary to facilitate their march. I flatter myself, from the provision that hath been made and is now making, that the time will not be long, nor the period distant, when they shall rendezvous at your Excellency's head-quarters, wherever they may be, or such other place to which they may be ordered. Nothing shall be neglected, in my power, speedily to effect this.

Soon after advice was forwarded to your Excellency by Mr. Bowdoin, that the State of Massachusetts Bay had ordered out about six thousand of their militia, to reënforce the Continental army, the General Court were informed, by General Schuyler, that the time for which the men, doing duty at Ticonderoga, engaged to serve, was near expiring; and that the forts there would, in all probability, be left in a short time too defenceless, unless they could be reënforced by the militia; the consequence of which might be extremely injurious to the cause of America. He therefore urged the Massachusetts to send him at Albany some of their militia, in the most pressing and energetic terms, in order that he might succour

---

* General Lincoln, at this time, had command of the Massachusetts militia. He was appointed a Major-General in the Continental army on the 19th of February following.

those forts, if he should find it necessary. The Court thereon ordered two of their most western regiments to march directly for Albany.

In consequence of an application from the Commissioners assembled at Providence from the New England States, appointed, among other things, to adopt measures for the immediate defence of the State of Rhode Island, and the neighbouring States, the Court of Massachusetts Bay have halted in that State the men raised to reënforce the Continental army in the counties of Plymouth, Barnstable, and Bristol, which will amount to ten or eleven hundred. The remainder, from the best returns I can obtain, will a little exceed four thousand, officers included.

I left Providence last Monday, in the forenoon. There were no late accounts from the Island of Rhode Island. A few days before, some ships, to the number of ten or twelve, had left it and gone up the Sound. Whether they had troops on board, or not, we could not learn. The accounts, with regard to the number of troops on the Island, are so various that no good judgment can be formed. Some positively affirm that there are not more than three thousand five hundred, others, with as much assurance, declare that there are nine thousand. From the best information I could obtain at Bristol and Howland's Ferry, their numbers do not much exceed, if any, five thousand men. Indeed, I have sometimes doubted, from their manœuvres, whether they amount to that number. I am, with the most perfect regard and esteem, Sir,

Your most obedient, humble servant,

BENJAMIN LINCOLN.

FROM THE PRESIDENT OF CONGRESS.

Baltimore, 6 January, 1777.

SIR,

The inclosed resolves, which I have the honor of transmitting, call for your immediate attention; and I am to request you will take measures in pursuance thereof, as soon as possible. General Lee's situation seems to be extremely dangerous and critical, and from General Howe's behaviour to him, it is highly probable he will be brought to a trial for desertion. General Lee, it is said by Mr. Eustace, his Aid-de-camp, having addressed two letters to General Howe, received them both back again, unopened, and inclosed under a cover directed to *Lieutenant-Colonel Lee*. I hope the flag, which Congress ordered to be sent to make inquiry into the manner in which he was treated, has been despatched, and a remonstrance, in consequence of it, should the information you have received of his treatment have rendered that step necessary.

You will please to propose an exchange of the six Hessian field-officers for him; and at the same time make inquiry whether the report which Congress have heard of Mrs. Stockton's being confined in a common jail by the enemy, has any truth in it or not.

By a letter, which Congress yesterday received from Mr. Morris, we are informed that General Cadwalader, with the troops under him, had joined your army; that the enemy were at Trenton; that the two armies were divided only by a creek; and that a general engagement was hourly expected. In the mean time Congress are infinitely anxious to hear the event, and humbly hope that victory has declared in favor of those whose sacred cause should inspire them with ardor, on every solemn appeal to that Being who hateth all injustice, tyranny, and oppression. I have the honor to be, with every sentiment of respect, Sir,

Your most obedient and very humble servant,

JOHN HANCOCK, *President.*

P. S. If the desire of Congress to procure General Lee's exchange cannot be effected, and the enemy, preferring the gratification of revenge to the civility they owe their Hessian auxiliaries, determine to keep or to abuse him, it will be very agreeable to Congress that their determination, with the inclosed resolve, be made known to the Hessians as fully as possible. To secure General Lee as effectually as may be from personal insult and injury, Congress have come to the present resolution; which you, Sir, are desired to convey to General Howe, with all convenient despatch. It will be very agreeable to Congress, that the Hessian field-officer intended to be exchanged for Colonel Ethan Allen, be sent to notify it to General Howe, taking his parole to return in a fixed time, if Colonel Allen is not returned in his place. It will fall within the wish of Congress, if Colonel Rahl, or one of the Hessian officers, should be also sent with the flag proposing the exchange of General Lee; but the propriety of it is submitted to you.

We have had an imperfect account of the engagement at Trenton, and anxiously wait for further particulars. It was in hopes of receiving them that I detained the express till this morning.

FROM ROBERT MORRIS, GEORGE CLYMER, AND GEORGE
WALTON.*

Philadelphia, 7 January, 1777.

SIR,

We were this day honored with your favor of the
5th instant, which arrived in time to forward the inclosures by post. We waited, with impatience, to
learn the consequence of your late movements, and
have been highly gratified; at the same time, we see
plainly some important event is still to happen. The
enemy must mean to evacuate the Jerseys, or give
you battle. The latter may be ruinous in its consequences to either party, and therefore it is probable
will only be sought for by those that have the superiority. This, we fondly hope, will fall to your lot, if
joined by General Heath and General McDougall,
and the Jersey militia, as we are taught to expect
will be the case. Should they lose a battle, or evacuate Jersey, surely they cannot afterwards make out
a decent paragraph for Gaines's infamous paper, after
being outgeneralled and obliged to abandon the country they thought themselves securely possessed of.

Your Excellency will find inclosed a paper herein,
drawn up by a Captain Gamble, lately a prisoner on
board the fleet in New York. He declares that the
treatment of both sea and land prisoners, in that

---

* Congress adjourned from Philadelphia to Baltimore on the 12th of
December, and assembled in the latter city on the 20th. The following
resolution was passed on the 21st: — " That Robert Morris, George Clymer, and George Walton, Esquires, be a Committee of Congress, with
powers to execute such Continental business as may be proper and
necessary to be done at Philadelphia."

place, is shocking to humanity. This man deserves credit, and his account of their ill usage is confirmed by all the prisoners that come from thence. As to the information that he gives at the bottom of his paper, he says he will forfeit his life if every tittle of it is not as near to the truth as possible for an inquisitive man, in his situation, to come at. We think this would be a good time to remonstrate to General Howe and Lord Howe against the base usage our people meet with, and to threaten immediate retaliation on the British prisoners in our possession, if they do not alter their conduct.

It is probable General Howe may say it is contrary to orders, and not with his knowledge, if our people suffer; but this is not sufficient. Our poor soldiers and sailors are perishing for want of food, fresh air, and cleanliness, whilst those of theirs, in our possession, are feasting on the fat of this land. They have said we treat them well through fear. It is time to convince them we are not afraid, although we are actuated by principles of humanity. But those principles now dictate the necessity of severe usage to British officers in particular, that they may hereafter make it a point, for their own sakes, to see proper care taken of those that fall within their power.

Depend on it, good Sir, we do not write in this style to gratify any feelings of our own. They are all repugnant to what we propose. Lieutenant Josiah has just called on us, and confirms the account of ill usage, &c. He says he was exchanged for Lieutenant Ball, and that no person has been given up for Lieutenant Boger, now in New York. There is a Captain Burke, that was formerly Captain Manly's Lieutenant in his successful cruise. Burke succeeded to the command of Manly's vessel; was taken by the Liverpool frigate, to which Mr. Boger belongs; and Captain Bellen sent Burke to New York for the express purpose of having him exchanged for Boger; and, as he is said to be a very good officer, has been ill used, and suffered a good deal, we dare say your Excellency will demand his release by the first flag. We have the honor to be, Sir,

Your Excellency's obedient servants,

ROBERT MORRIS,
GEORGE CLYMER,
GEORGE WALTON.

FROM BRIGADIER-GENERAL ARNOLD.

Providence, 13 January, 1777.

DEAR GENERAL,

Yesterday I arrived here, having previously done all in my power to forward on the militia from the Massachusetts Bay and Connecticut, upwards of six thousand of which I hope are in the Jerseys before this time.

There are, at this place and in the vicinity, about two thousand men, part of six thousand ordered from the New England States. The others are on their march, and expected in, in a few days. The enemy's force on Rhode Island, by the best intelligence, is five or six thousand; one half foreigners, and some few invalids. We are informed, by several persons who left Newport within a few days, that General Clinton is going home in the Asia, and has sent his baggage on board, and that the troops have orders to hold themselves in readiness to embark at a minute's notice, perhaps for New York. I believe they have no intention of penetrating the country at present. I beg leave, though late, to congratulate your Excellency on your success at Trenton. It was a most happy stroke, and has greatly raised the sinking spirits of the country.

We this minute have advice, by a letter from Governor Trumbull, of your further success near Princeton; and report says, Generals Putnam and Mifflin have killed and taken two regiments near Bristol. We believe this true, as the intelligence comes from Newport.* People in general are in high spirits. This seems a most favorable crisis to dislodge the enemy from the country. Heaven grant your Excellency may be able to effect it, and may peace and laurels crown your successes!

About twelve or fifteen hundred of the enemy are dispersed in all the farm-houses on Rhode Island. As soon as the militia arrives, I hope we shall be able to give a good account of some of them.

I beg leave to recommend to your Excellency, Captain Samuel Mansfield, to command a company of artillery. He was a Lieutenant of artillery last summer in the Northern Department, and afterwards Captain of a galley in two actions, and behaved with great prudence and bravery. Being anxious to continue in the service, and much wanted here, I have desired him to engage a number of men. If your Excellency should think proper to appoint him, his company will be soon filled up, and I dare be responsible for his conduct.

A Quartermaster is much wanted here. One is ap-

---

* This report proved to be erroneous.

pointed by the State for their own troops, but they are not able to furnish him with cash. I am, dear General,

Your most obedient, humble servant,

BENEDICT ARNOLD.

FROM MAJOR-GENERAL HEATH.

Williams's Tavern, 19 January, 1777.

DEAR GENERAL,

I have just received the honor of yours of the 14th and 17th instant.

Yesterday morning, about sunrise, our troops, in three divisions, arrived in the neighbourhood of Fort Independence ; the right division by the Albany Road, the centre by Stephen Ward's, and the left by East Chester. Upon our approach, the enemy fled to Fort Independence, leaving fifteen muskets at one place, and ten at another, besides blankets, &c.

I summoned the fort to surrender. I have taken the liberty to inclose a copy. The answer to the summons was verbal, and in substance, that, as the Americans were excepted, they, although Britons, had no answer to return. They afterwards fired a number of cannon at us from the fort, which we returned. We are just informed, by two deserters from the fort, that the garrison consists of about three hundred and fifty men; that the last night they had a twelve-pounder sent to the fort, and that General Agnew moved up yesterday with his brigade, and took post at the northernmost woody hill, between Fort Washington and King's Bridge, and about twelve hundred Hessians near the fort. Between two and three hundred Hessians are in the houses just over the bridge.

We took one light-horseman, with horse complete, and one soldier, and have had one man killed by a cannon ball this day. To-morrow we intend to make an attack upon the Hessians at the bridge, if they should not be reënforced. They have two pieces of cannon well posted. Our troops are all militia, and, although perhaps as good as any militia, yet they are not disciplined. Our numbers are about three thousand, but they begin to go home already. The want of covering, the weather cold, &c., causes many complaints. Much will depend on the success of our attack to-morrow.

I have approved of the sentence of the court-martial on Strang, and have ordered him to be executed on Wednesday next at eleven o'clock before noon.

A Hessian Major, son of one of their Generals, commands Fort Independence. I have the honor to be, very respectfully,

Your Excellency's most humble servant,
WILLIAM HEATH.

FROM WILLIAM DUER.

Camp in Westchester County, 28 January, 1777.

I beg leave to introduce to your Excellency's acquaintance Mr. Sacket, a member of the Convention of the State, a man of honor, and of firm attachment to the American cause.

He will communicate to your Excellency some measures taken by him and myself, which, if properly prosecuted, may be of infinite utility to the present military operations. I have, therefore, recom-

28 *

mended it to him to wait on you in person, in hopes that some systematical plan may be adopted and prosecuted for facilitating your manœuvres against the British army.

To say more in a letter, might be imprudent. I shall, therefore, content myself with observing, that Mr. Sacket is, as I know by experience, a person of intrigue and secrecy, well calculated to prosecute such measures as you shall think conducive to give success to your generous exertions in the cause of America.

Your Excellency will likewise receive from Mr. Sacket a confidential account of our operations in this quarter. I wish I could say they had been conducted in such a manner as to create, either a diversion in favor of the army in Jersey, or, at least, to drive the enemy from this county. On the contrary, it is obvious to every discerning person, that we have been insulted by a handful of traitorous banditti, and that we run a risk of either being routed or cut off by a night surprise, or of abandoning this part of the country with disgrace.

As I have been appointed, by the Convention of the State of New York, a member of a Committee for coöperating in the design formed by your Excellency for driving the enemy from this quarter, I esteem it my duty to inform you, that I have no manner of doubt but it has been in our power to cut off the communication of Fort Independence with York Island, and to make ourselves masters of the garrison, with a loss noways proportionable to the benefits which would inevitably result from such a measure. This is still in our power; but how long it will continue so, I will not pretend to determine. Certain I am, that, unless a decisive and systematic plan is devised and prosecuted in a very short time, your success will be counterbalanced by our disgrace; that many good officers and men, who have come down as volunteers, will return home; that the militia, should any come in, will grow languid; that our enemies will triumph; and that the timid Whigs, who have been roused from their late lethargy or despair, from your Excellency's successful efforts, will either relapse into the same supineness, or take an active part with our enemies.

It would be needless and impertinent in me to point out to your Excellency the very great advantages, which would result from our making ourselves masters of this county. I shall only content myself with observing that, if no other purposes were to be answered by this expedition but those of laying up magazines of forage for the next campaign, the raising of recruits for the Continental army, and preventing the disaffected from taking part with the enemy, it is an object worthy our greatest exertions.

Brigadier-General Parsons, who came down with us from Peekskill, is gone to Connecticut, not choosing, as I conceive, to run the risk of his reputation by a longer stay here. Colonel Dubois, who has come down with the York militia as a volunteer, and who has repeatedly offered his service to destroy King's Bridge, will, I fear, return to-morrow, despairing to see any thing effectual done.

Should your Excellency wish to know to what our want of success is to be attributed, I must beg leave to refer to your own judgment of the character of men; observing only that it is my private opinion that, if measures could be devised, without injuring the public service, that either General Mifflin, General Parsons, or General Clinton, could direct our opera-

tions in this part of the county of Westchester, that
the enemy would not only be driven from this county, but other measures might probably be devised for
pushing our success and harassing the enemy. At
the request of General Heath, I devised means of
his obtaining the best intelligence of the enemy's
strength and disposition. Would to heaven we had
profited by it! I write with an aching heart, and in
a great hurry, so that your Excellency will excuse
both my freedom and inaccuracy. I have long intended to return; but shall wait the return of Mr.
Sacket, in hopes that some more regular counsels
may be formed, and more vigorous measures prosecuted, in this quarter.

As I am informed that your Excellency is raising
several new battalions, the officers of which are to be
of your appointment, I beg leave to inform you that
Mr. John Livingston, a son of Mr. Robert Livingston,
lord of the manor of that name, is anxious to enter
the service in a regiment to be commanded by gentlemen. He is a young gentleman of a high spirit,
of honor, and undoubted bravery. I have, therefore,
no doubt but he will raise his own reputation, and
do justice to your appointment, if you should think
proper to give him the offer of a Lieutenant-Colonel's
commission. I beg to know from your Excellency
whether my application can be complied with. It is
with great reluctance I ever venture to recommend;
but I know this young gentleman so well, that I
will risk my reputation upon his behaving himself
with distinguished resolution, should he have an opportunity of embracing the military profession. I am,
with great respect,

Your Excellency's most obedient, humble servant,

WILLIAM DUER.

FROM MAJOR-GENERAL HEATH.

Burling's, near Ward's, 30 January, 1777.

DEAR GENERAL,

I have just received the honor of yours of the 27th instant. The last evening we moved back from the neighbourhood of King's Bridge; General Lincoln's troops to Dobbs's Ferry and Tarrytown; the Connecticut militia, to New Rochelle; and the York militia, towards White Plains. This remove was for the following reasons.

We could not reduce the fort by cannonade, being destitute of proper artillery. As to taking of it by storm, it is surrounded by *chevaux-de-frise*, hooked together; yet I think it might have been taken, if we had been so happy as to have had a few Continental troops. But our army is all militia, and your Excellency well knows that they are by no means adequate to such an enterprise. The houses in the vicinity are so scattered, that the troops were every hour exposed to surprise, if the enemy should make a sudden sally, or continually harassed by keeping out large guards exposed, in the open air, to the inclemency of the season; and, as there remained little or no probability of success, either against the fort or island, and the principal object now being to collect the forage, protect the well-disposed, and curb the disaffected, the Generals who were present in council, namely, Lincoln, Wooster, Ten Broeck, and Scott, were unanimously of opinion that, as the before-mentioned purposes could be as well answered by the troops falling back, as remaining so near the fort, and many inconveniences avoided, the manœuvre was advisable; and it was accordingly made.

We have collected considerable quantities of forage. At present, it is stored at Kingstreet and Wright's Mills. Large quantities are still uncollected.

The person who lately brought me intelligence from the city has, since I wrote your Excellency, mentioned one piece which, if true (and he thinks it is), is very extraordinary, namely, that General Carleton's army formed a junction with Howe's before the army went into the Jerseys; and that a small garrison only is left at Quebec. It is reported here, and gains credit, that the enemy have burnt Newport and left Rhode Island.*

Daniel Strang was executed at Peekskill, on Monday last, agreeably to his sentence. The Tories gave out that we dare not hang him. I have the honor to be

Your Excellency's most humble servant,
W. Heath.

FROM BRIGADIER-GENERAL ARNOLD.

Providence, 31 January, 1777.

Dear General,

By the best intelligence we have been able to procure of the enemy's force on Rhode Island, it consisted of about six thousand men; eleven regiments of British, and four of Hessians. Two thousand embarked the 21st instant, in twenty-four transports, and sailed from Newport three days since, supposed for New York, as they were seen off New London. Part

---

* All these reports were unfounded, except that a part of the enemy had sailed from Newport.

of the remainder, believed about fifteen hundred, are disposed over the Island in seeming great security. They have a small fort opposite Bristol Ferry, and are raising a work opposite Fogland Ferry. One of their frigates was lately drove from thence, and was yesterday replaced by a fifty-gun ship and two tenders, which we are preparing to attack, by guns on shore, and our galleys, which are ordered down.

At a Council of General Officers, held a few days since, it was advised to land a body of eight thousand men (if they can be procured) on Rhode Island, and attack the enemy in the following manner, namely;—Five thousand men, with proper artillery, to embark at Howland's Ferry and land nearly opposite Fogland Ferry, and to take post on a high ground, under cover of a thick wood, on the middle of the Island, six miles this side of Newport. Three thousand men to embark at Bristol and Howland's Ferry, and attack the enemy in the different posts, a diversion to be made by a party from Seconnet, who are to land three miles from Newport. At the same time, two fire-ships are to be sent into Newport among the transports; two frigates and two galleys are to be placed between Bristol and Howland's Ferry, which, with the batteries, will effectually secure our retreat. We are making every necessary preparation of boats, artillery, &c., which will be complete in two or three weeks. Nothing will be wanting but men. We have, at present, only four thousand. Not more than one thousand more (of the six ordered) can be expected. With this number, as they are chiefly raw militia, I believe your Excellency will not think it prudent for us to make a general attack. The deficiency I know of no way of making up but by calling in four or five Continental regiments from the States of Massachusetts Bay and New Hampshire. If this number can be procured, we have a good prospect of dislodging the enemy from Newport; if not, we must be content to harass them with small parties. I suppose Major-General Spencer has wrote your Excellency very particularly on the subject, and will wait for your directions in the matter.

This will be delivered to your Excellency by Captain Mansfield, whom, I recommended, in my last as a proper person to command a company of artillery. If your Excellency should think proper to appoint him, I beg the favor that he may be allowed to return here immediately. I am, with sentiments of great respect and esteem, Dear General,

Your affectionate and most obedient,

Humble servant,

BENEDICT ARNOLD.

P. S. I have inclosed a plan of Rhode Island and the adjacent country, by which you will observe the great difficulty of coming at the enemy, and the necessity of having a superior force, if we land on the Island.   B. A.

FROM MAJOR-GENERAL HEATH.

Westchester, 6 February, 1777.

DEAR GENERAL,

The last evening I received the honor of yours of the 3d and 4th instant, which has given me great pain. Perhaps I may venture to say, that no officer is more attentive to orders or more anxious to carry them into execution, than I am. When I received your Excellency's orders to march towards King's Bridge, nothing could be more agreeable than the manœuvre; but I cannot say the taking the command of a body of troops, entirely militia, was so. It was indeed far otherwise. Before I received your Excellency's orders to move myself towards King's Bridge, upon the application of the Committee of the State of New York, I appointed General Parsons to take the command of the troops destined for their secret expedition. He gave me his answer in writing, accepting the command in obedience to orders, but, at the same time, desiring that his answer might remain in writing, that it might appear, that although he cheerfully obeyed orders, yet that he considered the taking the command of a body of militia for such an attempt, to use his own words, as a sacrifice of his character. By your Excellency's orders to me, his has escaped, but it seems mine is to receive the fatal stab. As I feel myself much interested in this matter, your Excellency will bear with me to be a little explicit, and to recapitulate the whole expedition.

Upon my arrival before the fort, I summoned the garrison to surrender, as your Excellency is sensible is the practice on the first investing of a place ; and this in particular I did at the motion of a gentleman before I left Peekskill, as it was supposed the garrison consisted of Hessian troops ; and, from some preceding circumstances, it might answer a very good purpose. And although some of the enemy may laugh at a fort being summoned, and not taken, I believe they will scarcely publish the summons. After this I called a Council of War, as I did in every instance of importance during our continuance before the fort, and in every one of them the Council were unanimous. I have taken the liberty to inclose one

of them, to wit, that preceding our remove, by which
your Excellency will perceive that the landing of
Lord Percy, to surround us, was not so much as mentioned.

. The facts were briefly these.   The troops were
scattered in a circle of more than eight miles.   We
had tried to hut them, but the rain, preceding our
remove, had driven four of General Lincoln's regiments from their huts, with the loss of nearly all
their ammunition.   The enemy had sallied, early one
morning, and surprised one of our out-guards.   The
regiment nearest the place were struck with a panic,
and had quitted their quarters, leaving their baggage.
The troops were so scattered as not to be collected
in less than two or three hours; in which case, those
who were quartered within cannon shot of the fort,
as was the case, would be entirely cut to pieces before they could be supported.   A diffidence and uneasiness were discovered in even the bravest officers.
In such a situation, and a universal desire to get
more advantageously quartered, every officer objected
to a storm, as they apprehended the militia inadequate to such an enterprise.   Every purpose, it was
supposed, would be, and has been answered, by the
troops ·in their present cantonment, except that of
reducing the fort.

No officer could be more anxious to effect something to purpose than I have been during the expedition here, or more harassed, perplexed, and fatigued,
with an undisciplined militia; and if, after all this,
and having taken every step agreeably to the result
in the Councils of War, I am to be censured, it is
truly discouraging.   However, if there has been error
in judgment, we have all been in the dark, except
some who may be distinguished for their sense and

judgment. But, if I am not mistaken in them, their military propositions, in some instances, have been as laughable as my summons may be. It is not uncommon for those unacquainted with military operations to expect as much from undisciplined as disciplined troops, if their numbers are considerable; but, in our present case, the officers of artillery, one and all, informed me, that they could not be accountable for the artillery, if they were to be covered with militia; and every officer, acquainted with service, was wishing for a few Continental troops, when our conquest would have been easy.

I thank your Excellency for your secret admonition, but must entreat that you would be pleased to let me know who were your Excellency's informers, as you were pleased to mention that they were some who have been with me. I think, what your Excellency is pleased to mention with respect to the forage, we are pursuing. I am a little at a loss for your final determination, as to my conduct here. In your letter of the 3d instant, you are pleased to direct that, after fixing a number of troops in this quarter and at Peekskill, the remainder should immediately march forward and join you; and in your letter of the 4th, you are pleased to advise some further attempts on the fort. The last night I ordered a large scouting party to march, at one o'clock this morning, from Ward's, to surprise the out-guards near Fort Independence, and attempt whatever might appear practicable. I have not as yet heard from them. I had yesterday ordered some of the troops lower down, and to take quarters below Ward's. I shall immediately endeavour to make the necessary arrangement directed by your Excellency, and shall, *in obedience to your orders*, consult Colonel Duer; other-

wise I should not do it in military matters, although
I much esteem him for his good sense and judgment
in other affairs. It will, most probably, be several
days before the troops can move, in which time I
hope to hear again from you; and in the mean time
I can assure your Excellency, they shall not be idle.

I thank your Excellency for the leave you have
been pleased to grant me to ride to New England.
Nothing but necessity could have induced me to solicit the favor. I shall endeavour to return in about
four weeks from the time that I leave Peekskill,
which will give me about two weeks at home. I
have the honor to be,

Your Excellency's most humble servant,
WILLIAM HEATH.

FROM BRIGADIER-GENERAL SCOTT.

Fishkill, 14 February, 1777.

SIR,

Permit me to acknowledge the receipt of your favor by Mr. Sacket, by which I esteem myself much
honored. I wish I had it in my power to give you
a favorable account of our little expedition, which I
imagine would have been successful beyond expectation, had it not been for certain reasons. When I
found that it was all dwindled into a mere foraging
business, that our little corps was headed by three
Major-Generals and two Brigadier-Generals, while my
command, in point of numbers, was reduced to that
of a Major, I thought it my duty, as well to save
public expense as to be where I could be more useful, to return to the Convention. I left the command

of my little handful to Major Fish, who, with another Major of this State, very early, a few mornings ago, surprised and killed three light-horsemen of the enemy out of six, wounded another, and took one horse; and had it not been for the too great promptitude of the other Major, who killed one of the enemy with his own hand, the whole little party would probably have fallen into our hands. This effort, however, in a young man, though not altogether prudent, yet for a militia officer, whom I would much rather see rash than cowardly, is commendable. His name is Van Rensselaer. He was Major in my brigade, under Colonel Humphrey, in the last campaign. I am pleased to see our officers brave. Service will teach them discipline and prudence.

I am sorry to be obliged to inform you that our Convention, in spite of my every effort to prevent it, have resolved to adjourn to Esopus, for no other reason than because their lodging here was inconvenient. The reasons of a public nature against the removal are weighty. Permit me, Sir, to mention them. First, the danger that the blocking up of the channel will be neglected. Secondly, the danger that the internal enemies in Duchess and Westchester will rise up in arms. Thirdly, the danger of the oppression, and therefore the loss, of the well-affected in those counties. Fourthly, the danger that our foraging will be discontinued. And, fifthly, the danger that the New York troops will not be properly equipped for the field.

These, in my humble opinion, were sufficient to exclude from consideration every article of private convenience; and you would be surprised were I to inform you who were the principal agents in bringing about the resolve to adjourn. If, Sir, you should

29*

view the matter in the same light that I do, I am sure you would do every thing in your power to bring them back. I hope I may be honored in my opinion by a conformity of sentiments in you. Should this be the case, a line from you will, in consequence of the great deference I am sure they pay you, have the desired effect. Were the matter now to be moved, it could not be carried. They seized the lucky moment. If you should think it advisable to write to them on the subject, I beg you may do it without delay, and conceal the quarter from whence you obtained your information.

You may think it vanity in me, Sir, to add my application to that of our Convention, for the exchange of the four officers of my brigade, concerning whom they write to you. My only motive for doing it is, that perhaps my assurance of their merit, on a personal knowledge of them, may have some weight. I am, Sir, with every possible assurance of real respect and esteem,

Your most obedient, humble servant,

JOHN MORIN SCOTT.

FROM GOVERNOR TRUMBULL.

Lebanon, 21 February, 1777.

SIR,

I am honored with yours of the 1st instant, and although it would have made me very happy to have been able to procure a release of all our officers in captivity, I freely acknowledge and acquiesce in the justice and impartiality of the measures you have taken respecting them.

We have now granted to our proportion of the sixteen battalions the additional bounty of thirty-three dollars and one third, estimating that proportion at one thousand men. In making this estimate, we are governed by the proportion which the quota assigned by Congress to this State bears to the whole number to be raised, namely, as eight is to eighty-eight. This I trust will put the officers you have appointed in this State upon an equal footing with those of the eight regiments allotted to us before, and remove every impediment in the way of raising their men.

I am not insensible, that the step taken by the New England States, of granting an additional bounty to their quotas of the Continental army, is objected to, as tending to produce discontent and disorder in the army. You will, therefore, permit me to state the reasons which have prevailed to induce the giving it, and the manner in which this State hath been drawn in to accede to it.

The length and severity of our winters in this climate are such, that a soldier can neither clothe nor support himself, or a family, so cheaply at any time as he can in a southern climate. Many, indeed most of our soldiers, have small families at home dependent, in a good measure, upon the savings they can make out of their wages for subsistence, which must always be the case while most of our youth marry at the age of twenty-one years, or thereabouts. The almost total interruption of commerce, and the scarcity of materials for manufactures, have and must still greatly increase the prices of clothing and other articles, whilst the demand for all kinds of provisions for the army has likewise rendered every necessary article of subsistence much dearer than at the commencement of hostilities. At that time the wages given to a common laborer were about forty shillings per month; now ten dollars are rather less than a medium, and all articles of produce are risen in proportion. Add that the seaman is offered twenty dollars per month, and tradesmen and artificers in proportion. Neither is this chargeable to any ill principle, but the necessary consequence of drawing off so many of our men into the service. When these facts are considered, it was thought to be very apparent, that a New England soldier cannot, and in justice ought not to serve upon the same pay and allowances that were given in 1775, or that one from the Southern States, when his expense for clothing and subsistence for himself and family is so much less, now can. Our people in general are so fully persuaded of this difference, it is alleged that it would be fruitless, as well as unjust, to attempt to engage them upon it, and vain to expect success in the attempt.

These considerations induced the Massachusetts Assembly, in October, to offer an additional monthly pay. The Assembly of this State, who had before rejected the measure when proposed by some of their own members, followed their lead, and offered the same additional pay; but when they were advised of the disapprobation of Congress, and had your Excellency's objections laid before them, they cheerfully retracted, and determined to trust to the bounties and pay of Congress, with some encouragement in furnishing them with necessaries at prime cost, to induce them to enlist. In the mean time, all the other New England States offered large additional bounties; Massachusetts and New Hampshire, sixty-six dollars and two thirds; Rhode Island, twenty dollars. It was soon evident, that these bounties would entice a great part of our men into the service of the States con-

tiguous to us on the east and north, which, besides
the obstruction which would thence arise to the filling
up our own battalions, would be highly prejudicial to
the agriculture of this State, and, in effect, to the
general service, as the army must still depend, for a
very considerable part of its subsistence, on this State.

In this situation the matter rested until the enemy
took possession of Newport. It then became necessary to provide for the immediate defence of the New
England States, and Commissioners met at Providence
to concert proper measures for that purpose. They
immediately agreed to raise an army of six thousand
men for a temporary defence, until the Continental
army might be raised.

Sensible that an attempt to raise a separate army
for their own defence, must effectually obstruct the
raising a Continental army, and otherwise be liable
to great objections, they considered raising the Continental battalions speedily, as the only sure means
of defence against the enemy, should they fall upon
any of these States; and proceeded to deliberate upon
proper measures for this purpose.

The rapid increase of the prices of the necessaries
and conveniences of life operates strongly to discourage
soldiers from enlisting. These they attempted to limit
by recommending prices to be affixed by law, beyond
which they might not rise, by recommending that a
stop be put to emitting further bills of credit, and
measures to be taken to reduce the quantity now cir-
culating.

The number of men employed on board privateers
and merchant vessels, formed another obstacle to raising an army. They recommended an embargo upon
all privateers and merchant vessels, except those sent
after necessaries by permit, until the army was raised.

The bounties offered by the other States were alleged as an impediment to raising the quota for the army in this State and Rhode Island. The Commissioners from this State strongly urged, that the additional bounties should be withdrawn, and encouragement, by supplying necessaries at a certain price, be substituted in their place. In this they were overruled; and then, sensible of the mischief that must arise from the great bounties given by the other States, they consented, in case Massachusetts and New Hampshire would reduce their bounty to thirty-three dollars and one third, to recommend to this State to give the same bounty to our soldiers, which was agreed to, and recommended accordingly.

Our Assembly, with reluctance, for the sake of uniformity, and to avoid what they considered as a greater evil, acceded to the recommendation, and offered the proposed bounty.

I must leave the other New England States to give their reasons for the measures they have adopted, and only add, that it is my wish and desire that all jealousies and occasions of disunion and animosity of the several States, may be avoided and laid aside. It is not wonderful, that diversity of sentiments happens at a time that government is so far convulsed and unhinged. It is necessary, as far as possible, to become all things to all men, and not suffer our enemies to avail themselves of any discord or disunion among these States. I am, Sir, with great truth and respect,

Your obedient, humble servant,

JONATHAN TRUMBULL.

FROM THE PRESIDENT OF CONGRESS.

Baltimore, 25 February, 1777.

SIR,

From the resolves, which I have the honor of transmitting herewith, you will perceive the measures Congress have taken to reënforce your army at this juncture.

I have wrote to the Convention of New York to place a proper guard of militia at the passes in the Highlands, in case you should think proper to call to your assistance the troops under General Heath, which will be highly agreeable to Congress.

I have likewise wrote to the Governor of New Jersey, and to the Council of Safety of Pennsylvania, to call forth their militia at this important crisis. It is indeed devoutly to be wished, and is the earnest desire of Congress, that the army under your command may be made, not only strong enough to confine the enemy within their present quarters, and prevent them from getting supplies from the country, but totally subdue them before they can be further reënforced. You will, therefore, be pleased to write to the Colonels, or other commanding officers of the regiments that are raising in the New England States, as well as those of New York and New Jersey, and order them immediately to march the troops under their command, in the most expeditious manner, to head-quarters. Similar letters will be written by the Board of War to the commanding officers in Pennsylvania, Delaware, Maryland, and Virginia. I beg leave to refer your attention to the whole of the inclosed resolves.

Your favor of the 20th instant came to hand the

24th, and was immediately laid before Congress. I have the honor to be, with sentiments of the greatest esteem and respect, Sir,

Your most obedient and very humble servant,

JOHN HANCOCK, *President.*

P. S. In consequence of your letters, and one from Mr. Morris, Congress have suspended their remove to Philadelphia for a few days.

FROM ROBERT MORRIS.

Philadelphia, 6 March, 1777.

DEAR SIR,

I am honored with yours of the 2d instant. The good opinion you are pleased to entertain of me, makes me very happy, because there is no man's opinion I reverence more; and that very circumstance is, at the same time, the source of trouble in my mind, as you force me to abandon that idea of security which I was desirous of maintaining. It is truly lamentable, that we have never been able to this day to conquer that fundamental error made in the outset by short enlistments. It was not until conviction of the absolute necessity of it stared every man in the face, that the wholesome measure of enlisting for three years, or during the war, could be carried in Congress; and since it was carried there, it meets with insuperable obstacles, raised by the former practice; for the bounties, high wages, and short service, have vitiated the minds of all that class of people, and they are grown the most mercenary beings that exist.

I do not confine this observation to the soldiery merely, but extend it to those who get their livings by feeding and entertaining them. These are the harpies that injure us much at this time. They keep the fellows drunk while the money holds out; when it is gone, they encourage them to enlist for the sake of bounty, then to drinking again; that bounty gone, and more money still wanted, they must enlist again with some other officer, receive a fresh bounty and get more drink, &c. This scene is actually carrying on here daily, and does immense injury to the recruiting service; but still I hope our new army will be got together before long, at least so many as will enable you to put a good face towards your enemies; and if that is accomplished, I think they will not venture this way at present. It seems to be their object; and, in your situation, I really do not see what is to prevent their taking possession of it, unless the want of stores, forage, &c., retards their movements, or renders it impracticable for them to come on. In the mean time, the public stores are removing, and Congress has adjourned back to this place, many of the members are come up, and the rest on the road.* I do not expect they will make a House sooner than Monday; but your late despatches shall be delivered to the President as soon as he arrives.

I wish with you, Sir, that they had complied with General Lee's request; and when I sent forward those

---

* Congress remained in Baltimore from the 20th of December till the 27th of February, when they adjourned to meet in Philadelphia on the 4th of March.

despatches to Baltimore, I wrote my sentiments to some of the members; and although it would have been inconvenient for me, and I urged not to be appointed on that errand, yet I would have gone rather than he should have been disappointed.* Whether they will take up the matter again, I do not

---

* General Lee was at this time a prisoner in New York. He had written to the President of Congress the following letter.

"New York, 10 February, 1777.

" SIR,

" As it is of the greatest consequence to me, and I think of no loss to the public, I am persuaded that the Congress will comply with the request I am going to make. It is, that they will permit two or three gentlemen to repair to New York, to whom I may communicate what so deeply interests myself, and, in my opinion, the community. The most salutary effects may, and I am convinced will, result from it, and, as Lord and General Howe will grant a safe conduct to the gentlemen deputed, it can possibly have no ill consequences, unless the fatigue and inconveniency to the particular gentlemen who are appointed; to lighten which and save time, which, in the present situation of affairs, is a matter of the most material consideration, I cannot help expressing my wishes that some of those gentlemen, who at present compose the Committee at Philadelphia, might be nominated; but this must be referred to your better judgment. If my own interests were alone at stake, I flatter myself that the Congress would not hesitate a single instant in acquiescing in my request; but this is far from the case; the interests of the public are equally concerned, at least in the opinion of one who is and ever shall be most sincerely attached to their welfare.

"I am, &c.,   CHARLES LEE.

" P. S. The gentlemen deputed must pass through General Washington's camp, where passports will be ready for them."

After this letter was read, Congress resolved;

" That General Washington be directed to inform General Lee, that Congress are pursuing, and will continue to pursue, every means in their power to provide for his personal safety, and to obtain his liberty.

" That General Washington inform him of the steps taken to effect these ends, and at the same time acquaint him, that Congress judge it altogether improper to send any of their body to communicate with him; and that they cannot perceive how a compliance with his request will tend to his advantage or the interest of the public." *Journals, February* 21*st.*

know; but I much doubt it, as from the little conversation I have had with some of the members now here, they seem very averse to it. However, I expect this matter, as well as the confinement of the Hessian field-officers, will at least be referred to the consideration of a Committee, in consequence of your letters on the subject; and, if I can influence a compliance with your wishes, it will give me pleasure, for my own sentiments coincide with yours exactly in these two points.

At the same time, I must hint to you what I take to be one of the most forcible arguments that probably has been used in Congress against this measure. I have not heard that it was used, but it occurred to myself on reading General Lee's letters. I mean, the effect it may have at the Court of France, should they hear, as they undoubtedly would, that members of Congress visited General Lee, by permission of the British Commissioners. The meeting with Lord Howe, at Staten Island, last summer, injured Mr. [Deane's] negotiations much, and retarded supplies intended for us.

I am now at the 15th of March, and must apologize to you, sir, for not answering fully your letter, and not having sent this away long since; but I have been attacked by a weakness in my eyes, and writing is the most dangerous thing I can do whilst it continues. On this account I am obliged to absent myself from Congress, and refrain from business; but in all situations of life I shall ever remain, with the sincerest esteem, your Excellency's

Most obedient and humble servant,

ROBERT MORRIS.

Peekskill, 9 March, 1777.

My dear General,

I have called on General McDougall, and informed him, confidentially, of the state of our army. He says there are about six hundred Continental troops here, with two Massachusetts militia regiments. He is of opinion, that the Continental troops here should be sent forward, and that this State should garrison this post, for which purpose he will call on Mr. Jay, and consult with him upon the most effectual measures to bring it about.

Dear General, since I left the army I have been informed that General St. Clair is to take the command at Ticonderoga the ensuing campaign. Though I never wish to complain, I cannot help the disagreeable feelings, so common to mankind, when they find themselves slighted and neglected. When I had completed the disagreeable retreat from Canada, I was with circumstances of indignity. Since which, and before, every Major-General, except myself, has had the honor of commanding posts, separated from the main army. General Putnam has commanded at New York and Philadelphia; General Gates at Ticonderoga and Philadelphia; General Greene in the Jerseys, when the army was at New York; General Spencer at Rhode Island; and General Heath the forces in this State. I have never yet been thought worthy to intrust with the command of a separate post. I have felt those things most sensibly, and wish to know, to what it is owing. If it be to my want of prudence, resolution, or whatever other cause, I wish to know it, that I may rid the Continent of an officer who is unworthy to trust with command.

I once had the command in Canada by an act of Providence; and even malice itself cannot censure my conduct. I was soon deprived of the command, and rewarded with disgrace for saving the army and stores in that country. I know that Ticonderoga will become an important object with the enemy. They must try for it, and therefore he that has the command there will have the post of honor. I do therefore humbly claim it as my right, and as the first separate post intrusted to my care; and cannot think of the command being given to a younger officer, without conceiving myself a second time treated with neglect, which I well know my conduct has not deserved.

I wish your Excellency to forward me a line by the post upon this subject, which will be gratefully acknowledged by

　　　　Your Excellency's most obedient servant,
　　　　　　　　　　JOHN SULLIVAN.*

FROM BRIGADIER-GENERAL ARNOLD.

　　　　　　　　　　　Providence, 11 March, 1777.
DEAR GENERAL,

I am now to acknowledge your Excellency's favors of the 6th and 20th ultimo, and 3d instant. On receipt of the former, I was ordered to Boston, with the view of collecting four or five Continental battalions for our intended attack. On my return, General Spencer thought it necessary for me to go to Point Judith,

------

* See the answer to this letter in Washington's Writings, Vol. IV. p. 364.

from whence I returned last night, and was then presented with your Excellency's favors of the last date, prior to the receipt of which we had laid aside all thoughts of making a general attack on Rhode Island. The new levies of the Massachusetts Bay being all ordered to Ticonderoga, and those of Connecticut inoculated for the smallpox, deprives us of the aid of Continental troops, on whom we had placed our chief dependence.

When the attack was first proposed, we had reason to think your Excellency had a force superior to the enemy in the Jerseys. I am sorry to say, we now have reason to think the case is altered. After duly weighing the matter, and considering the difficulties and risk of attacking and making good a retreat, and the fatal consequences attending the failure of success, I was dubious of the propriety of the attack, as the enemy now rest secure and easy in their quarters. I am fully of opinion it will be imprudent to force them to action, until our new levies are in a manner complete. From our strength and numbers, which do not exceed four thousand raw militia, we have no reasonable prospect of succeeding against four thousand well-disciplined troops. Notwithstanding, the Assembly of this State have lately requested General Spencer to make an attack on the enemy on Rhode Island, which he seems inclined to do, and the militia are collecting for the purpose. It is proposed to attack the west end of the Island, with three thousand men. I am much averse to this plan, as I am fearful it will bring on a general action, and end in our disgrace, or cause the troops in Newport to embark, both of which I wish to avoid at this critical juncture. From some of our own people, and several deserters from the enemy, we are informed they are near four thousand strong. It is said two thousand have lately arrived at Newport from New York. I am rather inclined to think they are a body of men lately sent to Martha's Vineyard, for ten transports passed Point Judith this day week to the westward, and appeared full of troops. Twenty odd sail are gone to England, and fifty sail remain at Newport.

I am greatly obliged to your Excellency for interesting yourself so much in my behalf in respect to my appointment, which I have had no advice of, and know not by what means it was announced in the papers. I believe none but the printer has a mistake to rectify. Congress have doubtless a right of promoting those, whom, from their abilities, their long and arduous services, they esteem most deserving. Their promoting junior officers to the rank of Major-General, I view as a very civil way of requesting my resignation, as unqualified for the office I hold. My commission was conferred unsolicited, received with pleasure only as a means of serving my country. With equal pleasure I resign it, when I can no longer serve my country with *honor*. The person who, void of the nice feelings of honor, will tamely condescend to give up his rights, and hold a commission at the expense of his reputation, I hold as a disgrace to the army, and unworthy of the glorious cause in which we are engaged.

When I entered the service of my country, my character was unimpeached. I have sacrificed my interest, ease, and happiness in her cause. It is rather a misfortune than a fault, that my exertions have not been crowned with success. I am conscious of the rectitude of my intentions. In justice, therefore, to my own character, and for the satisfaction of my friends, I must request a court of inquiry into my conduct; and, though I sensibly feel the ingratitude of my countrymen, every personal injury shall be buried in my zeal for the safety and happiness of my country, in whose cause I have repeatedly fought and bled, and am ready at all times to resign my life. I shall cautiously avoid any hasty step, in consequence of the appointments that have taken place, that may tend to injure my country.*

Particular attention shall be paid to your Excellency's commands respecting the prisoners. I have the honor to be, with very great respect and esteem, your Excellency's

Most obedient and humble servant,

BENEDICT ARNOLD.

FROM THE PRESIDENT OF CONGRESS.

Philadelphia, 17 March, 1777.

SIR,

I have the honor to transmit to you sundry resolves of Congress, of a very important nature, to which I beg leave to solicit your attention.

The Congress, having had your letters of the 1st and 6th instant under consideration, have come to the inclosed resolve on the subject, by which you perceive they decline making any alteration in the

* Congress had recently appointed five Major-Generals, and had not included Arnold in the number, although they were all his juniors in rank. See Sparks's Life of Benedict Arnold, p. 85. On the 2d of May he was appointed a Major-General, in consequence of his brave conduct in resisting the enemy's forces on their retreat from Danbury, but the date of his commission still left his rank below that of the five Major-Generals who had been promoted over him.

resolve of the 6th of January, and that it was not their intention that Colonel Campbell should experience any other hardship than such confinement as is necessary to his security for the end they had in view when they passed that resolve.

The obvious distinction made by General Howe, in his treatment of General Lee, who is notoriously committed to the custody of the provost, and denied his parole, while our other officers are admitted to it, was the ground on which Congress proceeded when they passed that resolve, the intention of which was to show that, in proportion as severities against him were increased, the same treatment should be exercised on six field-officers.

The principle of retaliation was early adopted by the States of America, and, if adhered to, will be the most likely way to prevent our enemies from making distinctions, which have no other foundation but the gratification of their revenge; General Lee having an undoubted right to every indulgence that our other officers, prisoners among them, may receive.

I have wrote to the Governor and Council of Virginia, and likewise to Colonel Stephen, on the subject of the inclosed resolves.

The Congress have endeavoured to put a stop to foreigners coming over to America to enter the service, not only by directing the Committee of Secret Correspondence to write to the agents abroad to discourage them from such views, but by declaring that they shall not be employed unless they are well acquainted with our language.

Your several favors of the 20th, 23d, and 28th of February, and 1st and 6th of March, have been duly received and laid before Congress. I am also this minute honored with your favor of the 14th, which shall be laid before Congress as soon as possible. I have the honor to be, with sentiments of the greatest esteem, Sir,

Your most obedient and very humble servant,

JOHN HANCOCK, *President.*

FROM THE PRESIDENT OF CONGRESS.

Philadelphia, 26 March, 1777.

SIR,

I have the honor of transmitting such resolves of Congress as have passed since my last, which are either relative to your department, or necessary for your information. The Congress have authorized you to proceed in the exchange of prisoners, agreeably to the cartel at present existing, or such other regulations as you may think proper to make in the matter, provided the enemy will relax in their treatment of General Lee, and acknowledge him to be a prisoner of war, and as such entitled to be exchanged.

I congratulate you on the arrival of a vessel at this port, from France, with eleven thousand stand of arms in good order, and, I am informed, fit for immediate use. She has brought likewise fifteen hundred gun-locks, and a large quantity of flints. Six thousand eight hundred of the arms are public property. The balance, which belong to individuals, the Congress have empowered the Secret Committee to purchase immediately. I have wrote to General Gates to repair to Ticonderoga, agreeably to the inclosed resolve.

Colonel Clinton was yesterday appointed a Brigadier-General, in consequence of a very warm recommendation from the Convention of New York. As he is an officer of established good character, and is now engaged in obstructing the river, his station at the Highlands will be more convenient, and highly agreeable to the Convention of New York.

Your favor, by General Greene, was duly received, and a Committee appointed to confer with him, the result of which shall be immediately transmitted. I have the honor to be, with the most perfect esteem and respect, Sir,

Your most obedient servant,
JOHN HANCOCK, *President.*

FROM BRIGADIER-GENERAL ARNOLD.

Providence, 26 March, 1777.

DEAR GENERAL,

I was made very unhappy, a few days since, by hearing your Excellency was exceedingly ill with a fever. I soon after had the pleasure of hearing, by Mr. Learned, you were so far recovered as to be able to ride out. My fears have not entirely subsided. I am still anxious for your safety, and apprehensive your zeal for the public service will induce you to exert yourself before you are perfectly recovered.

I wrote your Excellency the 11th instant, since which our intended expedition against Rhode Island is laid aside. We now confine ourselves to a defensive opposition only. Desertions from the Island are frequent. The most intelligent persons agree that the enemy have six battalions of Hessians, and four of British troops; the whole about four thousand men. Several inhabitants, who came from Newport the evenings of the 23d and 25th instant, say that all the enemy's transport-ships are hauled off from the wharves, their water in, and sails bent, and ready for sailing. Sir Peter Parker has sent his baggage on board, and was to embark soon. It is said, by their seamen, that they are bound for New York. From appearances, they will doubtless soon leave Newport, and probably join General Howe.

In my last, I intimated to your Excellency the impossibility of my remaining in a disgraceful situation in the army. My being superseded must be viewed as an implicit impeachment of my character. I therefore requested a court of inquiry into my conduct. I believe the time is near at hand, when I can leave this department without any damage to the public interest. When that is the case, I will wait on your Excellency, not doubting my request will be granted, and that I shall be able to acquit myself of every charge malice or envy can bring against me.

General Spencer writes your Excellency very particularly by this opportunity. I have only to add my sincere wishes for your restoration to perfect health, and preservation in any danger, and am, very respectfully, dear General,

Your affectionate and most obedient servant,
BENEDICT ARNOLD.

Williamsburg, 29 March, 1777.

SIR,

I am very sorry to inform you, that the recruiting business of late goes on so badly, that there remains but little prospect of filling the six new battalions, from this State, voted by the Assembly. The Board of Council see this with great concern, and, after much reflection on the subject, are of opinion that the deficiency in our regulars can no way be supplied so properly as by enlisting volunteers. There is reason to believe a considerable number of these may be got to serve six or eight months. But, as you were pleased to signify to me that great inconveniences had arisen by the admission of transient troops at the camp, the Board do not choose to adopt the scheme of volunteers, until we are favored with your sentiments on the subject. I believe you can receive no assistance by drafts from the militia. From the battalions of the Commonwealth none can be drawn as yet, because they are not half full.

The volunteers will consist of men chiefly from the upper parts of the country, who would make the best of soldiers, could they continue so long in the service as to be regularly disciplined. They will find their own arms, clothes, and blankets, and be commanded by captains and subalterns of their own choosing; the field-officers to be chosen by the others. They will be subject to the Continental Articles of War, and I believe will be as respectable as such a corps can be expected, without training.

I cannot speak with any certainty as to their numbers. In a very little time, seven companies were made up in Augusta. In the other counties no great progress was made, because Government stopped it, on being informed that it was a prejudice to the regular enlistment. But . on the failure of this, the other may be revived, I believe, with success. Virginia will find some apology with you for this deficiency in her quota of regulars, when the difficulties lately thrown in our way are considered. The Georgians and Carolinians have enlisted probably two battalions at least. A regiment of artillery is in great forwardness. Besides these, Colonels Baylor and Grayson are collecting regiments, and three others are forming for this State. Add to all this our Indian wars and marine service, almost total want of necessaries, the false accounts of deserters, many of whom lurk here, the terrors of the smallpox, and the many deaths occasioned by it, and the deficient enlistments are accounted for in the best manner I can.

As no time can be spared, I wish to be honored with your answer as soon as possible, in order to promote the volunteer scheme, if it meets your approbation. I should be glad of any improvements on it that may occur to you. I believe about four of the six battalions may be enlisted, but have seen no regular [return] of their state. Their scattered situation, and being many of them in broken quotas, is a reason for their slow movement. I have issued repeated orders for their march long since. With sentiments of the highest esteem and regard, I have the honor to be, Sir,

Your most obedient and very humble servant,
PATRICK HENRY, JR.

Philadelphia, 4 April, 1777.

SIR,

The inclosed resolves of Congress, which I have the honor of transmitting, will naturally claim your attention, from their great importance. The regulations relative to the payment of the troops and the department of the Paymaster-General will, I hope, be the means of introducing order and regularity into that part of the army, where, it must be confessed, they were extremely wanted.

General Gates having laid before Congress the proceedings and sentence of a Court-Martial on a certain James Molesworth, who was accused and found guilty of being a spy, they immediately approved the same. He has since suffered the punishment due to his crime. From his repeated confession, it appears that Mr. Galloway was extremely active in engaging him to undertake this infamous business, and was the person employed to make the bargain with him. He says, indeed, Lord Howe was present; but, from the description he gave of his person, it is supposed he must be mistaken.

The Congress have directed General Gates to take General Fermoy with him to Ticonderoga, and such other French officers as he may think proper. General St. Clair, being ordered to Ticonderoga, but previously to repair to this city to await the further order of Congress, you will please to direct him to repair here accordingly, as soon as possible. I have the honor to be, with the most perfect esteem and respect, Sir,

Your most obedient and very humble servant,

JOHN HANCOCK, *President.*

Philadelphia, 9 April, 1777.

SIR,

Yesterday evening, the Congress completed the business of the Medical Department, and on so large and liberal an establishment that we may rationally expect the most beneficial effects will flow from it. Every encouragement is given to gentlemen of skill and reputation in that art to enter into our army; and a variety of regulations adopted to carry the plan more effectually into execution. As I have the honor of inclosing the resolves on this subject, I beg leave to refer your attention to them.

It is with particular pleasure I transmit the resolution of Congress directing monuments to be erected to the memory of Major-General Warren and Brigadier-General Mercer. Every mark of distinction shown to those illustrious men, who offer up their lives and liberty for the happiness of mankind, reflects the highest honor upon those who pay the tribute, and, by holding up to others the prospects of fame and immortality, will animate them to tread in the same path. I have the honor to be, with the greatest respect and esteem,

Your most obedient and humble servant,

JOHN HANCOCK, *President.*

FROM COLONEL PICKERING.

Salem, 9 April, 1777.

SIR,

I esteem it as a singular honor, done me by your Excellency, in offering me the post of Adjutant-General; and it pains me sensibly that I am obliged to decline it. It is an honor to which I did not aspire, because I did not account myself equal to the important business of the office. Your Excellency does not mistake my attachment to the interests of the United States. It is sincere and unalterable. But my military character, which you are pleased to mention as a motive to the appointment, is, in my own estimation, of no great account. I have, it is true, studied the rudiments of the military art, but have very small, or rather no pretensions to capacity and skill in the important scenes of war, and much fear I should disappoint your Excellency's expectations concerning me.

I have domestic reasons and private concerns, which powerfully urge my staying at home; but these I should not mention, did they exist alone. But, beside the command of a regiment of militia on the sea-coast, I hold divers civil offices, which are sufficient to engage my constant attention; those of Judge of one of the Maritime Courts, Judge of the Inferior Court of Common Pleas, acting Justice of Peace and Register of Deeds for the County of Essex. The exercise of these offices I could, without any very great inconvenience, quit for a season; and, therefore, at the time of making the late levy of militia, as there appeared some backwardness in the

31 *

people, I encouraged their engaging, and stepped forth and offered my own personal service.

Nevertheless, I would forever abandon all these employments, if I thought myself capable of doing more service to my country, by acting in the office to which your Excellency has been pleased to invite me. But, as I do not thus think of myself, and conceive it not difficult to find a person not otherwise employed, and, to say the least, as able to discharge the duties of the office as I, I must beg leave to decline it. I am, with the greatest veneration,

Your Excellency's most obedient servant,
TIMOTHY PICKERING, JR.

FROM RICHARD HENRY LEE.

Philadelphia, 10 April, 1777.

MY DEAR GENERAL,

The resolves of Congress, that you will receive by this messenger, you may be assured are not intended, by any means, to obstruct your views a single moment. If your judgment should incline you to think that the troops had better march to head-quarters as quick as possible, you have only to order it, and it will give pleasure to every good man here. The business of speedily reënforcing you will not be obstructed, but accelerated; because they now enter the city, where every day's stay is thirty days' injury to the great purpose of strengthening your hands; and should the enemy destine here, something like a military collection may produce a greater resort. If you will indulge my conjecture, I think they cannot purpose coming here, because the water securities against such a plan are really formidable, and the situation of the land, where the water obstructions are fixed, is such that great delay, and probable ruin, forbids the enterprise, as they cannot so fix land batteries as to remove the strong vessels that protect the *chevaux-de-frise*, added to the numerous fire-rafts and fire-ships that, in a narrow water, with strong current, may destroy their fleet.

Your army, Sir, feeble as it is, and the North River, are more tempting objects, because they are not strong, and because the defeat of the one and the acquisition of the other, would avail our enemies greatly.

My wishes are, Sir, and I think they correspond with the true interests of America, that you should quickly be possessed of a strong army; that your powers might be such as to gratify your wishes of crushing our enemies, before an addition of strength to them may render the business more difficult and uncertain. I think I well know your situation, and, from your excellent disposition, I know your feelings; and I do most ardently wish to make the former good, and to render the latter agreeable; and therefore whenever I can know either from yourself, all the powers I possess shall be exerted to accomplish both. The troops of Maryland are now under inoculation, and so are about one thousand Virginians from Baltimore to Wilmington inclusive. Here, we suppose, may be near one thousand of all kinds, who, by the new plan of encampment, will be in tents as quickly as the physicians can discharge them, or the officers collect them from this attractive scene of debauch and amusement. With every hearty wish for your health and prosperity, I remain, dear Sir,

Most affectionately yours,

RICHARD HENRY LEE.

FROM COLONEL PICKERING.

Salem, 14 April, 1777.

SIR,

I sent, by the express, an answer to your letter respecting the office of Adjutant-General, and gave what appeared to me sufficient reasons to excuse my declining to accept it; but I have since been uneasy lest you should deem them otherwise, and that I was too willing, under the civil offices I sustain, to shelter myself from the dangers and fatigues of war; an opinion which, if it has taken place, I wish to remove.

The case was this. I had concluded to accept the office; but, meeting with a number of unavoidable interruptions in the way of business, was unable to give my answer to the express till the evening, at eight o'clock, at which time I had directed him to call, and it was then, in fact, sealed up, and ready to be delivered; the same which I now inclose to your Excellency. But the express delaying his coming a full hour, I of course continued to revolve the matter in my mind, and, upon a review of the reasons on both sides of the question, those against my accepting the post, increased by the suggestions of my nearest friend, whose happiness and tranquillity of mind lay near my heart, preponderated, and occasioned the answer your Excellency has already received. Besides the reasons there given, others weighed with me, which I had not time to mention. The civil offices I sustain yield me an income that contents me, and, in a time of peace, would maintain my family. These I must have relinquished, without an expectation of resuming them. Consequently, had I taken the post of Adjutant-General, and some cause had arisen (an event far from impossible), rendering it expedient for me to quit the camp, I should have returned divested of the principal means of supporting my family.

Whenever I thought of a military employment, the condition of my eyes was no small discouragement to me. I am so near-sighted that I, although placed in the best situation, cannot, with any degree of accuracy, discern the position of a body of men beyond the size of a single regiment. It is true, in viewing distant objects, my spectacles help me to see nearly as well as people in general do with the naked eye; but they are frail things; and rain or snow beating against them (I found in the winter's campaign) so obstructs the vision as to render them almost useless. My business as Register of Deeds had, by my absence, got behindhand; it seemed to be daily increasing, and my office was not in such order as I wished to leave it in to a successor. These, with the reasons mentioned in my former letter, and many others of lesser moment, determined my answer in the negative. I regretted the proposal could not have been made me while at head-quarters, where I could have inquired particularly into the nature and extent of the office of Adjutant-General, and thence judged more certainly whether or not I was able to discharge the duties of it. The want of such information left doubts on my mind that were no small obstacle to my accepting it.

On the other hand, I am sensible that to support the army is of essential importance; that on the failure of it, besides the general calamity of my country, every prospect of advantage or enjoyment to me must vanish. I have been, therefore, ever ready to serve the public to the utmost of my power. But perhaps the comforts of civil life, the love of ease, the enjoyment of my friends, and the powerful allurements springing from the nearest connection on earth, have led me to mistake the object. From a sacred regard, therefore, to the interests of my country; from the ardent desire I have to approve myself to your Excellency; from the pain it has given me to deny the request of the last of men to whom I would refuse any thing, — I submit the whole matter to your Excellency's determination. If, upon a view of all circumstances, you judge it my duty to exchange the civil for a military life, I will do it. And then, should the office of Adjutant-General (for, from what conception I have of it, none would be more agreeable) be once more vacant, or any other post or employment present, to which you shall deem me competent, I will not again confer with flesh and blood, but instantly obey your Excellency's commands.

I beg your Excellency's pardon for imposing on your patience this second long letter. But I feared lest, by my backwardness, I might have offended. And I was led to make the above tender of my services, because your Excellency's good opinion of me, and the urgency of your request, have raised me to some importance with myself. I am, with the highest veneration and esteem for your Excellency, your Excellency's

Most obedient and most humble servant,
TIMOTHY PICKERING, JR.

FROM BRIGADIER-GENERAL GEORGE CLINTON.*

New Windsor, 18 April, 1777.

DEAR SIR,

Being from home when your Excellency's letter of the 31st ultimo was left at my house, prevented my answering it by the return of the express, and till now I have not had any other opportunity. Before the receipt of it, I had, in consequence of powers given me by the Convention of this State, ordered out about twelve hundred of the militia of this and Orange county; five hundred of them to relieve Colonel Pawling, at the post near Sydman's Bridge, and do the duties which had been assigned him, as the time for which his regiment stood engaged was expired; the remainder to reënforce the garrison of Fort Montgomery, and carry on the works necessary for its defence. I also ordered from Dutchess county eight hundred, and three hundred and fifty from Westchester, to reënforce the garrisons on the west side of Hudson's River, and to give protection to the inhabitants of the latter county, into which, for want of a proper force, the enemy make frequent incursions, and take off large droves of cattle, horses, and other supplies.

The unhappy affair at Peekskill,† and apprehension, entertained by our Convention, that the enemy might surprise and take our forts in the Highlands, induced me to take this step without waiting to get your

---

* Appointed a Brigadier-General in the Continental service on the 25th of March. He had previously commanded the New York militia.

† On the 23d of March the British made a descent upon Peekskill, and seized or destroyed the provisions and military supplies deposited there. See Washington's Writings, Vol. IV. p. 369.

Excellency's approbation of the measure. I would fain hope that it will not be disagreeable, as these troops, if wanted, are to continue in service till the 1st of August; yet they may be dismissed at any time before, and great pains have been taken to draw them out in such a manner as to promote the recruiting service, and I doubt not but it will be a means to complete our regiments for the standing army much sooner than they otherwise would have been. As yet, however, not above one half of the above number of militia have marched, and I much fear the whole will not easily be got out, if ever so much wanted.

I most sincerely thank your Excellency for the very polite and kind manner in which you are pleased to mention my appointment to a command in the Continental army. At the same time my precarious state of health, and want of military knowledge, would have rather induced me to have led a more retired life than that of the army, had I been consulted on the occasion, and at liberty of pursuing my own inclinations. But as, early in the present contest, I laid it down as a maxim not to refuse my best, though poor, services to my country, in any way they should think proper to employ me, on this principle I cannot refuse the honor done me by Congress in the present appointment; and shall be happy if, in my best endeavours to serve my country in the military line, I shall at any time prove so successful as to merit your Excellency's approbation.

We have, some considerable time since, drawn the chain across the river at Fort Montgomery; and as the tide, as it is now fixed, has not the least impression on it, and it is greatly strengthened by a number of anchors and cables, I am in hopes it will answer some good end. The works in the river near this place go on well, and I have not the least doubt but they will be effectual when completed; and had the Convention suffered me to have paid my whole attention to this business, it would have been the case nearly by this time. As it is, they are in great forwardness, and in a few days will become formidable. The companies for which I nominated officers, are successful in recruiting, two of them having already near thirty men each. I, through mistake, appointed a First-Lieutenant more than I was directed; and as he is an active person, and has enlisted a number of men, I wish he could be provided for. I am, with the highest esteem,

Your Excellency's most obedient servant,

GEORGE CLINTON.

FROM BRIGADIER-GENERAL McDOUGALL.

Peekskill, 29 April, 1 P. M., 1777.

SIR,

The wind blowing fresh northerly on Monday, and likely to continue for two or three days, when I received a little provision for the men, I marched, at ten at night, with about twelve hundred, and one field-piece, towards Bedford, in hopes to fall in with the enemy there, from the intelligence contained in Number Eight of the inclosure. At ten the next morning, I arrived at the south end of the town, at the road leading from Ridgefield, which is ten miles from Bedford. I had but just arrived there, when two expresses came in, and informed me that the enemy had left Ridgefield that morning at daybreak, and marched towards Norwalk, which is but seventeen miles from the former; and that they had met with no opposition all the morning. This intelligence deprived me of all hopes of coming up with them, in that distance, as they had rested at Ridgefield the night before, and we had marched twenty-one miles, through very rough ground, without sleep or refreshment. Although I hoped the public and my superiors would justify my risking this post, when there was some prospect of advancing the service, yet I considered it madness to risk it in a fruitless pursuit of the enemy, and therefore returned here this moment, after a very fatiguing march, which the troops endured with great patience.

Your favor of the 26th found me at Bedford, and that of the 28th two miles south of Croton Bridge. The inclosures will give all the intelligence I am possessed of. I am

Your Excellency's humble servant,

ALEXANDER McDOUGALL.

FROM COLONEL PICKERING.

Boston, 7 May, 1777.

SIR,

I had the honor to receive your Excellency's letter by Colonel Lee, conferring upon me the office of Adjutant-General; and since, notwithstanding all my objections, it is your Excellency's pleasure, I am happy to declare my acceptance of it. At the same time, I am constrained, from my real feelings, again to express my fears that I shall fall short of your

Excellency's expectations. Few people are competent judges of military abilities; and most are apt to form their opinions very superficially. Hence I have as often been mortified as pleased by the favorable sentiments which some have expressed concerning me, conscious that many times I did not merit their applause. I know not who have recommended me to your Excellency; I wish they may not have judged too favorably of my abilities. However, I am determined to exert myself to the utmost to serve your Excellency and my country; and if, after all, I fail of executing the office with propriety, seeing I at first declined it, partly from an apprehension of inability, your Excellency will acquit me of presumption in accepting it at your repeated request.

My affairs are complicated, but I will prepare to attend you with all possible despatch. General Glover accepts the post assigned him, and we shall doubtless go to head-quarters together. I am, Sir,

Your most obedient servant,
TIMOTHY PICKERING, JR.

FROM ROBERT MORRIS.

Philadelphia, 10 May, 1777.

DEAR SIR,

I have not taken the liberty of giving you any trouble for some time past; and, indeed, I never do it but with great reluctance, because I know how much your attention and time must be engaged in the most important pursuits.

The bearer of this, the Marquis Armand de la Rouerie, is entitled to my warmest recommendations, because he brought from his own country letters to me that I am obliged to attend to, and put great faith in, as they come from persons worthy of the utmost credit. One of them is from Mr. Deane, who not only mentions him as a gentleman of rank, good family, and fortune, but also as a man of great merit; desiring my particular attention to him, and that I should supply him with money, which will be repaid in France by a gentleman to whom America is under the most important obligations. You will, therefore, excuse and oblige me at the same time by your favorable attention to Monsieur Armand, for he chooses to pass by that name; and, should he want money, I will pay his drafts for what he stands in need of. I find he is a little disgusted at an appointment made for him by Congress this day; and I believe it was through the inattention of a Committee, which I shall get set right again in a short time.* I am, dear Sir, with the greatest esteem and affection,

Your obedient, humble servant,

ROBERT MORRIS.

FROM GENERALS GREENE, MᶜDOUGALL, KNOX, WAYNE, AND CLINTON.

Peekskill, 17 May, 1777.

MAY IT PLEASE YOUR EXCELLENCY,

We have examined the obstructions in the North River, and beg leave to observe, that the object is too important to be trusted to its present security. If those obstructions in the river can be rendered effectual, and the passes into the Highlands be pro-

---

* He was appointed a Colonel, but near the close of the war he was raised to the rank of Brigadier-General.

perly guarded, which can be done with about four or five thousand troops, the rest of the army will be at liberty to operate elsewhere.

To render the obstruction at Fort Montgomery complete, it will be necessary to have a boom across the river, and one or two cables in front of the chain, to break the force of the shipping before they come up to it. The two Continental ships should be immediately manned and fixed, and the two row-galleys be stationed just above the obstruction, which will form a front fire equal to what the enemy can bring against them. The fire from the ships and galleys in front, and the batteries upon the flank, will render it impossible for the shipping to operate there, if the obstructions in the river bring them up; which, with the additional strength proposed, we have great reason to expect.

The communication between the Eastern and Western States is essential to the Continent; and the advantages we shall have over the enemy by the communication, and the great expense that will be saved in transportation of stores, by having the command of the river, warrant every expense to secure an object of so great magnitude. We are very confident, if the obstructions in the river can be rendered effectual, the enemy will not attempt to operate by land, the passes through the Highlands are so exceeding difficult. We are, with the greatest respect and esteem,

Your Excellency's most obedient servants,
NATHANAEL GREENE, M. G.
ALEXANDER MCDOUGALL, B. G.
HENRY KNOX, B. G. Artillery.
ANTHONY WAYNE, B. G.
GEORGE CLINTON, B. G.

32 *

FROM THE PRESIDENT OF CONGRESS.

Philadelphia, 5 June, 1777.

SIR,

The inclosed resolves are all I have in charge from Congress to forward at this time.

General Mifflin having applied to Congress, in consequence of your letter to him, he has their permission to repair immediately to head-quarters, agreeably to his own desire. I have made him acquainted with this determination of Congress.

In order that you may be enabled to meet General Howe upon his own ground, who has long since offered rewards to induce the soldiers of the American army to desert, the Congress have authorized you to fix on such rewards or sum of money as you may judge proper, to encourage deserters from the enemy, both horse and foot. You will, therefore, be pleased to carry this resolve into execution in such way as you may think most expedient, and best suited to answer the end. I have the honor to be, with the utmost esteem and respect, Sir,

Your most obedient and very humble servant,

JOHN HANCOCK, *President*.

FROM BRIGADIER-GENERAL KNOX.

Camp, Middlebrook, 5 June, 1777.

SIR,

A resolution, of the 30th ultimo, has been shown to me by some French officers attached to the corps of artillery under my command, ordaining that all officers of artillery, engaged by Mr. Deane in France, shall take rank, in the American artillery, according to the dates of their brevet commissions in the French service.

I believe the Congress did not sufficiently consider the consequences of such a resolution, or that they had not full information to form it, consistent with that justice which is due their own officers.

The French Minister of Marine, or Minister of the Colonial Department, gave these officers brevet commissions, to be in force in their Colonies only, or rather on this Continent, of superior rank to those which they then held in France, in order to give them an ideal rank here. They have had the rank given to them implied in their brevet commissions, and some higher than they expected. But this resolution of Congress gives them another superiority, which perhaps was not intended. Nearly all the Captains now in the Continental artillery served for the last two campaigns as Captain-Lieutenants, and are such only of that class as distinguished themselves by their abilities and special services. They are arranged, in the different battalions of artillery, according to their seniority, but do not take rank as full Captains until the commencement of the present year; whereas the French officers' brevet commissions are dated in November and December, 1776.

The resolution of Congress pervades all the different ranks in the artillery, of Captains, Captain-Lieutenants, and Lieutenants, and supersedes all the officers in these different stations.

I confess that it surprises me much, and that I am totally unacquainted with the principles upon which it is founded. No military ones most certainly can be assigned. These French gentlemen, in general, have never been in so much actual service as the American officers, who are not accused of any demerits; but, on the contrary, their reputation, as a corps, is equal to any in the service. Why, then, should they all be superseded and disgraced? They have exerted themselves to recruit their companies on the new establishment, and marched them to camp.

I conceive the most fatal consequences will arise to the artillery, except this resolution be repealed, at least so far as respects the seniority of rank. All that can with propriety be done, is to give them commissions dated at the same time that Congress accepted their services. Any thing more will occasion the resignation of every officer of spirit in the corps, who, though they are actuated by every tie of attachment and interest in the service of their country, yet will infinitely prefer serving as volunteers, than under people who can have no other tie than the pay they receive, and who cannot give a single order that can be understood.

In justice to the merit of the officers under my command, and to promote the good of the service, I make this representation to your Excellency, begging that you would be pleased to transmit it to the Honorable Congress for their information. If they repeal the resolution, I shall be happy. If they do not, I shall be clear of any bad consequences which may follow. I am, with the greatest respect,

Your Excellency's most obedient servant,
HENRY KNOX.*

* General Washington sent a copy of this letter to Congress, and on the 10th of June the following resolution was passed;

"Resolved, that General Washington be informed, that that clause of the resolution of the 30th of May last, ' the rank of each class of the said officers to be settled by the date of their commissions from the King

FROM THE PRESIDENT OF CONGRESS.

Philadelphia, 13 June, 1777.

Sir,

You will perceive, from the inclosed resolves, the fixed determination of Congress to retaliate, as nearly as lies in their power, on our enemies, should they think proper to send any of their prisoners to Great Britain, or to any other part of the British King's dominions beyond sea. This resolution you will please to convey to General Howe, as soon as possible, as it is of the utmost importance.

If the sixteen additional battalions are not all provided with commanding officers, the Congress, in consequence of a letter from Governor Caswell (an extract of which I inclose to you), have recommended Colonel Abraham Shepherd to the command of one of the said battalions, and doubt not you will honor him with the appointment. I beg leave to request your attention to the whole of the resolves herewith transmitted.

Inclosed you have the observations of Monsieur Ducoudray on Billingsport, and the other fortifications in this river, which I forward for your perusal. Every possible measure is taking to render the fortifications complete.

I have the honor to be, with the utmost esteem and respect, Sir,

Your most obedient, and very humble servant,

JOHN HANCOCK, *President.*

---

of France,' intended only their relative rank among one another; but that their commissions in the American army be dated by General Washington on the day when they shall be filled."

Saratoga, 14 June, 1777.

DEAR SIR,

I do myself the honor to inclose your Excellency a letter to Congress, under flying seal. The variety of affairs, which claim my attention, does not permit me time to communicate to your Excellency and Congress, separately, such information as it may be necessary both should know. You will, therefore, please to excuse the mode I take.

Our numbers are so few to the northward, and we have so little prospect of their increasing, that should a disaster befall us at Ticonderoga, we should have very few troops indeed to oppose them. If the enemy should make an attempt to penetrate into the country, I shall probably be under the necessity of calling for assistance from Peekskill. Perhaps your Excellency may think proper to lodge an order with the commanding officer to comply with my requisition, if I should make one, ascertaining the number you may think proper to spare. Be assured that I shall not ask any aid, as long as there is a possibility of doing without.

Your letter of the 11th of May, to General Gates, was this day delivered to me by Brigadier-General Learned. The clothing for Colonel Shepherd's regiment, if at Ticonderoga, will be immediately sent down. I am, dear Sir, with the sincerest esteem,

Your Excellency's most obedient, humble servant,

PHILIP SCHUYLER.

FROM MAJOR-GENERAL SCHUYLER.

Fort Edward, 16 June, 1777.

DEAR SIR,

I did myself the honor to address you from Saratoga on the 14th instant. On the next day, Amsbury and Adams (mentioned in General St. Clair's letter, copy whereof I transmitted to Congress by letter under cover to your Excellency) arrived at Saratoga. What passed between us, and what information he gave, is noted in paper Number One. Number Two is the letter which was inclosed between the bottoms of the canteen.

If the information which Amsbury gives is to be relied upon, as I think it is, we shall soon be attacked at Ticonderoga; and although I think the force now there may be sufficient to hold that important post, yet I have no troops to oppose either Sir John Johnson, if he should penetrate to the Mohawk River, or any to prevent the communication between this and Fort George from being cut off; nor have I force, if these should not be attempted by the enemy, to march to the relief of Ticonderoga. In this situation, I am under the necessity of applying to your Excellency for a reënforcement.

From the time I left Albany till my return to that place, nothing, comparatively speaking, has been done towards throwing into Ticonderoga a stock of provisions of the meat kind; and of the little that is left there, I fear to learn that a very considerable part is damaged; and what is equally bad, if not worse, is, that we have very little hopes of a supply of fresh meat. A week or two may remedy the latter, but it may then be too late to convey a quantity to Ticonderoga. If, therefore, any salted pork or beef can be spared from Peekskill, or elsewhere, I wish it may be ordered up, without the least delay.

Should your Excellency order me a reënforcement, permit me to suggest, that, if there are no vessels at Peekskill or Fishkill to transport the troops to Albany, it may be proper, by express, to direct the commanding officer at Albany to send down from thence a sufficient number of sloops.

Such is the inattention, in this department, that not less than a thousand barrels of flour are now lying at this post, and only five wagons employed to carry it to Fort George, the distance of fifteen miles.

Permit me to beg that your Excellency will communicate the contents of this despatch to Congress, as I cannot find time to do myself the honor to write to them.

I shall (consulting with the General Officers at Ticonderoga) try to send an answer to Mr. Levius's letter, as from General Sullivan, in which I shall leave him to suppose (what I do not by any means believe) that General Sullivan has entered into his views. Your Excellency will please to mention my intention to General Sullivan, and to assure him that my only view is to serve the public. I am, dear Sir, most sincerely,

Your Excellency's most obedient, humble servant,
PHILIP SCHUYLER.

FROM MAJOR-GENERAL ARNOLD.

Coryell's Ferry, 16 June, 1777; 8 o'clock, P. M.

MY DEAR GENERAL,

I wrote your Excellency yesterday, that the boats, scows, &c., were sent up the river, eleven miles, to a place called Tohegan, except such as were necessary here, which would be secured from the enemy in case of their approach. Since which I have had no direct, and but very imperfect intelligence from your Excellency. I am at a loss if any part of your army has removed from Middlebrook, and more so of your Excellency's intentions. The enemy, I am informed, are at Somerset Heights, intrenching. General Sullivan is at Flemington, with sixteen hundred Continental troops, the Jersey militia, and one thousand men I have sent him from this place, half Continental, the others militia. I expect Colonel Bull here to-morrow, with five hundred State troops, part of two battalions engaged for the war.

General Mifflin wrote me yesterday, that the City militia will move this morning; I am informed there are about two thousand of them; they bring ten pieces cannon, and one royal howitzer, two hundred tents, one thousand felling axes, one thousand spades and shovels. One quarter part of the militia of this State are ordered out immediately, except two of the western counties. The whole, including the City militia, I am informed, will make ten thousand men. Three thousand of the Southern Continental troops are on their march, and will be in Philadelphia in the course of a week; six heavy pieces cannon, four galleys, and ten armed boats, are arrived at Bristol and Trenton ferries. The enemy must be desperate indeed, if they attempt to push for Philadelphia.

As the militia can be but illy spared at this busy season, I wish to know, as early as possible, your Excellency's orders respecting them; if you wish to have them in the Jerseys or on this side the Delaware. If the latter, for the defence of the passes on the

river, one half will effectually answer the purpose. I
have examined, and inclosed your Excellency a sketch
of the passes between this and Trenton Ferry. Four
or five thousand men, with a few pieces of cannon,
will effectually guard the whole, and as far down as
Philadelphia, with the assistance of the galleys and
armed boats, against twenty thousand men. Above
Coryell's Ferry, I am convinced the enemy will never
attempt to pass. I hope the troops will be ordered
for a different purpose, that of securing the enemy
where they are, in the Jerseys. If they are detained
here, I shall employ them in fortifying the banks of
the river against the passes.

I have sent off, this evening, *via* Flemington, four
wagons, and musket cartridges sixty-six thousand,
under an escort of seventy-five men. I have only
to add, with great respect and esteem, I am

Your Excellency's most obedient, humble servant,

BENEDICT ARNOLD.

FROM BRIGADIER-GENERAL REED.

Philadelphia, 18 June, 1777.

DEAR SIR,

By some accident Mr. Peters omitted sending me
your favor of the 14th instant, so that I did not
receive it till several days after he returned.* I
cannot sufficiently acknowledge the kind sentiments
which your letter breathes, nor express the satisfaction it has given me. If I had been capable of the

-----

* See this letter in Washington's Writings, Vol. IV. p. 540.

disingenuity, which might seem to appear, I should
certainly have guarded it; but, as my letter, to which
that was an answer, contained nothing that could
make any caution necessary, none was used. While
there was a prospect of General Lee's release, I pur-
posely avoided an explanation, as I hoped my letter
might have been preserved.* Certain I am, it contained no other sentiments than lamenting the loss
of Mount Washington, as occasioned, I frankly acknowledge, by hesitating too long between clashing
opinions, the want of assistance to enable your Excellency to bear the load of accumulated losses and
misfortunes, and to enable you to extricate yourself
from the difficulties which surrounded us.

I pressed him to hasten with his troops to our relief, as necessary to raise the spirits of our broken
army; and as General Greene's judgment had just
then proved so erroneous, I urged General Lee, by
every motive of regard to the cause, and his own
honor and safety, to hasten his march, that his judgment and experience might, in some degree, supply
that defect. To induce him to exert himself, I remember I told him that I knew you had a great
confidence in his abilities as well as the public, and
that the opinions of others had kept you in suspense.
I believed your own judgment was fixed. His answer,
you may recollect, followed these ideas, though min-
gled with those expressions, and a style which, you
may recollect, was peculiar to himself.

I gratefully remember the honor you often did me
in hearing my sentiments, and should have been sufficiently encouraged to have expressed my apprehen-

---

* A copy of the letter was afterwards procured. It is printed in the
Life and Correspondence of Joseph Reed, Vol. I. p. 255.

sions of any quality of the mind, whose operations
might prejudice the service and your own honor, if
my views and subject had led to it. But at that
time I had nothing more upon my mind, or in prospect, than the affair of Mount Washington, and a
speedy junction with General Lee. But I will not
trouble you any farther upon this subject than to
give you my most sincere thanks for the kind and
obliging manner in which you have relieved my
mind from the anxiety which the apprehended loss
of your favor and friendship had occasioned.

I saw Dr. Shippen yesterday, who surprised me
very much by mentioning that you had received no
letters from me on the subject of the late appointment.* I assure you, my dear Sir, I wrote immediately on receiving information of your kind intentions; and when I had determined, which I would not
do hastily or without advice of my friends, I wrote
immediately and sent the letter to Mr. Hancock's, as
the proper place to be forwarded. I confess my inclinations led me strongly to accept, and more especially when I was assured of your favor and friendship; but, upon a calculation of the expense which
would attend it, and for which the Congress have
not made any special provision, I found that in two
or three years I should probably sink my little fortune, and do injustice to the public or discredit the
station. This, added to the many promotions made
in the interior, were my principal reasons. My prospects in the civil line are considerable; these I must
also have sacrificed.

For all these I am sure you will make due allow-

---

* He had been appointed by Congress a Brigadier-General in the
Continental army on the 12th of May.

ances, and, I hope, not disapprove my declining the honor you intended me. I can hardly flatter myself with the hope of contributing any thing to your ease or honor, but my prayers and wishes for both will ever be as sincere as my attachment and respect are lasting and ardent. I have this morning seen a copy of your letter to General Arnold, expressive of your plan and views of the enemy's intentions. It cannot be unacceptable to you to know that it is highly approved. I have lately had a collection of English papers, by way of France. I read, with great pleasure, the encomiums which the British officers have wrote to their friends, not only on the virtue of your private character, but conduct of the war. The praise of an enemy cannot be suspected. Be assured you stand high in the opinions of the first military characters in Europe. As far as my poor opinion can go, I think your present system and plan have the fairest chance of success, and will meet with it, if some of those unforeseen strokes, to which war is subject, do not intervene. We have had a letter published here, which says we must fight or forfeit our honor. It is said to be wrote by some General Officer. I cannot think he intended it for publication. Your letter contains different, and, I think, juster sentiments upon this important point.

Colonel Moylan writes, that he thinks my knowledge of the country and people would be of use in the quarter where he is, and presses me to come up, which I shall do immediately, and pay my respects at head-quarters as soon as possible. I have been employed, for some time, in laboring an accommodation with the contending parties in this State, which, through General Armstrong's and Mifflin's influence, is at last effected, so as to afford the fairest pros-

33*

pects of bringing forth the force of this State. General Mifflin addressed the people at a town-meeting in your name, and requested them all to turn out; but, on trial, this was found impracticable. About four thousand, besides those in the field, will probably be the number, provided they can get arms, accoutrements, and tents; but there is at present so lamentable a deficiency in these articles, that I very much fear difficulties will arise after the men are procured. General Armstrong is indefatigable in his endeavours, and I hope will be more successful than at present he seems to expect.

I presume the hurry in which General Mifflin came, prevented a formal application from yourself to the persons in authority here. I would just hint it to your Excellency, as I observe they think themselves passed by in the mode which has been taken, and which, most probably, has been purely accidental.

I am too well acquainted with your many engagements to take up more of your time. Allow me only to add, that I am, with the most sincere respect and attachment, my dear General, your most obliged,

Affectionate, and obedient humble servant,

JOSEPH REED.

FROM THE PRESIDENT OF CONGRESS.

Philadelphia, 24 June, 1777.

SIR,

Your favor of the 23d, containing the agreeable intelligence that the enemy had retreated from Brunswick, I had the honor of receiving yesterday afternoon, and shall this morning, with the greatest pleasure, lay it before Congress.   Give me leave to congratulate you very sincerely upon this event; as it must be principally ascribed to the prudence and wisdom of your operations, which had so embarrassed the enemy as to reduce them to the necessity of acting in the manner they have done.   Should they be compelled finally to abandon the Jerseys, which I flatter myself will be the case, it will be the most explicit declaration to the whole world, that the conquest of America is not only a very distant, but an unattainable object. We have seen them, after penetrating some miles into our country, precipitately driven back, and in a moment obliged to evacuate towns, after keeping possession of them only a few months.

I do myself the honor to inclose you the resolves of Congress respecting the Commissary's Department, together with a list of the persons appointed to carry it into execution. I beg leave to request your attention to them, and to the other resolves herewith transmitted.

Your favor of the 20th instant was duly received, and immediately communicated to Congress.   I have the honor to be, with the greatest esteem, Sir,

Your most obedient and very humble servant,

JOHN HANCOCK, *President*.

FROM MAJOR-GENERAL SCHUYLER.

Albany, 28 June 1777; 11 o'clock, A. M.

DEAR SIR,

Your Excellency's favor of the 20th instant I had the honor to receive at Saratoga, in the evening of the 26th.

I am this moment favored with a letter of the 25th instant from General St. Clair, copy whereof I herewith transmit.* Should an accident happen to the garrison of Ticonderoga, and General Burgoyne make a push to gain the south part of the Lake, I know of no obstacle to prevent him. Comparatively speaking, I have not a man to oppose him; the whole number at the different posts at and on this side of the Lake, including the garrisons of Fort George and Skenesborough, not exceeding seven hundred men, and these I cannot draw away from their several stations, in every one of which they are already much too weak. It is therefore highly necessary that a strong reënforcement should, without delay, be sent me. If the sloops are not yet sent to bring the troops your Excellency has ordered to be kept in readiness at Peekskill, I shall push them off without delay.

As it is not probable that we shall in time be supplied with field-pieces from the eastward, I must entreat that the reënforcements may bring some up with them.

I have this moment also received a letter from Mr. Deane, the Indian Interpreter, an extract whereof I inclose to you. As the information tallies exactly with what I had before, it leads me to conclude that an irruption will be made from the [westward].

I shall apply for the aid of the militia of this and the neighbouring States, but I fear it will not be very powerful, as many must be necessarily left at home.

I have received a letter from the Commissary-General, which I think neither so temperate or decent as it should be. I shall take the first leisure hour to transmit you a copy, with my answer, in

---

* See this letter in the Appendix.

which, I believe, it will be evinced from authentic returns, that the scarcity of provisions in this department is, in a great measure, if not altogether, to be imputed to a want of attention in the persons whose duty it was to supply this department. I am, dear Sir, with great regard and esteem,

Your Excellency's most obedient, humble servant,

PHILIP SCHUYLER.

P. S. I have sent an express to General Putnam to hasten on the troops your Excellency had ordered to be in readiness for this quarter.

Since writing the above I have received another letter from General St. Clair, a copy whereof is inclosed. I am in pain about Fort George, but have no troops to throw in, and some time will necessarily elapse before the militia can be got to march.

FROM MAJOR-GENERAL SCHUYLER.

Saratoga, 7 July, 1777.

DEAR SIR,

Soon after I had despatched the letter, which I did myself the honor to address to your Excellency from Stillwater, I met with Lieutenant-Colonel Hay, Deputy Quartermaster-General, who was at Ticonderoga. He informs me, that on Saturday it had been agreed upon to retreat from Ticonderoga and Mount Independence; that between two and three o'clock on Sunday morning, General St. Clair, with the rest of the General Officers, and the army, marched out of the lines at Mount Independence; that Colonel Long, with about six hundred men, embarked on board our few vessels, and in bateaux; that, just before they arrived at Skenesborough, they were overtaken by the enemy's vessels and gunboats, and were obliged to abandon the vessels, in which we lost all our ammunition. Indeed, Colonel Hay assures me that not one earthly thing has been saved.

The troops under Colonel Long are arrived at Fort Ann. Where General St. Clair is, with the main body, I have not yet learnt. Colonel Hay imagined he would come by the way of Skenesborough. If so, he will fall in with the enemy, who have taken possession there. Captain Dantignac, who is just arrived here, confirms Colonel Hay's account, except as to General St. Clair, who he understood was to march to Number Four. This is not likely. I have despatched an officer to meet General St. Clair, and requested that he should march, by the shortest route, to Fort Edward. As I have related the above from memory, I may have omitted some, and misapprehended other circumstances.*

It is impossible to say what post we shall take. It depends on the route the enemy mean to pursue. My prospect of preventing them from penetrating, is not much. They have an army flushed with victory, plentifully provided with provisions, cannon, and every warlike store. Our army, if it should once more collect, is weak in numbers, dispirited, naked, in a manner, destitute of provisions, without camp equipage, with little ammunition, and not a single piece of cannon. In this situation, it is of the most urgent necessity, that your Excellency should afford me a very respectable reënforcement, besides that now com-

---

* See General St. Clair's letter to General Schuyler, dated July 8th, and other letters on this subject, in the Appendix.

ing up under Brigadier-General Nixon; for it will be impossible for me to keep the militia together any time in a country very thinly inhabited, in which they cannot find shelter, and must lie out exposed to the weather.

As the Continental troops have lost every thing, your Excellency will please to order up to me, the soonest possible, tents for four thousand men, five hundred camp kettles, a quantity of fixed musket ammunition, cartridge-paper, twelve pieces heavy cannon, with travelling carriages, sixteen field-pieces, and a considerable quantity of ammunition for them; a competent number of artillerymen, in addition to Major Stevens's corps, so as to be sufficient to manage the artillery; all the implements necessary to the artillery, horses, harness, and drivers; about six hundred intrenching tools, sorted, excluding pickaxes, of which we have a considerable number. Please also to send me a good engineer or two. I am, dear Sir, with great respect and esteem,

Your Excellency's most obedient, humble servant,
PHILIP SCHUYLER.

FROM MAJOR-GENERAL SCHUYLER.

Fort Edward, 9 July, 1777.

DEAR SIR,

Since I wrote you from Saratoga, I have not been able to learn what is become of General St. Clair and the enemy. The army followed the troops that came to Skenesborough as far as Fort Ann, where they were yesterday repulsed; notwithstanding which, Colonel Long, contrary to my express orders, evacuated that post. I am here, at the head of a hand-

ful of men, not above fifteen hundred, without provisions, little ammunition, not above five rounds to
a man, having neither ball, nor lead to make any;
the country in the deepest consternation; no carriages to move the stores from Fort George, which I
expect every moment to learn is attacked.   And
what adds to my distress, is, that a report prevails
that I had given orders for the evacuation of Ticonderoga, whereas not the most distant hint of such an
intention can be drawn from any of my letters to
General St. Clair, or any other person whatever.
I am informed, from undoubted authority, that the
garrison was reënforced with twelve hundred men at
least two days before the evacuation, and that eighty
head of cattle had got in, and a number of sheep.
What could induce the General Officers to a step
that has ruined our affairs in this quarter, God only
knows.

By the information of some of the prisoners I
learn, that the enemy have already a brigade on the
way from Skenesborough to this place.   General Nixon's is not yet come up; but, if it does, we shall
still be too weak to make any capital opposition.   I
will, however, throw as many obstructions in the enemy's route as possible.   A party is parading to fell
trees across the road between this and Fort Ann, to
take up all the bridges, drive off all the cattle, and
bring away the carriages.

I inclose your Excellency a proclamation of General Burgoyne, which he has caused to be industriously
spread through the country, and, I fear, will be attended with the most evil consequences to us.   I am,
dear Sir,

Your Excellency's most obedient, humble servant,

PHILIP SCHUYLER.

FROM MAJOR-GENERAL SCHUYLER.

Fort Edward, 14 July, 1777.

DEAR SIR,

On the 12th instant General St. Clair arrived here. As he fell in with Hudson's River about twelve miles below this, I ordered the troops to halt at Fort Miller, having no kind of shelter for them at any other place, and not even a sufficiency of boards at that. What the number is that have arrived I have not yet been able to learn, as the greatest confusion imaginable prevails here. General St. Clair supposes about fifteen hundred. Nor can I say what militia are in this quarter. I do not, however, suppose that our whole strength, in this department, exceeds four thousand five hundred men.

Colonel Warner, with the remains of his regiment, I have ordered to remain on what are commonly called the New Hampshire Grants, together with the militia from that part of this State. He has directions to drive off all the cattle and carriages; but whether he will be able to effect it is a doubt, as I am informed a very great proportion of the inhabitants are taking protections from General Burgoyne, as most of those in this quarter are also willing to do.

Two regiments of the militia from the State of the Massachusetts, under the command of Learned and Wells, who were sent up to supply, in part, the deficiencies of the other regiments from that State, are, to a man, gone home.

General Nixon arrived the night before last, with his brigade. From the slowness with which they moved from Albany to this, being four days marching forty-six miles, I was led to conclude that they were a formidable body; but to my great mortification, I find the whole to consist of five hundred and seventy-five, rank and file, fit for duty, and eleven sick. Several of these are nogroes, and many of them young, small, and feeble boys. Desertion prevails, and disease gains ground; nor is it to be wondered at, for we have neither tents, houses, barns, boards, or any shelter, except a little brush. Every rain that falls, and we have it in great abundance almost every day, wets the men to the skin. We are, besides, in great want of every kind of necessaries, provisions excepted. Camp-kettles we have so few, that we cannot afford above one to twenty men. Although we have near fifteen tons of powder, yet we have so little lead, that I could not give each man above fifteen rounds; and although I have saved about thirty pieces of light artillery, yet I have not a single carriage for them, so that my whole train of artillery consists of two iron field-pieces, which General Nixon brought up with his brigade.

I have, indeed, written to Springfield for the cannon which were there; but the answer I got was, that they were all ordered another way. I have also written for a variety of articles to that place and to Boston; not that I expect any thing will be sent me, but that I may stand justified, for I have never yet been able to get much of any thing from thence. In this situation I have only to look up to your Excellency for relief; and permit me to entreat you to send a reënforcement of troops, and such a supply of artillery, ammunition, and every other necessary, except provisions and powder, as an army ought to have, if it can possibly be spared.

An express has passed through the country from General Burgoyne to General Howe. The latter will, probably, on receipt thereof, immediately move up Hudson's River.

I inclose your Excellency copy of the proceedings of a Council of General Officers, held at Ticonderoga, a copy of which I beg you will transmit to Congress, and be so good as to mention that I have not time to do myself the honor to write them. It contains the principles on which the evacuation of that fortress took place.

If the enemy will permit us to pass unmolested, three days longer, to Fort George, I shall be able to bring away all the stores from thence, and then draw off the few troops we have there.

Yesterday, accompanied by the General Officers and engineers, I examined the country, and found a very defensible spot about four miles below this, to which place we are this day moving part of the army, and our stores. I propose remaining here until Fort George is abandoned, and as much longer as the enemy will permit me.

General Nixon, with his brigade, supported by about six hundred militia, is advanced to Fort Ann, to fell trees into Wood Creek, and into the road from Fort Ann to this place. I have also stationed a body of militia about five miles on this side of Fort George, to cover the retreat of the garrison now at that place.

We are informed that part of the enemy are still at Skenesborough, and that a body is coming by the way of Lake George. I hope it will not be very soon. Adieu, my dear Sir; and believe me, unfeignedly, and with great respect,

Your Excellency's most obedient, humble servant,
PHILIP SCHUYLER.

Fort Edward, 17 July, 1777.

SIR,

Your Excellency's letters of the 12th and 13th instant, to General Schuyler, have been by him communicated to me. Considering that my letter to him of the 5th, the day before I left Ticonderoga, was not delivered, and one I wrote to him whilst on the march to this place has miscarried, and that your Excellency has had no intimation of the motions and destination of our army, I do not wonder that you should have some doubts about the propriety of my conduct, though it gives me a very painful sensation to know myself, but for a moment, the subject of a doubt with you. I have, however, the strongest hopes, when your Excellency comes to be fully informed of our situation and force, you will not condemn me; and, although I am not solicitous about the opinion of the world, though very far from disregarding it, I wish to hold a character with your Excellency something more than merely negative.

Returns of the strength of my garrison were regularly transmitted to General Schuyler, and by him, no doubt, to you. By them, your Excellency will see, that our force consisted of little more than two thousand effectives. With these, I had lines and redoubts of more than a league in extent to defend. Judge how poorly they could have been defended by these numbers, had they been perfected, which they were very far from being. In fact, they were not defensible at all upon the Ticonderoga side, unless the enemy would have been so complaisant as to attack us in front of the old French lines, and take no notice of the flanks of them, which were both open. We had, last year, nine thousand men at these posts, and they were found barely sufficient for the defence of the works. The system was a little altered this season, but not so as to make a smaller number answer, but to make a greater number necessary.

The enemy had nearly invested us, nothing being wanting to complete it but their occupying a narrow neck of land, betwixt the East Creek and the Lake, on the Mount Independence side. This, I had information, would certainly take place in the course of the next twenty-four hours, and had been left open so long only with a view to intercept any cattle that we might bring in from the country, and then our communication would have been effectually cut off. We could have received neither supplies of provisions nor reënforcements, for, depend upon it, Sir, the militia of this country cannot yet be brought on to raise a siege.

But, it may be asked, why I had not called in the militia to assist in the defence of the posts. For this plain reason, I had not provision for them, and very little prospect of an effectual supply. When I first had notice of the approach of the enemy, there was no more than ten days' provision in store for the troops then upon the ground. To have called in the militia, in that situation, would have been certain ruin. So soon as a supply arrived, although but a scanty one, I did call for them, and about nine hundred joined me the day before the resolution to evacuate the posts was taken. They had come out in such a hurry, and almost entirely without clothes, they did not propose to remain but a very few days at the utmost. The term of Learned and Wells's regiments, which made part of the garrison, expired

34 *

also in two days, and the commanding officers had acquainted me that they could not prevail upon the men to remain beyond the time they were engaged for. Your Excellency knows, but too well, the disposition of these people on such occasions.

The batteries of the enemy were ready to open in three different quarters, and our whole camp, on the Ticonderoga side, was exposed to the fire of each; and, as soon as they did open, every man I had must have been constantly on duty, as, from our weakness, of which the enemy could not be ignorant, I had reason, every moment, to expect an assault. Judge, Sir, how long we could have sustained it, or whether our resistance must not have been a very feeble one indeed, especially when you take into the account that a great number were mere boys, and that not more than a tenth part were furnished with bayonets.

Revolving these circumstances in my mind, I was at no loss to determine what part I ought to take; but I thought it prudent to take the sense of the other General Officers. A copy of the Council has been transmitted to your Excellency by General Schuyler. They were unanimously of opinion that the posts ought to be evacuated immediately; wisely, in my judgment, considering that a retreat, even with the loss of our cannon and stores, if it could be effected, would be of infinitely greater service to the country, and bring less disgrace upon our arms, than an army, although a small one, taken prisoners, with their cannon and stores. I was fully in sentiment with them, and believe I should have ordered the retreat, if they had been of a contrary way of thinking.

But here, again, it may be asked why, when I found myself in the situation I have described, I did not retreat sooner, when every thing might have been saved. I have only to answer that, until the enemy sat down before the place, I believed the small garrison I had to be sufficient. The intelligence that Congress had received, that no serious attempt in that quarter was intended, as it gained credit with them, I never doubted, and was unwilling to be the occasion of drawing off any part of your army, as your operations might thereby be rendered less vigorous; and I knew, too, that you could very ill spare them. Besides, until the case became so urgent that I had no alternative but the evacuation of my posts, or the loss of the army, it did not lie with me to determine upon.

The retreat was begun a little before day, on the 6th instant, unperceived by the enemy, after having embarked as much of the stores and provision, and as many of the cannon, as was possible in the course of one very short night; and our march would probably have been unperceived for some time, if General Fermoy's house had not been set on fire. How that happened, I know not. I had previously given orders against burning any of the buildings, that our march might be the longer concealed; but it served to the enemy as the signal of our leaving the place, and, in consequence, they were upon the Mount before our rear was clear of it, and fired a few times upon it, but without effect.

Colonel Long, with his regiment, and a detachment from the other regiments, and the invalids with the hospital, were sent to Skenesborough, by water; while I took the road to the same place, through Castleton, with the body of the army. As the enemy were at least four times my numbers, I had nothing for it but a forced march; and I pressed it as much as possible, and reached Castleton that night, thirty miles from Ticonderoga, having, on our way, fallen in with and dispersed a party of the enemy, from whom we took twenty head of cattle, three British prisoners, and five Canadians.

The rear guard, under Colonel Warner, which, with those that had failed upon the march, amounted to a thousand, imprudently halted six miles short of Castleton, and wasted so much time in the morning, that they were overtaken and surprised by a strong detachment from Ticonderoga, which had been sent up the East Bay, which runs into the country very near the place where he was. They sustained the attack with great bravery, but were finally obliged to give way, with the loss of about fifty killed and wounded. On the first of the firing, I sent orders to two regiments of militia, who had left me the night before, and were lodged within two miles of Colonel Warner's post, to move up to his assistance, which had they done, that party would have been cut off. But, instead of that, they made all possible haste to rejoin me, and at the same instant I received the account of the enemy's being in possession of Skenesborough, and having taken and destroyed every thing that had been sent there.

I was then constrained to change my route, both that I might avoid the being put between two fires, and that I might be able to bring off Colonel Warner. I therefore sent him orders to retire to Rutland, where he would find me to cover him. A considerable part of his detachment joined me at that place, and he, with about ninety more, two days afterwards, at Manchester. A great many are still missing, though few, I believe, have fallen into the enemy's hands, as they did not pursue Colonel Warner but a very small distance, and, from all accounts, suffered much in the action. The ninth regiment followed Colonel Long towards Fort Ann, and were almost entirely cut off. I have despatched officers to Bennington and Number Four to pick up the stragglers who, I suppose, have taken these routes to New England; and, on the 12th instant, I joined General Schuyler, at this place, after a very fatiguing march.

Thus, Sir, I have laid before you, without the least reserve, every thing I can recollect respecting Ticonderoga, and the retreat from thence. Happy should I be, if my conduct therein meets with your approbation; and I can, with the strictest truth, affirm I was actuated by no motives but what sprang from a sincere regard for the public welfare. I have the honor to be your Excellency's

Most obedient and very humble servant,

ARTHUR ST. CLAIR.

FROM MAJOR AARON BURR.

Peekskill, 20 July, 1777.

HONORED SIR,

I was this morning favored with your Excellency's letter of 29th ultimo, and my appointment in Colonel Malcom's regiment. I am truly sensible of the honor done me, and shall be studious that my deportment in that station be such as will insure your future esteem.

I am, nevertheless, Sir, constrained to observe, that the late date of my appointment subjects me to the command of many who are younger in the service, and junior officers the last campaign. With submission, and if there is no impropriety in requesting what so nearly concerns me, I would beg to know whether it was any misconduct in me, or extraordinary merit or services in them, which entitled the gentlemen, lately put over me, to that preference; or, if a uniform diligence and attention to duty has marked my conduct since the formation of the army, whether I may not expect to be restored to that rank, of which I have been deprived rather, I flatter myself, by accident than design. I would wish equally to avoid the character of turbulent or passive, and am unhappy to have troubled your Excellency with a matter which concerns only myself; but, as a decent attention to rank is both proper and necessary, I hope it will be excused in one who regards his honor next to the welfare of his country.

I am not yet acquainted with the state of the regiment, or the prospect of filling it, but shall immediately repair to the rendezvous, and receive Colonel Malcom's directions. I have the honor to be, with the greatest respect,

Your Excellency's very humble servant,

AARON BURR.*

FROM CHARLES THOMSON.

Summerville, 21 July, 1777.

DEAR SIR,

Having lately met with an ordinance of the King of France, passed last December, for establishing the corps of engineers, I made a hasty translation of it,

---

* This letter is indorsed "not answered."

from which I apprehend some useful hints may be taken for establishing such a corps in this country. And as I know of no better hands into which it may be put for this purpose, I have taken the liberty to send you a copy.

You are doubtless informed of the four engineers sent over by Dr. Franklin and Mr. Deane, three of whom are arrived and taken into the service of the Continent, the first as Colonel, the second as Lieutenant-Colonel, and the third as Major of engineers. What probability there is of their being men of experience you will see by the inclosed ordinance, and the rank they held in the royal corps of engineers. Whether their being taken into the service as Colonel, &c., of engineers, will give them rank of those heretofore engaged simply as engineers, with similar ranks, will, I presume, be left to your determination agreeably to the rules of the army.

I congratulate you on the capture of General Prescott, and I hope soon to hear of the release of General Lee. The haughty instrument of tyranny will, I trust, abate his insolence, at least admit the propriety of now insisting on General Lee's release, "when you have an officer of equal rank to offer in exchange." Though I must confess I should be very glad, before any exchange even now took place, that a cartel was settled on such plain and equal principles as to remove all grounds of cavil. The Board of War have had the cartel settled between the French and English in the year 1759, lately reprinted, which you have undoubtedly seen.

I cannot forbear thinking that the posts held in the army ought to be attended as much, if not more, than nominal rank. Without this, our enemy will have greatly the advantage. Their General Officers have all regiments, so that there are but few Colonels. Ought not, therefore, Lieutenant-Colonels, or even Majors, when they command regiments, to be estimated as Colonels?

But I am transgressing my line, and I fear trespassing on your time. I am, Sir,

Your obedient, humble servant,
CHARLES THOMSON.

FROM JAMES LOVELL.*

Philadelphia, 24 July, 1777.

SIR,

So long ago as December 2d, 1775, direction was given by Congress to the Committee of Secret Correspondence to procure from Europe four good engineers. This was not, however, accomplished till the 13th of last February, when the bearer, the Chevalier Duportail, with M. La Radière, M. Gouvion, and one other officer, who is left sick in the West Indies, were engaged by Dr. Franklin and Mr. Deane to come over to America. I beg your Excellency to observe well, that these are the only officers, of any species, who have been procured from abroad by express direction of Congress. And this I do, because I am about to furnish you with several circumstances peculiarly within my knowledge, relative to a point of equity well worthy of your Excellency's attention.

The corps of engineers is very honorable in France, and officers from it are sought by different European powers. These gentlemen, who are come over into

---

* Member of Congress from Massachusetts, and for some time Chairman of the Committee of Foreign Affairs.

our service, made an agreement with our Commissioners to rise one degree from the rank they held at
home, upon a supposition that the practice of Europe
had been regarded here. But, when they arrived,
they found instances very different with respect to
officers in all other corps. It was their mishap, also,
to see a Major of artillery affecting to be exalted
four ranks, as a chief, in his proper line and theirs
also. They made a representation of these circumstances, and appealed to the equity of Congress. But
they had arrived at a time when the infatuation of
some here, and the wild conduct of one abroad, had
rendered a spirit of reformation absolutely necessary
as to the point of rank.

The ingenuous, however, must own, that there is
singular hardship in the case of these gentlemen.
The only officers ever sent for by us, procured by
the *real* political agents of Congress, coming out with
the good wishes of the French Ministry, being of undoubted rank and ability in their profession, find
themselves in the dilemma of becoming the first ex-
amples of our new reforming spirit, or else of going
home during a campaign, which their high sense of
honor will not allow. But, though the Chevalier Duportail was not made a Brigadier, yet it appeared too
gross to expose him to be directed, in his peculiar
line, by such as will readily acknowledge his pretensions, by regular education and discipline, to be greatly superior to their own. His commission prevents
this, and enables him so to distribute, in work, the
others who came with him, as to prevent them who
have been within a few months as long in service as
himself, from being interfered with by such as never
belonged to the Royal Corps of Engineers in France,
or perhaps but a very short time to any other.

Your Excellency cannot but wonder at the strange manner of wording the commission. I shall explain it with the greatest freedom. M. Ducoudray being employed as a good artillery officer to examine the arsenals in France, to see what cannon, &c., could be spared from them, acted with great industry in that employment, and much seeming regard to America. In the course of his transactions between the Compte de St. Germain and Mr. Deane, he was not blind to perceive that he might take occasion to serve himself. Besides being paid for his trouble and expenses in France, he procured an agreement from Mr. Deane, which has already been shown to your Excellency, and has affected you, doubtless, with the same surprise and indignation which it has excited in others, almost without a single exception.

I shall omit any remarks upon that treaty, or a long *too* ingenious memorial presented to Congress with it, except such as are strictly connected with the occasion of this letter. M. Ducoudray, having created himself to the command of artillery *and* engineers, persuaded Mr. Deane that it would be impossible to get any from the *military* corps of engineers, now called *royal*, because their demands would be so exorbitant, and that it would be also unnecessary, because we ought not to build fortified places in America to serve as secure holds to our enemy, when once taken from us; and that, therefore, a few *bridge and causeway-makers* would answer all the ends of military engineers. Such he brought with him, who were quite ready to fall under the command of an *artillery* direction, when not the lowest officer of the Royal Corps of Engineers would have submitted to such a novel pretence.

It is needless to inquire whether it be true, that

Mr. Deane acknowledged he had been surprised into this uncouth compact. It is sufficient that Dr. Franklin made an after one, which Mr. Deane also signed. Is not this in fact tantamount to a disavowal of the first treaty, so far as relates to the orders of Congress? For, if those orders were fulfilled by the first, why was a second treaty made? The agents show that there had been a deception, or that there had not been any attempt to follow the instructions of Congress as to engineers, in all the train attending M. Ducoudray.

Another remark may not be impertinent here. As these four engineers showed their treaty to the Compte de St. Germain, to whom they have also written from hence, it cannot be supposed that he would have permitted a Lieutenant-Colonel of the Royal Corps of Engineers, and two old Majors of the same, to come over hither to be under the immediate command of a young Major of artillery. It is not to be conceived. From whence I conclude that M. Ducoudray never let his exorbitant and whimsical treaty be known to that Minister of the War Department, who must have been shocked at the confusion of corps in the principles of contract.

Excuse me, dear General, I will not again wander from the point which I said I would explain. M. Ducoudray has given full scope to *his* species of ingenuity here, as in the neighbourhood of Mr. Deane. I have been told that he has said, if he could not be employed himself, he would bring it about that these others should not. This may be an absolute falsehood. But, I will own, it comes the nearest of anything which I can conceive of, to explain the delays which have taken place in regard to these engineers, who ought to have been sent to your Excellency

long ago. They have remained subject to the cruci-
fying expenses of this city, because their employment seemed to interfere with M. Ducoudray's pretensions, though those very pretensions had been rejected. Your Excellency would doubtless smile, if you
should ever hear, that even a number of *peasants* disputed three days about the difference between the
consequences of a man's being Colonel-in-chief, or
First Colonel, or Colonel to take rank and command
of all heretofore appointed, or Colonel-*commandant* of
engineers. Would not a Brigadier or Major-General
of engineers alike annul the supremacy of the differ-
ently-worded commissions? Or rather, do not the
four different modes give like command?

I shall pass from rank to pay. These gentlemen,
not only far from the prophesied exorbitancy in demand of rank, never received one shilling in France
as gratification; though others, who were *not sent
for*, received large sums, and claim pay from their
embarkation, and even pensions for life. But Dr.
Franklin, supposing it would be less trouble to himself and more agreeable to the engineers to see to
their own passages, stipulated their pay from the 13th
of February.

As no regulations have yet been made in regard
to cavalry or engineers, these gentlemen have received five months' pay as infantry, which will not refund
the expenses of their voyage. I am really uneasy,
when I find manly, honorable intentions do not meet
with at least equal emoluments with artful, suspicious,
tricking contractors. If these officers do not walk to
camp, it is not because they were furnished by the
Board of War with horses upon my application for
them; and yet the nature of their profession demands
a provision of the kind. Are they suddenly to re-

connoitre a camp, a river, a shoal, or a whole neighbouring country, through which an army is to march,
and to make the speediest return to the Generals, on
foot? I trust your Excellency, when asking for engineers, had ideas of something beyond what the
sinister views of an ambitious foreigner have sought
to inspire us with here; which is, forming a causeway,
or cutting a ditch, or planking a bridge. And I shall
consequently rest satisfied that you will receive the
officers, now presenting themselves to you, and secure
to them such honors and emoluments as you shall
find them to merit from their education and abilities,
exemplified under your command. No one has been more
backward than I in desiring to see foreigners in our
service, to the slight of my countrymen. And, except engineers, I could not admit the thought of our
wanting any military strangers, other than one or
two veteran Adjutants or Majors, who know our language well, and could serve as instructors at large to
our spirited and well-attached young American officers.

I wish these engineers could speak English better
than they do; but they can receive orders and give
them in English, and will speedily learn to speak.

I hope your Excellency will not think amiss of the
freedom I have taken at this time, both as to the
matter of my letter and the interruptive length of it.
I do not write officially, as of the Committee on Foreign Applications. In that capacity I have more than
once communicated to you proceedings of Congress,
in a style which might lead you to misconjecture my
individual opinion. I write as a friend to my country, and the reputation of its Congress, its army, and
agents abroad. I write as being well acquainted with
your Excellency, or, in other words, as thinking I

35*

know you. In short, I write because I had determined it to be my duty so to write. *That* path once determined, I never ask myself whether there may not be a lion in the way.

After the important kindnesses, which your Excellency has done me, I so far forgive the late injury of your apologizing for a *short* answer written by one of your hurried family, as not to revenge myself, by entreating you to excuse my *rough, uncopied* sheets to a violent headache. *Aliquando dormitat* did not appear an unnatural charge against Homer. *Nimium vigilat* would have appeared so against Scipio or Marlborough, and yet I am led by you to think they might have given provocation for it. With truest vows for your prosperity, I am your Excellency's

Obliged friend and humble servant,

JAMES LOVELL.

FROM BRIGADIER-GENERAL GEORGE CLINTON.

Fort Montgomery, 26 July, 1777.

DEAR SIR,

When I had the pleasure of seeing your Excellency at Ramapo, I mentioned that the terms, for which the two militia regiments stationed at this post were engaged in service, expired the last of this month, at which time, unless a reënforcement is sent here by General Putnam, the whole strength we shall have, at this important station, will be Colonel Dubois's regiment, two companies of artillery, and a detachment of about one hundred and fifty Continental troops under Lieutenant-Colonel Meigs.

I have this day wrote to General Putnam on the

subject, that he may so order matters as to furnish a reënforcement to this garrison, if he shall judge it expedient.

I have had a second call to attend at Kingston, and take the oath of office in consequence of my late appointment;* and as the new Legislature of this State are to meet on the 1st of August, it will be necessary that I shall leave this, so as to be there a day or two previous to their meeting.

This I have also mentioned to General Putnam, and requested leave of absence for an unlimited time, as the affairs of Government render it uncertain whether I shall be able, during the present campaign, to return to the command of this post.

It is with a degree of pain that I am under a necessity of asking permission, at this time, to quit the service, especially as the designs of the enemy are not fully known; and should the business of my new appointment admit of it, I will most cheerfully return to the army, until the fate of the present campaign is determined. I am, with much esteem,

Your Excellency's most obedient servant,

GEORGE CLINTON.

FROM MAJOR-GENERAL SCHUYLER.

Saratoga, 28 July, 1777.

DEAR SIR,

I am honored with your favor of the 24th instant, which I received half an hour ago, having just arrived from Moses Creek, where I keep my quarters.

---

* He had recently been chosen Governor of the State of New York

So far from the militia that are with me increasing, they are daily diminishing, and I am very confident that in ten days, if the enemy should not disturb us, we shall not have five hundred left; and although I have entreated this and the Eastern States to send up a reënforcement of them, yet I doubt much if any will come up, especially from the Eastern States, where the spirit of malevolence knows no bounds, and I am considered as a traitor.

I believe your Excellency has spared me all the troops you prudently could, but we are still too weak in this quarter, especially as sickness decreases us with great rapidity. Our men living entirely upon fresh meat occasions much disease. Salt meat we have none of, nor is any to be got in this quarter. If it can be spared from any post below, I wish a quantity may be ordered up.

I have informed you that, on the 26th, an advanced picket was attacked near Fort Edward. Last night a body of regular troops appeared at that place, however not in such force but that they suffered our men, about one hundred and fifty in number, to come off unmolested. I believe their main body will be down in a few days. We are preparing to receive them in the best manner we can.

I shall be happy to see General Lincoln. He may possibly be able to do something with the New England militia.

I do not think it would be prudent, at present, to send General Arnold to Fort Schuyler. I will try to send another General Officer to that place. I am, dear Sir, with great regard and esteem,

Your Excellency's most obedient, humble servant,

PHILIP SCHUYLER.

FROM MAJOR-GENERAL PUTNAM.

Peekskill, 31 July, 1777.

DEAR GENERAL,

I received your favor of the 28th instant, and have, according to your direction, ordered two brigades, namely, General McDougall's and Huntington's, to put their heavy baggage over the river, and to be in readiness to march on the arrival of further orders. I have sent Lieutenant-Colonel Dimon to the White Plains, with his regiment, to relieve Colonel Cortlandt's detachment there, consisting of his own, Colonel Livingston's, and a party from Colonels Durkee's and Chandler's regiments.

You may think it not necessary to keep a party at the White Plains, but, unless we do, the inhabitants will be ruined; their grass, grain, and cattle will all be taken off by the enemy. There are seven hundred militia at the forts and different posts, whose time is out to-day, and must be discharged. I have advised with General Clinton in respect to calling in the militia, and concluded that one thousand should be called for immediately, five hundred from Connecticut, and five hundred from this State; and an express was immediately sent off to Governor Trumbull, requesting them to be sent without delay. But the season of the year renders it very difficult and doubtful whether they will turn out or not. When the two brigades are marched, now under orders, there will be left on this side the river two small brigades, consisting of two thousand three hundred and forty-seven, of which two thousand and fifty-one are returned fit for duty. Five hundred must be kept at the White Plains for the reasons above mentioned, five hundred at the Forts Independence, Montgomery, and Constitution. A subaltern's guard is kept at Fredericksburg to guard the stores, another is necessary at Robinson's Mills for the same purpose, although, at present, the latter is only a sergeant's. The men for the ships and boats are principally out of these brigades, so that there will not be left a thousand men to keep up our guards, and to defend this important post and the passes. There are, I am well assured, five or six thousand troops at King's Bridge and Fort Washington.

You had not received my two last letters, I perceive, at the time of writing yours. You will see, Sir, by this stating, how exposed and weak we are at this post, as well as the whole Eastern country, in case an attack should be made on any part.

I am so unhappy as to differ from your Excellency with respect to the enemy's motions. Many considerations concur to evince that this post, or some more eastward, will be the real point of attack. This will divide and distract the New England militia, directly coincide with General Burgoyne's operation, who is making his way to Albany, divide the Continent, facilitate the junction of their forces, and cut off all communication between the Northern and Southern States. In addition to this, their fleet was seen from Blue Point, standing eastward, of which I wrote you in my last. To draw the forces from this post, so as to return and get possession of the passes through the Highlands, is, I conceive, an object of so much consequence, that no cost or pains would be spared by General Howe for the obtainment of it. If it is not absolutely certain that the enemy are gone for Philadelphia, it is certain they may come here or go eastward; and should they, as they will, if my conjectures are right, it is certain the consequences must be very serious and unhappy, on account of so many of the troops being gone to the southward.

If their real design is for this, or further eastward, it is very certain they would make as great show of a real intent to go to Philadelphia as possible. By a deserter, who came from King's Bridge day before yesterday, I learn that three hundred horses, with wagons, are come from Long Island to King's Bridge; that they are building a new redoubt that is to mount six guns, which will be finished this week, and then they design to come out with a great foraging party, as they say; but something more is doubtless intended. But, if no more, Colonel Dimon's regiment will be unequal to their force, and it may be thought imprudent for me to leave this post. I am further informed by a Captain that has been in their service and left them, that there were two thousand men on Staten Island, two regiments of Hessians, and Cortland Skinner's brigade. There is a report that General Burgoyne is at Saratoga. I am, most respectfully,

Your most obedient humble servant,
ISRAEL PUTNAM.

FROM MAJOR-GENERAL SCHUYLER.

Stillwater, 4 August, 1777.

DEAR SIR,

By the unanimous advice of all the General Officers, I have moved the army to this place. We propose to fortify our camp, in hopes that reënforcements will enable us to keep our ground, and prevent the enemy from penetrating further into the country. But if I should be asked from whence I expect reënforcements, I should be at a loss for an answer, not having heard a word from the Massachusetts on my repeated applications; nor am I certain that Connecticut will afford us any succour. Our Continental force is daily decreasing by desertion, sickness, and loss in skirmishes with the enemy; and not a man of the militia, now with me, will remain above one week longer. And whilst our force is diminishing, that of the enemy augments by a constant acquisition of Tories; but if we, by any means, could be put in a situation of attacking the enemy, and giving them a repulse, their retreat would be so extremely difficult that, in all probability, they would lose the greater part of their army. I am, dear General, most respectfully,

Your Excellency's most obedient, humble servant,

PHILIP SCHUYLER.

FROM GOVERNOR CLINTON.

Fort Montgomery, 9 August, 1777.

DEAR SIR,

Immediately on the receipt of your Excellency's letter, directing from one thousand to fifteen hundred of the militia of this and the State of Connecticut, to reënforce this garrison and the army under General Putnam, I issued orders for drawing out eight hundred and ten, including non-commissioned officers, from this State, for the above purposes. Since which I have been induced, from the situation of our affairs to the northward, in addition to the above numbers, to order out five hundred of the militia from the northern parts of Ulster and Duchess counties, one thousand from the county of Albany, and five hundred from the county of Tryon, to reënforce the army under the command of General Schuyler, and to continue in service until the first day of November next, unless your Excellency shall think proper to dismiss them before. Those from the two former counties, I have reason to believe, are by this time on their march, but I have not yet been advised what success they have experienced in getting the proportion allotted for the other counties. I fear, not so good as could be wished. The people in that quarter consider the Western frontier equally liable to the invasions of the enemy, and, influenced by this consideration, are unwilling to leave their families exposed, and join our army. As the enemy advance, many of the best of the inhabitants are employed in moving off their families and effects. Indeed, I have always observed that the militia of any part of the country most in danger, are, for the above reasons, least forward in opposing an enemy. Some, too, decline acting under those circumstances, from unworthy principles.

Your Excellency's letter of the 1st instant, dated at Chester, I received in Kingston, on Wednesday last, and thereupon ordered four regiments of militia to this place, three to join General Putnam at Peekskill, and one to occupy the post at the mouth of the Clove. The last of those ordered here arrived yesterday, and I learn from General Putnam, that those designed for him are also arrived at Peekskill. All the remainder of the militia of the State are under marching orders.

I never knew the militia come out with greater alacrity; but as many of them yet have great part

of their harvests in the field, I fear it will be difficult to detain them long, unless the enemy make
some movements that indicate a design of coming
this way suddenly, and so obvious as to be believed
by the militia. I cannot but express my surprise
that no reënforcements, as I have heard, have yet
arrived to our northern army from the eastward.
The want of confidence in the General Officers to
the northward, is the specious reason. To me it appears a very weak one. The mutilated and distressed
condition of this State renders our utmost exertions
to oppose the common enemy, in appearance but
little, better than one half of it being out of our possession. Common gratitude to a sister State, as well
as duty to the Continent at large, conspire in calling
on our eastern neighbours to step forth on this occasion, and more especially as they only are in a situation totally to destroy General Burgoyne's army, by
intercepting his supplies, and even cutting off his
retreat to the Lakes.

The detachment of eight hundred and ten for this
garrison and Peekskill is not yet completed, owing
to the body of the militia being so suddenly called
out, but will be effected immediately on their return
home; till which time I will endeavour to detain an
equal number of them here.

I have not yet received the late resolves of Congress for recruiting the army, alluded to in your Excellency's letter of the 4th instant. As soon as they
come to hand, I will do every thing in my power
to render them effectual, and forward the requested
information. I am, with much esteem,

Your Excellency's most obedient servant,
GEORGE CLINTON.

Stillwater, 12 August, 1777.

DEAR GENERAL,

Agreeably to your Excellency's orders, I waited upon General Schuyler, on my way to the militia who had assembled and were assembling at Manchester, on the Grants, received his instructions, and met the troops the 2d instant.   I found only five or six hundred there; but one regiment was on the road from the Massachusetts, and about thirteen or fourteen hundred from New Hampshire.   Before many of them arrived, I received General Schuyler's orders to join him, with all the troops excepting one small regiment.   Part of them began their march yesterday; the remainder were to leave the Grants this day.   The army here is to take post upon a small island in the Mohawk River, where it unites with the Hudson. That post is supposed to be more favorable than the one now occupied by them.

I am to return with the militia from the Massachusetts, New Hampshire, and the Grants, to the northward, with a design to fall into the rear of Burgoyne, who, from the best information we can obtain, hath left a very naked and uncovered rear, and, if possible, cut off his communication with the Lakes. This movement, probably, will cause him to reënforce the several posts of which he hath possessed himself, and which, at all hazards, he must attempt to maintain, or induce him to make a detachment with a view to attack us.   In either case, it will greatly weaken his main body, and may give the force here an opportunity to act against them with success.   The Massachusetts, I hear, have ordered out two thousand of their militia. From the best accounts we can obtain, the enemy are not more than six thousand strong. If Burgoyne falls down into the country this way, I see nothing but he must be ruined, unless supported by General Howe, which, by his movements, he undoubtedly expects.

I am happy to inform your Excellency, that I now enjoy my usual good state of health. I am, dear General, with sincere regard and esteem,

Your most obedient, humble servant,
BENJAMIN LINCOLN.

FROM THE PRESIDENT OF CONGRESS.

Philadelphia, 17 August, 1777; Sunday morning.

SIR,

The complaints of the want of men to the northward are so great and urgent, that Congress, with a view of affording them some assistance, have come to the inclosed resolve; by which you will perceive it is their desire that five hundred riflemen, under the command of an active officer, should be immediately sent into that department, to oppose the incursions of the Indians.

Your favor of the 16th instant, I was last night honored with, containing sundry inclosures, which shall be communicated to Congress to-morrow. The plan you have adopted and recommended for the defence of the River Delaware, is ordered to be carried into execution. As soon as Congress shall come into any resolves on the subjects of your several letters, the result shall be immediately transmitted. I have the honor to be, with the greatest respect, Sir,

Your most obedient, and very humble servant,
JOHN HANCOCK, President.

FROM MAJOR-GENERAL SCHUYLER.

Van Schaick's Island, in the mouth of the
Mohawk River, 19 August, 1777.

DEAR SIR,

I have the honor to congratulate your Excellency
on a signal victory gained by General Stark over a
detachment of about fifteen hundred of the enemy
near Bennington, on the 16th instant, an account
whereof I have this moment received in a letter from
General Lincoln, of which the following is a copy.

"Bennington, August 18th, 1777. Dear General,
the late signal success of a body of about two thousand troops, mostly militia, under the command of
Brigadier-General Stark, in this part of the country,
on the 16th instant, over a party of about fifteen
hundred of the enemy, who came out with a manifest design to possess themselves of this town, as
will appear by the inclosed, is an event happy and
important. Our troops behaved in a very brave and
heroic manner. They pushed the enemy from one
work to another, thrown up on advantageous ground,
and from different posts, with spirit and fortitude,
until they gained a complete victory over them.

"The following is the best list I have been able
to obtain of the prisoners, their killed and wounded,
namely: One Lieutenant-Colonel, one Major, five Captains, twelve Lieutenants, four Ensigns, two Cornets,
one Judge-Advocate, one Baron, two Canadian officers,
and three Surgeons, thirty-seven British soldiers, three
hundred and ninety-eight Hessians, thirty-eight Canadians, and one hundred and fifty-one Tories taken.
The number of wounded fallen into our hands, exclusive of the above, is about eighty. The number
36 *

of their slain has not yet been ascertained, as they fought on the retreat for several miles in a wood, but supposed to be about two hundred. Their artillery, which consisted of four brass field-pieces, with a considerable quantity of baggage, likewise fell into our hands. We have heard nothing of Burgoyne, or his army, for these two days past. The prisoners have been sent into the State of Massachusetts Bay, except the Tories. Shall wait your direction respecting them, as most of them belong to the State of New York. We have now about two thousand at or near this place.

"I am, dear General, with regard and esteem,
"Your very humble servant,
"BENJAMIN LINCOLN."

"N. B. We had about twenty or thirty killed in the action, and perhaps fifty wounded."

I also inclose copy of General Burgoyne's orders to Lieutenant-Colonel Baum, which were transmitted to me with the above.

I have great hopes that we shall soon have the satisfaction of learning, that General Arnold has raised the siege of Fort Schuyler. General Gates, I am informed, arrived last night at Albany. I am, dear Sir, with the most respectful sentiments,

Your Excellency's most obedient, humble servant,
PHILIP SCHUYLER.

Head-Quarters, 22 August, 1777.

SIR,

Upon my arrival in this department, I found the main body of the army encamped at Van Schaick's Islands, which are made by the sprouts of the Mohawk River joining with Hudson's River, nine miles north of Albany. A brigade, under General Poor, encamped at Loudon's Ferry, on the south bank of the Mohawk River, five miles from hence. A brigade, under General Lincoln, had joined General Stark at Bennington; and a brigade, under General Arnold, marched the 15th instant to join the militia of Tryon country, to raise the siege of Fort Stanwix.

Upon my leaving Philadelphia, the prospect this way appeared most gloomy, but the severe checks the enemy have met with at Bennington and Tryon county, have given a more pleasing view of public affairs. Particular accounts of the signal victory gained by General Stark, and of the severe blow General Herkimer gave Sir John Johnson and the scalpers under his command, have been transmitted to your Excellency by General Schuyler. I anxiously expect the arrival of an express from General Arnold, with an account of the total defeat of the enemy in that quarter. By my calculation, he reached Fort Stanwix the day before yesterday.

Colonels Livingston's and Cortlandt's regiments arrived yesterday, and immediately joined General Poor's division. I shall also order General Arnold, upon his return, to march to that post. I cannot sufficiently thank your Excellency for sending Colonel Morgan's corps to this army; they will be of the greatest service to it; for, until the late success this way, I am told the army were quite panic-struck by the Indians, and their Tory and Canadian assassins in Indian dress. Horrible, indeed, have been the cruelties they have wantonly committed upon the miserable inhabitants, insomuch that all is now fair with General Burgoyne, even if the bloody hatchet he has so barbarously used should find its way into his own head.

Governor Clinton will be here to-day. Upon his arrival, I shall consult with him and General Lincoln upon the best plan to distress, and I hope finally to defeat the enemy. I am sorry to be necessitated to acquaint your Excellency how neglectfully your orders have been executed at Springfield; not any of the musket ball, or lead, which you ordered so long ago to be sent to this department, is yet arrived, and I am exceedingly distressed for the want of it. Upon my arrival at Albany, I despatched an express to Colonel Hughes, with the inclosed return of ordnance stores wanted in this department, and directed what he could not furnish might be immediately ordered to be supplied from Springfield. Few of the militia demanded are yet arrived, but I hear of great numbers upon the march. Your Excellency's advice in regard to Morgan's corps, &c., &c., shall be carefully observed. My scouts and spies inform me, that the enemy's head-quarters and main body are at Saratoga, and that they have lately been repairing the bridges between that place and Stillwater.

As soon as times and circumstances will admit, I shall send your Excellency a general return of this army. I am, Sir,

Your Excellency's most obedient, humble servant,

HORATIO GATES.

FROM THE PRESIDENT OF CONGRESS.

Congress, 22 August, 1777; half past 1 o'clock, P. M.

SIR,

This moment an express is arrived from Maryland, with an account of near two hundred sail of Mr. Howe's fleet, being at anchor in the Chesapeake Bay. A copy of the letter, brought by express, I inclose to you, and to which I refer you. In consequence of this advice, Congress have ordered the immediate removal of all the stores and prisoners from Lancaster and York, in this State, to places of greater safety.

Congress have this moment come to the inclosed resolution, to which I beg leave to refer you; and, indeed, I need not add, as the whole matter is submitted to you. I will not detain the express only to say, that I am, with every sentiment of esteem and respect, Sir,

Your very humble servant,
JOHN HANCOCK, *President*.

FROM THE PRESIDENT OF CONGRESS.

Philadelphia, 1 September, 1777.

SIR,

Your several favors to the 30th ultimo, inclusive, I have had the honor of receiving, in the order of their dates.

From the inclosed resolves, you will perceive that the Congress have appointed a committee to collect and arrange the evidence relative to the evacuation of Ticonderoga, which will be afterwards transmitted to you, that a court-martial may be thereupon instituted for the trial of the General Officers who were in the Northern Department when the evacuation took place.

The great demand for arms to equip the militia, who are called into service, has induced the Congress to pass the inclosed resolve, directing that a number of workmen, conversant in the business of repairing firelocks, should be immediately detached from the militia, to be employed in repairing the arms in this city, there being between two and three thousand that in a short time may be rendered fit for use.

I have the pleasure to congratulate you on our further success in the Northern Department, in raising the siege of Fort Schuyler. The enemy, on the approach of General Arnold, fled with the utmost precipitation, leaving behind them their tents, ammunition, provision, &c. As I forward herewith several letters for you from that quarter, which I make no doubt contain an account of the matter, I beg leave to refer you to them for further particulars. I have the honor to be, with the greatest respect, Sir,

Your most obedient, and very humble servant,

JOHN HANCOCK, *President.*

FROM GOVERNOR HENRY.

Williamsburg, 5 September, 1777.

SIR,

Edmund Randolph, Esq., communicated to me that part of your last letter to him, in which you are pleased to take notice of your lady's reception at this place. I beg you to be assured, that every expression of regard falls far short of that which I feel, and shall retain through life, for such distinguished merit.

You are pleased also to observe, that you have not received any answer from me to your two favors of the 13th of April and 17th of May last. The latter has never been received; the former would have been answered, but really, when I have considered the extent, variety, and importance of the things which occupy your attention, I have been afraid of pestering you with letters. The scheme of embodying volunteers was no more thought of after the receipt of yours, in which it appeared to be against your wishes. In that, as in every military measure, I shall be solely guided by your opinions.

Upon the appearance of the British fleet, about three thousand militia were embodied. They have shown great alacrity. A third part of the militia of Prince William, Loudoun, Fairfax, Culpepper, Fauquier, Berkeley, Dunmore, and Frederic, is ordered to rendezvous at Fredericktown, in Maryland, and there to await your orders. I have thought it of great consequence to throw some troops on the eastern shore. But it is rather disagreeable to the militia, and, for want of more regulars, two companies only are gone there. Colonel N. Gist, with seventeen Cherokees, being here, chose also to go over, and is gone.

Although a good peace is made with the Cherokees, yet our south-western frontier is much harassed with small parties of Indians. General Hand expects pretty warm work about Pittsburg.

Could any particular assistance to you be rendered by Virginia, at this juncture, I should be made happy. Early intelligence of the enemy's motions may be of the highest moment, should they come down the Bay.

I beg leave to assure you of that perfect esteem, and high regard, with which I have the honor to be, Sir,

Your most obedient and very humble servant,

PATRICK HENRY.

FROM THE PRESIDENT OF CONGRESS.

Philadelphia, 6 September, 1777.

SIR,

You will perceive, from the inclosed resolves, that Congress, desirous of reënforcing the army at this critical period, have recommended to the States of Pennsylvania and New Jersey to order out immediately a considerable part of their militia; and I have no doubt of their compliance.

I have wrote to Governor Livingston on the subject, and informed him that, should he think proper to appoint General Dickinson to the command of the three thousand requested from that State, it will be extremely agreeable to Congress. That gentleman has, I understand, signified his readiness to act whenever called upon; and, as he possesses the confidence of the militia, and has talents equal to the task, I am persuaded the appointment will give general satisfaction.

Your favor of the 3d instant, and likewise of yesterday by the hands of General St. Clair, I have been duly honored with. The latter I shall lay before Congress this morning. I have the honor to be, with the greatest respect, Sir,

Your most obedient and very humble servant,

JOHN HANCOCK, *President.*

FROM THE PRESIDENT OF CONGRESS.

Philadelphia, 9 September, 1777.

SIR,

I have the honor to transmit, at this time, copies of the several letters from General Livingston and General Ducoudray to Congress. As Governor Livingston seems apprehensive of an irruption from the enemy on Staten Island, and says they are collecting there for this purpose, the Congress have directed General Putnam to hold in readiness fifteen hundred men, under the command of a Brigadier, to cross the North River when you may think proper to order it. A copy of the resolve I shall immediately forward to General Putnam.

The inclosed letter, from Monsieur Ducoudray, contains a proposal of forming a camp between Wilmington and Philadelphia, the propriety of which the Congress have referred entirely to you. Colonel Harrison's favor of the 7th instant was duly received. I beg leave to request your attention to the inclosures; and have the honor to be, with the greatest respect, Sir,

Your most obedient and very humble servant,

JOHN HANCOCK, *President*.

FROM THE PRESIDENT OF CONGRESS.

Philadelphia, 12 September, 1777;
4 o'clock, A. M.

SIR,

I am this moment favored with yours, by the express.* I am sorry for the unfortunate issue of

---

* The letter written at Chester, in the night after the battle of the Brandywine. See Washington's Writings, Vol. V. p. 57.

the day; but from the troops keeping up their spirits, I flatter myself it will still be in our power to retrieve the loss of yesterday.

I have thought proper, in consequence of the intelligence received this morning, to call the Congress together at six o'clock. I have the honor to be, with the utmost respect, Sir,

Your most obedient servant,
JOHN HANCOCK, President.

FROM MAJOR-GENERAL DICKINSON.

Elizabethtown, 20 September, 1777;
6 o'clock, P. M.

SIR,

I wrote your Excellency this morning, since which I have had the honor of receiving your favor of yesterday's date. Your Excellency will be much surprised to hear there are not more than one thousand of our militia now embodied, all of which are at this post. Since the receipt of your Excellency's letters, I have been considering in what way I could most speedily reënforce the army under your Excellency's command, as that is the object; and I am clearly of opinion, that the most expeditious is, to march the troops from this post, and collect what numbers I can upon our march. I shall, therefore, order all the guards called in before day, and march, with the utmost expedition, the routes directed. Your Excellency may be assured my utmost exertions shall not be wanting upon the present occasion.

I flatter myself I shall be able, in a short time, to bring on a reënforcement of two thousand men. Had it not been for the late unlucky alarm in this State,

I have great reason to believe, I should have crossed the Delaware with four thousand men. I have ordered General Wines to collect and march his brigade to this post, with all despatch. This State will be in a very defenceless situation, and there is little doubt but the enemy will soon be apprised of it, and make a visit. I am a little apprehensive many of the men will desert us before we cross the Delaware, having dreadful apprehensions from the vicinity of the enemy. Every precaution shall be used to keep them together, and bring them on speedily. I have the honor to be,

Your Excellency's most obedient servant,

PHILEMON DICKINSON.

FROM ELBRIDGE GERRY.*

Lancaster, 24 September, 1777.

SIR,

In consequence of your letter of the 22d, directed to the President, or any member of Congress, I have conferred with William Henry, Esq., of this place, upon the most expeditious method of collecting the arms and accoutrements in the hands of the inhabitants here; and he is of opinion that it may be accomplished by your warrant to him, grounded on the late resolution of Congress for that and other purposes. As there is not a prospect of having a Congress, or Board of War, for several days, to give him authority, and the articles are immediately wanted,

---

* Delegate in Congress from Massachusetts.

he has consented to proceed on the business without delay, in expectation that, on the receipt of this, you will give him full powers to justify his conduct, and date them the 22d, that the time of his transaction may comport with his commission.

With wishes of success to your Excellency, and the cause in which you are engaged, I remain, Sir, very respectfully,

Your most humble servant,

ELBRIDGE GERRY.

FROM THE PRESIDENT OF CONGRESS.

Yorktown, in Pennsylvania, 30 September, 1777.

SIR,

Since my departure from Philadelphia, I have to acknowledge the receipt of your favors to the 23d instant. I met the Congress on Saturday last, at Lancaster, and, upon consultation, it was judged most prudent to adjourn to this place, where we now are, and where we can prosecute business without interruption, and where your despatches will meet us.

I have just now received, by General Gates's Aid-de-camp, Major Troup, sundry letters, copies of which I have the honor to inclose to you, by which it appears that our affairs in the Northern Department wear a favorable aspect, and I hope soon to transmit you an account of an issue to the contest in that quarter.

I wish soon to receive the most pleasing accounts from you. We are in daily expectation of agreeable tidings, and that General Howe is totally reduced.

I beg leave to refer you to the inclosed papers; and am, with the utmost respect and esteem, Sir, Your most obedient and very humble servant,

JOHN HANCOCK, *President.*

FROM MAJOR-GENERAL GATES.

Head-Quarters, Camp, Behmus's Heights,
5 October, 1777.

SIR,

Since the action of the 19th ultimo, the enemy have kept the ground they occupied the morning of that day, and fortified their camp. The advanced sentries of my pickets are posted within shot, and opposite the enemy's. Neither side have given ground an inch. In this situation, your Excellency would not wish me to part with the corps the army of General Burgoyne are most afraid of. From the best intelligence, he has not more than three weeks' provision in store; it will take him at least eight days to get back to Ticonderoga; so that, in a fortnight at farthest, he must decide whether he will rashly risk, at infinite disadvantage, to force my camp, or retreat to his den. In either case, I must have the fairest prospect to be able to reënforce your Excellency, in a more considerable manner than by a single regiment.

I am sorry to repeat to your Excellency the distress I have suffered for want of a proper supply of musket cartridges from Springfield, or the materials to make them. The inclosed, from the Commissary of Ordnance Stores at Albany, will convince your Excellency of the truth of this assertion. My anxiety, also, upon account of provisions has been inexpressible; a

37 *

greater error has not been committed this war than
the changing the Commissaries in the middle of the
campaign. You, Sir, must have your grievances. I,
therefore, will not enhance them by enlarging upon
mine. I am, Sir,

Your Excellency's most obedient, humble servant,

HORATIO GATES.

FROM MAJOR-GENERAL PUTNAM.

Fishkill, 6 o'clock, Wednesday morning,
8 October, 1777.

DEAR GENERAL,

It is with the utmost reluctance I now sit down
to inform you that the enemy, after making a variety of movements up and down the North River, landed, on the morning of the 4th instant, about three
thousand men, at Tarrytown; and, after making an
excursion about five miles up the country, they returned and embarked. The morning following they
advanced up near King's Ferry, and landed on the
east side of the river; but in the evening part of
them reëmbarked, and, the morning after, landed a
little above King's Ferry, on the west side; but the
morning being so exceeding foggy concealed their
scheme, and prevented us from gaining any idea what
number of troops they landed. In about three hours
we discovered a large fire at the Ferry, which we
imagined to be the store-houses, upon which it was
thought they only landed with a view of destroying
the said houses.

The picket and scouts, which we had out, could not
learn the exact number of the enemy that were remaining on the east side of the river; but, from the

best accounts, they were about fifteen hundred. At this same time a number of ships, galleys, &c., with about forty flat-bottomed boats, made every appearance of their intentions to land troops, both at Fort Independence and Peekskill Landing. Under all these circumstances, my strength, being not more than twelve hundred Continental troops and three hundred militia, prevented me from detaching off a party to attack the enemy that lay on the east side of the river. After we had thought it impracticable to quit the heights, which we had then possession of, and attack the enemy, Brigadier-General Parsons and myself went to reconnoitre the ground near the enemy, and, on our return from thence, we were alarmed with a very heavy and hot firing, both of small arms and cannon, at Fort Montgomery, which immediately convinced me that the enemy had landed a large body of men at the time and place before-mentioned. Upon which, I immediately detached off five hundred men to reënforce the garrison. But before they could possibly cross the river to their assistance, the enemy, who were far superior in numbers, had possessed themselves of the fort. Never did men behave with more spirit and alacrity than our troops upon this occasion. They repulsed the enemy three times, which were in number at least five to one. Governor Clinton and General James Clinton were both present; but the engagement continuing until the dusk of the evening, gave them both an opportunity, together with several officers and a number of privates, to make their escape.

The loss of the enemy in this affair, Governor Clinton thinks must be very considerable. Our loss, killed and wounded, is by no means equal to what he might have expected. General James Clinton was wounded in the thigh, but I hope not mortally. Governor Clinton arrived at Peekskill the same evening, about eleven o'clock; and, with the advice of him, General Parsons, and several other officers, it was thought impossible to maintain the post at Peekskill with the force then present, against one that the enemy might, in a few hours, bring on the heights in our rear. It was, therefore, agreed that the stores ought to be immediately removed to some secure place, and the troops take post at Fishkill, until a reënforcement of militia should come to their aid.

I have repeatedly informed your Excellency of the enemy's design against this post; but, from some motive or other, you always differed with me in opinion. As this conjecture of mine has, for once, proved right, I cannot omit informing you that my real and sincere opinion is, that they now mean to join General Burgoyne, with the utmost despatch. I have written General Gates, and informed him of the situation of our affairs in this quarter. Governor Clinton is exerting himself in collecting the militia of this State. Brigadier-General Parsons I have sent off to forward in the Connecticut militia, which are now arriving in great numbers. I therefore hope and trust that, in the course of a few days, I shall be able to oppose the progress of the enemy. Time will not permit me to add any thing more respecting the engagement, only that our loss (I believe, from the best information,) does not exceed two hundred and fifty, killed, wounded, and taken prisoners. This evening I intend writing you again, but am now very busy. I am, dear General, with sincere regard,

Your very obedient, humble servant,

ISRAEL PUTNAM.

FROM MAJOR-GENERAL PUTNAM.

Fishkill, 8 October, 1777.

DEAR GENERAL,

Since I wrote you this morning, I have waited on Governor Clinton, to consult about our present circumstances, and fix upon the most effectual measure that could be pursued against the enemy, who are now landing a considerable number of troops at Fort Constitution, and proceeding up the river with their ships, galleys, flat-bottomed boats, &c. They will, from all appearance, be at the *chevaux-de-frise* in the space of an hour. They well know the situation of our troops, and I sincerely believe that their intentions are to make all expedition to get above us. I do not think weighing the *chevaux-de-frise* is a matter of great moment to them.

If they cannot effect it with the greatest ease, they will proceed up the river with the flat-bottomed boats, and such small vessels as can convey the baggage of the troops, stores, &c., to Half-Moon. If they attempt to march by land, on the west side the river, Governor Clinton will annoy them as much as possible with about four hundred Continental troops, which I yesterday detached over, and the militia, which he is now collecting. If this side should be their route, I will, with the remainder of the Continental troops and the Connecticut militia (which, I am happy to inform your Excellency, are coming in very fast), oppose them to the utmost of my power. All our stores, baggage, &c., except a few barrels of flour and bread, are removed from Peekskill. I have now a small guard at that place, and, if I can with any safety remove it from thence, I shall be glad. All the ordnance stores, which are not immediately wanted, I have ordered to the eastward. All our baggage, except what is absolutely necessary, I shall send off in the morning to some place of security; after which my troops will be light, and I flatter myself will either be able to fight them, or keep pace, should they keep upon the water.

I have the pleasure to inform you that many more of our troops made their escape than what I was at first informed of. Colonel Dubois, who is one of the number, this day collected near two hundred of his regiment, that got off after the enemy were in the fort. About five o'clock the enemy demanded a surrender of the fort; but, to their surprise, and the honor of our commanders, they had an answer that it should be defended to the utmost of their power. This renewed the action with double ardor, which continued till quite dark, when the enemy (who, we have since learnt, were five thousand in number) forced our lines; after which, our troops would not surrender, but fought with bayonets, swords, &c., in such a manner as reflects the highest honor on our noble garrison. General James Clinton was wounded with a bayonet in his thigh, and a number of other officers and men with the same weapon.

Yours, of the 1st instant, I have this day received. The ten pieces of artillery you mention were ordered from Springfield by Congress, two of which, from a request of General James Clinton, were sent to Fort Montgomery; two I have with me; and the other six are on the other side the river, with Governor Clinton. I am, dear General, with great regard,

Your obedient, humble servant,

ISRAEL PUTNAM.

P. S. General Clinton* commands the enemy in person, with two other General Officers.

* Sir Henry Clinton, the British General.

FROM THOMAS MᶜKEAN.

Newark, [Delaware] 8 October, 1777.

SIR,

By the captivity of President McKinly, of the Delaware State, on the 12th of last month, and the absence of the Vice-President, the command in chief devolved on me, as Speaker of the Assembly, agreeably to the Constitution. I had some time before accepted the office of Chief Justice of Pennsylvania, and, at the time this unfortunate event happened, was out of the Delaware State, but thought it my duty to my country to repair thither, which I did on the 20th following. On my arrival, I found that all the records and public papers of the county of Newcastle, and every shilling of the public money, together with the fund belonging to the Trustees of Newark Academy, and upwards of twenty-five thousand dollars in the Continental Loan-Office, &c. &c., had been captured at Wilmington, at the same time the President was taken by the enemy. The people were dispirited and dispersed; and the Tories, and less virtuous part that remained, were daily employed in supplying the British troops, both in Wilmington and at Newcastle, on board the ships of war, with all kinds of provisions.

Among other things, I called out the one half of the militia into actual service, and ordered the remainder to be in readiness to march at an hour's warning; and, to render the service as easy and as agreeable as possible, allowed the Colonel or commanding officer of every battalion in the State to assign posts to the militia within the bounds of the battalion. My intention was afterwards to reduce the number of posts, and to strengthen those nearest the enemy, and, if a sufficient force could be collected, to advance towards them. Above ten days were employed in this experiment, almost in vain. The Whigs in Sussex county are said to be rather too few to keep the Tories there quiet, the latter being most numerous. The same is said of Kent county, and the militia there absolutely refuse to march out of that county. In Newcastle county the lower class of the people have got an opinion that, by remaining quiet, they will not be molested, and seem unwilling to join their officers, or that any troops should be assembled in their neighbourhood; and many of the officers and better sort of the inhabitants apprehend that, by attempting any thing without the assistance of the others, they will expose themselves to certain destruction.

This, Sir, is a true portrait of the Delaware State, at present, and I really fear a total defection, without some effectual remedy is speedily applied. There are so many virtuous and brave men in the State, who will be sacrificed to their inveterate enemies, by leaving them in their present situation, that my blood runs cold at the reflection. The only remedy I can suggest is, to have a regiment of Continental troops forthwith despatched here to Newark. This will give new life to the virtuous, who will immediately join them; and, from their example and through their influence, I make no doubt most of the lower class will come forth. By this means, our internal enemies will be kept in awe, and, by securing some of them (which must be done), the spirit of the rest will be broken, and our foreign enemies will be no longer supplied with necessaries, and, very probably, be obliged either to throw in more troops to Wilmington, which will, in proportion, weaken their army op-

posed to you, or to abandon it entirely. If a greater
force could be spared from the main army (say five
hundred good men), with some officers of abilities, and
some field-pieces, the reconquest of Wilmington might
be meditated.

Upon the whole, Sir, you will judge for yourself,
and the common good, and do what you think best
at this critical period. If you are in force, you will
spare as many men as requisite; if not, the Delaware State must take its fate, and not occasion the
loss of a battle, which may prove more injurious to
the common cause, though I shudder at the thought.

With heart-felt gratitude to the Divine Disposer
of all events, and next, to you, I received an account
of your success on Saturday last, from some Quakers returning to Nottingham, in Chester county, and
to Elkridge, in Baltimore county, from their yearly
meeting at Philadelphia, which you broke up on Saturday night, by the actions of the day. These men
would not relate a single word of any thing that
happened at Philadelphia, during the eight days they
were there; saying they did not go there to carry or
to bring news, and seemed unwilling even to stop so
long as to make this speech. However, I compelled
them to stop, made them dismount, and examined
them separately, and in private. They said, at first,
they had no news, &c. I mention these minute circumstances to satisfy you that their account, being
given with great reluctance, was that of the Tories
and the English themselves.

It is, in brief, as follows; — That you attacked the
picket of the enemy, consisting of four or five hundred men, near Beggarstown, about three o'clock in
the morning, and drove them until supported by the
British light infantry, at which time you had taken

nine field-pieces, and killed or taken most of the picket; that the infantry were driven near two miles into Germantown; that they are all cut off except a very few; that, at Germantown, there were thirty-five of some English General's guard killed, and it was supposed he himself was taken prisoner; that, during the action, all the British troops, except part of a regiment of grenadiers, not exceeding fifty, went from Philadelphia, and joined General Howe, who commanded in person; that the main body of the enemy were at the end of Germantown next Phila-delphia, and, upon their advancing, were once repuls-ed by you; but afterwards, about nine o'clock, oblig-ed the Americans to retreat to the ground they oc-cupied the day preceding; that General Agnew was killed; and John Pierpoint, one of the examinants, said, he saw two Hessian Generals brought into the city wounded, one of them mortally, the other not so badly; that a great number of Colonels and many other officers were killed, and about a thousand men; that one hundred wagons, and upwards, came into the city after night, about nine o'clock, with the wound-ed; some had three, others seven, and between these numbers, in them, according to the severity of their wounds, as they were told; that a Virginia regiment had grounded their arms, and, with others, amounting in the whole to five hundred rebels, were taken pri-soners by the English, and that General Wayne was killed; but they heard of no other American officer of distinction that was.

They further said, they heard that the English could never form until they joined their main body below Germantown, and that you had the advantage of the ground; that a wounded Hessian told one of them, that he had fought French and Spaniards, but that the rebels would beat them both; and that he had never seen men fight as they did; and, in fine, that though the English had got the ground, which they called the victory, it was agreed, on all hands, that the British had not met with so great a loss since they came to America.

John Pierpoint, who seemed willing enough to tell all he knew, informed me that the Delaware frigate was given up by the pressed men on board; that there were but two brass cannon, twelve-pounders, fired from the fort upon the frigate, and but one man killed in the fort, and one in the frigate; that she was manned with English, and lay above the town on Sunday morning, when he came away; that the English had strong lines, some heavy cannon, and a fortification, about half way between German-town and the City, as he was told; that the Quakers could get no provender but hay for their horses; that butter had sold from three shillings and nine-pence to five shillings a pound; and that a famine was expected by the citizens in general, though some said they might subsist for a month. A Mr. Husbands told me he saw upwards of two thousand troops at Chester, on Monday last, escorting wagons, that were loaded from thirteen ships which lay there; that four men-of-war were then at the *chevaux-de-frise*, and that he saw two hundred and fifty Hessians, who had crossed Schuylkill on the same day, proceeding down the neck towards Delaware, it was supposed, to forage, plunder, &c. This is all that seems, in any degree, worth communicating; indeed, none of it is perhaps worth your reading; however, if any use can be made of it, you have it.*

If your Excellency attacks and disables a thou-

---

* It is needless to say that the above statements are, in many parts, inaccurate.

sand of the enemy a week, and you are constantly reënforced equal to the numbers you lose, as I trust you will be, you must soon prove triumphantly victorious, and get the game, though you should not throw sixes.

Your answer, by the express, will oblige one who prays for your success and happiness, and professes himself to be, with the utmost regard, your Excellency's most obedient

And devoted humble servant,

THOMAS McKEAN.

FROM THE REVEREND JACOB DUCHÉ.

[Philadelphia], 8 October, 1777.*

SIR,

If this letter should find you in Council, or in the field, before you read another sentence, I beg you to take the first opportunity of retiring, and weighing its important contents. You are perfectly acquainted with the part I formerly took in the present unhappy contest. I was, indeed, among the first to bear

---

* This extraordinary letter was immediately transmitted by Washington to Congress. In a letter to the President of Congress, dated October 16th, which accompanied it, he wrote as follows; —

"I yesterday, through the hands of Mrs. Ferguson, of Graham Park, received a letter, of a very curious and extraordinary nature, from Mr. Duché, which I have thought proper to transmit to Congress. To this ridiculous, illiberal performance, I made a short reply, by desiring the bearer of it, if she should hereafter, by any accident, meet Mr. Duché, to tell him I should have returned it unopened, if I had had any idea of the contents; observing, at the same time, that I highly disapproved the intercourse she seemed to have been carrying on, and expected it would be discontinued. Notwithstanding the author's assertion, I cannot but suspect that the measure did not originate with him, and that he was induced to it by the hope of establishing his interest and peace more effectually with the enemy."

my public testimony against having any recourse to threats, or indulging a thought of an armed opposition.

The current, however, was too strong for my feeble efforts to resist. I wished to follow my countrymen as far only as virtue, and the righteousness of their cause, would permit me. I was, however, prevailed on, among the rest of my clerical brethren of this city, to gratify the pressing desires of my fellow-citizens, by preaching a sermon to the second city battalion. I was pressed to publish this sermon, and reluctantly consented. From a personal attachment, of near twenty years' standing, and a high respect for your character, in private as well as public life, I took the liberty of dedicating this sermon to you. I had your affectionate thanks for my performance, in a letter, wherein was expressed, in the most delicate and obliging terms, your regard for me, and your wishes for a continuance of my friendship and approbation of your conduct. Farther than this I intended not to proceed. My sermon speaks for itself, and wholly disclaims the idea of independency. My sentiments were well known to my friends. I communicated them, without reserve, to many respectable members of Congress, who expressed their warm approbation of it then. I persisted, to the very last moment, to use the prayers for my Sovereign, though threatened with insults from the violence of a party.

Upon the declaration of independency, I called my vestry, and solemnly put the question to them, whether they thought it best, for the peace and welfare of the congregation, to shut up the churches, or to continue the service, without using the prayers for the Royal Family. This was the sad alternative. I concluded to abide by their decision, as I could not have time to consult my spiritual superiors in Eng-

38*

land. They determined it most expedient, under such critical circumstances, to keep open the churches, that the congregations might not be dispersed, which we had great reason to apprehend.

A very few days after the fatal declaration of independency, I received a letter from Mr. Hancock, sent by express to Germantown, where my family were for the summer season, acquainting me I was appointed Chaplain to the Congress, and desired my attendance next morning, at nine o'clock. Surprised and distressed, as I was, by an event I was not prepared to expect; obliged to give an immediate attendance, without the opportunity of consulting my friends, I easily accepted the appointment. I could have but one motive for taking this step. I thought the churches in danger, and hoped, by this means, to have been instrumental in preventing those ills I had so much reason to apprehend. I can, however, with truth, declare, I then looked upon independency rather as an expedient, and hazardous, or, indeed, thrown out *in terrorem*, in order to procure some favorable terms, than a measure that was seriously persisted in, at all events. My sudden change of conduct will clearly evince this to have been my idea of the matter.

Upon the return of the Committee of Congress appointed to confer with Lord Howe, I soon discerned their whole intentions. The different accounts which each member gave of this conference, the time they took to make up the matter for public view, and the amazing disagreements between the newspaper accounts and the relation I myself had from the mouth of one of the Committee, convinced me there must have been some unfair and ungenerous procedure. This determination to treat on no other

strain than that of independency, which put it out
of his Lordship's power to mention any terms at all,
was sufficient proof to me that independency was the
idol they had long wished to set up, and that, rather
than sacrifice this, they would deluge their country
with blood.   From this moment I determined upon
my resignation, and, in the beginning of October,
1776, sent it, in form, to Mr. Hancock, after having
officiated only two months and three weeks; and
from that time, as far as my safety would permit,
I have been opposed to all their measures.

This circumstantial account of my conduct, I think
due to the friendship you were so obliging as to express for me, and, I hope, will be sufficient to justify
my seeming inconsistencies in the part I have acted.

And now, dear Sir, suffer me, in the language of
truth and real affection, to address myself to you.
All the world must be convinced you are engaged in
the service of your country from motives perfectly
disinterested.   You risked every thing that was dear
to you, abandoned the sweets of domestic life, which
your affluent fortune can give the uninterrupted enjoyment of.   But had you, could you have had, the
least idea of matters being carried to such a dangerous extremity?   Your most intimate friends shud-
dered at the thought of a separation from the mother
country, and I took it for granted that your sentiments coincided with theirs.   What, then, can be the
consequence of this rash and violent measure, and
degeneracy of representation, confusion of councils,
blunders without number?   The most respectable characters have withdrawn themselves, and are succeeded by a great majority of illiberal and violent men.
Take an impartial view of the present Congress, and
what can you expect from them?   Your feelings

must be greatly hurt by the representation of your native Province. You have no longer a Randolph, a Bland, or a Braxton, men whose names will ever be revered, whose demands never ran above the first ground on which they set out, and whose truly glorious and virtuous sentiments I have frequently heard with rapture from their own lips. Oh! my dear Sir, what a sad contrast of characters now presents; others, whose friends can ne'er mingle with your own. Your Harrison alone remains, and he disgusted with the unworthy associates.

As to those of my own Province, some of them are so obscure, that their very names were never in my ears before, and others have only been distinguished for the weakness of their understandings, and the violence of their tempers. One alone I except from the general charge; a man of virtue, dragged reluctantly into their measures, and restrained, by some false ideas of honor, from retreating, after having gone too far. You cannot be at a loss to discover whose name answers to this character.

From the New England provinces can you find one that, as a gentleman, you could wish to associate with, unless the soft and mild address of Mr. Hancock can atone for his want of every other qualification necessary for the seat which he fills? Bankrupts, attorneys, and men of desperate fortunes, are his colleagues. Maryland no longer sends a Tilghman and a protestant Carroll. Carolina has lost her Lynch; and the elder Middleton has retired. Are the dregs of Congress, then, still to influence a mind like yours? These are not the men you engaged to serve; these are not the men that America has chosen to represent her. Most of them were chosen by a little, low faction, and the few gentlemen that are

among them now are well known to lie on the balance, and looking up to your hand alone to turn the
beam. 'Tis you, Sir, and you only, that support the
present Congress; of this you must be fully sensible.
Long before they left Philadelphia, their dignity and
consequence were gone; what must it be now, since
their precipitate retreat? I write with freedom, but
without invective; I know these things to be true,
and I write to one whose own observation must have
convinced him that it is so.

After this view of the Congress, turn to the army.
The whole world knows that its only existence depends upon you; that your death or captivity dis-
perses it in a moment, and that there is not a man
on that side the question, in America, capable of succeeding you. As to the army itself, what have you
to expect from them? Have they not frequently
abandoned you yourself, in the hour of extremity?
Can you have the least confidence in a set of undisciplined men and officers, many of whom have been
taken from the lowest of the people, without principle, without courage? Take away them that surround your person, how very few are there you can
ask to sit at your table! As to your little navy, of
that little, what is left? Of the Delaware fleet, part
are taken, and the rest must soon surrender. Of
those in the other provinces, some are taken, one or
two at sea, and others lying unmanned and unrigged
in your harbours.

And now, where are your resources? Oh! my
dear Sir, how sadly have you been abused by a faction void of truth, and void of tenderness to you and
your country! They have amused you with hopes of
a declaration of war on the part of France. Believe
me, from the best authority, it was a fiction from the

first. Early in the year 1776, a French gentleman was introduced to me, with whom I became intimately acquainted. His business, to all appearance, was to speculate in the mercantile way. But, I believe, it will be found that in his country he moved in a higher sphere. He saw your cause. He became acquainted with all your military preparations. He was introduced to Congress, and engaged with them in a commercial contract. In the course of our intimacy, he has frequently told me, that he hoped the Americans would never think of independency. He gave me his reasons. "Independency can never be supported, unless France should declare war against England. I well know the state of her finances. Years to come will not put them in a situation to enter upon a breach with England. At this moment, there are two parties in the Court of Versailles; one enlisted under the Duke de Choiseul, the other under the Count Maurepas. Choiseul has no chance of succeeding, though he is violent for war; Maurepas must get the better; he is for economy and peace." This was his information, which I mentioned to several members of Congress. They treated it as a fable, depending entirely on Dr. Franklin's intelligence.

The truth of the matter is this; — Dr. Franklin built upon the success of Choiseul. Upon his arrival in France, he found him out of place, his counsels reprobated, and his party dwindled into an insignificant faction. This you may depend upon to be the true state of affairs in France, or the court of Dr. F.; and, further, by vast numbers of letters found on board prizes taken by the king's ships, it appears that all commerce with the merchants, through whom all your supplies have been conveyed, will be at an end, the letters being full of complaints of no remittances from America, and many individuals having generally suffered.

From your friends in England you have nothing to expect. Their numbers have diminished to a cipher; the spirit of the whole nation is in activity; a few sounding names among the nobility, though perpetually ringing in your ears, are without character, without influence. Disappointed ambition has made them desperate, and they only wish to make the deluded Americans instruments of revenge. All orders and ranks of men in Great Britain are now unanimous, and determined to risk their all with content. Trade and manufactures are found to flourish, and new channels are continually offering, that will perhaps more than supply the loss of the old.

In America, your harbours are blocked up, your cities fall one after another; fortress after fortress, battle after battle is lost. A British army, after having passed unmolested through a vast extent of country, have possessed themselves of the Capital of America. How unequal the contest! How fruitless the expense of blood! Under so many discouraging circumstances, can virtue, can honor, can the love of your country, prompt you to proceed? Humanity itself, and sure humanity is no stranger to your breast, calls upon you to desist. Your army must perish for want of common necessaries, or thousands of innocent families must perish to support them; wherever they encamp, the country must be impoverished; wherever they march, the troops of Britain will pursue, and must complete the destruction which America herself has begun. Perhaps it may be said, it is better to die than to be made slaves. This, indeed, is a splendid maxim in theory, and perhaps, in some instances, may be found experimentally true; but when there is the least probability of an happy accommodation, surely wisdom and humanity call for some sacrifices to be made, to prevent inevitable destruction. You well know there is but one invincible bar to such an accommodation; could this be removed, other obstacles might readily be removed.

It is to you, and you alone, your bleeding country looks, and calls aloud for this sacrifice. Your arm alone has strength sufficient to remove this bar. May Heaven inspire you with this glorious resolution of exerting your strength, at this crisis, and immortalizing yourself as friend and guardian to your country! Your penetrating eye needs not more explicit language to discern my meaning. With that prudence and delicacy, therefore, of which I know you possessed, represent to Congress the indispensable necessity of rescinding the hasty and ill-advised declaration of independency. Recommend, and you have an undoubted right to recommend, an immediate cessation of hostilities. Let the controversy be taken up where that declaration left it, and where Lord Howe certainly expected to find it left. Let men of clear and impartial characters, in or out of Congress, liberal in their sentiments, heretofore independent in their fortunes,—and some such may be found in America,—be appointed to confer with his Majesty's Commissioners. Let them, if they please, propose some well-digested constitutional plan, to lay before them at the commencement of the negotiation. When they have gone thus far, I am confident the usual happy consequences will ensue; unanimity will immediately take place through the different provinces; thousands who are now ardently wishing and praying for such a measure, will step forth, and declare themselves the zealous advocates for constitutional liberty;

and millions will bless the hero that left the field of war, to decide this most important contest with the weapons of wisdom and humanity.

Oh! Sir, let no false ideas of worldly honor deter you from engaging in so glorious a task. Whatever censures may be thrown out by mean, illiberal minds, your character will rise in the estimation of the virtuous and noble. It will appear with lustre in the annals of history, and form a glorious contrast to that of those who have fought to obtain conquest, and gratify their own ambition by the destruction of their species and the ruin of their country. Be assured, Sir, that I write not this under the eye of any British officer, or person connected with the British army, or ministry. The sentiments I express are the real sentiments of my own heart, such as I have long held, and which I should have made known to you by letter before, had I not fully expected an opportunity of a private conference. When you passed through Philadelphia, on your way to Wilmington, I was confined, by a severe fit of the gravel, to my chamber; I have since continued much indisposed, and times have been so very distressing, that I had neither spirit to write a letter, nor an opportunity to convey it when written; nor do I yet know by what means I shall get these sheets to your hands.

I would fain hope that I have said nothing by which your delicacy can be in the least hurt. If I have, I assure you it has been without the least intention, and, therefore, your candor will lead you to forgive me. I have spoke freely of Congress and of the army; but what I have said is partly from my own knowledge, and partly from the information of some respectable members of the former, and some of the best officers of the latter. I would not offend the meanest person upon earth; what I say to you I say in confidence, to answer what I cannot but deem a most *valuable purpose*. I love my country; I love you; but to the love of truth, the love of peace, and the love of God, I hope I should be enabled, if called upon to the trial, to sacrifice every other inferior love.

If the arguments made use of in this letter should have so much influence as to engage you in the glorious work which I have warmly recommended, I shall ever deem my success the highest temporal favor that Providence could grant me. Your interposition and advice, I am confident, would meet with a favorable reception from the authority under which you act.

If it should not, you have an infallible recourse still left; negotiate for your country at the head of your army. After all, it may appear presumption, as an individual, to address himself to you on a subject of such magnitude, or to say what measures would best secure the interest and welfare of a whole Continent. The friendly and favorable opinion you have always expressed for me, emboldens me to undertake it, and which has greatly added to the weight of this motive. I have been strongly impressed with a sense of duty upon the occasion, which left my conscience uneasy, and my heart afflicted, till I fully discharged it. I am no enthusiast; the course is new and singular to me; but I could not enjoy one moment's peace till this letter was written. With the most ardent prayers for your spiritual as well as temporal welfare, I am your most

Obedient and humble friend and servant,

JACOB DUCHÉ.

APPENDIX.

APPENDIX.

No. I.

OPERATIONS IN CANADA.

MAJOR JOHN BROWN TO GOVERNOR TRUMBULL.

Crown Point, 14 August, 1775.

MAY IT PLEASE YOUR EXCELLENCY,

On the 24th of last month, by the General's order, I set out for Canada with four men, with directions to penetrate the country, and get all the intelligence that could be had in regard to the military preparations making there by the king's troops, Canadians, or Indians; what the situation of St. John's, Chamblee, Montreal, and Quebec; how many troops at each place; whether the Canadians designed to take up arms against us; whether any reënforcements had arrived in the Colony, &c.

I arrived in Canada on the 30th. Had a tedious and fatiguing march through a vast tract of swamp lying on the west side of the Lake, in which I lodged three nights. But I pass by the particulars of the adventure; how pursued and surrounded by a large party of the enemy, when in a house; escaping out of a back window, and pursued two days, on my return; notwithstanding which I continued in the country four days, being protected by the Canadians, who, I can assure you, are our friends, without whose protection I must have fallen into the hands of the enemy. It is impossible for me to describe the kindness received from the French, as also their distressed situation, being threatened with destruction from the king's troops by fire and sword. Though they refuse to take up arms against the Colonies, they wish and long for nothing more than to see us, with an army, penetrate their country. They engage to supply us with every thing in their power. The Indians are determined to act in conjunction with the Canadians. Colonel Guy Johnson has arrived at Montreal with a party of three hundred, mostly tenants, unacquainted with arms. There are also some Indians arrived with him, *via* Oswego. They held a Council with the Iroquois and St. Louis, and are determined to act with the Canadians, except it be to go on discovery.

The regulars are fortifying St. John's; have raised two batteres, which mount nine guns each. They have intrenched and picketed out some distance from their other works. Two large row-galleys, of sixty or eighty feet in length each, are on the stocks, and will be finished soon. They mount twelve guns each. There are about seven hundred of the king's troops in Canada; near three hundred at St. John's, about fifty at Quebec, the remainder at Montreal, Chamblee, and at the upper posts. Now, Sir, it is time to carry Canada. It may be done with great ease and little cost, and I have no doubt but the Canadians would join us. There is great defection among them. They have lately raised a mob, seized on the French officers lately appointed, and taken away their commissions. They were under arms several days, and it seemed that the king's troops durst not resent it; but their captain, with one of my men (a Canadian) whom I sent to Montreal to do business, are both taken prisoners and in close hold. This, I imagine, will raise the resentment of the Canadians to a higher pitch than any thing that has yet been done.

I left the country on the 3d instant, being informed by the Canadians that two scouts, of fifty men each, were sent out often; the one up the Lake, the other to Montreal. I steered to the east north-east three days, and came to the Bay of Missisco, where I got a small canoe ; and, on the 10th instant, arrived at the Point.

Should a large reënforcement arrive in Canada, it will turn the scale immediately. The Canadians must then take up arms, or be ruined.

It seems that some evil planet has reigned in this quarter this year, for notwithstanding the season far advanced, and a fine opportunity presents of making ourselves masters of a country, with the greatest ease, which, I fear, may cost us much blood and treasure, if delayed, New York have acted a droll part, and are determined to defeat us, if in their power; they have failed in men and supplies.

I beg your Honor's pardon for troubling you with this letter; but, as every friend and well-wisher to the success of our arms is curious as to the probability of the success, I have taken it on me to acquaint your Honor of the state of Canada, which doubtless you may have from the General in a more perfect manner. It is by Mr. Bennet's motion, in part, that I give your Honor this trouble. I hope, as my paper, ink, and eye-sight are bad, that you will pass by mistakes. I am, Sir,

Your Honor's most obedient, humble servant,
JOHN BROWN.

COLONEL ETHAN ALLEN TO GENERAL SCHUYLER.

September 14, 1775.

Wednesday, the 6th of September, set out from Isle-aux-Noix. On the 8th instant, I arrived at Chamblee; found the Canadians in that vicinity friendly; they guarded me under arms night and day, escorted me through the woods, as I desired, and showed me every courtesy I could wish for. The news of my being in this place excited many Captains of the militia, and respectable gentlemen of the Canadians, to visit and converse with me, as I gave out I was sent by General Schuyler to manifest his friendly intentions towards them, and delivered the General's written manifesto to the Chiefs of the Caghnawaga Indians, demanding the cause why sundry of the Indians had taken up arms against the United Colonies.

They sent two of their Chiefs to me, who plead that it was contrary to the will and orders of their Chiefs. The king's troops gave them rum, and inveigled them to fight General Schuyler; that they had sent their runners and ordered them to depart from St. John's, averring their friendship to the Colonies. Meanwhile the Sachems held a general council, sent two of their Captains and some beads of a wampum belt as a lasting testimony of their friendship, and that they would not take up arms on either side. These tokens of friendship were delivered to me, agreeably to their ceremony, in a solemn manner, in the presence of a large auditory of Canadians, who approved of the league and manifested friendship to the Colonies, and testified their good will on account of the advance of the army into Canada. Their fear, as they said, was, that our army were too weak to protect them against the severity of the English government, as a defeat on our part would expose our friends in Canada to it. In this dilemma, our friends expressed anxiety of mind.

It furthermore appeared to me, that many of the Canadians were watching the scale of power, whose attraction attracted them. In fine, our friends in Canada earnestly urged that General Schuyler should immediately environ St. John's; that they would assist in cutting off the communication between St. John's and Chamblee, and between these forts and Montreal. They furthermore assured me that they would help our army to provisions, &c.; and that, if our army did not make a conquest of the king's garrisons, they would be exposed to the resentment of the English government, which they dreaded, and consequently, that the attempt of the army into Canada would be to them the greatest evil. They furthermore told me, that some of the inhabitants, that were in their hearts friendly to us, would [resolve] to extricate themselves and take up arms in favor of the crown; and, therefore, it was of the last importance to them that the army immediately attack St. John's, which would cause them to take up arms in our favor.

Governor Carleton threatens the Canadians with fire and sword, except they assist him against the Colonies, and the Seignieurs urge them to it. They have withstood Carleton and them, and keep under arms throughout most of their parishes, and are now anxiously watching the scale of power.

This is the situation of affairs in Canada, according to my most painful discoveries, given under my hand, upon honor, this 14th day of September, 1775.

ETHAN ALLEN.*

---

* In his published "Narrative," Allen speaks of this expedition as follows; — "I advanced with the army to Isle-aux-Noix, from whence I was ordered by the General to go, in company with Major Brown and certain interpreters, through the woods into Canada, with letters to the Canadians, and to let them know that the design of the army was only against the English garrisons, and not the country, their liberties, or religion. And having, through much danger, negotiated this business, I returned to the Isle-aux-Noix the forepart of September, when General Schuyler returned to Albany; and, in consequence, the command devolved upon General Montgomery, whom I assisted in laying a line of circumvallation around the fortress at St. John's." Allen's Narrative, p. 7.

GENERAL MONTGOMERY TO GENERAL SCHUYLER.

Camp, near St. John's, 19 September, 1775.

DEAR SIR,

I take the opportunity of Fulmore's * return with the Oneidas, to acquaint you of our arrival here on the 17th, in the evening. Yesterday, I marched, with five hundred men, to the north side of St. John's, where we found a party of the King's troops, with field-pieces. This party had beaten off Major Brown † a few hours before, who had imprudently thrown himself in their way, depending on our more early arrival, which, through the dilatoriness of our young troops, could not be sooner effected. The enemy, after an ill-directed fire for some minutes, retired with precipitation; and lucky for them they did, for had we known their situation, which the thickness of the woods prevented our finding out till it was too late, not a man of them would have returned. The old story of *treachery* spread among the men; as soon as we saw the enemy, we were trepanned, drawn under the guns of the fort, and what not. The woodsmen ‡ were not so expert at forming as I expected, and too many of them hung back; had we kept silence at first, before we were discovered, we should have got a field-piece or two.

I have left the five hundred men at the joining of the two roads; § this day I have sent them intrenching tools.

Things seem to go on well among the Canadians. It is strongly reported, that the King's stores are embarked at Montreal, in order to be removed. I have sent Colonel Allen to Chamblee, in order to raise a corps. Send me money as fast as possible, my dear General. Guy Johnson and Claws have repre-

---

[The following are notes by General Schuyler in the copy of the letter sent to General Washington.]

* Fulmore, an Indian Interpreter, who attended the Deputies of the six nations to Caghnawaga.

† Major Brown I had sent with one hundred of our men, and about thirty-four Canadians, towards Chamblee, to keep up the spirits of the Canadians, and join the army at St. John's, as soon as it should arrive there.

‡ Woodsmen, I suppose the New Hampshire people and Green Mountain Boys.

§ Joining of the roads which lead to Chamblee and Longueil, opposite to Montreal.

sented us as beggarly miscreants, who have nothing to give away to the Indians, nor to pay for what we get. Fulmore will give you an account of our Council.

I have great dependence on your presence, to administer to our many wants.

I most earnestly hope this will find you relieved from the acuteness of your pain; a perfect cure, in so short a time, can hardly be expected. Believe me, dear Sir, with the fullest esteem and respect,

Your most obedient servant,
RICHARD MONTGOMERY.

P. S. On the 17th, at night, Major Brown intercepted eight carts going to the fort, laden with rum and gun-carriages for the vessel; these things were hid in the woods, and were not recovered by the enemy on Brown's discomfiture.

COLONEL SETH WARNER TO GENERAL MONTGOMERY.

Laprairie, 27 September, 1775.

MAY IT PLEASE YOUR HONOR,

I have the disagreeable news to write to you, that Colonel Allen hath met with a defeat by a stronger force, which sallied out of the town of Montreal, after he had crossed the river about a mile below the town. I have no certain knowledge of Allen as yet, whether he is killed, taken, or fled. But this defeat hath put the French people into great consternation; they are much concerned for fear of a company coming over against us. Furthermore, the Indian Chiefs were at Montreal, at the time of Allen's battle, and there was a number of the Caghnawaga Indians in the battle against Allen, and the people are very fearful of the Indians; there were six in here last night, I suppose sent as spies. I asked the Indians concerning their appearing against us in every battle; their answer to me was, that Carleton made them drunk, and drove them to it; but they say they would do so no more.

I should think it proper to keep a party at Longueil, and my party is not big enough to divide, if I tarry here. I should be glad of my regiment, for my party is made up with different companies, and different regiments, and my reputation is not so good as I could wish for. Subordination to your orders is my pleasure. I am, Sir, with submission,

Your humble servant,
SETH WARNER.

P. S. This morning arrived, from Colonel Allen's defeat, Captain Duggan, with the following intelligence. Colonel Allen is absolutely taken captive into Montreal, with a few more, and about two or three killed, and about as many wounded. The living have not all come in. Something of a slaughter made among the King's troops.* From yours to serve,

SETH WARNER.

GENERAL MONTGOMERY TO GENERAL SCHUYLER.

Camp, near St. John's, 28 September, 1775.

DEAR SIR,

Since my last of the 24th, we have opened a battery of two twelve-pounders, upon the ship-yards and schooner. She was obliged immediately to haul near the wharf, or rather as near the north end of the fort as she could get. This battery is screened from the guns of the fort by an epaulement, in a good measure.

I fear I have neither men nor ammunition to carry on any attack with success; to which purpose, it would be absolutely necessary to occupy a very advantageous piece of rising ground on the west side, and there erect my battery to rack their defences. The largest of the mortars is useless, and on the mortars I principally depended for distressing the garrison. The weather has been and is still so exceedingly bad, and the encampment so swampy, that I feel exceedingly for the troops; and withal, provisions so scanty, flour as well as pork, that it will require, not only good fortune, but despatch, to keep us from distress. I hope the thirteen-inch mortar and more powder are on the way.

Allen, Warner, and Brown are at Laprairie and Longueil, with a party of our troops, and some Canadians. How many, I cannot tell. They all speak well of the good disposition of the Canadians. They have a project of making an attempt on Mon-

---

* Allen gives a particular account of this adventure in his Narrative, pp. 8 – 14.

treal. I fear the troops are not fit for it. Carleton has certainly left that town, and it is in a very defenceless state.

As the garrison is shut up, I hope the Kennebec expedition will meet with no obstruction in the attack upon Quebec. Should any thing not go well, I tremble for the fate of the poor Canadians, who have ventured so much. What should I do with them should we be obliged to evacuate the country! Though I hope this will not be the case. If possible, do not let us want ammunition, my dear General. I have seen Mr. Livingston. He has a considerable body of Canadians in arms at Chamblee, is very active, and they have great confidence in him, I believe. I wish to have him taken notice of by the Congress, in a manner suitable to his services, and the risk he runs. I am, my dear Sir, with the warmest wishes for the recovery of your health,

Your faithful, humble servant,

RICHARD MONTGOMERY.

GENERAL MONTGOMERY TO GENERAL SCHUYLER.

Camp, south side of St. John's, 6 October, 1775.

DEAR GENERAL,

Your vigilance and foresight have saved us from the difficulties that threatened us. We are no longer afraid of starving. I wait now with impatience for the arrival of those troops, mentioned in your last, which I believe, from the number of boats on the way, will soon be here, to take the advantageous post I formerly spoke of, on a hill to the westward.

Since my last, I have had some proposals of an accommodation, through the channel of the Caghnawagas, from the formidable St. Luc le Corne, and other principal inhabitants of Montreal. To-morrow is appointed for a conference at Laprairie. I have sent Major Brown to manage it. Macpherson goes with him, and Mr. Livingston of Chamblee will attend. The result of this negotiation I hope soon to make you acquainted with. Mr. St. Luc's character gives me all the reason in the world to be on my guard against him. I shall insist on some substantial proof of his sincerity. Mr. Livingston, some days ago, took post at Hazen's house, with near two hundred Canadians. They are erecting a battery there, which seems to make the garrison very uneasy.

Yesterday they attacked them with their row-galley, but were beaten back without loss on the side of the Canadians. No certain intelligence yet of Arnold's arrival, though there are flying reports to that purpose. I wish he was at Quebec, with all my heart. I believe there is nothing to oppose him. I am extremely happy you have sent for more powder. I believe we have not more than two and one-half tons. This I am afraid will not do. Send us as many men as you can possibly furnish with provisions. I am greatly in want of them. Our feebleness has intimidated the Canadians from embarking in so uncertain an adventure. Were I strong enough to send five hundred men to Montreal, it would certainly declare for us; at least I have great reason to think so. The miserable weather we have had has distressed us much, but I hope it is now over.

Let the hard cash come as soon as possible, that our reputation may hold good.

Mr. Carleton has not departed, as I informed you. We want both iron and steel, and turner's tools. The large mortar is ready to play. I shall send some more boats in a few days.

I am, &c., &c.,

RICHARD MONTGOMERY.

GENERAL MONTGOMERY TO GENERAL SCHUYLER.

Camp, near St. John's, 13 October, 1775.

DEAR GENERAL,

Some time ago I informed you of my intentions to make my approaches on the west side, as soon as the expected reënforcement enabled me to undertake it. I had had a road cut to the intended ground, and some fascines made, when I was informed by Major Brown, that a general dissatisfaction prevailed; that unless something was undertaken in a few days, there would be a mutiny; and that the universal sense of the army was to direct all our attention to the east side. The impatience of the troops to get home has prevented their seeing the impossibility of undertaking this business sooner, the duty being hard for the troops, even on the present confined state of operations.

When I mentioned my intentions, I did not consider I was at the head of troops who carry the spirit of freedom into the field, and think for themselves. Upon considering the fatal consequences which might flow from a want of subordination and discipline (should this ill humor continue), my unstable authority over troops of different Colonies, the insufficiency of the military law, and my own want of powers to enforce it, weak as it is, I thought it expedient to call the Field-Officers together. Inclosed I send you the result of our deliberations.

RICHARD MONTGOMERY.

Result of the Proceedings of a Council of War, held at St. John's, October 13th, 1775.

I proposed establishing a battery of all our spare heavy cannon, on the rising ground exactly opposite the stone house in the north redoubt (in the west face of which there is but one embrasure open), at the distance of about four hundred yards, securing this battery with a work capable of being well defended by two hundred men. From this battery our approaches might be continued to the ditch, and by the time we arrived there, the fraise around the berme would be destroyed, the rampart in a ruinous state, and the large house (which is said to be their principal barrack) would be destroyed, as every shot that missed the rampart, must take the house. Two four-pounders on the east side would answer the end of securing the west rampart in reverse, and thereby slackening the opposition of the enemy.

By this mode of proceeding, if our ammunition held out, there would be, in my opinion, some prospect of success, notwithstanding the superior artillery of the garrison, which could not be mounted in its proper place in time enough to prevent the erection of our battery. The Field-Officers were, to a man, of opinion that my reasons were insufficient, being afraid the designed ground was at this season too wet for approaches, and strongly of opinion our heavy cannon on the east side would more effectually distress the enemy by annoying their buildings, the fort having a gentle slope to the river, and (which was urged as the strongest motive) by destroying their schooner. In vain I represented, that even if every building was destroyed, the garrison would not surrender without a probability of an assault, which could never arise from any attack on the opposite side of the river; that the vessel could not be destroyed, because she would change her place in such a manner as to elude our batteries; that we had little powder or time to throw away on experiments; that I had a moral certainty they would find themselves mistaken; and finally that they must take it upon themselves, for I would not oppose the general sense of the army, and should enforce the measure by every effort in my power.

I cannot help observing, to how little purpose I am here. Were I not afraid the example would be too generally followed, and that the public service might suffer, I would not stay an hour at the head of troops whose operations I cannot direct. I must say I have no hopes of success, unless from the garrison's wanting provisions.

RICHARD MONTGOMERY.

BROOK WATSON TO WILLIAM FRANKLIN, GOVERNOR
NEW JERSEY.

Montreal, 19 October, 1775.

DEAR SIR,

I had the pleasure to write you from Quebec, the 18th ultimo, per the Cillery, Captain Hardie; since which I have been much alarmed by a letter from Boston, dated the 5th ultimo, advising of Halifax being taken; but I was soon relieved by a letter from Mr. Butler, dated the 1st September, which was soon followed by others of the 16th and 21st, by which I learn, to my great comfort, that the Province was not in any immediate danger. Nor do I conceive these people will be so mad as to send a body of men, where, let their success be ever so great, they cannot winter them. Indeed, the Admiral's orders to destroy their vessels will, if executed, effectually prevent their crossing the Bay of Fundy.

It is my opinion General Gage cannot winter the army in Boston, and that he will soon be obliged to quit it. If so, part of them must winter at Halifax, and part at Quebec, where they are indeed much wanted; for such is the wretched state of this unhappy Province, that Colonel Allen, with a few despicable wretches, would have taken this city on the 25th ultimo, had not its inhabitants marched out to give them battle. They fought, conquered, and thereby saved the Province for a while. Allen and his banditti were mostly taken prisoners. He is now in chains on board the Gaspee. This little action has changed the face of things. The Canadians before were nine tenths for the Bostonians. They are now returned to their duty, many in arms for the King, and the parishes, who had been otherwise, are daily demanding their pardon, and taking arms for the Crown. St. John's is still invested. They have in the fort eight hundred men, well fortified and appointed. There is little danger of its being taken; yet I cordially wish for a few battalions of the King's troops to chase them out of the country. Our weather has been remarkably fine and mild, or they would soon be moving.

The Adamant is nearly loaded. I hope to sail from Quebec about the 10th of next month, and to arrive in England before Parliament shall adjourn for the holidays. Let me entreat you to remit the balance of Mr. Louberbahler's account. Every shilling is a relief at this time of general distress.

My good wishes attend Mrs. Franklin and the children; and I pray you to believe, that I am, dear Sir,

Your faithful, humble servant,

BROOK WATSON.

GENERAL MONTGOMERY TO GOVERNOR CARLETON.

Camp, before St. John's, 22 October, 1775.

SIR,

I have received information, from different quarters, that the prisoners you have made are treated with cruel and unnecessary severity, being loaded with irons; and that Colonel Allen himself meets with this shocking indignity.

Your character, Sir, induces me to hope I am ill informed; nevertheless, the duty I owe the troops committed to my charge, lays me under the necessity of acquainting your Excellency that, if you avow this conduct and persist in it, I shall, though with the most painful regret, execute with rigor the just and necessary law of retaliation upon the garrison of Chamblee, now in my possession, and upon all others who may hereafter fall into my hands. I must be understood to stipulate for those unfortunate Canadians, your prisoners, who have thrown themselves into the arms of the United Colonies for protection, whose enraged countrymen have with difficulty been restrained from acts of violence on the garrison of Chamblee.

I shall expect your Excellency's answer in six days. Should the bearer not return in that time, I must interpret your silence into a declaration of a barbarous war. I cannot pass this opportunity, without lamenting the melancholy and fatal necessity which obliges the firmest friends of the Constitution to oppose one of the most respectable officers of the Crown. I am, &c.,

RICHARD MONTGOMERY.

MAJOR PRESTON TO GENERAL MONTGOMERY.

St. John's, 1 November, 1775.

SIR,

I am credibly informed that the prisoner you permitted to pass here this evening is frequently subject to fits of insanity, and therefore cannot lay much stress on what he says.

Equally anxious to prevent the further unnecessary effusion of blood, and zealous to maintain the honor of his Majesty's arms, I now inform you that, should no attempt be made to relieve this place within the space of four days, I will then offer to you my proposals relative to a surrender. The low state of my provisions, the destruction of artillery stores, tools, &c., are points with which the deserter was not well acquainted. In whatever way the fate of this garrison may be determined, I flatter myself it will never depend on the assembling of Canadians, who must have rendered themselves equally contemptible to both parties. I am, Sir, &c.,

CHARLES PRESTON,
Major of the 26th Regiment, commanding at St. John's.

GENERAL MONTGOMERY TO MAJOR PRESTON.

1 November, 1775.

SIR,

The advanced season of the year will not admit of your proposal. I do assure you, upon the honor of a gentleman, that what the prisoner has informed you of is true, as far as has come to my knowledge. However, if it wants further confirmation, Mr. Depane, of Montreal, who is also my prisoner, will, I believe, give you the same intelligence.

Having now acquitted my conscience, I must, to save time and prevent trouble, acquaint you, if you do not surrender this day, it will be unnecessary to make any future proposals. The

40 *

garrison shall be prisoners of war without the honors of war, and I cannot insure the officers their baggage. Should you wish to send an officer to Mr. Depane, who is on board the sloop, you have my permission. Captain Stewart carries an order for that purpose. Should you still be inclined to persist in a useless defence, you will immediately fire a cannon without shot, as a signal.   I am, &c.,

RICHARD MONTGOMERY.

GENERAL MONTGOMERY TO GENERAL SCHUYLER.

Camp, near St. John's, 3 November, 1775.

MY DEAR GENERAL,

I have the pleasure to acquaint you the garrison surrendered last night. This morning, we take possession; to-morrow, I hope the prisoners will set off. Inclosed you have the capitulation, which I hope will meet your approbation and that of Congress.

I have ventured to permit an officer or two to go to their families, which are in some distress, at Montreal, upon their parole. They can't do us any harm, and there would have been a degree of inhumanity in refusing them. When we had played on the fort some hours from our battery of four twelve-pounders, on the north-west, and another, of two twelve-pounders and two four-pounders, on the east side, some prisoners arrived who had been taken in an action with Governor Carleton, at Longueil. He made an attempt to land with thirty-four boats, full of men. Warner's detachment, consisting of the Green Mountain Boys and second regiment of Yorkers, repulsed them with loss; took two Indians and two Canadians prisoners. We have buried three Indians, and it is supposed many in the boats must have been killed; we had not a man even wounded. This, I believe, is his last effort.

One of the above-mentioned prisoners I sent into the fort to inform Major Preston of the circumstances of the action, that he might judge what prospect he had of relief. It had the desired effect; the garrison having been on half allowance for some time.

I am making the necessary preparation to proceed immediately to Montreal, by way of Laprairie, as the enemy have armed vessels in the Sorel. Send everybody you possibly can immediately down, as it is much to be apprehended many of the men on this service will insist on returning home when their times are expired. It will not be necessary to keep people with arms for the present at Ticonderoga. Several men of rank in Canada are among the prisoners. I have permitted them to remain at Crown Point till the return of two gentlemen they send to their friends for money, &c. They pleaded hard to return home; but they are too dangerous to let loose again.

I have this moment received your letter of the 27th October. Not a word of Arnold yet. I have sent two expresses to him lately; one by an Indian, who promised to return with expedition. The instant I have any news of him, I will acquaint you by express.

Colonel Easton and Major Brown, with that corps, and Mr. Livingston, with, I believe, one thousand Canadians, are going towards the mouth of the Sorel, and pushing Colonel Allan McLean before them. McLean had many Canadians, but they joined him through fear of fire and sword; you may judge easily how they will fight. I send you a list of stores, articles, &c., and am, my dear Sir, with respect and esteem,

Your much obliged, humble servant,
RICHARD MONTGOMERY.

Neither Macpherson nor Rensselaer have commissions.

P. S. *Half after six.* Just received your favor of the 31st October; a good deal of artillery stores, but we have not time to ascertain them.

COLONEL ARNOLD TO GENERAL MONTGOMERY.

St. Marie, 2 1-2 leagues from Point Levy,
8 November, 1775.

DEAR SIR,

Your favor of the 29th ultimo, I received at ten o'clock this morning, which gave me much pleasure. I heartily congratulate you on your success thus far. I think you have had great reason to be apprehensive for me, the time I mentioned to General Washington being so long since elapsed. I was not then apprised, or indeed apprehensive, of one half the difficulties we had to encounter, of which I cannot at present give you a particular detail. I can only say we have hauled our bateaux up over falls, up rapid streams, over carrying-places, and marched through morasses, thick woods, and over mountains, about three hundred and twenty miles, many of which we had to pass several times to bring over our baggage. These difficulties the soldiers have, with the greatest fortitude, surmounted; and about two thirds of the detachment are happily arrived here, and within two days' march, most of them in good health and high spirits. The other part, with Colonel Enos, returned from Dead River, contrary to my expectation, he having orders to send back only the sick, and those that could not be furnished with provisions.

I wrote to General Schuyler the 13th of October (by an Indian I thought trusty), inclosed to my friend in Quebec; and, as I have had no answer from either, and he pretends to have been taken sick at Quebec, I make no doubt he has betrayed his trust; which I am confirmed in, as I find they have been some time apprised of our coming in Quebec, and have destroyed all the canoes at Point Levy, to prevent our passing. This difficulty will be obviated by birch canoes, as we have about twenty of them, with forty savages, who have joined us, and profess great friendship, as well as the Canadians, by whom we have been very friendly received, and who will be able to furnish us with a number of canoes.

I am informed, by the French, there are two frigates and several small armed vessels lying before Quebec, and a large ship or two, lately arrived from Boston. However, I propose crossing the St. Lawrence as soon as possible, and, if any opportunity offers of attacking Quebec with success, I shall embrace it; otherwise, I shall endeavour to join your army at Montreal. I shall, as often as in my power, advise you of my proceedings, and beg the favor of hearing from you by every opportunity.

The inclosed letter to his Excellency General Washington, I beg the favor of your forwarding by express.

I am, very respectfully, dear Sir, your most obedient, humble servant,

BENEDICT ARNOLD.

P. S. Since writing the above, I have seen a friend from Quebec, who informs me a frigate of twenty-six guns, and two transports, with one hundred and fifty recruits, arrived from St. John's, Newfoundland, last Sunday, which, with the inhabitants who have been compelled to take up arms, amount to about three hundred men; that the French and English inhabitants in general are on our side, and that the city is short of provisions. I shall endeavour to cut off their communication with the country, and make no doubt, if no more recruits arrive, to bring them to terms soon, or at least keep them in close quarters until your arrival here, which I await with impatience; but, if St. John's should not have surrendered, and you can possibly spare a regiment this way, I think the city must of course fall into our hands.

GENERAL MONTGOMERY TO THE INHABITANTS OF MONTREAL.

12 November, 1775.

GENTLEMEN,

My anxiety for the fate of Montreal induces me to request, that you will exert yourselves among the inhabitants to prevail on them to enter into such measures as will prevent the necessity of opening my batteries on the town. When I consider the dreadful consequences of a bombardment, the distress that must attend a fire (at this season especially), when it is too late to repair the damage which must ensue, how many innocent people must suffer, and that the firm friends of liberty must be involved in one common ruin with the wicked tools of despotism, my heart bleeds at the dire necessity which compels me to distress that unfortunate city. I conjure you, by all the ties of humanity, to take every possible step to soften the heart of the Governor, who, if he be sincere in his professions to the people committed to his charge, must commiserate their condition. In vain will he persist in a resistance, which can only be attended with misery to the inhabitants and with lasting disgrace to his own humanity. I am, gentlemen, with earnest wishes for the success of your negotiation,

RICHARD MONTGOMERY.

P. S. I have just heard it has been falsely and scandalously reported that our intentions are to plunder the inhabitants. I have only to appeal to your own observation, whether such a proceeding be consistent with our conduct since we have entered this Province.

ARTICLES OF CAPITULATION,

Made and entered into between Richard Montgomery, Esq., Brigadier-General of the Continental Army, and the Citizens and Inhabitants of Montreal, represented by the subscribers,

John Porteous, Pierre Panet, John Blake, Pierre Mezière, James Finlay, St. George Duprée, James McGill, Louis Carrignant Richard Huntly, François Mathiot, Edward William Grey, and Pierre Guy, duly elected for that purpose.

ARTICLE I.   That the citizens and inhabitants of Montreal, as well individuals as religious orders and communities, without any exceptions, shall be maintained in the free possession and enjoyment of their rights, goods, and effects, movable and immovable, of what nature soever they may be.

ARTICLE II.   That the inhabitants, French and English, shall be maintained in the free exercise of their religion.

ARTICLE III.   That trade, in general, as well within the Province as in the upper countries, and parts beyond the seas, shall be carried on freely as heretofore, and passports shall be granted for that purpose.

ARTICLE IV.   That passports shall also be granted to those who may want them for the different parts of this Province or elsewhere, on their lawful affairs.

ARTICLE V.   That the citizens and inhabitants of the town and suburbs of Montreal shall not be compelled, on any pretence whatever, to take up arms against the Mother Country; nor to contribute, in any manner, towards carrying on war against her.

ARTICLE VI.   That the citizens and inhabitants of the town and suburbs, or any other part of the country, who have taken up arms for the defence of this Province, and are taken prisoners, shall be set at liberty.

ARTICLE VII.   That Courts of Justice shall be established for the determination of property, and that the Judges of the said Courts shall be elected by the people.

ARTICLE VIII.   That the inhabitants of the town shall not be subjected to lodge troops.

ARTICLE IX.   That no inhabitants of the country, or savages, shall be permitted to enter the town until the Commandant shall have taken possession, and provided for the security thereof.

JOHN PORTEUS,   PIERRE PANET,
R. HUNTLY,   MATHIOT,
JOHN BLAKE,   CARRIGNANT,
EDWARD W. GREY,   MEZIÈRE,
JAMES FINLAY,   ST. GEORGE DUPRÉE,
JAMES McGILL,   GUY.

Montreal, 12 November, 1775.

GENERAL MONTGOMERY'S ANSWER.

I do hereby certify, that the above articles were presented to me, to which I have given the following answer; —

The city of Montreal, having neither ammunition, artillery, troops, nor provisions, and having it not in their power to fulfil one article of the treaty, can claim no title to a capitulation.

The Continental army have a generous disdain of every act of oppression and violence; they are come for the express purpose of giving liberty and security. The General, therefore, engages his honor to maintain, in the peaceable enjoyment of their property of every kind, the individuals and religious communities of the city of Montreal.

The inhabitants, whether English, French, or others, shall be maintained in the free exercise of their religion.

The present unhappy contention between Great Britain and her Colonies puts it out of his power to engage for freedom of trade to the mother country; nor can he make a general promise of passports; as far as it may consist with the safety of the troops and the public good, he shall be happy to promote commerce, and, for that purpose, promises to grant passports for the upper countries, when required.

The General hopes to see such a virtuous Provincial Convention assembled, as will enter with zeal into every measure that can contribute to set the civil and religious rights of this and her sister Colonies on a permanent foundation. He promises for himself, that he will not compel the inhabitants of the town to take up arms against the Mother Country, or contribute towards the expenses of carrying on the present war.

The Continental army came into this province for its protection; they, therefore, cannot consider their opposers as taking up arms for its defence.

It is not in the General's power to engage for the return of prisoners; motives of humanity will induce him to use his interest for their return to their families, provided it can be done without endangering the public safety.

Speedy measures shall be taken for the establishing Courts of Justice upon the most liberal plan conformable to the British Constitution.

The inhabitants shall not be burdened with troops but when necessity requires it; of which necessity the General must be judge.

The inhabitants of the country, and savages, shall not enter the town till the guards are posted.

To-morrow morning, at nine o'clock, the Continental troops shall take possession of the Recollect Gate. The proper officers must attend, with the keys of all public stores, upon the Quartermaster-General at nine o'clock at the Recollect Gate.

This engagement is understood and declared to be binding on any future commanding officer of the Continental troops, that may succeed me in this district.

RICHARD MONTGOMERY,
Brigadier-General Continental Army.

Montreal, 12 November, 1775.

GENERAL MONTGOMERY TO GENERAL SCHUYLER.

Montreal, 13 November, 1775.

MY DEAR GENERAL,

The badness of the weather, and worse roads, have put it out of my power to get here before yesterday. A favorable wind enabled, the night before, Mr. Carleton to get away, with his little garrison on board ten or eleven little vessels, reserved for that purpose, and to carry away the powder and other important stores. I don't despair of getting hold of the powder yet. No diligence shall be wanting for that purpose. By intercepted letters, I find that Colonel Arnold is certainly arrived in the neighbourhood of Quebec; that the king's friends are exceedingly alarmed, and expect to be besieged; which, with the blessing of God, they shall be, if the severe season holds off, and I can prevail on the troops to accompany me. The Lizard, man-of-war, is arrived there; she has brought twenty thousand pounds sterling, and one hundred marines. They have had some other little reënforcements of recruits for McLean's regiment, and artificers, to the amount, in all, including marines and sailors, of four hundred and fifty men. One of the brigs is arrived with clothing and arms for the *faithful* Canadians, as Mr. Carleton with propriety terms them.

This morning we have taken possession of the town; I send you their articles of capitulation, with my answer, and hope it may meet with approbation.

I can't help feeling great uneasiness till I know the determination of the troops with respect to engaging for six months longer. I was obliged, at St. John's. to promise all such their dismission as chose it, to coax them to Montreal.

Indeed, Wooster's regiment showed the greatest uneasiness. I make no doubt of retaining as many as will hold the ground already gotten; but it is of the utmost importance to finish this business at once, that the Ministry may have no hopes left of carrying on their infernal plan in this important quarter. At any rate, it will be highly expedient to throw in a large body of troops, as soon as the ice will bear, in order to make a vigorous attack on Quebec, before the arrival of succours in the spring, should it not fall into our hands this winter; but, should this instance of good fortune crown our labors, some advantageous post must be chosen below Quebec, where a large corps of troops, strongly posted, a boom over a narrow channel, and floating batteries, may baffle all attempts from Europe. I am told a difficult pass, termed the Travers, will answer this purpose. If your health will not permit you to engage in this affair, I think Lee ought, by all means, to have the command here. I send some choice letters of that worthy and steady friend of the Colonies, Brook Watson, whose zeal is only to be equalled by his sincerity. You will think them of importance enough, I believe, to be communicated to General Washington and the Congress. Your friend, Mr. William Smith, has been pretty well humbugged by this gentleman.*

I am exceedingly sorry Congress have not favored me with a Committee. It would have had a great effect with the troops, who are exceedingly turbulent, and indeed mutinous. My vexation and distress can only be alleviated by reflecting on the great public advantages, which must arise from my unparalleled good fortune.

I shall clothe the troops completely, who engage again. I find with pleasure that my politics have squared with the views of Congress, and shall lose no time in calling a Convention, when my intended expedition is finished.

Will not your health permit you to reside at Montreal this winter? I must go home, if I walk by the side of the Lake, this winter. I am weary of power, and totally want that patience and temper, so requisite for such a command.

I will take it as a favor, if you will send Harry Livingston with your despatches for Congress.

I wish some method could be fallen upon of engaging *gentlemen*

---

* For an extract from one of the letters of Brook Watson, here alluded to, see Washington's Writings, Vol. III. p. 142.

to serve; a point of honor, and more knowledge of the world, to be found in that class of men, would greatly reform discipline, and render the troops much more tractable.

The officers of the first regiment of Yorkers and artillery company, were very near a mutiny the other day, because I would not stop the clothing of the garrison of St. John's. I would not have sullied my own reputation, nor disgraced the Continental arms, by such a breach of capitulation, for the universe; there was no driving it into their noddles, that the clothing was really the property of the soldier; that he had paid for it, and that every regiment, in this country especially, saved a year's clothing to have decent clothes to wear on particular occasions.   I am, &c.,   RICHARD MONTGOMERY.

COLONEL ARNOLD TO GENERAL MONTGOMERY.

Point Levy, 13 November, 1775.

DEAR SIR,

The foregoing is a copy of my last by the two Indians you sent by express the 29th ultimo, who, I hear this moment, are taken five leagues above this; since which, I have waited two or three days for the rear to come up, and in preparing ladders, &c. The winds have been so high, these three nights, that I have not been able to cross the river. I have near forty canoes ready; and, as the wind has moderated, I design crossing this evening. The Hunter sloop, and Lizard frigate, lie opposite to prevent us; but I make no doubt I shall be able to avoid them. I this moment received the agreeable intelligence, *via* Sorel, that you are in possession of St. John's, and have invested Montreal. I can give no intelligence, save that the merchant ships are busy, day and night, in loading, and four have already sailed.   I am yours, &c.,

BENEDICT ARNOLD.

COLONEL ARNOLD TO GENERAL MONTGOMERY.

Colvil Place, 1 1-2 miles from Quebec,
14 November, 1775.

DEAR SIR,

I wrote you yesterday from Point Levy, by an express sent

from Sorel, by Colonel Easton, of my intention of crossing the St. Lawrence, which I happily effected between nine and four in the morning, without being discovered, until my party of five hundred men were nearly all over, when a frigate's barge, coming up, discovered our landing and prevented our surprising the town. We fired into her, and killed three men.

I am this minute informed, by a gentleman from town, that Colonel McLean had determined to pay us a visit this morning, with six hundred men and some field-pieces. We are prepared, and anxious to see him. Others from town inform me, that the inhabitants in general had laid down their arms. By the best information, they are in the greatest confusion, very short of wood and provisions, much divided, and refused provisions from the inhabitants; and if blocked up by a superior force, must, as soon as the frost sets in, surrender.

I have thought proper to despatch the bearer to inform you of my situation, as also with a request I have to make. I must refer you to him for particulars; as I have been so unfortunate in my former letters, I do not choose to commit every intelligence to writing. It is the current report here, that you have invested Montreal and cut off their retreat. This I hope is true, and that I shall soon have the pleasure of seeing you here. I am, dear Sir, with great respect,

Your obedient, humble servant,
BENEDICT ARNOLD.

P. S. Since writing the foregoing, the enemy found means to make prisoner of one of our out-sentinels. I immediately invested the town, as near as possible, with my troops, which has occasioned them to set fire to the suburbs of St. John's; and several of the houses without the wall are now in flames.   B. A.

COLONEL ARNOLD TO LIEUTENANT-GOVERNOR CRAMAHÉ.

Camp, before Quebec, 14 November, 1775.

Sir,

The unjust, cruel, and tyrannical acts of a venal British Parliament, tending to enslave the American Colonies, have obliged them to appeal to God and the sword for redress. That Being, in whose hands are all human events, has hitherto smiled on their virtuous efforts.   And, as every artifice has been used to make the innocent Canadians instruments of their cruelty, by instigating them against the Colonies, and oppressing them on their refusing to enforce every oppressive mandate, the American Congress, induced by motives of humanity, have, at their request, sent General Schuyler into Canada for their relief.   To coöperate with him, I am ordered by his Excellency, General Washington, to take possession of the town of Quebec.

I do, therefore, in the name of the United Colonies, demand immediate surrender of the town, fortifications, &c., of Quebec, to the forces of the United Colonies under my command; forbidding you to injure any of the inhabitants of the town in their persons or property, as you will answer the same at your peril. On surrendering the town, the property of every individual shall be secured to him; but if I am obliged to carry the town by storm, you may expect every severity practised on such occasions; and the merchants, who may now save their property, will probably be involved in the general ruin.

I am, Sir, your most obedient, humble servant,

BENEDICT ARNOLD.

COLONEL ARNOLD TO LIEUTENANT-GOVERNOR CRAMAHÉ.

15 November, 1775.

SIR,

I yesterday sent the inclosed with a flag and officer, who, approaching near the walls of the town, was, contrary to humanity and the laws of nations, fired on, and narrowly escaped being killed.   This I imputed to the ignorance of your guards, and ordered him to return this morning, and, to my great surprise, he was received in the same manner as yesterday.   This is an insult I could not have expected from a private soldier, much less from an officer of your rank; and, through me offered to the United Colonies, will be deeply resented; but at any rate, cannot redound to your honor or valor.

I am informed you have put a prisoner, taken from me, into irons.   I desire to know the truth of this, and the manner in which he is treated.   As I have several prisoners taken from you, who now feed at my own table, you may expect that they will be treated in the same manner in future as you treat mine.

I am, Sir, your obedient servant,

BENEDICT ARNOLD.

COLONEL ARNOLD TO GENERAL MONTGOMERY.

Camp, before Quebec, 16 November, 1775.

DEAR SIR,

My last was of the 14th instant, advising you of my crossing the St. Lawrence, and being before Quebec; since which I have not had the pleasure of hearing from you. I then informed you of my situation and prospects. Fearing that may have miscarried, I have thought proper to despatch the bearer, a merchant of Quebec, and particular friend of mine, who has been kind enough to offer his service, and will inform you more fully than in my power to write. I am very anxious to hear from you, and much more to see you here. I am, dear Sir, with great esteem,   Your obedient, humble servant,

BENEDICT ARNOLD.

GENERAL MONTGOMERY TO GENERAL SCHUYLER.

Montreal, 19 November, 1775.

DEAR GENERAL,

I wrote to you the other day, in a great hurry, by express, sending a letter for General Washington from Colonel Arnold. I have this morning had another express from Colonel Arnold, acquainting me he has crossed the river to the Quebec side; that he had been near surprising the town; that it was closely invested; that they were in the greatest confusion within, the inhabitants having refused to take arms. A scarcity of provisions and wood must bring the garrison to terms, were a blockade alone to be the measure adopted. Mr. Carleton is *in statu quo*, about fifteen miles on this side of Sorel, where I hope they will not let him pass. I suppose Mr. Carleton is on board the fleet, which left this upon my arrival; as I have never had any account of his making his escape. I have not yet been able to adjust the new-formed corps, or get our warm clothing ready to go down, touching which I am exceedingly impatient, Arnold having no artillery, and being in want of warm clothing.

I have appointed a Mr. Mason, one of our friends in this town, postmaster, till the pleasure of Congress be known.

I find Mr. Price so active and intelligent, so warm a friend

41 *

to the measures adopted by Congress, that I wish to have him mentioned in the strongest terms to Congress.

I have set a regiment on foot of Canadians, James Livingston, Colonel, to be engaged twelve months, should this unhappy controversy last so long.

I have made the inhabitants acquainted with the views of Congress relative to this province, declaring I should call a Convention on my return from Quebec. I have had some conversation with Pére Flacquet, a Jesuit at the head of the society here, and esteemed a very sensible fellow; he complained of some little indignities shown their order, particularly in making part of their house the common prison by his Majesty's Governors. I promised redress, and hinted, at the same time, the great probability of that society enjoying their estate (notwithstanding Sir Jeffery Amherst's pretensions), should this province accede to the General Union.

I hope this hint may be of service; the priests hitherto having done us all the mischief in their power in many parishes. They will not yet give the people absolution. However, I have shown all the respect in my power to religion, and have winked at this behaviour in the priests, for fear of giving malice a handle.

I wish I could have apprised you, in time, of your obligations to Captain McKay. He generously offered Mr. Carleton, if he would give him two hundred men, to go and burn the new church at Saratoga last summer. He is so inveterate a fellow that I think, if the other prisoners should be indulged in returning to their families this winter, he ought not to be permitted to enter this province. When a Convention is assembled, I propose requesting the return of the other gentlemen, on their parole. The inhabitants are our friends on both sides of the river to Quebec; our expresses go without interruption backwards and forwards; a young man who is got out of Quebec, informs me, that the Lieutenant-Governor, the Chief Justice, and several others, have put their baggage on board ship, and that no ship is permitted to sail; this looks as if they despaired of making a defence. Colonel McLean has threatened a [sally,] and Arnold is apprised of it, and his troops wish for it.

I hear there is a considerable quantity of powder at Niagara; perhaps this may be thought an object worthy of attention; they have been very apprehensive of an attack from the Virginians in that quarter all this summer.

I fear Carleton has thrown a great quantity of powder into the river. I have desired a severe message to be delivered to him on that subject.

Farewell, my dear Sir, and believe me, with all regard and respect, Your most obedient servant,

RICHARD MONTGOMERY.

P. S. Hard money should be sent down. I can get some thousands here from Price, though not sufficient to answer all expenses, and it is too soon to offer paper.

COLONEL ARNOLD TO GENERAL MONTGOMERY.

Point-aux-Trembles, 20 November, 1775.

DEAR SIR,

I wrote you the 14th and 16th instant from before Quebec, which I make no doubt you have received. I have this minute the pleasure of yours of the 17th instant. I heartily congratulate you on your success, and hope, as fortune has so far been favorable, and is generally so to the brave, it may in future be equal to your warmest wishes.

It was not in my power, before the 18th, to make an exact scrutiny into the arms and ammunition of my detachment, when, upon examination, great part of our cartridges proved unfit for service, and, to my great surprise, we had no more than five rounds for each man, and near one hundred muskets unfit for service. Add to this, many of the men invalids, almost naked, and wanting every necessary to make them comfortable. The same day I received advice from my friends in town, that Colonel McLean was making preparation, and had determined in a day or two to come out and attack us; and, as his numbers were greatly superior to ours, with a number of field-pieces, and the limits of Quebec are so extensive, I found it impossible entirely to cut off their communication with the country, without dividing the small number of men I have (about five hundred and fifty effective), so as to render them an easy sacrifice to the besieged. I therefore concluded it most prudent to retire to this place, and ordered the main body to march at three o'clock yesterday morning, and waited, with a small detachment, to watch the motions of the enemy until the main body were out of danger. They all arrived here last night. I have procured leather sufficient to shoe them all in a day or two, the only article of clothing to be had in this part of the country. Inclosed is a memorandum of clothing absolutely necessary for a winter's campaign, which I beg the favor of your forwarding to me as soon as possible. Should it be troublesome, I have desired the bearer, Captain Ogden, a young gentleman and volunteer from the Jerseys, to procure them, and some other articles the officers are in want of, and beg the favor of your order to forward them on.

Captain Napier, in the snow, and a small schooner, passed us yesterday, and is now at Quebec. The two frigates were laid up the 18th; their guns and men all taken on shore. They are getting all the provisions they possibly can out of the country, and are doubtless determined to make the best defence. From the best accounts I can get, their force is about nineteen hundred men, namely; landed from the frigate and two transports from St. John's, one hundred and fifty recruits; Colonel McLean's regiment, one hundred and seventy irregulars; from the Lizard, two hundred seamen and marines; from the Hunter sloop, one hundred; on board Captain Napier, one hundred and fifty, which make seven hundred and seventy;—inhabitants, French and English, on their side, one hundred and thirty; ditto, obliged to bear arms against their inclination, and who would join us if an opportunity presented, six hundred; neutrals, four hundred; total, eighteen hundred and seventy. You will, from the above account, be better able to judge of the force necessary to carry the town. If my opinion is of any service, I should think two thousand necessary, as they must be divided at the distance of three or four miles, to secure the passes effectually; and as there is no probability of cannon making a breach in the walls, I should think mortars of the most service; the situation for heaving shells being extremely good, and I think, of course, would soon bring them to compliance; if not, time and perseverance must effect it before they can possibly be relieved.

Colonel Allen and his party have been some time since sent to England in irons. Mr. Walker I have not heard of. I have ordered Captain Ogden to send down all the powder and ball on the road. If he should not be able to procure sufficient, I make no doubt of your forwarding it as soon as possible. The inhabitants are very friendly, and give all the assistance they dare to do at present. Had we a sufficient force to blockade the garrison, I make no doubt of their coming to our assistance in great numbers. As it will doubtless take some time in bringing down your artillery, would it not be better, if you can spare them, to send down five or six hundred men, who, joined to my little corps, will be able to cut off their communication with the country?

I am, dear General, &c.

BENEDICT ARNOLD.

P. S. My hard cash is nearly exhausted. It will not be sufficient for more than ten days or a fortnight, and, as the French have been such sufferers by paper money, I do not think it prudent to offer it to them at present.   B. A.

COLONEL ARNOLD TO GENERAL WASHINGTON.

Point-aux-Trembles, 20 November, 1775.

MAY IT PLEASE YOUR EXCELLENCY,

My last, of the 14th instant, was from Point Levy. The same evening I passed the St. Lawrence without obstruction, except from a barge, into which we fired, and killed three men; but, as the enemy were apprised of our coming, and the garrison augmented to near seven hundred men, besides the inhabitants, it was not thought proper to storm the place, but cut off their communication with the country, until the arrival of General Montgomery. We accordingly invested the town with about five hundred and fifty effective men, took possession of the Nunnery, and Colonel C.'s house, about half a league from town. We marched up several times near the walls, in hopes of drawing them out, but to no effect, though they kept a constant cannonading, and killed us one man.

On the 18th, having intelligence that Captain Napier, in an armed snow, with near two hundred men, having made his escape from Montreal, was very near, and that the garrison, furnished with a number of good field-pieces, intended attacking us the next day, I ordered a strict examination to be made into the state of our arms and ammunition, when, to my great surprise, I found many of our cartridges unfit for use, which, to appearance, were very good, and that we had no more than five rounds to each man. It was judged prudent, in our situation, not to hazard a battle, but retire to this place, eight leagues from Quebec, which we did yesterday, and are waiting here with impatience the arrival of General Montgomery, which we expect in a few days.

I have been obliged to send to Montreal for clothing for my people, about six hundred and fifty in the whole, who are almost naked, and in want of every necessary. I have been as careful of cash as possible, but shall soon have occasion for hard money. As the French have been such sufferers from paper heretofore, and mine so large, I thought it not prudent to offer it them at present. I have written to General Montgomery my situation and wants, which I expect will be supplied by him. Had I been ten days sooner, Quebec must inevitably have fallen into our hands, as there was not a man then to oppose us. However, I make no doubt General Montgomery will reduce it this winter, if properly supported with men, which, in my opinion, cannot in the whole be less than two thousand five hundred, though it may possibly be effected with a less number. The fatigue will be severe at this season and in this inclement climate. I have the honor to be, with the greatest respect, your Excellency's most obedient and very humble servant,

BENEDICT ARNOLD.

GENERAL MONTGOMERY TO GENERAL SCHUYLER.

Montreal, 24 November, 1775.

MY DEAR GENERAL,

I am ashamed of dating my letter from hence; you will be surprised at my long stay here, but day after day have I been delayed without a possibility of getting to Arnold's assistance. His last letter I inclose to you, together with one for General Washington.

To-morrow, I believe, I shall sail with two or three hundred men, some mortars and other artillery. It is with great indignation I hear Lieutenant Halsey, whom I left as Assistant Engineer at St. John's, to put the barracks in a proper state for the reception of a garrison, has run away without leave, taking with him the artificers I had left to carry on the work. This behaviour deserves the severest punishment. I beg he may be made an example of; he is a fit subject of it, and deserved to have been dismissed for endeavouring to persuade the soldiers to return from St. John's, and not to proceed to Montreal. Lieutenant Graham, of the fourth regiment, and several others, can prosecute him.

It will be necessary to send hard money here immediately, as paper will not yet go down. Price has lent me five thousand pounds, York money; Walker has been so fortunate as to get home, being retaken in one of the vessels. Poor Allen is sent to England in irons. Should any accident befall him, I hope Prescott will fall a sacrifice to his manes.*

I sent by Mr. Schuyler a return of provisions, taken in the vessels. I wish Lee could set off immediately for the command here. I have thoughts of disarming the Tories in this town; not so much from any apprehensions I have of them, as to quiet the jealous apprehensions of the troops. Several Commissioners and other officers are flown without settling their accounts. I hope those people will incur the heavy censure of Congress. One, Mr. Waterhouse, who was appointed by Colonel Bedel, and whose conduct must be inquired into, having, I fear, made great waste of public stores; one, Mr. Stewart, who acted at Laprairie; one, Mr. Power, who acted at St. John's. Lieutenant-Colonel Warner has, I believe, large accounts unsettled. In short, there are great abuses to be rectified.

I wish exceedingly for a respectable Committee of Congress. I really have not weight enough to carry on business by myself. I send you the two Indians taken in Carleton's attack. I forgot to make you this present before.

With respect to the Canadian soldiery, I think you may venture to send them back. The   I should imagine might influence in some measure the choice of representation for a Convention. I am, my dear General, with sentiments of real esteem and respect, your most affectionate, humble servant,

RICHARD MONTGOMERY.

P. S. The Indians are of the Conosadago. I have not, I believe, more than eight hundred effective here. However, I can have as many Canadians, as I know how to maintain; at least I think so, while affairs wear so promising an aspect.

---

* The British General Prescott had recently been captured. He was charged with cruel treatment to Ethan Allen, who had been taken prisoner, and was confined on board the schooner Gaspee with irons upon his hands and feet, by order of Prescott. General Washington wrote to General Howe on the subject, and threatened to retaliate upon General Prescott whatever treatment should be received by Colonel Allen. See Washington's Writings, Vol. III. p. 202.

GENERAL MONTGOMERY TO GENERAL SCHUYLER.

Holland House, near the Heights of
Abraham, 5 December, 1775.

DEAR GENERAL,

I have been this evening favored with yours of the 19th ultimo. I return you many thanks for your warm congratulations. Nothing shall be wanting on my part to reap the advantage of our good fortune. The season has proved so favorable as to enable me to join Colonel Arnold at Point-aux-Trembles, where I arrived with the vessels Mr. Prescott made us a present of.* They carried the few troops, about three hundred, who were equipped for a winter's campaign, with the artillery, &c. Colonel Livingston is on his way with some part of his regiment of Canadians.

Mr. Carleton, who is, I suppose, ashamed to show himself in England, is now in town, and puts on the show of defence. The works of Quebec are extremely extensive, and very incapable of being defended. His garrison consists of McLean's banditti, the sailors from the frigates and other vessels laid up, together with the citizens obliged to take up arms, most of whom are impatient of the fatigues of a siege, and wish to see matters accommodated amicably. I propose amusing Mr. Carleton with a formal attack, erecting batteries, &c., but mean to insult the works, I believe towards the Lower Town, which is the weakest part. I have this day written to Mr. Carleton, and also to the inhabitants, which I hope will have some effect. I shall be very sorry to be reduced to this mode of attack, because I know the melancholy consequences. But the approaching severe season, and the weakness of the garrison, together with the nature of the works, point it out too strongly to be passed by.

I find Colonel Arnold's corps an exceeding fine one, inured to fatigue, and well accustomed to cannon shot (at Cambridge). There is a style of discipline among them much superior to what I have been used to see this campaign. He himself is active, intelligent, and enterprising. Fortune often baffles the sanguine expectations of poor mortals. I am not intoxicated with the favors I have received at her hands, but I do think there is a fair prospect of success.

---

* He joined Arnold at Point-aux-Trembles on the 3d of December, and they arrived at Quebec the next day.

The Governor has been so kind as to send out of town many of our friends, who refused to do military duty; among them several very intelligent men, capable of doing me considerable service. One of them, a Mr. Antill, I have appointed Chief Engineer. Mr. Mott and all his suite have returned home.

Be so good as to show Congress the necessity I was under of clothing the troops, to induce them to stay, and undertake this service at such an inclement season. I think, had their Committee been with me, they would have seen the propriety of grasping at every circumstance in my power to induce them to engage again. I was not without my apprehensions of not only being unable to make any appearance here, but even of being obliged to relinquish the ground I had gained. However, I hope the clothing and dollar bounty will not greatly exceed the bounty offered by Congress.

Whilst the affair of Chamblee was in agitation, Major Brown, as I am well informed, made some promises to the Canadians who engaged on that service, which I believe I must, from motives of policy as well as justice, make good; namely, to share the stores, except ammunition and artillery. When matters are settled, I shall pay them in money, it being inconvenient to part with the provisions.

Upon another occasion I have also ventured to go beyond the letter of the law. Colonel Easton's detachment at the mouth of the Sorel was employed on the important service of stopping the fleet. They were half naked, and the weather was very severe. I was afraid that not only they might grow impatient, and relinquish the business in hand, but I also saw the reluctance the troops at Montreal showed to quit it. By way of stimulant I offered, as a reward, all public stores taken in the vessels to the troops who went forward, except ammunition and provisions. Warner's corps refused to march, or at least declined it. Bedel's went on, and came in for a share of the labor and honor. I hope the Congress will not think this money ill laid out.

With a year's clothing of the seventh and twenty-sixth, I have relieved the distresses of Arnold's corps, and forwarded the clothing of some other corps. The greatest part of that clothing is a fair prize, except such as immediately belonged to the prisoners taken on board. They must be paid for theirs, as it was their own property. We shall have more time hereafter to settle this affair.

Should there be any reason to apprehend an effort next spring to regain Canada, I would not wish to see less than ten thousand men ordered here. The Canadians will be our friends so long as we are able to maintain our ground, but they must not be depended upon, especially for defensive operations. The great distance from any support or relief, renders it, in my opinion, absolutely necessary to make the most formidable preparations for the security of this important Province. What advantages the country below Quebec affords for defence, I cannot yet assert, but the Rapids of Richelieu, some miles above, may be defended against all the navy and all the military force of Great Britain, by such a body of troops as I have mentioned, provided with sufficient artillery, row-galleys, and proper vessels fitted for fire-ships.

Some time since, you desired a return from General Wooster of the men he had discharged between Albany and Ticonderoga. I was afraid there might be something disagreeable to him in the desire, and, as it was too critical a time to put anybody out of humor, I therefore suppressed it. I shall now make him acquainted with your pleasure on that head.

There are several appointments I have thought necessary to make, which I shall soon make known to you. I hope the Congress will not yield to any solicitations to the prejudice of the troops who have borne the burden of the service here. I have paid particular attention to Colonel Arnold's recommendations. Indeed, I must say, he has brought with him many pretty young men.

I do not know that I informed you, that it was in vain to think of engaging the troops for twelve months. The 15th of April, which allows them time to plant their corn upon returning home, was all I dared to ask. I hope the proper measures will be taken for sending fresh troops into the country before that time.   I am, &c.,

RICHARD MONTGOMERY.

GENERAL MONTGOMERY TO GOVERNOR CARLETON.

Holland House, 6 December, 1775.

SIR,

Notwithstanding the personal ill treatment I have received at your hands, notwithstanding the cruelty you have shown to the unhappy prisoners you have taken, the feelings of humanity induce me to have recourse to this expedient to save you from the destruction which hangs over your wretched garrison.   Give me leave to inform you, that I am well acquainted with your situation; a great extent of works, in their nature incapable of defence, manned with a motley crew of sailors, most of them our friends, and citizens who wish to see us within their walls, a few of the worst troops that call themselves soldiers, the impossibility of relief, and the certain prospect of wanting every necessary of life, should your opponents confine their operations to a single blockade, point out the absurdity of resistance.   Such is your situation.

I am at the head of troops accustomed to success, confident of the righteous cause they are engaged in, inured to danger and fatigue, and so highly incensed at your inhumanity, illiberal abuse, and the ungenerous means employed to prejudice them in the minds of the Canadians, that it is with difficulty I restrain them, till my batteries are ready, from insulting your works, which would afford them the fair opportunity of ample vengeance and just retaliation.

Firing upon a flag of truce, hitherto unprecedented, even among savages, prevents my following the ordinary mode of conveying my sentiments.   However, I will at any rate acquit my conscience. Should you persist in an unwarrantable defence, the consequence be upon your own head.   Beware of destroying stores of any sort, public or private, as you did at Montreal, or in the river; if you do, by heavens there will be no mercy shown.

RICHARD MONTGOMERY.

GENERAL MONTGOMERY TO GENERAL WOOSTER.

Head-Quarters, before Quebec, 16 December, 1775.

DEAR GENERAL,

The bearer, Mr. Melchior, I sent express to St. John's for artillery stores.   Be so good as to give him all the assistance in your power, particularly in money matters.   Yesterday we opened a battery of five guns and a howitzer, and, with very little effect, I attempted to summon the Governor by a flag of truce.   He would not receive any letter.   The enemy have very heavy metal, and I think will dismount our guns very shortly.   Some they have already rendered almost useless.   This gives very little uneasiness; I never expected any other advantage from our ar-

tillery, than to amuse the enemy, and blind them as to my real
intention.

I propose, the first strong northwester, to make two attacks by
night, one with about a third of the troops on the Lower Town,
having first set fire to some houses, which will in all probability
communicate their flames to the stockade lately erected on the
rock, near St. Roc suburbs; the other upon Cape Diamond bas-
tion, by escalade. I have not time to point out my reasons for
this particular attack. Let it suffice that it is founded on the
nature of the ground, works, and the best intelligence I have been
able to procure. However, I am not certain whether or no the
troops relish this mode of proceeding. I am fully convinced of the
practicability. But should it not appear in the same advantageous
light to the men, I shall not press it upon them, well knowing
the impossibility of making troops act with the necessary vigor,
on such an occasion, if their minds are possessed with imaginary
terrors.

We are exceeding weak, it is true, but the enemy are so too,
in proportion to the extent of their works; and as they know
not where they will be attacked, all must be guarded. Indeed,
their apprehensions for the Lower Town, induce them to bestow
their greatest attention on that quarter. I hope the arms, lead,
and flints are on their way. I could wish for a reënforcement,
if to be spared. We have not much above eight hundred men
fit for duty, exclusive of a few ragamuffin Canadians.

I believe you will not think it proper to let the contents of this
letter go abroad. Should you have no accounts of any cash on
the way, I must beg you will send an express to hasten it. I
shall soon be exceedingly distressed, if a supply don't arrive. I
must therefore beg you to raise what you can, for fear of accidents. Let a considerable number of shirts be sent down as
soon as possible. Our men are much in want of them. I must
refer you to Mr. Melchior for particulars. Believe me, dear Sir,
with much esteem,

Your affectionate, humble servant,

RICHARD MONTGOMERY.

GENERAL MONTGOMERY TO GENERAL SCHUYLER.

Head-Quarters, 18 December, 1775.

MY DEAR GENERAL,

I have been near a fortnight before Quebec, at the head of

upwards of eight hundred men ; a force, you will say, not very adequate to the business in hand. But we must make the best of it. It is all I could get. I have been so used to struggle with difficulties, that I expect them of course.

I hope the troops will be sent down as soon as possible, for should we fail in our first attempt, a second or a third may do the business, before relief can arrive to the garrison. Possession of the town, and that speedily, I hold of the highest consequence. The enemy are expending the ammunition most liberally ; and I fear the Canadians will not relish a union with the Colonies, till they see the whole country in our hands, and defended by such a force as may relieve them from the apprehensions of again falling under the ministerial lash. Were it not for these reasons, I should have been inclined to a blockade, till towards the first of April, by which time the garrison would probably be much distressed for provisions and wood.

With anxious wishes for the recovery of your health, and best respects to your family, if you be returned home, I am, my dear Sir, your very affectionate and obliged, humble servant,

RICHARD MONTGOMERY.

GENERAL MONTGOMERY TO GENERAL SCHUYLER.

Head-Quarters, before Quebec, 26 December, 1775.

MY DEAR GENERAL,

When last I had the honor to write, I hoped before now to have had it in my power to give you some good news. I then had reason to believe the troops well inclined for a *coup-de-main*. I have since discovered, to my great mortification, that three companies of Colonel Arnold's detachment are very averse from the measure. There is strong reason to believe their difference of sentiment from the rest of the troops arises from the influence of their officers. Captain *   , who has incurred Colonel Arnold's displeasure by some misconduct, and thereby given room for harsh language, is at the bottom of it, and has made some declarations which I think must draw upon him the censure of his country, if brought to trial. Captain   and Hubbard seem to espouse his quarrel. A Field-Officer is concerned in it, who wishes, I suppose, to have the separate com-

* The blanks are in the copy sent by General Schuyler to General Washington.

42*

mand of those companies, as the above-mentioned Captains have made application for that purpose. This dangerous party threatens the ruin of our affairs. I shall at any rate be obliged to change my plan of attack, being too weak to put that in execution I had formerly determined on. I am much afraid my friend   is deeply concerned in this business. I will have an *éclaircissement* with him on the subject. I will hereafter acquaint you more particularly with this matter. In the mean time, I wish you would not mention names, for I know not whether the situation of affairs will admit of doing the public the justice I could wish.

Strain every nerve to send a large corps of troops down, the instant the Lake is passable. It is of the utmost importance we should be possessed of Quebec before succours can arrive; and I must here give it to you as my opinion, and that of several sensible men acquainted with this Province, that we are not to expect a union with Canada till we have a force in the country sufficient to insure it against any attempt that may be made for its recovery. I believe I have mentioned this in my last, but I can't help repeating it again. One difficulty occurs to me. How are those troops to be paid here? The Continental money will not be received by the inhabitants. I had distributed part of it to the troops at Montreal; few would receive it. The consequence was, the soldier offered it for less than its value, and so it became depreciated. One scheme has occurred to me, which I shall communicate by this opportunity to Price and our other friends at Montreal. If they can send down to the army such articles as soldiers choose to lay out their money upon, employing sutlers for that purpose, who will receive our paper, the troops may then be paid in Continental currency, which will not be depreciated; the soldier will not grumble, as he may be regularly paid; and, by degrees, the inhabitants may acquire confidence in it, seeing our merchants take it freely. What hard cash can be mustered might pay the contingencies of the army, such as transportation of baggage, &c., and purchase provisions.

I am amazed no money is yet arrived. The troops are uneasy, and I shall by and by be at my wits' end to furnish the army with provisions. I am the more surprised, as I am credibly informed cash arrived from Philadelphia at Ticonderoga three weeks since. I have almost exhausted Price, having had upwards of five thousand pounds York from him. I must take this opportunity of acknowledging his services. He has been a faithful friend to the cause indeed. His advice and assistance, upon every occasion, I have been much benefited by; and when I consider that he has been the first mover of those measures which have been attended with so many and great advantages to the United Colonies, I can't help wishing the Congress to give him an ample testimony of their sense of his generous and spirited exertions in the cause of freedom.

Having so early reported to you my determination to return home, I take it for granted measures are taken to supply my place. Should not anybody arrive shortly for that purpose, I must conclude Congress mean to leave the management of affairs in General Wooster's hands; and therefore, if this business should terminate in a blockade, I shall think myself at liberty to return. However, if possible, I shall make an effort for the reduction of the town. I will shortly comply with several articles of directions, which I have received from you, and which I deferred in hopes of complying with them before now, in peaceable possession of Quebec. The strange divided state of the troops all this campaign has prevented my sending returns, having never been able to get one with any tolerable exactness. The three discontented companies are within a few days of being free from their engagements. I must try every means to prevent their departure, and in this matter I am much embarrassed. Their officers have offered to stay, provided they may join some other corps. This is resentment against Arnold, and will hurt him so much, that I don't think I can consent to it. I am, dear Sir, with great respect and esteem,

Your most obedient and affectionate, humble servant,

RICHARD MONTGOMERY.*

COLONEL ARNOLD TO GENERAL WOOSTER.

General Hospital, 31 December, 1775.

DEAR SIR,

I make no doubt but General Montgomery acquainted you with his intentions of storming Quebec as soon as a good oppor-

* Five days after the date of this letter, General Montgomery was slain in the assault on Quebec.

tunity offered. As we had several men deserted from us a few days past, the General was induced to alter his plan, which was to have attacked the Upper and Lower Town at the same time. He thought it most prudent to make two different attacks upon the Lower Town; the one at Cape Diamond, the other through St. Roc. For the last attack, I was ordered, with my own detachment and Captain Lamb's company of artillery. At five o'clock, the hour appointed for the attack, a false attack was ordered to be made upon the Upper Town.

We accordingly began our march. I passed through St. Roc, and approached near a two-gun battery, picketed in, without being discovered, which we attacked. It was bravely defended for about an hour; but, with the loss of a number of men, we carried it. In the attack, I was shot through the leg, and was obliged to be carried to the hospital, where I soon heard the disagreeable news that the General was defeated at Cape Diamond; himself, Captain Macpherson, his Aid-de-camp, and Captain Cheeseman, killed on the spot, with a number of others not known. After gaining the battery, my detachment pushed on to a second barrier, which they took possession of. At the same time, the enemy sallied out from Palace Gate, and attacked them in the rear. A field-piece, which the roughness of the road would not permit our carrying on, fell into the enemy's hands, with a number of prisoners. The last accounts from my detachment, about ten minutes since, they were pushing for the Lower Town. Their communication with me was cut off. I am exceedingly apprehensive what the event will be; they will either carry the Lower Town, be made prisoners, or cut to pieces.

I thought proper to send an express to let you know the critical situation we are in, and make no doubt you will give us all the assistance in your power. As I am not able to act, I shall give up the command to Colonel Campbell. I beg you will immediately send an express to the Honorable Continental Congress, and his Excellency General Washington. The loss of my detachment, before I left it, was about twenty men, killed and wounded; among the latter is Major Ogden, who, with Captain Oswald, Captain Burr, and the other volunteers, behaved extremely well. I have only time to add that I am, with the greatest esteem, &c.,

BENEDICT ARNOLD.

P. S. It is impossible to say what our future operations will be, until we know the fate of my detachment.

COLONEL ARNOLD TO GENERAL WOOSTER.

General Hospital, 2 January, 1776.

DEAR SIR,

I wrote you, three days since, of our defeat, and the death of General Montgomery and others, with all the information I then had of the matter. We have been in suspense, with regard to my detachment, until this afternoon, when Major Meigs was sent out, with a flag, for the officers' baggage, who, he says, are all taken prisoners, except Captain Hendricks, Lieutenant Humphreys, of the riflemen, and Lieutenant Cooper, who were killed in the action. General Carleton says our loss, in killed and wounded, is a hundred. Major Meigs thinks it does not exceed sixty, and about three hundred taken prisoners, who are treated very humanely. These brave men sustained the force of the whole garrison for three hours, but were finally obliged to yield to numbers, and the advantageous situation the garrison had over them. Several other officers, I am told, are slightly wounded.

We had the misfortune of losing one brass six-pounder in the engagement, and all our mortars were taken from St. Roc the evening after the engagement. This was the fault of some of the officers who commanded, as they might very easily have been brought away, agreeably to my positive orders for that purpose. Our force, at this time, does not exceed eight hundred men, including Colonel Livingston's regiment of two hundred Canadians, and some scattered Canadian forces, amounting to two hundred more. Many of the troops are dejected and anxious to get home, and some have actually set off. I shall endeavour to continue the blockade, while there are any hopes of success. For God's sake, order as many men down as you can possibly spare, consistent with the safety of Montreal, and all the mortars, howitzers, and shells, that you can possibly bring. I hope you will stop every rascal who has deserted from us, and bring him back again.

Every possible mark of distinction was shown to the corpse of General Montgomery, who was to be interred in Quebec this day. Had he been properly supported by his troops, I make no doubt of our success. We are short of cash. Not more than four or five hundred pounds, and only twenty barrels of salt pork. If any can be spared from Montreal, I think best to bring it down, and all the butter.

I beg you will transmit a copy of this letter to the Honorable Continental Congress, and another to his Excellency, General Washington. I think it will be highly necessary, with the reënforcement which, I make no doubt, Congress will send, that they should order all the large mortars and howitzers at Crown Point, Ticonderoga, and Fort George, on to this place. Monsieur Pallasier, who has a furnace at Three Rivers, assures me that he can cast any size and number of shells between this and the beginning of April. I hope the Honorable Continental Congress will not think of sending less than eight or ten thousand men to secure and form a lasting connection with this country.

I am in such excessive pain from my wound (as the bones of my leg are affected), I can only add, that I am, with the greatest esteem, dear Sir,

Your most obedient and very humble servant,
BENEDICT ARNOLD.

N. B. Many officers here appear dispirited. Your presence will be absolutely necessary. I do not expect to be in a capacity to act this two months.

GENERAL ARNOLD TO THE CONTINENTAL CONGRESS.*

Camp, before Quebec, 11 January, 1776.

GENTLEMEN,

I take the liberty most heartily to condole with you on the loss of the great, amiable, and brave General Montgomery, and those brave men who fell with him. By his death the command of the army devolves on me; of course, I have carefully examined his instructions from the Honorable Continental Congress, and their resolutions respecting this country. I find it strongly recommended to him to conciliate the affections of the Canadians, and cherish every dawning of liberty which appears among them, and to assure them of the protection and friendship of the Congress, and to endeavour to form, on a lasting basis, a firm union between them and the Colonies, by forming a Provincial Congress, and from that body giving them a full representation in the grand Continental Congress. This,

---

* Arnold was appointed a Brigadier-General by Congress on the 10th of January.

I am confident, the General labored with the greatest assiduity, and with as great a degree of success as could be expected under the present state of affairs.

The disposition of the Canadians is very favorable to your wishes; the only bar of consequence is Quebec. As this is the key, so, in a great measure, it governs the whole country, who having been so long habituated to slavery, and having, as yet, but a faint sense of the value of liberty, are naturally timorous and diffident, and want every possible encouragement to take an active part. This bar removed, I humbly conceive every other obstacle to a firm and lasting union with Canada will of course be removed. So long as Quebec remains in the hands of the enemy, it will not be in our power to assist and protect them; of course, we cannot expect their hearty exertions in our favor. Quebec appears to me an object of the highest importance to the Colonies, and, if proper methods are adopted, must inevitably fall into their hands before the garrison can be relieved.

The whole garrison of Quebec, including men, women, and children, is supposed, by a gentleman who left town the beginning of December, to be four thousand; a gentleman of veracity assures me, that Mr. Alsop, the King's Commissary, told him, in confidence, that there were not one thousand barrels of flour in the town; and it was notorious among the merchants, that there were not eight thousand bushels of wheat, and no conveniency for flouring it. Provisions of meat were known to be much less than those of bread, though they had some quantity of fish. It is generally agreed they had short of four months' provision on the 1st December. This cannot be exactly ascertained, as the Governor denied the inhabitants liberty of viewing the stores, or giving them any satisfaction in regard to the quantity.

It appears a blockade must answer our purpose; it is possible it may not. Will it be prudent to trust an object of such vast importance to the event? With submission, I think it will not. What is to be done? A sufficient force employed to reduce it by a regular siege, or assault? If the first is attempted, an addition of three thousand men to our present force will, I make no doubt, be thought necessary; if the latter, at least five thousand. The former, with a vast expense and great waste of ammunition, may prove unsuccessful; the latter, from the extensiveness of their works, I think cannot; and five thousand men will hardly be a sufficient garrison, if the place is taken.

I beg leave to recommend the sending a body of at least five thousand men, with an experienced General, into Canada as early as possible; and, in the mean time, that every possible preparation of mortars, howitzers, and some 'heavy cannon should be made, as the season will permit our raising batteries by the middle of March, which may very possibly be attended with success, as we can place our mortars under cover within two hundred yards of the walls, and within one thousand of the centre of the town; and, if supplied with shells, carcasses, &c., can set fire to it, whenever we please, which I make no doubt would reduce the garrison to terms. I am well assured more than one half of the inhabitants of Quebec would gladly open the gates to us, but are prevented by the strict discipline and watch kept over them; the command of the guards being constantly given to officers of the Crown, known to be firm in their interest.

The garrison consists of about fifteen hundred men, great part of whom Governor Carleton can place no confidence in, or he would not suffer a blockade, and every distress of a siege, by seven hundred men, our force consisting of no more at present, including Colonel Livingston's regiment of two hundred Canadians. I have arranged my men in such order as effectually to blockade the city, and to assist each other as early as possible, if attacked. The men are obliged to lie on their arms constantly, and to mount guard every other night. Their duty is exceedingly hard. However, the men appear alert and cheerful, though wanting many necessaries, which cannot be procured here. I expect General Wooster from Montreal with a reënforcement every minute. I have withdrawn our cannon from the battery, and placed them round the magazine, which contains a considerable quantity of powder and ordnance stores, which I am fearful of removing, lest it should make unfavorable impressions on the Canadians, and induce them to withdraw their assistance, and Governor Carleton, presuming on our panic, to sally out. I thought it most prudent to put the best face on matters, and betray no marks of fear.

We are in great want of cash. Our finances have never afforded any of consequence to the troops, who make heavy complaints, not without reason. We have often been reduced to a few johannes, and never able to procure more than ten days' sustenance beforehand. Our whole dependence has been on Mr. Price, who has done every thing in his power, and is the only resource we have at present. I have received two petards from Mons. Pallasier at Three Rivers, who assures me he can supply us with shells by the 1st of April. Inclosed is a list of officers, killed and wounded in the unfortunate attack on Quebec. The prisoners and missing amount to about four hundred. Governor Carleton has permitted the baggage of both officers and men to be sent in, and (strange to tell) treats them with humanity. I think myself in justice bound to acknowledge the good conduct and intrepidity of both officers and men of my detachment, who undauntedly marched up in the face of the enemy's cannon; in particular the volunteers, and Captain Oswald, who signalized himself in the attack on their battery, and is now a prisoner.

I hope, gentlemen, my being confined to my bed with my wound, and a severe fit of the gout, will apologize for the incoherency and incorrectness of my scrawl; and that you will believe me, with the greatest respect and esteem, Gentlemen, yours, &c.,

BENEDICT ARNOLD.

GENERAL ARNOLD TO THE CONTINENTAL CONGRESS.

Camp, before Quebec, 12 January, 1776.

GENTLEMEN,

Since writing the inclosed, General Wooster has acquainted me he cannot leave Montreal, but has sent down Colonel Clinton, to whom I shall resign the command, until my wound will permit my doing duty, which my surgeon thinks will be four or six weeks. Colonel Clinton acquaints me we cannot expect more than two hundred men from Montreal. I have put on foot the raising a regiment of three or four hundred Canadians, which I make no doubt of effecting. They are to have the same pay and to be under the same regulations as the Continental forces. I make no doubt the exigency of our affairs will justify the step I have taken (though without authority for so doing), and that it will be approved of by the Honorable Continental Congress. I am, &c.,

BENEDICT ARNOLD.

GENERAL ARNOLD TO THE CONTINENTAL CONGRESS.

Camp, before Quebec, 24 January, 1776.

GENTLEMEN,

I wrote, on the 11th instant, advising you of our present

situation and that of the enemy, and took the liberty of presenting you my sentiments on a future plan of operation, for which
my zeal for the public service, I hope, will apologize; since
which I have made an estimate (which I now inclose) of such
artillery stores, ammunition, &c., which I imagine will be necessary. If it is thought proper to carry on a siege in form, of
this I can be no judge, as I know not if powder can be spared
from below, or shot, shells, &c., sent up in season. The artillery, except a thirteen-inch mortar (at Crown Point), is all in
this country. I have also inclosed a list of such ammunition,
stores, &c., as we have on hand. A list of such articles as can
be procured at Montreal, St. John's, and Chamblee, will be taken
and sent you by General Wooster.

I had encouragement from Monsieur Pallasier, at Three Rivers,
of being furnished with shot, shells, &c., in all the month of
March. I have this minute received advice from him, that the
want of coal will prevent his supplying those articles before May.
As coal is his only objection, I have wrote him to procure it, at
all events, if it can be done, to supply shells, &c., by the 1st
of April; of which the bearer, Major Ogden, will inform. This
measure, I hope, will meet your approbation, as the expense of
bringing shells from below will be great, and, if not wanted here,
the cost will be trifling.

It is very probable the city would surrender before half, or
perhaps one quarter, of the shot, shells, &c. in my memorandum
were expended; but, if they should make an obstinate resistance,
perhaps the whole will be necessary. A gentleman now present
assures me, that the King's magazines, containing upwards of
three thousand barrels of powder, were all full, and that three
hundred barrels, his private property, taken from him by Government, was obliged to be stored in a private vault. Add to this
ten thousand stand of arms, seven thousand of which are new,
and arrived last summer; also seven thousand complete suits of
new clothing, with a large quantity of artillery stores, two frigates with a number of other vessels in the harbour, &c., &c.
The above-mentioned articles, exclusive of securing an extensive
country in our interest, and liberating three or four hundred of
our brave men, appear an object of the greatest importance to
us under our present circumstances. I make no doubt every
necessary measure will be adopted for reducing the city.

Yesterday arrived here a reënforcement of one hundred men
from Montreal; sixty men are soon expected. We are still very

weak-handed; of course the duty severe; however, the enemy have not dared to come out, though they are double our numbers. Desertions from the garrison are frequent. They are in want of fuel, and have attempted to supply themselves by cutting down the houses in St. Roc's suburbs (under their guns,) to prevent which I have burnt most of them, with several vessels they had broke up. Every artifice is used by Governor Carleton to procure provisions, and induce the Canadians to take arms against us, to no effect, though seconded by the clergy, our bitter enemies. I make no doubt of continuing the blockade until a proper reënforcement arrives to make use of more coercive measures.

Major Ogden, the bearer of this to Montreal, who came out with me a volunteer, proposes going down to Philadelphia. I beg leave to recommend him as a gentleman who has acted with great spirit and activity through our fatiguing march, and at the attack on Quebec, in which he was wounded.

General Montgomery, on his arrival in this country, was pleased to appoint Mr. John Halsted Commissary. He is a gentleman who has been very active and zealous in our cause, is a merchant, and capable in his department, in which I beg leave to recommend his being continued.

Our finances are low; we have been obliged to beg, borrow, and squeeze to get money for our subsistence; and, but for Mr. Price, who has been our greatest resource, we must have suffered.

I have the agreeable intelligence from General Wooster, that the Paymaster is at hand. I am, with great esteem, very respectfully, Gentlemen, &c.

BENEDICT ARNOLD.

GENERAL ARNOLD TO THE PRESIDENT OF CONGRESS.

Camp, before Quebec, 1 February, 1776.

DEAR SIR,

I have the pleasure of acquainting you, that we still hold our ground before Quebec, and keep the enemy closely blockaded, though we have received but a small reënforcement of one hundred and fifty men from Montreal. The enemy have, within these ten days, sallied out twice at Palace Gate, with about four or five hundred men, with a view of seizing two field-pieces we have on that side. Our men advanced briskly to attack them, when they made a precipitate retreat, under cover of their guns. I make no doubt of holding our ground, as we expect a reënforcement daily, which we are anxiously waiting for, as the duty is very severe.

I have taken the liberty, in former letters to the Honorable Continental Congress, to give my opinion in regard to men and measures necessary for the reduction of Quebec. The necessary ways and means for supporting those men, I have omitted, as General Montgomery, in his lifetime, transmitted you his sentiments on the matter, as well as on the necessary measures for forming a lasting union between this country and the Colonies. I have only to observe, if the Capital is taken, I believe paper money will soon have a currency.

Major John Brown, who came down with General Montgomery, with about one hundred and sixty men, collected from different regiments, now assumes and insists on the title of Colonel, which he says the General promised him at Montreal. That the General promised him promotion, he told me some time before his death. When Major Brown wrote to remind him of his promise, the General handed me his letter, and told me, at the same time, as Colonel Easton and Major Brown were publicly impeached with plundering the officers' baggage, taken at Sorel, contrary to articles of capitulation, and to the great scandal of the American army, he could not, in conscience or honor, promote him (Major Brown), until those matters were cleared up. He then sent for Major Brown, and told him his sentiments on the matter very freely; after which I heard of no further application for promotion. This transaction, Colonel Campbell, Major Dubois, and several gentlemen were knowing to. As Colonel Easton and Major Brown have, doubtless, a sufficient share of modest merit to apply to the Honorable Continental Congress for promotion, I think it my duty to say, the charge before mentioned is the public topic of conversation at Montreal, and among the officers of the army in general; and, as such conduct is unbecoming the character of gentlemen or soldiers, I believe it would give great disgust to the army in general, if those gentlemen were promoted before those matters were cleared up.

This will be delivered you by Mr. David Hopkins, a gentleman who came out a volunteer with me. His spirited conduct, both on our march, and since our arrival in this country, merits my recommendation to your notice, of which I think him worthy.

I am, &c.,   BENEDICT ARNOLD.

P. S. The contents of the inclosed letter I do not wish to be kept from the gentlemen mentioned therein. The public interest is my chief motive for writing. I should despise myself were I capable of asserting a thing in prejudice of any gentleman, without a sufficient reason to make it public.

BENEDICT ARNOLD.

GENERAL ARNOLD TO GENERAL SCHUYLER.

Montreal, 20 April, 1776.

DEAR GENERAL,

I hope you will pardon my neglect in not writing to you for so long a time, when I acquaint you that I have, from time to time, communicated every material intelligence to General Wooster, who, I make no doubt, has transmitted the same to you. The 1st instant, he arrived at the camp before Quebec; on the 2d, I had, on an alarm, occasion to mount my horse, who unluckily fell on me, and violently bruised my lame leg and ankle, which confined me until the 12th, at which time I left the camp, and arrived here yesterday. Had I been able to take an active part, I should by no means have left the camp; but as General Wooster did not think proper to consult me in any of his matters. I was convinced I should be of more service here than in the camp, and he very readily granted me leave of absence, until recovered of my lameness.

Inclosed is a list of our force before Quebec, which, I am sorry to say, is so very inconsiderable, and illy supplied with every requisite to carry on a siege, that I am very dubious of their success. The 2d instant, we opened a battery of three guns and one howitzer, on Point Levy. Another battery of six guns, two howitzers, and two small mortars, on the Heights of Abraham, and one of two guns, at the Traverse, were nearly completed when I came away. To supply the whole, there are only three or four tons of powder, and ten or twelve of shot; an engineer and a few artillery men. Two fire-ships, one at Orleans, and one at Point-aux-Trembles, were nearly completed, to attempt burning their ships, as soon as the ice will admit of it. We have few seamen, and not one commander, to man those vessels, or I should conceive great hopes of their success.

Our army are supplied with provisions to the 10th of May, after which time their only resource for meat is from below. This

43 *

country, which is not plentiful at best, is nearly exhausted of beef. We can procure a supply of flour, if furnished with cash. I am now stretching our credit for that purpose, which is at a low ebb. I cannot help lamenting, that more effectual measures have not been adopted to secure this country in our interest, an object which appears to me of the highest importance to the Colonies. Colonel Hazen, who is a sensible, judicious officer, and well acquainted with this country, has shown me his letter to you, of the 1st instant. I am sorry to say, I think most of his remarks too true; and if we are not immediately supported with eight or ten thousand men, a good train of artillery well served, and a military chest well furnished, the ministerial troops, if they attempt it, will regain this country, and we shall be obliged to quit it, the fatal consequences of which are too obvious.

On my way up, I carefully examined the rapids of Richelieu, fifteen leagues above Quebec, which appear to me a very important post. The channel runs near the shore, and few ships can go up without anchoring near the shore, at the foot of the Rapids, where a battery of ten or twelve guns, and three or four gondolas above, will, in my opinion, effectually secure the pass, as no ships larger than a frigate can go up. I have despatched Lieutenant Johnson, of the train, to Crown Point, for four eighteen and eleven twelve-pounders, with what shot are at that place, for the above purpose, as we have very little time to fortify. I have directed him to bring down a gondola, which, I am told, is at Crown Point. We ought to have six or eight of them immediately, to secure the river, and prevent our communication being cut off with the army before Quebec. The row-galley that was at St. John's has been drove over the Falls, stove to pieces, and the gondola cut to pieces; so that we have only one gondola, mounting a twelve-pounder, and in a shattered condition.

Timber and plank for those ordered to be built here have been procured, and nothing will be done until they arrive from below. Intrenching tools are much wanted. We have very few. I have found it necessary to order Colonel Bedel, with two hundred men, to the Cedars, a very important post, fifteen leagues above this, to prevent any goods being sent to the upper country, and to guard against a surprise from the enemy or their Indians. I have also sent a Captain and sixty men to Carringon. We have left at this garrison about five hundred men, about half of whom are waiting an opportunity to return home. We are waiting with the greatest anxiety to receive supplies of men and ammunition from below. Every thing is at a stand for want of those resources, and, if not obtained soon, our affairs in this country will be entirely ruined. I am, with great respect and esteem, dear General,

> Your obedient and humble servant,
> BENEDICT ARNOLD.

GENERAL ARNOLD TO GENERAL SCHUYLER.

Montreal, 30 April, 1776.

DEAR GENERAL,

I have the pleasure to acquaint you of the safe arrival of the gentlemen from Congress, in good health and spirits.*

At a Council of War, held this morning, it was agreed to fortify, at Richelieu and Jacques Cartier, two important posts, the last eleven, and the former fifteen leagues above Quebec; also to set on foot and build immediately four row-galleys or gondolas, at Chamblee, under my direction; and that Colonel Hazen have the overseeing of the workmen, procuring materials, &c., of which I make no doubt the Committee of Congress will advise you, as also our prospects and resources in this country, which are very slender. I hope no time will be lost in hurrying on provisions, &c.

On my arrival here I sent Colonel Hazen to command at St. John's, Chamblee, &c. I have this minute received a letter from Lieutenant-Colonel Buell, acquainting me of his being appointed to command at those places, and having orders to build a storehouse, for which there are no materials to be procured at present. I fancy you have not been apprised of the store-rooms at St. John's and Chamblee, which are capable of holding two thousand barrels of provisions, and want little repairing.

We have engaged a number of French carpenters and bateaumen to be employed at Chamblee under the direction of Colonel Hazen, who is so well acquainted both with the Falls and inhabitants of the country, that a more useful man could not be employed at those posts. Perhaps you will think best that Colonel Buell should remain at this place, or go down to Richelieu, where I apprehend he will be of the greatest service; his want of the French tongue is a great hinderance to business here.

---

* Franklin, Chase, and Carroll, Commissioners from Congress, " to promote, or to form a union between the United Colonies and the peo-

I should be glad that the small hawsers and anchors at Ticonderoga might be sent to St. John's for the gondolas; and if fifty or a hundred good seamen could be engaged out of the troops coming up, to man them, with proper officers to command them, it will forward the matter much.

We have received no material advice from Quebec lately. Our last was the 24th ultimo, when our batteries were playing on the town. Expect soon to hear their effect. I am, very respectfully, dear General,

> Your obedient and humble servant,
> BENEDICT ARNOLD.

THE COMMISSIONERS IN CANADA TO GENERAL SCHUYLER.

Montreal, 10 May, 1776.

DEAR SIR,

Colonel Campbell arrived here early this morning from Quebec. He informs that five ships of war arrived there last Monday, the 5th, about sunrise, namely, two large ships, two frigates, and a tender. The enemy made a sally on Monday, between ten and eleven o'clock, in a body, supposed not to be less than a thousand. Our forces were so dispersed, that not more than two hundred could be collected at head-quarters.

In this situation a retreat was inevitable, and made in the utmost precipitation and confusion, with the loss of our cannon on the batteries, provisions, five hundred stand of small arms, and a bateau load of powder, going down with Colonel Allen. Colonel Campbell believes the loss of men inconsiderable, except the sick in the respective hospitals, amounting in the whole to about two hundred, so ill as not to be removed, who have fallen into the enemy's hands.

Our army are now on their way to the mouth of the Sorel, where they propose to make a stand. Colonel Greaton's battalion is arrived there; and we expect the residue of the brigade under the command of General Thompson, is arrived before this at St. John's. From the present appearance of things it is very pro-

---

ple of Canada," according to the instructions with which they were furnished. *Journals of Congress, March 20th,* 1776. They arrived in Montreal on the 29th of April. Franklin remained there but a few days. The other two continued till near the time when the American troops evacuated Canada.

bable we shall be under the necessity of abandoning Canada, at least all except that part which lies on the Sorel. We may certainly keep possession of St. John's till the enemy can bring up against that post a superior force, and an artillery to besiege it.

A further reënforcement will further increase our distress; an immediate supply of provisions from over the Lakes is absolutely necessary for the preservation of the troops already in this Province. As we shall be obliged to evacuate all this country, except that part of it already mentioned, no provisions can be drawn from Canada; the subsistence, therefore, of our army will entirely depend on the supplies it can receive, and that immediately, from Ticonderoga.

We need not mention the propriety of immediately fitting out the vessels at the place to bring over our provisions, and the sending off bateaux, and constructing more, for drawing the troops out of Canada, should we be constrained, by superior force, to take that measure; and in the interim to bring provisions.

It is probable, a considerable part of the bateaux now on the St. Lawrence will be destroyed, or fall into the enemy's hands. We mention this circumstance to show the necessity of constructing more.

We can form no opinion of the force brought into Quebec by the enemy. Colonel Campbell mentions that information, received at our camp before Quebec, was, that fifteen sail of ships were in the river, though only five were come up, as before mentioned.

We received your favor of the 2d instant, directed to B. F. We are, with great respect and regards, dear Sir,

Your most obedient, humble servants,
BENJAMIN FRANKLIN,
SAMUEL CHASE,
CHARLES CARROLL, *of Carrollton.*

CHARLES CARROLL AND SAMUEL CHASE TO DR. FRANKLIN.*

Montreal, 10 May, 1776.

DEAR SIR,

We are fully sensible of the great risk of taking post at Dechambeau. We have suggested, in writing, the difficulties and

---

* Dr. Franklin had recently left Montreal and returned to Congress.

reasons which have occurred to us against that measure, to General Arnold. Our army's remaining at Dechambeau, will depend in great measure on the strength of the enemy's land forces, and their activity and diligence in following up the blow they have already given our small and shattered army. Before this, no doubt, General Thomas has received some information of the enemy's numbers and of their motions. We are inclined to think a retreat will be made, first to St. John's and then to the Isle-aux-Noix.

Our letter to General Schuyler will give you all the information we have in our power to give, respecting the possibility of subsisting our army in Canada. We are of the opinion, that General Sullivan's brigade ought to be stopped at Fort George, till General Schuyler can send over with them a sufficient supply of pork, not only for the subsistence of that brigade, but of the rest of the army in Canada. Flour we are in hopes of procuring in sufficient quantities to support the army, at least for four months, provided we can keep possession of the country adjacent to the River Sorel, for the space of three weeks.

We sincerely wish the perfect reëstablishment of your health. Our stay at this place is uncertain. We shall be cautious to retreat in time to St. John's. We understand there is but a very small garrison there, and exceedingly negligent. No sentries posted in the night. This information we had from Mr. Price, who was an eye-witness of this negligence. Do speak about it. We are, with great esteem, dear Sir,

Your affectionate, humble servants,
CHARLES CARROLL, <i>of Carrollton</i>.
SAMUEL CHASE.

GENERAL ARNOLD TO THE COMMISSIONERS IN CANADA.

Sorel, 15 May, 1776.

GENTLEMEN,

I wrote you the 12th instant, by express, since which I have purchased twenty-seven hundred bushels of wheat of Captain Cuthbert, at four shillings and sixpence, lawful money, payable in our paper bills of exchange, or an order on Congress, which shall be most agreeable to you. It is now sending to the mills. I have also received two hundred barges of flour from below, and expect a quantity more every moment; also three tons flour, which I had engaged before I left Montreal. I make no doubt in a few days of collecting a magazine of flour sufficient for ten thousand men three months. A Commissary I sent out to purchase provisions, returned yesterday with twenty oxen. I have put the people to half an allowance of meat, and added to their bread. I make no doubt of supporting the army until provisions can come over the Lakes.

Mr. Bonfield, a gentleman of character, arrived here yesterday; he left Sully on Thursday last, Dechambeau on Saturday morning, where General Thomas was, with only nine hundred men; Colonel Maxwell was at Jacques Cartier, but the number of men with him Mr. Bonfield could not tell. Mr. Bonfield saw a number of the regular officers and inhabitants of Quebec before he left Sully, who acquainted him that on Monday, the 6th instant, arrived at Quebec one sloop of war with fourteen guns, one twenty and one fifty-gun ship, from England, with two companies of the twenty-seventh regiment, and one company of marines, which were immediately landed, who, with the garrison that came out the same afternoon, made a body of one thousand men, commanded by General Carleton, from whom our people made a most precipitate retreat, without ever firing a gun. On the 8th, arrived a frigate of thirty guns, and a large Indiaman, with five hundred men from Halifax, part of General Howe's army, the whole of which were on their passage for Quebec; and six thousand Hessians, it is said, are on their way from England. If the latter is true, we shall doubtless have our hands full. Colonel Allen is come out in the ships from England, in irons (it is given out), to receive his trial for rebellion, and to be executed here.*

I am sorry to inform you that all the carriages, except five, which came with the heavy cannon, were sent down, as they came over the Lakes, and fell into the enemy's hands. I have wrote to Colonel Hazen to put others in hand immediately, to replace them. We are making every possible disposition of defence in our power, and I make no doubt of securing this post in a few days. None of the enemy's ships have been able to ascend the Richelieu as yet. I make no doubt Mr. Price will take effectual measures to supply with provisions the garrison

---

* This was a mistake. Colonel Ethan Allen was sent home from England, and exchanged as a prisoner of war.

of Montreal, Chamblee, St. John's, and the Cedars. Inclosed you have a letter to Mr. Evans, which fell into my hands, which contains a piece of intelligence worth noticing.

I should be glad to know your sentiments in regard to inoculation, as early as possible. Will it not be best, considering the impossibility of preventing the spreading of the smallpox, to inoculate five hundred or a thousand men immediately, and send them to Montreal, and as many more every five days, until the whole receive it, which will prevent our army being distressed hereafter; and I make no doubt we shall have more effective men, in four weeks, than by endeavouring to prevent the disorder spreading; a period so near, that the enemy will not, with any considerable force, be able to reach this place by that time.

A Quartermaster-General and Commissary are much wanted here. I have so much on hand, that I can hardly get one minute to write. You will be kind enough to excuse haste and incoherency, and believe me, with the greatest respect and esteem, Gentlemen,

Your obedient, humble servant,
BENEDICT ARNOLD.

GENERAL ARNOLD TO THE COMMISSIONERS.

Sorel, 17 May, 1776.

GENTLEMEN,

I have the pleasure of your letter by General Thompson and Colonel St. Clair, who arrived safe here last evening. Herewith you have a letter from General Thomas, who is hourly expected here. It came by an express, who told me he had orders to deliver the letter to me, and wait my answer. I apprehended there might be some mistake in the superscription, and took the liberty of opening it, which you will excuse.

I am very happy to find you are in sentiments with me in respect to the smallpox. General Thompson and all the officers agree with us, and think it advisable to inoculate Colonel Patterson's regiment at Montreal, Colonel Bedel's at the Cedars, and the troops posted at Laprairie and Longueil at those places. It is thought most advisable to send all the troops at Montreal here who have had the smallpox, and to send five or six hundred men from this to Montreal, who will be at no expense of getting up, as they can row themselves. It will be very difficult to provide them quarters on the Sorel, except at such a distance as will render it extremely difficult to visit and supply them with provisions and other necessaries. This difficulty will be obviated at Montreal, as they will be near together, and may be quartered on the inhabitants (if the barracks are not sufficient); and, among the whole, a sufficient number of men will be found well to keep the garrison. The distance of time you mention between inoculating them will doubtless be most prudent. As soon as General Thomas arrives, I expect a Council of War will be immediately held. I shall be for keeping Dechambeau by all means, if it can be done without too great a hazard of our army. Our own strength (which at present is uncertain), and the advice which we may receive of the numbers and designs of the enemy, must govern our movements. I believe the difficulty of provisions may be got over; but the smallpox, and gondolas to secure our navigation and retreat, are very great obstacles in our way.

We have here about three tons of powder. There is a quantity at Chamblee; how much, I am uncertain. The distribution of the bateaux is already made, and twenty are sent from this to St. John's. Immediately on my arrival here, I sent to Maska. I have received from thence one hundred and seventy-six bags of flour, — I believe the same you refer to. As soon as Mr. Bonfield arrives, I shall employ him to collect all the flour in this neighbourhood, who will, at the same time, call on Mr. Belfeuil, and receive such goods as may answer our purpose. I have in contemplation the sinking a *chevaux-de-frise* at the islands five miles below this, where the channel is very narrow; but the water is so high we cannot fortify at present. Two other vessels will be ordered to Montreal the first fair wind. I beg my respectful compliments to the ladies, who, I hear, are returned with you; and am, with great affection and esteem, Gentlemen, &c.,

BENEDICT ARNOLD.

GENERAL ARNOLD TO THE COMMISSIONERS.

La Chine, 25 May, 1776.

GENTLEMEN,

One of our men this moment came in, who was taken at the

Cedars. He made his escape this morning, and says we have lost only ten privates killed; the rest are prisoners at St. Ann's and the Cedars. The enemy lost double that number. They were last night within three miles of us, with three hundred savages, fifty regulars, and two hundred and fifty Canadians, with our two pieces of cannon; but, on hearing we had a large body of men here, they made a precipitate retreat. He left them above Point Clare. They have only twenty-one canoes, which will carry eight or nine men on an average.

I intend to send off four hundred men in bateaux immediately, to proceed to the Isle Perot, and endeavour to cut off the enemy's retreat. I expect they will make some stay at Fort St. Ann's, by which it may possibly be effected. Pray, hurry on the men as fast as possible. I shall push them on from this immediately. We have so much water-craft, that we can always keep up a communication between those on land and those on water, and be able to act in concert. I am, Gentlemen, &c.,

BENEDICT ARNOLD.

SAMUEL CHASE AND CHARLES CARROLL TO GENERAL THOMAS.

Montreal, 26 May, 1776.

SIR,

We are favored with yours of yesterday from Chamblee. We went to Sorel on purpose to learn the condition of our army, and to know the sentiments of the General Officers respecting the future operations of the campaign. We expected to have had the pleasure of meeting with you there. On our way to Sorel, we were informed of your being taken ill with the smallpox, and that you had left the camp. We hoped to have found you at Chamblee; and to converse with you on the state of our affairs in this country, was the principal end of our journey thither. Unluckily, we passed you on the road.

In the present situation of the army, we think it would be impracticable to occupy and fortify the posts of Dechambeau and Jacques Cartier. We are sorry to find so little discipline in the army, and that it is so badly provided in every respect. We have some time since written pressingly to Congress for hard money, without which we believe it impossible to relieve our wants. The most immediate and pressing necessity is the want of flour. We have advised General Wooster to issue an order to the Town Major to wait on the merchants or others having provisions or merchandise for sale, and request a delivery of what the soldiers are in immediate want of, and pledge the faith of the United Colonies for payment; and have given it as our opinion, that, on refusal, our necessity requires that force should be used to compel a delivery. We have advised the General to issue a similar order to Messrs. Price and McCarty. The General has complied with our advice in both instances, and yesterday evening despatched an express to St. John's, with a letter to those gentlemen. We wrote to them by the same opportunity our sentiments. Flour is not to be procured in any considerable quantity on this Island, unless immediate steps be taken to secure large quantities of wheat, and have it ground up into flour with the utmost despatch. The army will be reduced to the greatest straits for want of bread. We most earnestly entreat you to turn your attention to this matter, and to use all the means which your prudence will suggest to procure flour for the troops. None is to be expected, at least for some time, from over the Lakes. Our soldiers will be soon reduced to the dreadful alternative of starving, or of plundering the inhabitants. The latter will surely happen, if our troops should not be supplied with bread in a regular way. Their other immediate wants may in some measure be relieved by compelling a delivery of some goods on the same terms with wheat and flour. This, however, we confess a violent remedy, which nothing can justify but the most urgent necessity, and therefore cannot be long pursued without drawing on us the resentment of the inhabitants. In short, Sir, without a speedy supply of hard money, it appears to us next to impossible to remain in Canada, even if we had no enemy but the inhabitants to contend with.

We have already mentioned the bad discipline of the army. It is no doubt, in a great measure, owing to the cause assigned in one of your letters, the short enlistments; but there appear to us other causes. The officers are not sufficiently active; nor do they seem actuated by those disinterested principles and generous sentiments which might be expected from men fighting in so just and glorious a cause. We would not be understood to cast a general reflection. There are many officers, we are satisfied, who act upon the noblest motives; but it gives us pain to assert, on the best information, that there are several whose conduct has too plainly proved them unworthy of the character and trust conferred on them by their countrymen.

We have mentioned our sentiments with freedom. We shall always give our opinions with the same. We mean not to dictate, but to advise with you and the general officers on the most effectual ways and means of extricating ourselves from our present difficulties, and promoting the general service. As by this time the virulence of your disorder, we hope, is abated, we recommend a meeting of the General Officers at Chamblee, to consult about and agree upon the future operations of the war in Canada. The inclosed copy of General Arnold's last letter will give you the best intelligence respecting the affair at the Cedars, and the actual state of the enemy, and our forces on this Island. Colonel Dehaas marched yesterday evening from this town, at six o'clock, with four hundred men to La Chine. We flatter ourselves we shall drive the enemy off the Island, redeem our prisoners, and recover our post at the Cedars. We are, with sincere wishes for your speedy recovery,

Sir, your most obedient, humble servants,
SAMUEL CHASE,
CHARLES CARROLL, *of Carrollton.*

GENERAL ARNOLD TO THE COMMISSIONERS.

St. Ann's, 27 May, 1776.

GENTLEMEN,

I wrote you from La Chine, yesterday morning, that the army marched at six o'clock for this place. We arrived here with the main body at six o'clock in the afternoon, when we discovered several of the enemy's bateaux taking our unhappy prisoners off an island at one league distance from us. Words cannot express our anxiety, as it was not in our power to relieve them. Our bateaux were a league behind, coming up the rapids very slowly. I sent several expresses to hurry them. However, it was sunset before they arrived and I could embark all my people; previous to which arrived some Caghnawaga Indians whom I had sent early in the morning to the savages, demanding a surrender of our prisoners, and, in case of refusal, and that any of them were murdered, I would sacrifice every Indian who fell into my hands, and would follow them to their towns and destroy them by fire and sword. The answer I received was, that they had five hundred of our prisoners collected together, and that if we offered to land and attack them at Quinze Chiens, where they were posted, they would immediately kill every prisoner, and give no quarter to any who should fall into their hands hereafter.

Words cannot express my feelings at the delivery of this message. Torn by the conflicting passions of revenge and humanity, a sufficient force to take ample revenge, raging for action, urged me on one hand; and humanity for five hundred unhappy wretches, who were on the point of being sacrificed if our vengeance was not delayed, plead equally strong on the other. In this situation, I ordered the boats to row immediately for the island, where our prisoners had been confined. We there found five unhappy wretches, naked, and almost starved; the rest, they informed me, were all taken off by the savages just before, except one or two, who, being unwell, were inhumanly butchered. I immediately ordered the boats to row for Quinze Chiens, about four miles from the island on the main land. There the enemy had two brass six-pounders, were intrenched round the church, and well fortified. They began firing upon us, when we approached within three quarters of a mile of the shore, with their cannon and small arms. We rowed near in shore without returning a shot. By this time it was so dark we could not distinguish a man on shore, and, as we were unacquainted with the ground, and our people much fatigued, I judged it most prudent to return to St. Ann's.

On our arrival, I called a Council of War, who were unanimous for attacking the enemy early in the morning; and, at two o'clock in the morning, Lieutenant Parke was sent to me with a flag and articles for exchange of prisoners, entered into by Major Sherburne and Captain Forster. One article was, that there should be an exchange of prisoners of equal rank, and that our troops should be under an obligation not to take up arms again; but the King's troops were to be at full liberty. This article I rejected, and despatched Lieutenant Parke to acquaint Captain Forster that I would enter into articles for exchange of prisoners on equal terms, which, if he refused, my determination was to attack him immediately; and, if our prisoners were murdered, to sacrifice every soul who fell into our hands. Captain Forster agreed to these terms, and sent them back signed. As they were not so explicit as I judged necessary, with some alterations and explanations I returned them. Inclosed you receive a copy, as finally agreed to. This matter was finished at six o'clock this

44*

evening, and to-morrow morning part of the prisoners are to be sent to Caghnawaga.

You may be surprised that six days were allowed for the delivery of the prisoners, and that hostilities should in the mean time cease. This does not include the savages. Captain Forster pretended it was not in his power to fix on any particular time for that purpose, but would engage, on his honor, to deliver them as soon as possible; and proposed, if it could be done in less time, hostilities should then commence, of which Captain Forster is to determine and acquaint me this evening. The base, hypocritical conduct of the King's officers, their employing savages to screen them in their butcheries, their suffering their prisoners to be killed in cool blood, I will leave with you to comment on. I observed to Captain Forster, that it appeared very extraordinary to me, that he could influence the savages to deliver up the prisoners, and could not keep them from being murdered in cool blood, or prevent their being stripped naked, contrary to the agreement made with the garrison at the Cedars.

I intend being with you this evening, to consult on some effectual measures to take with these savages, and still more savage British troops, who are still at Quinze Chiens. As soon as our prisoners are released, I hope it will be in our power to take ample vengeance, or we nobly fall in the attempt. I am, &c.,

BENEDICT ARNOLD.

P. S. A party of fourteen or fifteen Canadians, taken at the Cedars, are excluded from the above treaty; Captain Forster alleging that he had positive orders from government for that purpose.

———

ARTICLES FOR EXCHANGE OF PRISONERS.

After the maturest deliberation on the customs and manners of the savages in war, which I find so opposite and contrary to the humane disposition of the British Government, and to all civilized nations, and to avoid the inevitable consequences of the savage customs in former wars (which by their threats and menaces I find is not changed), that of their putting their prisoners to death, to disencumber themselves in case of their being attacked by their enemy; I have, therefore, in compliance with the above disposition in Government, and the dictates of humanity, thought fit to enter into the following articles of agreement with General Arnold, in the name of the power he is employed by, and of the officers and soldiers, who shall be released by this agreement, whose rank and numbers shall be indorsed on this cartel.

1st. That there shall be an exchange of prisoners faithfully made, returning an equal number of his Majesty's troops of the same rank with those released by this agreement, as soon as possible, within the space of two months, allowing a moderate time for casualties that may render the performance of this article impracticable.

2d. That the prisoners shall be conducted in safety, with all possible convenience and despatch that circumstances will permit to the south shore of the River St. Lawrence, from which they are to repair to St. John's, and return to their own countries immediately, without committing any waste or spoil on their march thither, allowing ten or twelve to go to Montreal to transact their private affairs.

3d. That the prisoners so returned shall not, under any pretext whatsoever, either in words, writing, or signs, give the least information to Government enemies, or their adherents now in arms, in the least prejudicial to his Majesty's service.

4th. That hostages be delivered for the performance of these articles to the full, according to the sense and spirit of the agreement, without any equivocation whatsoever.

5th. That the security of the subscribers be given to the inhabitants for all the waste and spoil committed by the detachments under Colonel Bedel, on fair accounts, attested and signed, being delivered, and for which the hostages are not to be answerable.

It being our full intention to fulfil the above articles, we mutually sign and interchange them as assurances of performance.

Given under our hands this 27th day of May, 1776.

VAUDREUIL.

GEORGE FORSTER,
Captain Commanding the King's troops.

Article 2d. The prisoners shall be sent to the south shore of St. Lawrence within one league of Caghnawaga, and from thence to St. John's and their own country, except twelve, who have liberty to go to Montreal, for which purpose six days shall be allowed, and hostilities to cease on both sides.

Article 4th. Four Captains shall be sent to Quebec as hostages, and remain there until prisoners are exchanged.

Article 5th. The Continental troops, from principle, have ever avoided plundering. Upon proof being made of any waste committed by Colonel Bedel's detachment, reparation shall be made. Given under our hands this 27th of May, 1776, at St. Ann's.

BENEDICT ARNOLD,
Brigadier-General of the Continental troops.

GEORGE FORSTER,
Captain Commanding the King's troops.

Two Majors, nine Captains, twenty subalterns, four hundred and forty-three soldiers. But if the prisoners can be conducted in less time, this truce to cease on the return of the last boats employed on this service, on notice given.

GEORGE FORSTER,
Captain Commanding the King's troops.

May 27th, 1776. Answer. If Captain Forster will choose to have hostilities commence in less time than six days, it will be perfectly agreeable to me, provided the time is fixed on, and notice given this evening.

BENEDICT ARNOLD,
Brigadier-General.

GENERAL ARNOLD TO GENERAL SULLIVAN.

Montreal, 5 June, 1776.

DEAR GENERAL,

I have complied with your orders, as far as in my power, respecting the destination of the troops. I intended setting off this day for Sorel, but have been much hindered by taking the goods in town. Every possible obstacle has been thrown in my way. However, I shall secure many articles much wanted by the army. Yesterday, Colonel Dehaas, with his detachment, set off for Sorel. Last night and this morning I have received intelligence of four or five hundred savages and Canadians being on the Island, with the intention of attacking our post at La Chine; and, as the garrison is so weak we can spare few men from it, I have thought proper to order Colonel Dehaas to return. I think it absolutely necessary some effectual methods should be taken with the savages immediately, or we shall be obliged to keep up a large force here. I shall be con-

tinually harassed with them. This affair will prevent my joining you at Sorel as soon as I could wish. It will not be in
my power to take an account of the goods, and send them off,
these three days.

I believe the enemy below will not advance very suddenly.
I make no doubt you will have time to prepare for them, and
that we shall be reënforced in time to secure this part of the
country. I have ordered Colonel Bedel, his Major, and Captain Young, to Sorel for their trial.

An express arrived here from Three Rivers yesterday. I
must refer you to General Thompson for the advice he brought.
We have only two pieces of cannon here, and no matrosses.

With great esteem and affection, I am, dear General,

Your obedient, humble servant,

BENEDICT ARNOLD.

GENERAL SULLIVAN'S INSTRUCTIONS FOR GENERAL THOMPSON.*

Sorel, 6 June, 1776.

DEAR SIR,

You are to march as soon as possible with Colonel Irvine's
and Colonel Wayne's regiments, together with those of Colonel
St. Clair now remaining at this place, and join Colonel St.
Clair at Nicolet, and take command of the whole party; and
unless you find the number of the enemy at Three Rivers to
be such as would render an attack upon them hazardous, you
are to cross the river, at the most convenient place you can,
and attack them. You will pay particular attention to the preservation of your bateaux, keeping them at a convenient distance
above the shipping, which lies at or near the Three Rivers.
I would by no means advise to an attack, if the prospect of
success is not much in your favor, as a defeat of your party
at this time might prove the total loss of this country.

Sir, as I have (without flattery) the highest opinion of the
bravery and good conduct of yourself and the officers you command, I forbear attempting particular instructions, being well
assured, that neither prudence nor resolution will be wanting to
answer the great purpose we have in view. I have the highest opinion of the bravery and resolution of the troops you

---

* General Thomas had died of the smallpox, at Sorel. General Sullivan took command there on the 4th of June.

command, and doubt not but, under the direction of a kind Providence, you will open the way for our recovering that ground, which former troops have so shamefully lost. Wishing you the greatest success and safety, I am, dear Sir,

Your most obedient servant,

JOHN SULLIVAN.

GENERAL ARNOLD TO GENERAL SCHUYLER.

Montreal, 6 June, 1776.

DEAR GENERAL,

I this moment received a letter from General Sullivan at Sorel, dated at 4 o'clock yesterday evening, informing me that a body of the King's troops and a number of ships were between him and Three Rivers, and that he soon expected to be attacked. I have sent every man that could be spared to his assistance, but am fearful he will be obliged to abandon his post. If the enemy land on that side, I am fearful they will endeavour to possess themselves of Chamblee and St. John's. If they come upon this side (on which they are at present), we must evacuate this town. Some days since the sick and baggage have been removed to St. John's. I am now removing a parcel of goods I have seized for the use of the army. I expect to have all over this evening. I shall retain only four or five hundred men to garrison the place, until I receive orders to leave it, or am obliged to quit it by superior force. Out of upwards of eight thousand men in this country, not five thousand effectives can be mustered. The smallpox has broke and divided the army in such a manner that it is almost ruined.

Our want of almost every necessary for the army, and repeated misfortunes and losses, have greatly dispirited the troops. Our enemies are daily increasing, and our friends deserting us. Under these discouragements and obstacles, with a powerful army against us, well disciplined, and wanting in no one article to carry on their operations, it will be a miracle, if we keep the country. My only expectation is to secure our retreat to St. John's or the Isle-aux-Noix, where it will doubtless be thought necessary to make a stand; for which purpose all the bateaux and vessels on your side the Lake, that can be spared, should be sent over. Our gondolas we shall be obliged to destroy. Others ought immediately to be taken in hand to secure the

Lake. The enemy, I am well informed, have brought a number with them, framed and done to put up in a short time.

The want of a little attention in time has lost us this fine country. I hope for better things on your side, and that, in the rotation of fortune, something better will turn up for us here. In every vicissitude of fortune, I am, with great esteem and affection, dear General,

Your obedient, humble servant,

BENEDICT ARNOLD.

GENERAL ARNOLD TO GENERAL SCHUYLER.

Montreal, 10 June, 1776.

DEAR GENERAL,

I received your letter of the 28th ultimo to the Honorable Commissioners, respecting the Oneidas, the 6th instant. There was a meeting of those Indians and several other tribes at Caghnawaga, some of whom agreed to deliver up the hatchet received from Governor Carleton last year, and remain neuter in the present dispute. On the 7th they came to Montreal, when, after the usual speeches and ceremonies, the St. Francis, Caghnawagas, and Conosadagas gave up the hatchet. The Oswagatchas pretended they had no authority for doing it; to whom I observed we were ready to receive them as friends, but if they preferred war to peace, we were ready to meet them as enemies; that we had it in our power to destroy them whenever we pleased, which they would soon be convinced of, if they did not lay down the hatchet. The Oneidas received the presents you desired, except the blankets and clouts, which could not be procured in town, having all been sent to Chamblee. I gave them an order on the Quarter-master there, but find, since, that they went directly to St. John's, and did not receive them.

General Thompson left the Sorel three days since, with two thousand men, for Three Rivers, where are about three or four hundred of the enemy intrenching. One frigate, a brig, and eight sloops and schooners are above Richelieu. I expect every moment to hear of an action between General Thompson and the enemy. A number of Indians and some regular troops are about this place, waiting, as is said, for a reënforcement from above, and for Governor Carleton to advance, when I expect we shall have an opportunity of seeing them here.

I have received your instructions respecting the Tories and their effects. Most of the former had absconded. Great part of the latter is secured. I have sent to St. John's a quantity of goods for the use of the army, some bought and some seized. I am in hopes of fixing on some method, in a day or two, of having them made up, as they are much wanted. I am, very respectfully, dear General,

Your obedient, humble servant,

BENEDICT ARNOLD.

GENERAL ARNOLD TO GENERAL SULLIVAN.

Chamblee, 10 [11 ?] June, 1776.

DEAR GENERAL,

I went to St. John's yesterday, where I found every thing in the greatest confusion; not one stroke done to fortify the camp; the engineer a perfect sot; at that place and this, near three thousand sick. I have given orders that the sick draw only half rations in future. I have ordered Colonel Antill to St. John's, and an *abatis* and lines to be immediately begun, to inclose the two old forts, and an encampment sufficient to hold six thousand men.

I am fully of opinion not one minute ought to be lost in securing our retreat, and saving our heavy cannon, baggage, and provisions. The enemy will never attack you at Sorel. Their force is doubtless much superior to ours, and we have no advice of any reënforcements. Shall we sacrifice the few men we have, by endeavouring to keep possession of a small part of the country, which can be of little or no service to us? The junction of the Canadians with the Colonies, an object which brought us into this country, is now at an end. Let us quit them, and secure our own country, before it is too late. There will be more honor in making a safe retreat, than hazarding a battle against such superiority, which will doubtless be attended with the loss of men, artillery, &c., and the only pass to our country. These arguments are not urged by fear for my personal safety. I am content to be the last man who quits this country, and fall, so that my country rise. But let us not fall all together.

The goods I seized at Montreal and sent to Chamblee, under the care of Major Scott, have been broken open, plundered, and huddled together in the greatest confusion. They were taken in such a hurry it was impossible to take a particular account of them. Each man's name was marked on his packages. When Major Scott arrived at Chamblee, he received your positive orders to repair to Sorel. The guard was ordered to return, and the goods to be delivered to Colonel Hazen, to be stored. He refused receiving or taking any care of them, by which means, and Major Scott's being ordered away, the goods have been opened and plundered, I believe, to a large amount. It is impossible for me to distinguish each man's goods, or ever settle with the proprietors. The goods are delivered to Mr. McCarty. This is not the first or last order Colonel Hazen has disobeyed. I think him a man of too much consequence for the post he is in. I am giving him orders to send directly to St. John's all the heavy cannon, shot, powder, bateaux, valuable stores, and the sick. I go to Montreal immediately, and beg to have your orders as soon as possible for my future conduct. I am, with respect and estęem, dear General,

Your obedient, humble servant,
BENEDICT ARNOLD.

P. S. If you should think proper to retire to St. John's, will it not be best to order a number of carts to be ready here from the neighbouring parishes, and enforce your order by sending a number of armed men to secure them?

GENERAL ARNOLD TO GENERAL SCHUYLER.

St. John's, 13 June, 1776.

DEAR GENERAL,

I wrote you a few days since, from Montreal, that I had seized a parcel of goods for the use of the army, by particular orders from the Commissioners of Congress. Our hurry and confusion was so great when the goods were received, it was impossible to take a particular account of them. Every man's name was marked on his particular packages, with intention of taking a particular account of them at Chamblee, or St. John's, where the goods were ordered to be stored. Major Scott was sent with them, with orders to have them stored under the care of Colonel Hazen, who commanded at Chamblee. On his arrival there, he received orders from General Sullivan to repair to Sorel. Colonel Hazen refused taking the goods into store, or taking any charge of them. They were heaped in piles on the bank of the river. Colonel Hazen finally received them, and placed sentinels over them. They were, however, neglected in such a manner, that great part were stolen or plundered. On receiving this intelligence, I repaired to Chamblee; the goods were sent to St. John's by Colonel Hazen, in different parcels, all under the care of a French Corporal, and through them, I found the goods broken open, plundered, and all mixed together in the greatest confusion, and great part missing. Mr. McCarty has General Sullivan's orders, and is now receiving the goods. I have sent over to Ticonderoga a quantity of nails and goods, the property of Thomas Walker, Esq., and ordered them to be stored there, and delivered to his order.

We have a report here, that on Sunday last our army, of about two thousand men, under the command of General Thompson, attacked the enemy near Three Rivers, and were repulsed, with the loss of twenty men and some bateaux. We have received no particular accounts of this matter, though several days have elapsed since the affair happened.

Near one half of our army are sick, mostly with the smallpox. If the enemy have a force of six or eight, and some say ten thousand men, we shall not be able to oppose them, sick, divided, ragged, undisciplined, and unofficered, as we are. If we are not soon reënforced, I tremble for the event. A loss of our heavy cannon, which is all ordered to Sorel, must ensue, if not of our army, as our retreat is far from being secured. Not one stroke has been struck to secure our encampment here. I have ordered men out to-morrow morning to inclose our encampment and the two old forts with an *abatis* and breastwork.

Dr. Stringer is in a disagreeable situation. Three thousand men are sick here and at Chamblee, and no room or conveniency for them. I should advise his going to the Isle-aux-Noix, was there any conveniency for the sick, or boards to make any. I have wrote General Sullivan on the occasion. I have ordered the frames of the vessels here taken in pieces, and sent to Crown Point. The timbers are all numbered, and easily put together again.

If any more men are ordered for this country, let me entreat you to hurry them on, and all the water-craft. I am, dear General,

Your affectionate, obedient, humble servant,
BENEDICT ARNOLD.

GENERAL ARNOLD TO GENERAL SCHUYLER.

Chamblee, 13 June, 1776, 10 o'clock, P. M.

DEAR GENERAL,

Since writing the foregoing, I arrived here, and met Dr. Center, who left Sorel at 12 o'clock this day. He informs me that General Thompson, Colonel Irvine, Drs. McKenny and McCawley, Lieutenants Bird and Curry are prisoners, and about forty men missing. General Thompson has wrote for his baggage, which has been sent to him. Burgoyne is with the enemy. Seventy transports, and, by the best accounts, ten thousand troops, are arrived in Quebec. The whole force we can muster does not exceed four thousand effectives, when they are all collected. I have wrote General Sullivan my opinion very freely, which is, to collect our whole force at St. John's immediately, and secure our retreat. I am told his intention is to remain at Sorel, until attacked by the enemy. I believe there will be little danger of it. I make no doubt the enemy will pass Sorel, and, as soon as in possession of Montreal, march immediately for St. John's, and endeavour to cut off our retreat. In which case, if we save our army, the cannon and heavy baggage must fall into the hands of the enemy.

All the craft on your side the Lake, in my opinion, ought immediately to be sent to St. John's, and a number of gondolas built as soon as possible to guard the Lake. You may expect soon to hear of our evacuating Canada, or being prisoners. I go to Montreal in the morning, where I shall remain until I have orders to quit it, or am attacked, when it will be too late. I am, respectfully, dear General,

Yours, &c.,

BENEDICT ARNOLD.

GENERAL SULLIVAN TO GENERAL SCHUYLER.

Isle-aux-Noix, 19 June, 1776.

DEAR GENERAL,

By a strange reverse of fortune we are driven to the sad necessity of abandoning Canada. I had the most sanguine hopes of collecting our army together, and driving the enemy below Dechambeau, in which I doubt not I should have succeeded, had not Burgoyne, with a strong party, arrived in Canada, and reached the Three Rivers the night before our people made the unfortunate attack upon that place under General Thompson. The particulars of this engagement I have not before had in my power to give you. I find our loss to amount to about a hundred and fifty. Colonel Wayne sustained the greatest, as his men began the attack, and behaved with great bravery, as did the Colonel himself. In short, all the officers behaved with great spirit, except some few of low rank; and had not the number of the enemy been so superior, I doubt not the point would have been carried, in which case I should have pushed for Dechambeau, which, if secured, would have given us the command of the country. But this defeat convinced us that we came too late for the important purpose.

I was determined, however, to hold Sorel, as it seemed the pleasure of Congress. But, after taking unwearied pains to fortify that post, and to collect the main body of the army to defend it, I found but twenty-five hundred at that place, and about a thousand more at the other garrisons, most of the latter being under inoculation, and those regiments, which had not the smallpox, expecting every day to be taken down with it. At the same time the British fleet, to the amount of thirty-six sail, had advanced into the Lake near us, and sixty-six lay at Three Rivers. The encampment of the enemy was, to appearance, very large, and every account proved their number to be exceedingly superior to ours. The Canadians, too, as far as the enemy advanced, were obliged to take arms or be destroyed. In this state of affairs I was much embarrassed, yet was determined to hold my ground at all hazards.

But, to my great mortification, I found myself at the head of a dispirited army, filled with horror at the thought of seeing their enemy. Indeed, I was much surprised to see the scattered remains of this army, when I had them collected together. The smallpox, famine, and disorder, had rendered them almost lifeless. The flight from before Quebec, the fate of those at the Cedars, and the total loss of Sherburne's party, had, before my arrival with my brigade, destroyed all spirit among these troops; but, upon our arrival, their spirit seemed to return. But, when they found this party defeated, and the number of the enemy increasing, I found a great panic again taking place among both officers and soldiers. I had no less, I believe, than forty officers, who begged leave to resign their commissions upon the most trivial pretences, and this even ex tended to Field-Officers. The prevailing opinion was, that the enemy, instead of attacking our works, would get round us, and cut off our communication with the upper country, and destroy our retreat. This, indeed, they had completely in their power, as we had not force to dislodge them. I soon found, that however strongly I might fortify Sorel, my men would in general leave me upon appearance of the enemy.

In this state of affairs I called a Council of all the Field-Officers, with the Baron de Woedtke, and they were almost unanimously for quitting the ground. General Arnold was not present, but his opinion you have, as well as that of Colonel Hazen and Colonel Antill, in the inclosed letters. I then immediately decamped, taking with us every article, even to a spade. The enemy, having a fair wind, was at our works in an hour after we left them. Our guards at Bertier, not coming in at the time they were ordered, were met by the enemy, forced to leave nine bateaux, and take to Chamblee by land. This was all the loss we sustained. We retreated as far as Chamblee. This post not being tenable, we removed our bateaux over the rapids, with all the baggage and stores, except three pieces of cannon, which were too heavy to bring over the rapids, and indeed they were but bad pieces of ordnance at best. I then proceeded to St. John's, where every thing arrived in safety. We burnt the garrison at Chamblee, with the gondolas and vessels there, leaving nothing but ruin behind us in the fort. We pulled up all the bridges in our way to St. John's. General Arnold did the same in the other road from Montreal, from which place he made a very prudent and judicious retreat, with an enemy close at his heels.

When we got to St. John's, another Council was held, where it was unanimously agreed, that to attempt holding St. John's would be to expose the whole army to inevitable ruin, as our communication might be easily cut off, and the whole army fall a sacrifice. Previous to this, I received the resolves of Congress for six thousand militia, which I laid before the Council. They were all of opinion, that this would rather weaken than strengthen our army, and further, that they could not possibly arrive in season to save us from a powerful army close at our heels. They were fully of opinion that, in the present unhealthy state of the army, it would be best to move to Crown Point, fortify that post, and build armed vessels to secure the navigation of the Lake. Upon this we immediately stripped the garrison of every

article, took our bateaux, and retreated to this island. Further
than this I could not go, without your or General Washington's
orders, or the directions of Congress. I therefore send on the
sick, the looks and numbers of which will present you with the
most dismal spectacle ever furnished from one army in this quarter of the globe. I have sent on General Arnold to give directions at Crown Point, and receive your orders. The men, who
are fit for duty, I shall retain here, ready to execute any orders
you will please to communicate.

Thus, dear General, I have given you an imperfect account
of my unfortunate campaign. Claiming no merit, except in making a safe and regular retreat, and although driven to it by inevitable necessity (as the Grand Post was lost before my arrival, and put beyond my power to regain), and although it was
before an army much more powerful than mine, yet I am sufficiently mortified, and sincerely wish I had never seen this fatal
country, unless I had arrived in season to have done some good
to my country, and answered the expectations of Congress. Dear
General, believe me to be, with the greatest respect,

Your most obedient servant,

JOHN SULLIVAN.

GENERAL ARNOLD TO GENERAL SCHUYLER.

Ticonderoga, 30 July, 1776.

DEAR GENERAL,

Your favor of the 20th instant I received last night. I am
sorry to hear your treaty with the Indians is so long retarded.
You must have an infinite deal of trouble with them, which I am
fearful will prejudice your health; and your presence is much
wanted both at Skenesborough and this place. I wrote you from
the former place on the 25th instant, at which time only two
companies of carpenters were arrived, one from Philadelphia, and
the other from Connecticut; since which the whole have arrived,
to the number of two hundred. I left them such directions as I
thought necessary, and orders to begin four row-galleys, nearly of
the construction of those built in Philadelphia, to carry four
pieces heavy and two pieces light cannon each. The two largest
schooners are at Crown Point, the sloop goes this morning, and
four gondolas will follow in two or three days. I intend to visit
Skenesborough on Monday next. I shall be happy to accelerate

the business all in my power, and to take as much trouble from off your hands as possible, as I am sensible you have more than your share of it.

A Frenchman, arrived here in fifteen days from St. François, confirms the intelligence respecting the Indians, and adds that all the tribes in Canada were determined on a neutrality; that the troops were busy in building bateaux and several large vessels at St. John's. General Carleton has given the French inhabitants notice of his intention of crossing Lake Champlain the last of August, or beginning of September, and that he should depend on their joining him. If we are supplied with the articles I wrote for, we shall soon be in a condition to give him a proper reception.

Inclosed is a return of the ordnance stores, shot, &c., &c., by which you will observe there are many articles wanting to complete the same, as also there is a great deficiency of shot in particular, grape, double-headed, chain, and round, which will be very serviceable among vessels and bateaux. More heavy cannon will be wanted for the row-galleys. The four now building will carry eight twenty-fours, and eight eighteens. Four others will be set up soon, and will require an equal number of guns. To supply the row-galleys and lines, we have only eleven pieces, and ten twelve-pounders, which may answer, though not so well as heavier guns. If they are substituted, eleven pieces will still be wanting, with shot, &c., which I wish may be sent up, if they can possibly be procured. With the approbation of General Gates I sent to Connecticut for three hundred seamen. The express had orders to call on you (if returned), and take your instructions in the matter. As it was uncertain, if you were returned, I wrote to Captain Varick desiring him to give the express a warrant on the Paymaster-General for one thousand pounds, to pay the bounty of the seamen, as the treasury was empty. He has proceeded on to General Washington. We are informed, that of the four regiments coming from Boston, there is a very considerable number of seamen, who are daily expected. I am, &c.

BENEDICT ARNOLD.

GENERAL GATES'S INSTRUCTIONS TO GENERAL ARNOLD.

Upon your arrival at Crown Point, you will proceed with the

fleet of the United States under your command, down Lake
Champlain, to the narrow pass of the Lake made by the Split
Rock, or to the other narrow approach down the Lake, made
by Isle-aux-Têtes and the opposite shore. You will station the
fleet in the best manner to maintain the possession of those
passes, according as your judgment shall determine, cautiously
avoiding to place the vessels in a manner, which might unne-
cessarily expose them to the enemy's heavy artillery from the
shore. You will most religiously observe, that it is my positive
order that you do not command the fleet to sail below the pass
of the Isle-aux-Têtes, above mentioned, incessantly reflecting,
that the preventing the enemy's invasion of our country is the
ultimate end of the important command with which you are
now intrusted. It is a defensive war we are carrying on;
therefore no wanton risk or unnecessary display of the power
of the fleet is at any time to influence your conduct.

Should the enemy come up the Lake, and attempt to force
their way through the pass you are stationed to defend, in that
case you will act with such cool, determined valor, as will
give them reason to repent their temerity. But if, contrary to
my hope and expectation, their fleet should have so increased
as to force an entrance into the upper part of the Lake, then,
after you shall have discovered the insufficiency of every effort
to retard their progress, you will, in the best manner you can,
retire with your squadron to Ticonderoga. Every vessel in the
fleet being furnished with a bateau, you will have it in your
power to keep out scout-boats at night, and occasionally to annoy the enemy's small craft. In the daytime your boats can
act, when opportunity offers, under cover of the cannon of your
fleet.

As the most Honorable the Congress of the United States
rest a great dependence on your wise and prudent conduct in
the management of this fleet, you will on no account detach
yourself from it, upon the lesser services above mentioned. A
resolute but judicious defence of the northern entrance into this
side of the Continent, is the momentous part which is committed to your courage and abilities. I doubt not you will secure
it from further invasion.

As I am entirely unacquainted with marine affairs, I shall
not presume to give any directions respecting the duty and discipline of the seamen and marines on board the fleet.

I have traced the great outline of that service which your

country expects from the rank and character you have acquired. I have, as is my duty, fixed the limits beyond which you are not to go. But you must communicate that restriction to nobody. I wish, on the contrary, that words, occasionally dropped from you with that prudence which excludes every sort of affectation, and which I believe you possess, may, together with all your motions, induce our own people to conclude it is our real intention to invade the enemy, which, after all, may happen. It will keep up their spirits, without affecting your reputation, whatever may be the event.

It only remains for me to recommend you to the protection of that Power, upon whose mercy we place our hopes of freedom here, and of happiness hereafter. You will frequently report the state and situation of your fleet, and of every interesting occurrence.

Given at Ticonderoga, this 7th day of August, 1776.

HORATIO GATES, *Major-General.*

GENERAL ARNOLD TO GENERAL SCHUYLER.

Skenesborough, 8 August, 1776.

DEAR GENERAL,

Your favor of the 31st ultimo was delivered to me on the 4th instant. I feel very sensibly for you in your disagreeable situation. I wish the fatigue and anxiety you undergo may not impair your health; and that you may succeed in your expectation with the savages, and soon give us the pleasure of seeing you here.

Captain Varick has been very active and industrious in procuring the articles for the navy. Many are arrived at Ticonderoga, and proper steps taken to procure the others. The carpenters go on with great spirit. Eight gondolas will be completed in a few days. One row-galley is gone to Ticonderoga, and will soon be fitted and armed. Three others will be launched in ten days or a fortnight. Four others will be set up in a few days, great part of the timber being cut. Iron, sails, cordage, and anchors will be wanted in a few days. About two tons of the former is here, and six tons will be wanted to complete the galleys in hand; twelve or fifteen tons will be necessary for the galleys to be set up. It will expedite the building if six or eight tons can be sent up in spikes from five to seven inches long, chiefly about six inches.

General Gates transmitted to you, last week, the testimony of two French Captains, lately from Canada, which is contradicted by a Lieutenant B. Whitcomb, who was lately sent from Crown Point to St. John's, which place he left the 31st ultimo. He went down on the east side as far as Chamblee, and returned on the west. Says he observed about forty bateaux at St. John's, and some others building, but no large vessels; believes there were about two thousand men there, and one thousand between St. John's and Chamblee.

This afternoon I returned to Ticonderoga, and in a few days propose to go down the Lake with the vessels completed, about ten sail.

The militia come in very slowly; not more than fifteen hundred have arrived. Our work at Ticonderoga goes on briskly. The line will be completed in ten days or a fortnight.

I am, with every sentiment of friendship and esteem, dear General, your obedient, humble servant,

BENEDICT ARNOLD.

GENERAL ARNOLD TO GENERAL GATES.

Button-Mould Bay, 31 August, 1776.

DEAR GENERAL,

The 24th instant, I left Crown Point; the 25th, at night, anchored at Willsborough. The same night came on a violent storm at northeast; the next day, at two, P. M., was obliged to weigh anchor and return to this place, where the whole fleet arrived the same evening, except the Spitfire, Captain Ulmer, who could not clear the shore, and was obliged to come to an anchor again, and rode out the storm, though exposed to the rake of Cumberland Bay, fifty miles long. The hard gale made an amazing sea; and, when I expected to hear the gondola was foundered, or drove on shore, she joined us, having received no damage, though a light bateau, veered astern of her, was sunk with the sea breaking over her. The severe weather prevented my despatching Lieutenant Whitcomb before yesterday morning. The first fair wind, I will follow him. I should have gone this evening, but the breeze is so light, night would have come on before we could have reached a safe place of anchorage.

I have had no advice from St. John's or Isle-aux-Noix. The earliest intelligence I receive shall be communicated to you immediately. I am very anxious to hear from New York, and make no doubt when you receive any material advices, I shall soon be acquainted with them.

Inclosed is a return of the strength of the fleet, by which you will observe that seventy-four men are wanting to complete the numbers proposed for the vessels, which are barely sufficient when complete. I should be extremely glad they were sent to us soon. If you think proper to send them, the bearer, Lieutenant Calderwood, will take charge of them.

Mr. Gilliland has the only good draught I know of Lake Champlain, which, he says, was delivered to Captain Bush for you. It will be of great service to me, as I have no draught of the Lake.

If a good officer can be procured to act as Captain of the Royal Savage, I think he might be of service in case any accident should happen to me. The present Master is not fit for the command in chief, though a good man in his present station.

I suppose by this time General Schuyler has paid you a visit. Please to make my respectful compliments to him, if arrived, and let him know I will write him very particularly as soon as I arrive at the other end of the Lake.

I am, with real affection and esteem, dear General, your obedient, humble servant,

BENEDICT ARNOLD.

Willsborough, 2 September, 1776.

DEAR GENERAL,

I intended sending the foregoing from Button-Mould Bay, but waited for a boat that I had sent to this place for a barrel of fresh salmon, which I had designed for you. The late freshets have broke the dam, so that none can be caught till it is mended. Mr. Gilliland sent you a few salted ones, very indifferent, which we have eaten, expecting to send you some fresh ones.

Yesterday, at noon, we left Button-Mould Bay, and arrived here last night. Before we passed the Split Rock, we saw two sail astern, which we supposed were the Lee and a gondola. They have not yet joined us. We are now under way, with a fresh southerly breeze, and expect to be at the Isle-aux-Têtes before night. I hope soon to have it in my power to send you a very full account of the strength of the enemy by sea and land. I hope no time will be lost in forwarding the three galleys. When they have joined us, I am very confident the enemy will not dare attempt crossing the Lake.

I beg my congratulatory compliments to General St. Clair on his promotion. When the enemy drive us back to Ticonderoga, I have some thoughts of going to Congress, and begging leave to resign. Do you think they will make me a Major-General?

Entre nous, I have received a letter from Samuel Chase, Esq., in which he mentions your letter to John Adams, Esq., and desires an explanation. I will send it to you when I have time to answer it.

I am, with every friendly wish, very respectfully, dear General, your obedient, humble servant,

BENEDICT ARNOLD.

GENERAL ARNOLD TO GENERAL GATES.

Windmill Point, 7 September, 1776.

DEAR GENERAL,

I wrote you the 2d instant, from Willsborough, by Lieutenant Calderwood. The same evening, anchored at Schuyler's Island; and, on the 3d instant, arrived safe at this place, which is four or five miles from the Isle-aux-Têtes, and seven miles from the Isle-la-Motte. We found the Isle-aux-Têtes occupied by the enemy, and several hundred men encamped between that and us, who, the evening of our arrival, made a precipitate retreat. I have posted my guard-boats at a point running into the Lake, about one mile below us. The enemy's boats have several times appeared on the Lake, with a view of decoying our boats; but I have never suffered them to be pursued. Lieutenant Whitcomb arrived here the 5th instant, in the evening, and went off the same night, with three men, for St. John's, on the west side. I sent off Ensign McKay early the next morning, on the east side, with three men. They are to send me intelligence from time to time. I expect to hear from them to-morrow.

Early yesterday morning the boats were ordered on shore, to cut fascines to fix on the bows and sides of the gondolas, to prevent the enemy's boarding, and to keep off small shot. One of the boats went on shore (contrary to orders) before the others were ready. They were attacked by a party of savages, who pursued them into the water. They all reached the boat; but, before they could row off, three were killed and six wounded. The party was headed by a regular officer, who called to our people to resign themselves. On our firing a few shot among them, they immediately dispersed. A party was sent on shore, who found a laced beaver hat, the button marked forty-seventh regiment.

The Lee and gondola arrived here yesterday morning. We are moored in a line across the Lake, in such a manner that it will be impossible for a bateau to pass us. I hope the galleys are nearly completed. The force of the enemy is uncertain; however, they have this advantage, that they can man all their bateaux with soldiers, whenever they think proper to attack us; and our vessels are so low that numbers may carry them by boarding. This must be attended with great loss on their side, as I am positive that they will not be able to surprise us. If I find the enemy have a considerable naval force, I design to retire to Cumberland Head, or Schuyler's Island, until joined by the three galleys, which will be superior to all our present force, when the whole are joined.

I believe the Isle-la-Motte will be the best stand, as the enemy can bring nothing against us by land, nor will they dare to come on the Island; and, by our guard-boats, we can prevent any boats going from Missisco Bay. As you have more troops at Ticonderoga than you want, will it not be prudent to send up one thousand or fifteen hundred men, who might encamp on the Isle-la-Motte, and be ready at all times to assist us, if attacked? Twenty men to a bateau will be sufficient. They might load under cover of the vessels, push out and fire, and retire under cover again; and, if the enemy's boats should make their principal attack on any particular vessel, those bateaux might assist her. Each should be fixed for a swivel in each end; and, if they are arrived, one should be fixed in them. If you should think it necessary to send a detachment, it will be necessary to bring intrenching tools, that they may cover themselves from small-arms.

We have but very indifferent men in general. Great part of those who shipped for seamen know very little of the matter. Three or four good gunners are wanted. Inclosed is a list of our sick, who increase fast. I have sent up, in three bateaux, twenty-three men, who will be of no service for some time.   I wish fifty-eight seamen could be procured and sent down.

I inclose you a letter from Samuel Chase, Esq. You will observe he requests an explanation of your letter to Mr. Adams. He observes, my character is much injured by a report prevailing in Philadelphia, of my having sequestered the goods seized in Montreal. As you have had an opportunity of hearing that matter canvassed on the trial of Colonel Hazen, I beg you will be kind enough to write your sentiments to him on the matter. I cannot but think it extremely cruel, when I have sacrificed my ease, health, and great part of my private property in the cause of my country, to be calumniated as a robber and thief, at a time too when I have it not in my power to be heard in my own defence.

The 15th August, when we left Ticonderoga, the fleet was victualled for thirty days, which time is elapsed, except six days. We have on board the fleet six or eight days' provision, besides twenty barrels of flour, left at Crown Point, to be baked, and ten barrels of pork, which I have ordered Lieutenant Calderwood to bring down, which will serve the fleet to the 20th. As the Lake is often very difficult to pass for a number of days, we ought to have at least one month's provision on hand. Major G. goes up with the sick, to whom I must refer you for particulars. We are very anxious to hear from New York. I hope soon to have that pleasure by one of the galleys, which I think must be completed by this time.

Please to make my compliments to the gentlemen of your family, and believe me, with much respect, esteem, and affection, dear General, yours, &c.,

BENEDICT ARNOLD.

GENERAL ARNOLD TO GENERAL GATES.

Schuyler's Island, 12 October, 1776.
DEAR GENERAL,
    Yesterday morning, at eight o'clock, the enemy's fleet, consisting of one ship, mounting sixteen guns, one snow, mounting the same number, one schooner, of fourteen guns, two of twelve, two sloops, a bomb-ketch, and a large vessel (that did not come up), with fifteen or twenty flat-bottomed boats, or gondolas, carrying one twelve or eighteen-pounder in their bows, appeared

off Cumberland Head. We immediately prepared to receive them. The galleys and Royal Savage were ordered under way. The rest of our fleet lay at an anchor.

At eleven o'clock they ran under the lee of Valcour Island, and began the attack. The schooner, by some bad management, fell to leeward, and was first attacked. One of her masts was wounded, and her rigging shot away. The Captain thought prudent to run her on the point of Valcour, where all the men were saved. They boarded her, and at night set fire to her.

At half past twelve the engagement became general, and very warm. Some of the enemy's ships, and all their gondolas, beat and rowed up within musket shot of us. They continued a very hot fire, with round and grape-shot, until five o'clock, when they thought proper to retire to about six or seven hundred yards' distance, and continued the fire until dark.

The Congress and Washington have suffered greatly. The latter lost her First Lieutenant, killed, Captain and Master wounded. The New York lost all her officers, except her Captain. The Philadelphia was hulled in so many places that she sunk about one hour after the engagement was over. The whole killed and wounded amounted to about sixty. The enemy landed a large number of Indians on the Island, and each shore, who kept an incessant fire on us, but did little damage. The enemy had, to appearance, upwards of one thousand men in bateaux, prepared for boarding. We suffered much for want of seamen and gunners. I was obliged myself to point most of the guns on board the Congress, which I believe did good execution. The Congress received seven shot between wind and water, was hulled a dozen times, had her mainmast wounded in two places, and her yard in one. The Washington was hulled a number of times, her mainmast shot through, and must have a new one. Both vessels are very leaky, and want repairing.

On consulting with General Waterbury and Colonel Wigglesworth, it was thought prudent to return to Crown Point, every vessel's ammunition being nearly three fourths spent, and the enemy greatly superior to us in ships and men. At seven o'clock Colonel Wigglesworth, in the Trumbull, got under way. The gondolas and small vessels followed, and the Congress and Washington brought up the rear. The enemy did not attempt to molest us. Most of the fleet is this minute come to an anchor. The wind is small to the southward. The enemy's fleet is under way to leeward, and beating up. As soon as our leaks are stopped, the whole fleet will make the utmost despatch to Crown Point, where I beg you will send ammunition, and your further orders for us. On the whole, I think we have had a very fortunate escape, and have great reason to return our humble and hearty thanks to Almighty God, for preserving and delivering so many of us from our more than savage enemies. I am, dear General,

Your affectionate, humble servant,

BENEDICT ARNOLD.

P. S. I had not moved on board the Congress when the enemy appeared, and lost all my papers and most of my clothes on board the schooner. I wish a dozen bateaux, well manned, could be sent immediately, to tow up the vessels in case of a southerly wind.

I cannot, in justice to the officers in the fleet, omit mentioning their spirited conduct during the action.

GENERAL ARNOLD TO GENERAL SCHUYLER.

Ticonderoga, 15 October, 1776.

DEAR GENERAL,

I make no doubt, before this, you have received a copy of my letter to General Gates, of the 12th instant, dated at Schuyler's Island, advising of an action between our fleet and the enemy's, the preceding day; in which we lost a schooner and gondola. We remained no longer at Schuyler's Island than to stop our leaks and mend the sails of the Washington. At two o'clock, afternoon, the 12th, weighed anchor, with a fresh breeze to the southward. The enemy's fleet, at the same time, got under way. Our gondolas made very little way ahead.

In the evening the wind moderated, and we made such progress that, at 6 o'clock next morning, we were about off Willsborough, twenty-eight miles from Crown Point. The enemy's fleet were very little above Schuyler's Island. The wind breezed up to the southward, so that we gained very little by beating or rowing. At the same time the enemy took a fresh breeze from the north-east, and, by the time we had reached Split Rock, were alongside of us. The Washington and Congress were in the rear; the rest of our fleet were ahead, except two gondolas sunk at Schuyler's Island. The Washington galley was in such a shattered condition, and had so many men killed and wounded, she struck to the enemy, after receiving a few broadsides. We were then attacked in the Congress galley, by a ship mounting twelve eighteen-pounders, a schooner of fourteen sixes, and one of twelve sixes, two under our stern, and one on our broadside, within musket shot.

They kept up an incessant fire upon us for about five glasses, with round and grape shot, which we returned as briskly. The sails, rigging, and hull of the Congress were shattered and torn in pieces; the First Lieutenant and three men killed; when, to prevent her falling into the hands of the enemy, who had seven sail around me, I ran her ashore in a small creek, ten miles from Crown Point, on the east side, when, after saving our small arms, I set her on fire, with four gondolas, with whose crews I reached Crown Point, through the woods, that evening, and very luckily escaped the savages, who waylaid the road in two hours after we passed. At four o'clock yesterday morning I reached this place, exceedingly fatigued and unwell, having been without sleep or refreshment for near three days.

Of our whole fleet, we have saved only two galleys, two small schooners, one gondola, and one sloop. General Waterbury, with one hundred and ten prisoners, was returned by Carleton last night. On board of the Congress, we had twenty odd men killed and wounded. Our whole loss amounts to eighty odd. The enemy's fleet were last night three miles below Crown Point. Their army is doubtless at their heels. We are busily employed in completing our lines and redoubts, which, I am sorry to say, are not so forward as I could wish. We have very few heavy cannon, but are mounting every piece we have. It is the opinion of Generals Gates and St. Clair, that eight or ten thousand militia should be immediately sent to our assistance, if they can possibly be spared from below.

I am of opinion the enemy will attack us with their fleet and army at the same time. The former is very formidable, a list of which I am favored with by General Waterbury, and have inclosed. The season is so far advanced, our people are daily growing more healthy. We have about nine thousand effectives; and, if properly supported, I make no doubt of stopping the career of the enemy. All your letters to me, of late, have miscarried. I am extremely sorry to hear, by General Gates, you are unwell. I have sent you, by General Waterbury, a small box, containing all my public and private papers and accounts, with a

46 *

considerable sum of hard and paper money, which I beg the favor of your taking care of. I am, dear General,

Your most affectionate, humble servant,

BENEDICT ARNOLD.*

GENERAL ARNOLD TO GENERAL SCHUYLER.

Ticonderoga, 24 October, 1776.

DEAR GENERAL,

Your kind favor of the 17th I received four days since. I am greatly obliged to you for the friendship you express on my safety and having escaped the enemy.

I am extremely glad to hear the militia are coming to our assistance. I believe the enemy, from the best accounts we can collect, are endeavouring to fortify Crown Point. I am afraid we shall not be able to detain a sufficient garrison for this place from the troops now here.

A boom will be laid across the Lake this day, and a bridge to-morrow from Ticonderoga to Mount Independence. We cannot ascertain the strength of the enemy. In a few days we shall be ready to make a trial of their force, if they think proper to attack us. I have only time to add my most respectful compliments, and that I am, with every friendly wish, dear General,

Your affectionate and obedient, humble servant,

BENEDICT ARNOLD.

---

* Sir Guy Carleton, in his letter to Lord George Germain, describing this action, dated October 14th, states the English forces as follows; — "Inflexible, 18 twelve-pounders; schooner Maria, 14 six-pounders; schooner Carleton, 12 six-pounders; radeau Thunderer, 6 twenty-four and 6 twelve-pounders; two howitzers; gondola, Loyal Convert, 7 nine-pounders; twenty gun-boats, each a brass field-piece, some twenty-fours to nines, some with howitzers; four long-boats, with each a carriage-gun, serving as tenders; twenty-four long-boats, with provisions."

Captain Douglas, writing to the Admiralty Office from Quebec, on the 21st of October, said; — "The prodigies of labor which have been effected since the rebels were driven out of Canada, in creating, re-creating, and equipping a fleet of above thirty fighting vessels of different sorts and sizes, and all carrying cannon, since the beginning of July, together with the transporting over land, and afterwards dragging up the two rapids of St. Terese and St. John's thirty long-boats, the flat-bottomed boats, a gondola weighing above thirty tons, and above four hundred bateaux, almost exceed belief." Almon's *Remembrancer*, Vol. III. p. 84.

GENERAL GATES TO GENERAL SCHUYLER.

Ticonderoga, 31 October, 1776.

SIR,

Monday morning, between eight and nine o'clock, our advanced guard-boat, down the Lake, made the signal for the approach of the enemy's fleet. In about one hour, five of their largest boats or gondolas appeared in sight, and a number of troops, Indians, and Canadians, were seen landing upon Three-Mile Point. Soon after, two of the armed boats stood over to the east side of the Lake, inclining upwards, as if sent to reconnoitre. When they came considerably within shot, they were fired upon from two redoubts very near the shore, and by a row-galley which is stationed to cover the boom. They thereupon retired. In the mean time, the enemy's troops were distinctly seen to land upon the back of the Point; and, presently after, thirteen small bateaux and birch canoes crossed from the west to the east side of the Lake into a bay, about four miles below our redoubts.

Upon these threatenings of an attack, our lines, redoubts, and posts were all manned; and as the motions of the enemy seemed to indicate they were gathering their main force upon the west side of the Lake, as if intending to make their push there, I ordered three regiments (Poor's, Read's, and Greaton's) from Mount Independence, to reënforce this side. The orders were instantly obeyed, and nothing could exceed the spirit and alertness which were shown by all officers and soldiers in executing every order that was given. About four, in the evening, the boats and canoes that had passed to the west side of the Lake returned, and the enemy were seen plainly to reëmbark at the Three-Mile Point. I immediately ordered the guard-boat to resume her station; and, by sunset, it was observed the body of the enemy had retired.

By the information I receive daily, I find that General Carleton continues in his post, and that three large vessels are anchored near Putnam's Point; a little below which, all the light infantry, grenadiers, and a large body of Indians and Canadians, are encamped. Chimney Point and Crown Point are also occupied by the enemy. Yesterday I received the inclosed intelligence from Newbury, Coos.

If Sir John Johnson did actually march at the time he is said to have done it, he must be upon the Mohawk River now; or, if he aims at Fort George, Dayton's regiment cannot be better stationed than there. Surely, your Oneidas will give you all the necessary information upon this head. But how could Sir John get back, if he should meet with a check? I have seen the Mohawk River fast frozen on the 10th of November.

Colonel Lewis set off yesterday morning by Skene. He has memorandums of our wants, and will be with you as soon as this letter. Colonel Gansevoort writes me for spades. You must answer his demand, for I cannot.

We received the good news you sent us from New York with joyful hearts. It was immediately made public to the army, in the manner you advised. I am, Sir,

> Your most obedient, humble servant,
>
> HORATIO GATES.

GENERAL GATES TO THE PRESIDENT OF CONGRESS.

Ticonderoga, 5 November, 1776.

SIR,

I have the honor to congratulate Congress upon the retreat of Lieutenant-General Sir Guy Carleton, with the fleet and army under his command, from Crown Point, Saturday last. The works being put into the best order, the boom and bridge of communication finished, and every necessary preparative for defence made, I determined to send a detachment down each side of the Lake to beat up the enemy's quarters at their advanced post on Putnam's Point and the opposite shore. About eight at night, the detachment, under the command of Major Delap, proceeded down the east side of the Lake; and the other, under Colonel Connor, down the west side. Sunday morning, Major Delap, with his detachment, took possession of Putnam's Point, which the enemy had just abandoned, and immediately detached a subaltern, with a small party, to reconnoitre Crown Point. The officer having returned, reported that he saw the enemy embark, a number of their vessels under sail, and the whole preparing to get under way. Colonel Connor, on taking possession of the post opposite to Putnam's Point, found that likewise abandoned. Yesterday an officer, with a party whom I sent to Crown Point, returned and reported he had been at Crown Point, with the inhabitants there; that the enemy were all gone from that post, and the inhabitants would come this day to Ticonderoga, to make their submission, and beg the protection of the United States.

I cannot help observing, here, that the removal of our army from Crown Point to Ticonderoga was a most fortunate and salutary measure; for, had it continued at Crown Point after the disaster that befell our fleets, the enemy might have cut off all our resources, by stationing their fleet above the Point. Desperate must then have been the situation of our army. I have the honor to be

Your Excellency's most obedient, humble servant,

HORATIO GATES.

END OF VOL. I.